Telepopulism

Telepopulism

Media and Politics in Israel

Yoram Peri

STANFORD UNIVERSITY PRESS

STANFORD, CALIFORNIA 2004

Stanford University Press
Stanford, California
© 2004 by the Board of Trustees of the
Leland Stanford Junior University. All rights reserved.

Printed in the United States of America
on acid-free, archival-quality paper

Library of Congress Cataloging-in-Publication Data
Peri, Yoram.
Telepopulism : media and politics in Israel / Yoram Peri.
p.   cm.
Includes bibliographical references and index.
ISBN 0-8047-4876-4 (alk. paper)—ISBN 0-8047-5002-5 (pbk. : alk. paper)
1. Television broadcasting—Israel.   2. Television and politics—Israel.
3. Television in politics—Israel.   4. Mass media—Israel.   I. Title.
PN1992.3.I75 P47 2004
302.23'45'095694—dc22   2003023439

Original Printing 2004

Last figure below indicates year of this printing:
13   12   11   10   09   08   07   06   05   04

Typeset by BookMatters in 10/12 Sabon

Contents

Telepopulism

Introduction

The Union of Media and Politics in Israel

Media and politics are tightly intertwined in the State of Israel, and have been since the beginnings of the Zionist movement, when the state was only a dream. Their union began with Binyamin Ze'ev Herzl's coverage in 1889 of the Dreyfus trial. Herzl, the founding father of Zionism, was the Paris correspondent of the Viennese paper *Die Presse*. The scandal, in which a Jewish officer in the French army was falsely accused of being a spy, unraveled the depth of anti-Semitism in French society. Appalled by the scandal, Emile Zola published his historic op-ed, "J'accuse," on the entire front page of the newspaper *L'aurore*. In the history of journalism, Zola's article emerges as a reference point for advocacy of moral and social causes. Herzl was an assimilated Jew from Vienna, and the Dreyfus trial proved to be his traumatic encounter with the "Jewish problem." Ultimately, it caused him to acknowledge that the only solution to the Jewish problem was for Jews to establish a separate sovereign state. He thus founded the Zionist movement whose goal was to create a national home in the Holy Land. One of his first gestures as movement leader was to start a weekly magazine called *Die Welt*.

The close ties between politics and media continued after Herzl's premature death at the age of forty-four in 1904. Exactly fifty years after he proclaimed, "If you will it, it is not a dream," the Jewish state was formed. Since that time, journalists and men and women of letters have stood at the helm of the national movement. Nachum Sokolov, Herzl's successor at the head of the World Zionist Organization, was also a journalist, and the Journalists' House in Tel Aviv is named after him.

The movement has achieved even more, however, than the establishment of political sovereignty; it has also birthed the revival of the Hebrew language. The man who led this effort in Palestine was Eliezer Ben-Yehuda, who established the first secular Hebrew newspaper there in 1885.

In the 1920s and 1930s, the formative years of Jewish society and pol-

itics in the Land of Israel, journalists were at the head of two major political movements that later became the Labor Party and Likud Party. Berl
Katzenelson was the founder and the first editor of *Davar*, the paper of
the social democratic party, which was dominant in Israel for forty-four
years. Leading the rival Revisionist movement, from which the Likud
Party later emerged, was Ze'ev Jabotinsky, a well-known journalist and
editor of *Do'ar Hayom*. His colleague and rival in this movement was
Meir Grossman, the man who established the Jewish Telegraphic Agency
(JTA), which still exists.

Even after the state was established, journalists continued to lead political parties and state institutions. The list of politicians who also worked
as editors at *Davar* is long and includes Zalman Shazar, the third president of Israel, Moshe Sharett, Israel's first foreign minister and second
prime minister, as well as leaders of many other parties.[1] Indeed, Israeli
journalists were keenly aware of their political status, as evidenced in a
statement by Arie Dissenchik, the editor of *Maariv*, who said that "journalism was the main carrier of the Zionist idea. Newspapers built the
Land of Israel with letters before the JNF [the Jewish National Fund that
bought land in Palestine to give to Jewish settlers] acquired and developed
the land" (Harshefi 1977: 226).

Although Dissenchik's description is somewhat exaggerated, typical of
the hubris of the editor of Israel's largest newspaper in the 1970s, there is
certainly a significant amount of truth in it. Words and intellectual activity were instrumental to the success of twentieth-century leaders of anti-
colonial national liberation movements, and as a result, their journalistic
work was different from the profession practiced today. These leaders'
attachment to the written word was inherent in national movements that
lacked political or military power. This was particularly true of Zionism
in its early days: for the Jewish nation, as Emmanuel Levinas wrote, par-
aphrasing Heine, "books, and not land, carried it through time."[2]

Jewish preoccupation with the written and spoken words, including
emergent magnetic, electronic, and digital formats, also results from an
exceptionally tight web of social ties in Israel. The high level of "social
density" that exists in Israel today is expressed by the fact that interpersonal connections and communication are extremely important. One
recent example is the remarkably high usage of cellular phones, which in
Hebrew are called the "*pele*-phone," meaning "magic phone." Israelis
only began using these phones in 1993, but by 2000 cell phones were
already being used by one out of three Israelis — the third-highest penetration rate in the world. In 1998, Israelis ranked second in the world in
their number of cell phone conversations per capita (1,100 calls on average per person annually) and held the world record for length of cell

phone conversations, averaging 150 minutes a month per person.[3] The abundant use of cell phones and the loud conversation style of Israeli culture have privatized the Israeli public sphere.

These close social ties are expressed both in primary social systems — family ties in Israel are much stronger than in many urban, Western, modern societies — as well as in larger social networks (Katz et al. 1992).[4] Camaraderie is an Israeli national value and receives an almost mythical aura through art, literature, and folk songs. This social density is expressed not only in interpersonal communication but also in the extensive consumption of mass media. Any tourist who uses public transportation in Israel will note that bus drivers do not forget to switch on the radio news every half hour.[5]

The same applies to the consumption of written and broadcast news. Eight out of ten adult Israelis regularly read a daily newspaper, six out of ten viewers watch the main television news broadcast every evening — compared with a bit more than four out of ten in the United States. This boundless need for news is in part explained by the external reality in which Israelis live: almost one hundred years of prolonged conflict with their neighbors, and outbreaks of war occurring almost once a decade. Living in Israel means living in an area where existential surprises are a daily matter, and it is well known that the media have a special role in crisis situations. Added to these dramatic events are Israeli national characteristics such as dynamism, energy, agitation, and overactivism. Taken together, it is easy to understand why the mass media are as necessary in Israel as water is to a traveler in the desert.

Close ties between politics and media have thus always existed in Israel. This relationship took a dramatic turn in the 1990s, however. In this period, two revolutions occurred simultaneously — the communication revolution and the political transformation. Although Israel belongs to the group of developed states, the media revolution reached it quite late — about ten years after similar transformations in Western European states. During the 1990s newspapers lost their status, and commercial multichannel television — "neotelevision," in Umberto Eco's terminology (1990) — became the hegemonic medium. Israeli culture quickly moved from the written age to the visual era.

Israel still lags behind the United States and other advanced societies in its development into a network society (Castells 1995).[6] It is too early to speak of a "digital citizen," "virtual community," or "cyberspace democracy." All of these are titles of books or articles that deal with the impact of computer-mediated communication (CMC) and new media on postmodern society and culture in developed states. However, the fact that parallel to the communication revolution Israel also went through a political transformation has made the country into a testing ground for the new sociopolitical phenomenon of "mediapolitik."

During the 1990s, one million immigrants from the former Soviet Union joined the five million people already living in Israel. This tremendous change in Israel's demographic equation brought a significant cultural transformation with it, as the melting pot model was replaced with pluralism, if not multiculturalism. During this period Israel was also thrust into the era of globalization, after many years of being the most planned economy in the free world. It was transformed from being a net exporter of oranges in the 1950s into being a major arms producer in the 1980s, and emerged in the 1990s as the Silicon Valley of the Middle East. Today, Israel is a major center for high-tech research and development in the world.

A digital divide has thus been created, which has further polarized the social cleavages in this already deeply divided society. To add to this, the country continues to suffer from the colonial situation that has existed since 1967: Israel rules over more than 3.5 million Palestinians. This situation has intensified the painful ongoing struggle over the national identity and the Zionist *leitkultur* — the dominant or superculture of society. In sum, these factors have intensified in Israel the crisis that most mature democracies go through: that of achieving legitimacy.

Scholars in many fields of social science have argued that Israel is an excellent laboratory for researching social processes. What happened in the 1990s in the field of political communication provides further evidence of this. The synergy caused by the two revolutions created a tectonic shift in Israeli politics. Parties that were the cornerstones of the political structure are now in demise. Instead of a party-state, Israel is morphing into a media-centered democracy.

The phenomenon of the mediatization, or medialization, of politics has been analyzed by political communication researchers for more than a decade. Mediatization is the process whereby the media, particularly television, invade the center of politics, become the arena for political action, influence political processes, and even become a dominant political actor. However, an analysis of the Israeli case shows that these changes are in fact much deeper. The relations between media and politics in Israel have been shaped in a completely new way, as they never had been before. Politics has lost its autonomy and has been dissolved into the media space. Media and politics have become intertwined in a symbiotic or fusionist manner, and politics has now adopted the logic of the media.

The first part of this book analyzes mediapolitik. Chapters 1 and 2 describe the Israeli communication revolution of the 1990s. Chapter 3 deals with the political transformation, and Chapter 4 describes the pattern of relations that have existed between the media and politics throughout Israel's existence. Chapters 5, 6, and 7 deal extensively with the new mediapolitik formation. In this framework I will also treat some of the issues that have occupied media scholars for some time. The first is the question of who influences whom — do journalists have sway over politicians, or vice versa? Has politics become media-driven, or has it tended to be guided more by political substance than by media antics?

The term "mediapolitik" provides a way out of this dilemma, as the answers to these questions cannot be found solely among journalists or politicians. In this book, I show that the distinction between political and media institutions in a media-centered democracy has lost its meaning. It overlooks the uniqueness of this new phenomenon created at the end of the twentieth century. Although the system has been created out of the combination of two ingredients, in fact it has an intertwined and fusionist nature.

An important question that arises in dealing with this new pattern of media-centered democracy — one frequently dealt with by media scholars — is also tackled in this study. Many experts have been troubled, and rightly so, by the negative impact that multichannel, market-driven media have had on the democratic system. They have expressed worries that the news media harm the public space; do not supply citizens with the breadth of knowledge necessary for informed, active, democratic citizenship; turn citizens into consumers of infotainment; reduce social trust and shake the legitimacy of the government; lower public involvement in social policy matters; reduce voter turnout; and create a spiral of cynicism. Critics argue that these types of media do not enable inclusiveness and a deliberative democracy, and in the end they create a "democracy without citizens," a "sound-bite society," and a "republic of denial."

These scholars have not been concerned about the power of the media as such; indeed, strong journalism has always been perceived as a positive element in democracies because of its power to place limitations and constraints on governments. Their worry has been, rather, that the penetration of market values into political communication was detrimental to the democratic model of an informed citizenry that actively participates in the political process.

The dilemma today has changed, however, because the media have become part and parcel of the political sphere in the new mediapolitik. To borrow from Bourdieu, the mere intrusion of the journalistic field into the political arena is the problem. Bourdieu expressed his worry that television would take control over all fields of cultural production and would insert heteronomic principles into these fields, rather than leaving them intact as autonomous spheres. He therefore called on scientists and artists to safeguard autonomy of the cultural fields and redefine the boundaries of each, and to break free from the idea that the media must have a monopoly over the means of the distribution of their products.

Is such a solution realistic for the political field as well? Can the political arena that has been overtaken by media logic regain its independence? Today, in the visual culture, when visibility is the sine qua non for political action and a basis of legitimacy for political power, is it possible to revert to the situation that existed before the fusionist model? Must we not admit that the media are now an integral part of the political arena and even of government? We have now to ask how to require the same principles from the media that democracy demands from politicians to prevent tyranny, to ensure accountability, and to keep power in citizens' hands.

The question that one must ask is, on the one hand, what tools should citizens be given in order to stand up to the power of the media, and on the other hand, how should the media itself behave in this new situation? Do the rules of behavior that were suitable in the past, when the media stood outside the halls of power and confronted the government, fit the new mediapolitik? What kind of social responsibility should be given to the media, and how should they behave so as not to harm democracy?

TELEPOPULISM AND COMMUNITARIANISM

Mediapolitik was not the only product of the social laboratory in Israel in the 1990s. The accelerated processes that took place there also created something else, something even more distinctive than the first product: telepopulism, a political genre that emerged in several states at the close of the twentieth century, most prominently in Italy, Bolivia, and Peru. Populism is certainly not a new phenomenon; it appeared in various forms in different places long before the advent of television. Contemporary populism, which has been called "new populism," "neopopulism," or "postpopulism," has its own particular features. However, in some cases, television's role has been so central to the emergence and the continuing existence of this new political construct that there is warrant for using a new term — "telepopulism."

Telepopulism is the embodiment of populism in the era of mediapolitik and is the most concrete expression of the new symbiosis between media and politics. It is the political formation whereby television serves a critical function and acts as the major tool in the hands of the populist leaders. However, in contrast with media outlets in the past — radio or the town square — in telepopulism the medium of television itself creates conditions that foster the development of populism. It constitutes a cultural and social infrastructure that enables the ascent of populist leaders. This phenomenon will be dealt with in the second section of the book, in Chapters 8 through 11. As in the first section, in the second section the particular Israeli case can also be used for comparative research and for general and theoretical propositions concerning the relation between media and politics.

The collapse of the old political order and a host of new social and cultural trends encouraged the development of populism in Israel in the 1990s. These developments, particularly the process of globalization, barely harmed the hegemonic elites at the top of the mediapolitik structure. They possessed a large amount of symbolic capital, controlled the old center of society, and ended up gaining from globalization. With the collapse of the previous political system, they were able to use their human and cultural capital to quickly integrate themselves into the new system. Many of them were able to weave new social ties beyond the limited boundaries of the nation-state and to adopt the new cosmopolitan culture of the global class.

The crumbling structures did, however, severely damage several other social groups: "Old Israelis," who could not integrate into the new economy tumbled down the rapidly upward-moving escalator of social mobility; those immigrants who could not adjust to the new homeland; and the youth who grew up on the periphery of society realized that the economic growth had surpassed them and that they were doomed to remain marginal. Israel, which had the highest level of economic equality in the democratic world for the first forty years of its existence, descended in the 1990s to the bottom of the comparative tables. Now, at the beginning of the new century it is second only to the United States in inequality indexes. The income gap between the poorest and the richest families is now 1:12, and the Gini coefficient that measures income distribution using a scale from 0 to 1, now exceeds 0.5, whereas it was previously fixed at less than 0.4.[7]

Certain populist moods and tendencies existed in Israel before the 1990s, encouraged particularly by Likud leader Menachem Begin during his term as prime minister from 1977 to 1983. However, the social changes of the late 1980s and early 1990s brought about the return of populism in a new form. Some Israeli social groups were intensely anxious during that period due to the social instability and status incongruency, typical of transition periods, particularly during modernization and accelerated economic development. The excluded groups had a deep sense of deprivation, could not put forward their claims for inclusion and entitlement in the new politics, were unable to express their wishes and dreams, and felt excluded from shaping Israeli's symbolic order with their own worldviews and perceptions. These groups reorganized themselves for a counterreaction, which expressed itself primarily in the cultural and identity spheres. The most radical manifestation of this was the ascent of Jewish fundamentalism and the spread of folk religious practices. A much wider reaction was the creation of the politics of identity and recognition. All of these groups became potential candidates for a neopopulist reaction to the old order.

What was now needed in order to trigger this potential populism was a leader who fit into this new world — someone who could gather the unorganized masses into a counterhegemonic bloc that would have a direct link to the populist leader. A leader with nationalistic ideology and rhetoric could lead this new political movement, which adopts principles of direct democracy, antistatism, social protest, and ethno-centricity by using the new political tool — television. The new leader who made use of television to mold this movement in the 1990s was Benjamin Netanyahu.

Netanyahu's news management style put him on a collision course with the media. The need of the telepopulist leader to use the media to build his position and then to control media outlets in order to solidify it necessarily creates a severe reaction by journalists. And so Netanyahu, the politician who understood the media better than anyone and was the best at manipulating them, unintentionally turned them into forceful opposition to him. Indeed, as is shown in Chapter 11, it was the desire of the media to resist his manipulation and to keep their autonomy that made them mobilize against Netanyahu and contribute to his downfall in 1999.

Although the telepopulist leader can inspire a wealth of hope among disenfranchised classes, his answers cannot solve the real problems of mature democracies. Such a solution is in fact a mirage: it is presentation, not representation. Indeed, as opposed to those who were caught up in the populist solution — under the influence of the leader who created symbolic meaning, prestige, and recognition — there were many in Israel who sought a different answer, one that supplied genuine belonging and participation. This was done by cultural groups based on communitarian principles. Indeed, the transformation from class politics to identity politics quickly created several cultural groups at the subnational level, which included Russian-speaking immigrants, Israeli Palestinians, ultraorthodox, religious nationalists, and to a lesser degree "southerners."[8] These were mnemonic communities that were formed on the basis of traditions, whether renewed or invented.

Like the new populist solution, the communitarian response also took shape in a media-saturated society, and the media were a significant force in its formation. Whereas national mainstream media supported the populist solution, small, alternative media helped the cultural groups. Indeed, alternative media played a major role in the constitution of the separate collective identities of each co-culture within Israeli society and had a major part in the constitution of the new sectarian or multicultural society.

This part of the story — the creation of the sectorial society and the role of the small media — appears in Chapters 12 and 13. Beyond presenting a historical description, that section of the book attempts to deal with the question of the impact of both mainstream and alternative media on the future development of Israeli society. Will the tendency to split the public sphere into small, secluded sphericules that create a mosaic of closed sectors continue? Will these changes possibly even bring about the disintegration of society, or will they cause the crystallization of a deep multicultural framework?

The different themes that are raised in the three parts of the book — the new mediapolitik, telepopulism, and the alternative media of the sectarian society — will be synthesized in the Conclusion and the perspectives of journalists will also be considered. The book ends by drawing conclusions regarding measures that should be taken in order for society to better respond to the challenges imposed by the media's new role as part of the body politic.

As for method, the book endeavors to present an empirically anchored theory of media-political relations in advanced democracies and uses Israel as a case study. I have used an integrated system, which includes both historical and analytical approaches and relies on extensive content analysis of newspapers and magazines in Israel, making wide use of primary sources. I have also collected relevant data from other sources, including journalists' surveys, public opinion polls, and press council statistics. This approach seemed fitting for research that attempts to span a period of more than fifty years and to encompass many diverse factors. I was also aided by my students in the Department of Communication at the Hebrew University of Jerusalem, who conducted a series of empirical studies. Together we did viewer and listener research, analyzed changes in news style and talk shows, and examined the small media of various co-cultural groups.

I also made use of ethnographic methodology, which included extensive interviews with members of the political and media elite in Israel, and added my impressions as a participant-observer of politics and the media. I was able to do so because over the course of a thirty-year career, I have been involved with political communication in three circles: journalism, politics, and academe.

My journalistic career began at the daily newspaper *Davar*, where I was a reporter, investigative journalist, columnist, managing editor, and, finally, editor in chief. I was also a member and president of the Association of Editors of Daily Newspapers and a member of the Press Council. I was involved in politics for several years as well, first as the spokesman of the Labor Party during Golda Meir's term as prime minister in the 1970s, then as the representative of the party in international organizations, and finally as political advisor to the late Prime Minister Yitzhak Rabin.

My academic research has revolved around different aspects of political sociology, particularly in Israel. I focused first on the role of the military in Israeli politics and society, and later on the relationship between the media, politics, and society. This triangle of professional journalism, political involvement, and academic research has given me a broad and multilayered perspective and hopefully a deeper sense of political communication in Israel, as well as a comparative and theoretical view.

This book is the fruit of four years of work, and I would like to thank the many people who assisted me at different stages of the process. First and foremost, I am grateful to Elihu Katz, a teacher-turned-colleague. One never ceases being overwhelmed by his originality and creativity and continuously learning from him. The many conversations I had with Daniel Hallin have helped me immensely to develop ideas presented in the book. Michael Gurevitch's comments contributed to the improvement of the first drafts. Special thanks are due to my colleagues and students at the Hebrew University of Jerusalem, especially Gadi Wolfsfeld, for many years of friendly collaboration. My warm appreciation goes to Hazel Arieli for helping me with the language and style.

I was assisted in this research by several foundations, including the Eshkol Institute of the Social Sciences Faculty at the Hebrew University of Jerusalem and the Truman Institute at that university. I am thankful for the Fulbright scholarship that I received in 2000. Thanks are also due to the School of International Service at the American University, Washington, D.C., and particularly to its dean, Louis Goodman, for providing me with a stimulating atmosphere for research and writing in 2001.

I owe more than I can express in words to my family: my wife, Pnina, for years of friendship, love, and sacrifice; and my children, Daphne, Jonathan, and Alma. They all continue to pay the price of my dedication to my work.

PART ONE

The Emergence of "Mediapolitik"

CHAPTER ONE

The Media Revolution of the 1990s

THE PEOPLE OF THE BOOK AND VISUAL CULTURE

"The three most important events that took place in Israel in the last decade of the twentieth century were the wave of immigration from the former Soviet Union, the Oslo Accords, and the inauguration of Channel 2 broadcasting," declared Uri Shinar, CEO of Reshet, one of the three companies that operate commercial television in Israel, in November 1998.

This provocative statement may raise some eyebrows. Indeed, the first two developments wrought tremendous change in Israeli society in the 1990s. The latest wave of immigration brought approximately one million Jews to Israel within a ten-year span. This group now constitutes the largest ethnic group in the country, approximately 17 percent of the population. Their arrival dramatically altered the character of Israeli society and ushered in a new era of multiculturalism. The 1993 Oslo Accords were no less significant in transforming the country; these accords expressed mutual recognition between the Israeli and Palestinian national movements after one hundred years of bloody conflict, leading to the assassination of Israeli Prime Minister Yitzhak Rabin in November 1995 and expediting progress toward the establishment of an independent Palestinian state. Is it not extremely arrogant to place the launching of commercial television on a par with these two other historic events?

The answer, in fact, is no. If we replace the phrase "the inauguration of Channel 2 broadcasting" with "the beginning of the era of multichannel commercial television," the words do not sound exaggerated, but instead hint at the kind of dramatic transformations that commercial television brought to Israeli politics, culture, and society in the 1990s. Simply put, it was a media revolution. During the 1990s, a commercial channel and tens of cable and satellite channels were added to the one existing public television station. These were also the years when VCRs and remote controls became popular and when the Internet was introduced. These together made significant structural modifications to the media landscape. Foremost, the 1990s ushered in a new cultural era in which television became a hegemonic actor in Israeli society.

The transformations that commercial television caused are especially dramatic when seen in the light of Jewish culture's deep connections to and emphasis on written traditions. The Jewish people have always ascribed profound significance to words, particularly to the written word. According to tradition, God created the world with a word. In contrast, attitudes toward visual representations among Jews have traditionally been negative. The Ten Commandments, for example, explicitly forbid the use of pictures and "graven images." Jews have often liked being referred to as "the people of the Book," a people that for almost two thousand years carried a written text that gave one a sense of the homeland from one diasporic community to another. For many years, Jewish authors were even named after the books that they wrote.

Zionism sought to constitute the modern Jewish nation first and foremost by creating a new text. This was done by reviving the ancient Hebrew language that had been used for hundreds of years only in religious ceremonies and by putting it into daily practice. Even the first daily newspapers founded in Palestine at the beginning of the twentieth century emerged from the ideological aim of turning Hebrew into a living language. In the absence of other assets, Hebrew language and culture served the Jewish community as an appropriating power and distinguished it from other societies. The new Hebrew culture was the ultimate project for the creation of a national identity (Z. Shavit 1998). Because of this centrality of the written word to Jewish culture, the arrival of television in Israel caused an especially dramatic revolution — it brought about the visualization of the culture.

Although speech is an essential tool of communication, people are in fact more visual than verbal (Hay 1986). When we are confronted with communicational texts, we first receive the visual message. Of all the senses, the quickest one is the eye, which identifies movement in space (Alger 1989). This ability is ingrained in our nature as human beings and derives from our survival instinct. Our greatest dangers come from predators that move in space; thus the eye is the essential tool for identifying and defending oneself against such enemies.

Despite this fundamental and age-old dependence on the visual, it was only the twentieth century that was labeled the "the age of the image." During this time moving pictures were added to the written word and the spoken voice, and the eye gained supremacy over the ear. This era started in the 1920s with the advent of the feature film and film art, further developing in the 1950s and 1960s with the emergence of television, and culminating in the 1980s and 1990s with the transformation of television, combined with the introduction of video and computer-based media. This visual-oriented century has led most theorists to agree that one of the distinctive features of postmodern societies is the dominance of the image within these societies.

Images are critical in contemporary culture because visual culture focuses on the visual as a place where meaning is created and contested. A picture is perceived as "admissible evidence" in the search for truth, as compared with information that is processed through the other senses. One sees this belief in such expressions as "to see the truth," and "a picture is worth a thousand words." Further evidence of this phenomenon is seen in the role that television footage has on the judgments of public opinion and politicians in modern wars. Television, rather than the actual battles on the ground, often is a decisive factor in determining which side was right and even which side won the war.

One of the most striking features of the new visual culture that has developed since the introduction of television is its influence on everyday life: modern life increasingly takes place on the TV screen. "The audiovisual mass media currently makes up the bulk of the world's symbolic environment" (Graber 2001: 95). Furthermore, visual culture does not depend on pictures themselves, but rather on the modern tendency to visualize existence (Mizroeff 1999). There is a growing tendency to picture things that are not in fact visual themselves. I do not, however, intend to expand on the issue of the impact of the visual revolution on culture at large, as media scholars such as Ong, McLuhan, or Meyrowitz have done, or even to examine its influence on Israel culture. The focus here will be instead on the changes that the new visual culture has wrought in the political arena, with a subsequent analysis of the concept of mediapolitik, or media-centered democracy.

The professional literature is saturated with the negative impacts of visualization on politics. The most prominent of these theories is the argument that before the advent of network newscasts campaigns were largely discursive, based on the spoken and written word (Schudson 1982). With the introduction of television into the political field, the nature of discourse during political campaigns was irrevocably altered. A frequently cited example is the famous Kennedy-Nixon debate from the 1960 U.S. presidential campaign, the political campaign that ushered in the era of televisual politics. While radio listeners claimed that Republican candidate Richard Nixon had won the debate, television viewers argued that Democrat John F. Kennedy had been the better speaker, mainly as a result of Nixon's sweating and nervous appearance. Twenty years later, it became apparent that U.S. President Reagan's huge popularity was due largely to his public image. Although the majority of Americans held opinions on policy issues that contradicted the president's, yet they reelected him in a landslide victory in 1984. Since the 1980s, polls have indicated that many voters are willing to vote for a candidate with whom they disagree on the issue because they "personally like him or her. Indeed, a third of Ronald Reagan's voters came from such support" (Meyrowitz 1992).

Since 1980, we know as a basic fact of campaigns that voters judge candidates in a completely different way when they use different senses. A given candidate's level of public support is significantly different when he relies solely on his words rather than his visual message. Because people trust the visual more than the verbal message, the image in fact becomes the prominent message of the campaign (Graber 1984).

The problem, according to this approach, is that television plays to the emotions rather than to the rational capacities of the viewer — something that derives from the essence of the medium. "What visual syntax lacks, especially in comparison to verbal language, is a set of explicit devices for indicating causality, analogy, or any other relationship other than those of space or time" (Messaris 1997: xviii). The structure of the "visual sentence" is based on the establishment of an argument by putting one picture next to another, thus creating a temporal or spatial relationship (not an explicit causal one) between them. Interpretations of this kind can be created only in the viewer's mind because they are not engrained in the substance of the text, but rather in the visual juxtaposition of the images or texts. Therefore, the range of interpretations of visual texts is much wider than the spoken or written text.

Written texts, by contrast, deal with the realm of linear, rational logic. Reading encourages rationality, as the sequential prepositional character of the written word forces one to deal with the abstract, or what Walter Ong calls "the analytical management of knowledge" (Alger 1989: 61). An argument that logically follows from this proposition is that the visual culture of television has transformed rational democracy, where debate is conducted using words, arguments, counterarguments, reason, and discourse into a model of democracy where the legitimacy of policy issues derives foremost from the personalities of the politicians shown on the TV screen.

One of the most important outcomes of the visualization of politics is its creation and furthering of the personalization of politics. Following this, the field of image management was widely developed. If we find, for example, in a public opinion poll conducted at the beginning of a political campaign that honesty is considered by voters as the most important characteristic of a given candidate, we will use tools of persuasive communication and visual argumentation to make our candidate seem more honest. Knowing that direct eye contact creates a sense among television viewers of a trustworthy person, all we have to do is to train our candidates to look straight into the camera when speaking.

The transformation from verbal to visual messages has caused an expansion of image-conscious political marketing, with an emphasis on style and the building of a politician's public persona. A wide avenue has thus opened up for political manipulation. Despite the seemingly cynical tone of such an idea, one example of such manipulation is the growing use of the "natural sound." Following the negative criticism of political publicity, candidates rarely speak during their political commercials. To resolve this problem, the "natural sound" was invented, which is "an editing technique that employs a few words of the candidate's speech without intending to convey information" (Adatto 1993: 6).

Although I have described at length only one of the negative effects of visualization on politics, there is a plethora of similar arguments. One, related to the previous criticism, is the argument that newsworthiness considerations are distorted because television newscasts prefer to air stories that have eye-catching images. Another is that the visual excels in emotional arousal compared to nonvisual stimuli; thus the quality of thinking elicited by audiovisual messages is shallow and short on rationality (Robinson and Davis 1990). Television distracts people from analyzing the substance of political issues. Furthermore, the fact that television brings images of the world into one's living room misleads viewers into believing that they are powerful and can easily change the world (Hart 1994).

Another criticism is that television distorts political reality. As Griffin describes it, visual imagery unavoidably alters the spatial and temporal dimensions of reality, creating mediated versions of people, places, and events that are fundamentally different from unmediated experiences (Griffin 1992). One reason for this phenomenon is the fact that television makes extended use of the technique of melodrama (Wagner-Pacifici 1986). Other causes include the argument that reality is skewed because most news stories are constructed by stringing together nonconsequential vignettes, and "television does present a caricature of the political world" (Graber 2001: 121). In addition, scholars have argued that pictures excel in presenting events but that they are somewhat less adept at analyzing them (Graber 2001). Also, the fact that imagery invokes a very distinct aspect of politics, including an emphasis on surface over substance, a reliance on stereotypes and pseudocrises, and the focus on journalists as actors, all of which distort the viewer's sense of political consequences (Bennett 1998).

These criticisms relate to the specific impact of the visual dimension of television on politics. The influence that television culture as a whole had on the political arena, however, was in fact much larger and deeper. Numerous media scholars have dealt with the negative impact that television had on democratic culture: a decrease in public trust, an increase in dissatisfaction with political institutions, a decrease in social capital and the level of political participation, and eventually the de-politicization of society. Although these arguments continue to form the basis of a plethora of articles and books, one can discern a new intellectual current that emphasizes the positive impacts of the visual on society and politics. Doris Graber provides a forceful discussion of this trend:

> Audiovisual rhetoric helped viewers to create new schemas and enrich existing ones . . . audiovisuals can convey abstractions . . . pictures are especially useful for resolving tangible evidence to citizens about major problems and possible solutions. . . . Audiovisuals have been widely praised for illuminating some of the most crucial social and political events of the twentieth century, giving viewers a clear, more lasting picture of what actually occurred than words alone could have done. (Graber 2001)

She further argues that the emotions that the visual arouse are crucial for the decision-making process, since "there is a symbiotic relationship between feeling and cognition. Emotional involvement therefore is essential to sound decision making" (Graber 2001: 72–79). Pippa Norris's book *A Virtuous Circle: Political Communication in Postindustrial Societies* is one of the most significant treatises of this new school of thought (2000). Norris and others contend that although these negative impacts might be relevant to the United States, they cannot be used as a general rule when analyzing other societies, many of which show trends of increased political interest and involvement.

Indeed, the Israeli case refutes many of the negative-impact theories.[1] Although it is true that the level of public trust of politicians and political institutions in Israel decreased by more than 20 percent during the 1990s, the knowledge and interest in Israeli politics did not diminish.[2] Meanwhile the previously high levels of political involvement continued and even increased. During the 1990s, approximately 80 percent of eligible voters went to the polls, and on the night of the 1999 elections, people in eight out of ten Israeli homes were glued to the television, watching the special-election broadcast on both noncable TV channels.

The communication revolution caused an enlargement of interest and knowledge of politics. Israelis are avid consumers of political information. More than 71 percent read a daily paper, and nearly 84 percent read a weekend newspaper (published on Friday, as there are no papers on Saturday). They also spend a significant amount of time reading. One-third devote up to half an hour per day to reading newspapers, one-third read papers for between half an hour and an hour, and one-quarter spend more than an hour a day reading papers. The average viewership of the evening news was about 60 percent during the 1990s — 40 percent on the commercial channel and the remaining 20 percent on the public channel (Tokatly 2000: 201) — compared to only 46 percent in the United States (Sparks and Tulloch 2000: 228).

The political newspaper columns are highly preferred to any other column, both by readers of the highbrow *Haaretz* (65 percent) and by tabloid consumers (55 percent). Israelis usually get their news information from more than one source. More than two-thirds of weekend newspaper readers in Israel read two weekend papers, and radio listening and television watching is frequent. In contrast, more than two-thirds of Americans rely on television alone for their news information (Castells 1997: 313). Even among television viewers, news programs are the most preferred, much above entertainment and other television genres. News is the first priority for more than 50 percent of viewers, compared to 25 percent who prefer entertainment (Adoni and Nossek 1997: 104). Three or four out of the ten highest-rated television programs at the end of the 1990s were news and current-affairs programs, and at the end of January 2002, when the new commercial channel was launched, its highest-rated broadcasts were news programs.[3]

A glance at the tabloids provides additional evidence of the high level of political engagement. Like the highbrow papers, the Israeli tabloids deal primarily with politics. The attempts to develop a supermarket press, such as the American *National Inquirer*, the British *Sun*, or the German *Das Bild*, failed in Israel. In tabloids, sex, sports, and crime, human stories and soft news take center stage. Not so in the Holy Land. There is very little paparazzi intrusion in the private lives of celebrities and no media coverage of politicians' sex lives or sexual preferences. The tabloid style is expressed in huge headlines, color print, an abundance of graphic elements, fewer opinion columns, the lessened importance of the op-ed page, as well as a certain type of sensationalist rhetoric, language, and editorial style. However, even in tabloids, politics and political news stand above all else.

Does this continued emphasis on news and politics mean that television has not changed the political habits of Israelis, their information consumption, or the substance of the information they consume? On the contrary, television has created a much deeper change in Israeli society: it has transformed the entire nature of Israeli politics. In order to fully examine this phenomenon, one must start with the beginning of the story. Because all chapters in Israeli history start and end with wars, we begin with the Six-Day War of 1967.

The effects of the communication revolution on political behavior in Israel more closely resemble the changes that occurred in European parliamentary democracies such as Germany and Italy than those that took place in the United States, with its presidential and majoritarian system.[4] As has happened in the United States, public attitudes toward politicians became more negative and public mistrust of national institutions grew. However, as distinct from the United States, Israelis' interest and participation in politics increased in the 1990s, albeit in a different form.

Although the new media culture did not create a "democracy without citizens" in Israel, as it did in some countries (Entman 1989), the synergy of the political and media revolutions generated a real change: it created a new kind of politics, mediapolitik, or media-centered democracy.

TELEVISION COMES TO THE HOLY LAND

Israeli television broadcasting began in June 1968. The introduction of this medium had hitherto been prevented by one man, David Ben Gurion. The "old man," as he was known, derived his power from having served as prime minister and defense minister from the day when he declared the establishment of the Jewish state in May 1948, until his voluntary retirement in 1963. Ben Gurion liked the Platonic model of the philosopher-king. He read a great deal, was an avid collector of books, and wrote voluminously. Like Churchill, he not only made history but also wrote the history of the period himself; unlike his British counterpart, however, he did not wait until his retirement to do this. Ben Gurion also devoted a great deal of time to reading newspapers and wrote to them, especially when he was involved in political controversies. With his turbulent temperament these were not rare occasions. He even liked movies and used to go to one of the few cinemas that existed in Jerusalem at that time. But television — that was another matter.

Ben Gurion considered television a negative and superfluous invention. Any doubts he may have had about this were dispelled one day in the early 1950s, when he stopped over in London to visit his son and grandchildren while on his way back from a session of the United Nations in New York. When he entered the apartment, he expected his grandchildren to run up to him, throw their arms around him, and hug him, but this did not happen. Sitting on the floor, their eyes riveted to the TV set, they turned round to glance at him for a moment and then turned back to the program. "When he told me this story upon his return to Israel, I saw that he still hadn't got over it," said Yitzhak Navon, his confidential secretary at the time, and later the fifth president of Israel in the 1970s. "It was clear to me that the old man was saying in his downright way: that's a mind-destroying device. It wastes time and addles the brain. We won't have it in our country."[5]

Was that the only reason? Ben Gurion the ascetic certainly saw television as an unnecessary luxury that did not suit the young, poor, pioneering society that he aspired to mold as a "light unto nations." Perhaps this authoritative leader also secretly feared television's potential ability to challenge the traditional loci of political power? In any case, it is doubtful whether there is another case of a democratic state in which one man was able to prevent the introduction of the cultural artefact that is so symbolic of the second half of the twentieth century.

Ben Gurion's successor, Levi Eshkol, who was a more easy-going, warm, and open-minded man, had to wait until he had settled into his position as prime minister before he could enable Israelis to discover the wonders of the new magic box. But he, too, decided to introduce television only when he was convinced that it could be a useful tool for the government. Following the Six-Day War in June 1967, more than a million and a half Palestinians in the West Bank of Jordan and the Gaza Strip came under Israel's control. Eshkol's colleague, Information Minister Israel Galili, sought tools that could help him to influence this population's political attitudes, and television seemed to be an effective option.

At that time, more than thirty thousand Israelis already had TV sets in their homes and they watched broadcasts from Jordan, Egypt, and Syria. Galili explained that the time had come to use this tool for propaganda in the opposite direction. He also argued that Israeli television could penetrate into the living rooms of tens of millions in the Arab states surrounding Israel and serve as a weapon in the ongoing war with them. Therefore, on September 17, 1967, the Israeli government decided to establish television as an emergency measure, broadcasting four hours a day in Arabic and only half an hour in Hebrew.

It was indeed symbolic that the new television began to broadcast on Independence Day and that the first broadcast was a review of a huge military parade through the streets of east Jerusalem, newly conquered from the kingdom of Jordan. It was no less symbolic that the TV camera dwelt on Prime Minister Levi Eshkol and his protégé, Chief of Staff Yitzhak Rabin, while completely ignoring the popular Defense Minister Moshe Dayan, their sworn political rival. When Dayan complained of media discrimination, he received an answer that left him speechless: "The TV cameraman was a foreigner and simply didn't recognize Dayan and therefore did not shoot him." Although it is hard to imagine that any journalist could have failed to identify the charismatic leader with the black eyepatch who was the hero of the Six-Day War, no one even bothered to question the Dutch cameraman (Gil 1986).

Even after general television was instituted, the political establishment still related to it like the ancient Ionians related to the fire that Prometheus brought down from the mountains: as a demonic invention whose harm exceeded its benefit.[6] Following this logic, Levi Eshkol thought that if one must have television, there was no need for expensive color TV: black-and-white television was good enough.[7] However, the futility of the attempt to halt such technological progress is graphically demonstrated in the story of the "antieraser," a product that became a distinct concept in Israel's cultural history.

Before Israeli television was established, a significant portion of the population had already acquired color TV sets to receive broadcasts from the Arab states. The infrastructure of the new Israeli television was prepared in advance for color broadcasting. In order to prevent mass buying of color sets, however, the government decided to operate an electronic device in the broadcasting stations, converting color broadcasts into black and white. The press, predictably, mocked this patent and called it "the eraser." It was not long before the Israeli public, which doesn't like to take no for an answer, found a technical way to overcome the prohibition, and the antidote soon appeared on the market — a small electronic device installed in the TV set that cancelled the effect of erasing the color. The name given to this invention was, not surprisingly, the "antieraser."

The device was expensive, costing IL5,000 when the price of a TV set was IL44,000, but the public bought it. When it became clear that most of the pubic could see color television, and those who could not, preferred the color broadcasts from Jordan, the government gave in. Television and public pressure had overcome the politicians.[8] Within ten years, color TV was installed in 80 percent of households (unlike the United States, for example, where only 10 percent of households acquired color TV in the first ten years of commercial color TV). This device both reflected and promoted the end of the ascetic age in Israeli society (Blondheim 1998).[9]

TELEVISION OUSTS THE NEWSPAPERS

In the early 1980s, illegal broadcasts began to appear throughout the country. These were the endeavors of agile entrepreneurs who were not especially impressed by the law that gave a monopoly to the Israeli Broadcasting Authority. In 1985, legislation to regulate cable TV broadcasting was initiated, and two years later, the Telecommunication Law was passed. The legislation procedure took only a few months; thus, unlike in most other countries, in Israel cable TV preceded off-air commercial television broadcasting. The government was quick to approve cable broadcasts because these were planned as regional broadcasts, covering only local news and not national news. Government ministers did not consider that these broadcasts would create a new forum, entailing concern about who might control it. Therefore, cable TV was not the object of special attention, despite its great potential in terms of communication (Lachman-Messer 1997: 71).

During the legislation processes for the second terrestrial channel, beginning in 1990, experimental broadcasts were conducted on this channel. Since it was to be a national channel financed by advertising and including a news company — elements that did not exist in cable TV — the legislation process was longer and more complicated. Finally, the new television company was established in September 1993, and one year later its news department began broadcasting.

The public lost no time in connecting to cable TV. By the time Channel 2 started broadcasting at the end of 1993, three and a half years after the introduction of cable TV, 60 percent of households in Israel were already connected to cable TV. This figure has since increased to 90 percent, with 70 percent actually subscribing to cable service. Only about 100,000 homes, either in outlying villages or belonging to members of ultraorthodox groups who are forbidden to watch television for religious reasons, are not connected to cable TV (Tokatly 2000). Such a high rate of cable TV generally characterizes small countries with multilingual populations that border on larger, cable TV supplier states, as in the case of Switzerland and the Benelux countries.[10] This is not, however, the case in Israel.

For a fee of less than U.S.$50 a month, cable TV offers its subscribers about fifty channels, some of them broadcasts relayed from satellites. Six of these are in Hebrew or with Hebrew subtitles; others broadcast in the variety of languages spoken by a diverse Israeli population. Since the legislature's intention was to establish the cable broadcasts as regional broadcasts, the law determined that there would be five companies. In practice, beyond a small extent of regional newscasts and broadcasting of current events on one channel, all the companies jointly run the regional broadcasts and provide their subscribers with most of the channels. For this purpose, they also established a joint programming company, ICP. The dream of regionality was shattered by the companies' commercial interests, but the multichannel age had already begun.

To sum up, until 1968 the Israelis did not have exposure to television at all. For the next twenty-five years, they were exposed to one monopolistic channel, which was controlled completely and later influenced by the government. The television consumers of the 1990s lived in an

entirely different reality, one of "open skies." Instead of one channel providing newscasts of half an hour a day, the viewers of the 1990s were
exposed to a second rival channel, which was under public supervision
but owned by private companies. In addition, they were now able to
view, on a twenty-four-hour-a-day basis, satellite channels that relayed
news and current events programs from the BBC, Sky News, or French,
Turkish, German, Spanish, Italian, Russian, and Arabic stations, as well
as American channels such as CNN.

In 2000 competition was introduced into multichannel broadcasting
with the launching of the "Yes" channel, operated by Direct Broadcast
Satellite (DBS). In order to compete with "Yes," the veteran cable companies decided to supply their subscribers with more channels and
divide the market into more specific target groups. They added dozens
of new channels and also upgraded to a digital cable format. In March
2000 the Knesset approved the establishment of a third terrestrial channel, Channel 10 (now the second commercial channel), which began
broadcasting soon afterward. In 2001, the first steps were taken to also
introduce designated channels: a full-time news channel, an Israeli
music video channel, a Jewish heritage channel, as well as channels in
Russian and Arabic.

A quantitative expression of the entrance into the television era is
reflected in the graphs of Israelis' cultural consumption. In 1970, two
years after the television era began, most of the adult population spent
about one hour per day (fifty-four minutes to be precise) watching the
single channel, which broadcast only a few hours a day. Twenty years
later, they were already watching television almost two hours a day, and
in 1988 this number increased by forty-two more minutes. Children spent
even more time in front of the set — averaging around four hours a day.[11]

Meanwhile, a media explosion was occurring in radio as well. For
decades, only two radio broadcasters had existed in Israel, Kol Israel (the
Voice of Israel) and Galei Zahal — the IDF (Israel Defense Forces) broadcasting station. Until 1965 the former was a government department under
the supervision of the director-general of the prime minister's office. It later
acquired the status of a public authority, subordinate to a public council,
following the BBC model. Galei Zahal, with one channel broadcasting
fewer than twenty-four hours a day, was the "army radio," subject to the
authority of the defense minister and the chief of staff. Its chief editor's title
was "Commander of Galei Zahal." In the 1980s some pirate radio stations
began to be heard on the airwaves. Most of these were local, but two of
them operated on a nationwide scale and had a distinctly political character: the Voice of Peace, operated by left-wing peace activist Abie Nathan;
and Channel 7 operated by the nationalist settlers on the West Bank.

In the wake of the liberalization in broadcasting and the legislation establishing a Second Authority for Radio and Television in 1993, an array of local commercial radio stations was in operation two years later. The established stations, Kol Israel and Galei Zahal, were not long in rising to the commercial challenge, and they, too, added more and more channels. The cliché that politicians were so fond of using to describe Israel in the 1950s — a Western island in a hostile Arab sea — sounded very true to anyone sitting in front of the radio receiver in those days, unable to receive more than two Hebrew-speaking channels. Today, the thirty-six automatic buttons on the digital car radio cover only a small proportion of the Israeli radio stations broadcasting in Hebrew. Fourteen stations broadcast under the aegis of the Second Authority for Radio and Television. Added to these are more than one hundred pirate stations. With radio, as with television, the proliferation of channels is only one dimension of the transition. Other dimensions include the split in mass broadcasting and the development of narrowcasting of the various Israeli co-cultures.

Print journalism also underwent a dramatic change in the course of the 1990s. The number of Hebrew dailies dropped from fourteen to seven in ten years, and the public sphere disintegrated into many different small public "sphericules," to use Todd Gitlin's term (1999). An unprecedented flowering of small-circulation dailies, weeklies, and periodicals in foreign languages, particularly Russian, among the co-cultures that comprise the new Israeli social mosaic followed.[12]

Despite the fact that television broadcasting had begun as far back as the 1970s, and although the overall circulation of the print media had grown, it was in the 1990s that television replaced the press as the dominant medium. All at once, Israeli culture entered the visual era. A comparative study examining cultural consumption in Israel in previous decades states explicitly, "In 1990 television ousted the newspaper and became the medium that best met the diverse needs of the Israeli public" (Katz et al. 1992). The study by Katz and his associates was based on the "uses and gratification" approach (Adoni and Nossek 1997: 99). This theoretical approach, despite its popularity among functionalist scholars, hides more important dimensions of the cultural phenomenon, beyond the response to the conscious needs of the media-consuming public. The 1990s were the era of consolidation of the "television society" in Israel.

FROM SERVICE TO BUSINESS

Two major developments occurred in Israel's media in the 1990s. First, the monopoly on public broadcasting in radio and television was broken, and a multichannel system was developed both in the print and electronic media. Second, the media became a true industry during this time, acting out of commercial considerations for the purpose of maximizing profits. These changes are no different in principle from the processes that occurred in many other developed countries, except that in Israel they occurred later. Even in Scandinavia, these processes were completed by the 1980s, and they acquired a specific form as a result of local constraints (Syvertsen 1997). An example particularly close to the Israeli case is that of the "ethereal revolution" in Italy, where five hundred television stations and two thousand radio stations sprang up as soon as the monopoly on public broadcasting was lifted in 1980, with far-reaching effects on the culture and later on the politics of Italian society (Mazzoleni 1987b).

During the 1990s the Israeli media became an industry no different in character from other economic sectors in the late-capitalist market. While Israel's mass-media map had for decades included only a handful of organizations, most of them controlled by the government or political parties, it now became an enormous web of corporations with an annual turnover of hundreds of millions of dollars. As soon as Channel 2, the commercial channel, went into operation, its financial growth rate went far beyond expectations. In 1994, the three commercial time-sharing broadcasters grossed IS330 million, in 1995 IS449 million, and more than IS570 million in 1996, an increase of 72 percent in two years. This pace continued in the following years, as the commercialization of the media engendered rapid growth in advertising, with television commercials accounting for 40 percent of the national advertising budget (Blondheim 1998: 338).

Commercialization led to a redefinition of the aims of the media organizations, shifting from a social orientation based on the ideology of public service, to an industry based on a market-oriented ethos with profitability as its central goal. In order to justify their new stockholders' investments, communication firms focused on economizing and maximizing profit. The immediate result was that the one clear division in news organizations between editorial decisions about the nature of the product and the marketing of the product disappeared rapidly. The Israeli news media became a platform for its owners to sell advertising space; thus, in the 1990s a new word entered the Israeli cultural scene — "rating." The Hebrew language did not even have a word for this concept.

Naturally, the great apostle of the rating gospel was commercial television, but public service broadcasting, including radio, was soon captivated by its magic. Although the mission of "selling an audience to the advertisers" was designed for the commercial channel, the public service Channel 1 — whose revenue is provided by license fees — also adopted the ratings principle and eschewed its traditional role of "selling the media product and its contents to the audience" (Curran 1986). This adaptation of public service broadcasting is familiar in many countries and was described by Bourdieu as "homogenization and banalization" (1999: 50). Others, somewhat less critical, described it as "convergence" (Merten 1994; Pfetsch 1996b). However, it is not inevitable; in this respect Sweden is an excellent example.

Like Israel, Sweden was governed for close to forty years by a social-democratic party, which stubbornly prevented the commercialization of public broadcasting. Finally, at the end of the 1980s, with the collapse of the welfare state, the barrier in the media was also broken down. The success of the commercial channels soon led the public service broadcasting to adopt the new style. However, neither the audience nor the media professionals concurred with this trend, and after a few years, the public service channels developed their own quality style, distinguishing them from commercial broadcasting. The entrance into the dual track era — commercial channels alongside public service broadcasting — considerably reduced the media dependence on politics without detracting from the public broadcasting's consciousness of public service and social responsibility (Machill 1999).

With respect to the treatment of public affairs in news broadcasts, European researchers found that in most European countries public television did not emulate the "infotainment" of commercial television; on the contrary, in many cases the latter even adopted part of the professional style of the former. "Contrary to what one might expect, news programs on the public channels did not move to the periphery of or outside prime-time in order to compete with popular drama on commercial television" (Brants 1998: 321).

In Israel, by contrast, the commercial approach was swiftly internalized, not only by those with financial interests in the media but also by those with an interest in culture in general. Although a high rating was a necessary condition for profitability in the commercial media, on the public channel it became a professional criterion. In the new media the guiding principle was "vox populi, vox Dei," and not just because of the profit motive. A high rating became an artistic criterion. Popularity, rather than any standard of quality, is what gives status to cultural products both in the arts and in other cultural spheres. Thus through the mechanism of rating commercial logic has been enforced on the cultural products.

The changed nature and aims of the news organizations also affected their management styles. The professional journalists and editors who had headed these organizations in the past were replaced in the second half of the 1990s by experts in administration, marketing, or financial management. The evening paper *Maariv*, for example, had previously been headed by a group of senior journalists — Azriel Carlebach, Arie Dissenchik, Shalom Rosenfeld, Shemuel Schnitzer, and Moshe Zak — who had resigned from *Yediot Ahronot* and had established the paper in 1948. In the 1990s, however, the paper was bought by two businessmen, Ya'akov Nimrodi and his son Ofer. The publisher also appointed himself editor in chief. The commercial character of the modern media inevitably led to increased intervention by publishers in editorial decisions.[13]

Commercialization also brought about a change in the status of the Journalists Association, both in their wage structure and their professional approach. Until the 1970s, almost all journalists were members of this trade union and worked according to a collective agreement that determined the principle of tenure at work and set the salary scale, with the gap between the lowest and highest grade not exceeding 1:4. When the media became a business the publishers pressed for more flexibility in the labor market. Consequently by the end of the decade more than half of the journalists in Israel were working on personal contracts without tenure. At the same time, publishers were prepared to pay high salaries to top journalists. With the launching of Channel 2 broadcasting, a new class had arisen: journalists and anchormen who were television celebrities. Concurrently, the wage gap in the profession jumped to 1:20.[14]

The weakening of the Journalists Association undermined the job security of those working in the media sector. "The journalist's status and resistance vis-à-vis his paper's publisher and editor have been considerably eroded in recent years and his dependence on them has grown," said attorney Haim Tzadok, president of the Press Council and former minister of justice in Yitzhak Rabin's government.[15] Moreover, it led to the weakening of the professional and ethical control mechanisms of the press community. There was no one to resist the harmful effects of commercialization on the profession. For example, journalists began to appear in commercials, despite their colleagues' criticism that this compromised their professional integrity and contravened the ethical code of the Journalists Association. When the watchdogs tried to bring up these cases in the Journalists Association, the new stars preferred to leave the union rather than forfeit the income of tens of thousands of dollars for half-minute commercials.

The profession was badly damaged by the fact that the most famous and prominent journalists, particularly political analysts, became hosts of talk shows and even entertainment shows while continuing to act as though they were journalists. When they became celebrities, with the significant effect on their bank balance, many of them lost a sense of mission that had characterized not only the previous generation but also themselves ten years earlier. Now very few of them still see their profession as *beruf* (a calling). "Carlebach did not sell newspapers," wrote Shemuel Schnitzer, editor of *Maariv*, about the founder and legendary editor of his paper, "he sold a vision."[16] In the Israel of 1999 a political journalist could establish a private company and sell its products — political interviews — to the commercial channel, his profits being a direct function of the program's rating. What will the considerations of such a journalist be in choosing his guests or formulating his questions? Professional considerations, like those that guided him in the past, or the wish to increase his profits? Journalistic judgment or commercial imperatives?

The Israeli media market, where news programs are extremely popular, did not suffer the negative consequences that are typical of other countries with market-driven journalism. In the United States, for example, diminishing resources brought about a decrease in investments in news programs and particularly in international news programs, which carry heavy production costs. Such a decrease did not occur in Israel, whose market was already operating under small budgets and economic constraints. However, the commercial competition that began in the 1990s, particularly between the two television channels, as well as between the two most popular newspapers, did cause significant damage to the Israeli media, as the Nimrodi case reveals.

"THE WIRETAPPING AFFAIR"

The Israeli media's new preoccupation with market considerations spawned growing competition between news organizations to an extent that would have been unacceptable in the past. Furthermore, such competition brought the industry down to an unprecedented level of degradation, in an event that came to be known as the "Wiretapping affair." This was a case of industrial espionage between the two largest newspapers, *Maariv* and *Yediot Ahronot*. It even reached the point where a daily newspaper editor was accused of planning to murder a key figure in the scandal.

A short time after starting his new job as editor of *Maariv* in 1992, veteran journalist Dan Margalit resigned. A series of actions by his publisher, Ofer Nimrodi, including intervention in the appointment of correspondents, setting journalists' salaries, and intervention in editorial judgments in order to promote his financial, personal, or social interests, led Margalit to the conclusion that his concept of editorial independence was very different from that of Nimrodi. Some time afterward it emerged, according to Margalit, that his publisher intended to blackmail commercial companies by preparing incriminating reports and then agreeing not to publish them in exchange for advertising in his paper. Margalit confided in the editor of *Yediot Ahronot*, Moshe Vardi, but found no consolation. In both papers, young publishers had taken over from the old ones during the 1990s, Vardi told him, "and like young colts they insist on showing that they are capable too, and we have to let them" (Margalit 1997: 234). Margalit decided to resign, but meanwhile the ball had started rolling. The complaints of attempted blackmail of advertisers dissolved in a prolonged legal battle that ended in 1999. However, in 1995 the "Wiretapping affair" hit the headlines, shocking the media and political world in Israel more than any other scandal had before.

It began in 1992, when Hachsharat Hayishuv, an investment group owned by the Nimrodi family, acquired *Maariv* and decided to break *Yediot Ahronot's* monopoly of the tabloid market. The strategy they chose was not to redesign *Maariv* differently from *Yediot* but, on the contrary, to make it look exactly the same. Therefore *Maariv's* format, structure, and even contents were changed until it became an identical twin of *Yediot Ahronot*. It very soon appeared that the two papers were more than similar. Somebody in one of the papers knew what was going to be published in the other the next day and copied it exactly.

In 1994 police investigators began to discover incidents of industrial espionage, at first by *Maariv* against *Yediot*, and later in the other direction. Both newspapers had employed private investigators and began wiretapping one another. Those employed by *Maariv* were charged, one of them turned state witness, and they were then tried, found guilty, and sentenced to prison terms. However, what made this a public scandal was the fact that charges were also pressed against people on the management and editorial boards of the two papers for ordering the wiretapping, and even against the publishers and editors, Arnon (Noni) Moses and Moshe Vardi of *Yediot Ahronot* and Ofer Nimrodi of *Maariv*. The investigation by the police and state attorney and the legal proceedings went on for several years. Finally, at the end of 1998, *Yediot* came out of the scandal almost unscathed. Its publisher did not have to face a trial, and the editor, Vardi, was sentenced to two months suspended sentence for listening to the wiretapped conversations, although the presiding judge had determined that he had not ordered them. *Maariv*, on the other hand, was badly hit when its publisher and editor in chief, Ofer Nimrodi, was found guilty of ordering the wiretapping and later, of disrupting the legal proceedings as well.

When the charge sheet against him was submitted to the court, some argued that a newspaper editor who was responsible for scrutinizing the behavior of public figures should not continue his job with such a severe indictment hovering over him. As a result, Nimrodi suspended himself from his role as editor, although he remained deeply involved with the paper as its publisher. The entire professional community reacted critically to this episode, the major attack being launched by *Haaretz* editor Amos Schocken. Nimrodi replied by criticizing Schocken and even accused *Haaretz* of biased coverage of the scandal because of its financial ties to *Yediot* (*Yediot* had loaned *Haaretz* U.S.$10 million a few years earlier).

The editor of *Haaretz*, however, did not remain silent in the face of these attacks. He revealed that the editors of all three papers had met at night for a secret meeting initiated by Nimrodi, who had suggested that the three would declare a truce in their coverage of the "affair" and agree to only report on the court proceedings. Schocken, however, refused to join this deal, and in reprisal *Maariv* revealed that *Yediot* had helped *Haaretz* financially. The mutual exposures, revelations, and accusations intensified the fear of many journalists that they were becoming pawns in the battle of the publishers. There were increasing manifestations of internal protest in the two evening newspapers, leading to the resignation of several journalists, among them Amnon Abramovitch, a senior journalist at *Maariv* who was widely regarded as a man of conscience with considerable public prestige.

After a prolonged trial Nimrodi confessed to most of the clauses in the indictment in a plea bargain, and in July 1998 he was sentenced to eight months in jail and a fine of more than IS1 million. The criticism of him now referred to the fact that after being found guilty of such a severe felony, he continued to act as publisher of the paper. The Press Council's Board of Ethics considered the scandal and found Nimrodi undeniably guilty of violating the ethical code that determines that

a newspaper and a journalist will act with honesty and integrity and will not make improper use of their position, their role, or their power to publish. In view of the respondent's status and role, and the severity, character and scope of the transgression as described, we censure the respondent and declare that he is not worthy to be included in the community of journalists, which he injured and on which he arrogantly cast so much disgrace and dishonor.[17]

Nimrodi went to jail, but when he finished serving his term, he resumed his role of publisher of the newspaper, of which he is also the owner. Two weeks after his release from prison, in April 1999, he threw a wedding party in his home and invited many distinguished guests. These invitees included Yitzhak Navon, past president of Israel, both former prime ministers and future contenders for the position, ministers, Knesset members, and various celebrities. Nimrodi was still the publisher of

Maariv, and the politicians, cognizant of the importance of good relations with the proprietor of the second largest newspaper in the country, demonstrated their friendship.

That was not, however, the end of the scandal. At the end of 1999, it exploded again, this time with even greater force. Nimrodi was now accused of attempting to suborn witnesses who were about to testify against him during the investigation, attempting to disrupt the process of the investigation by using his contacts with the top brass of the police, as well as by bribing senior officers. Following this there were accusations that while in jail he had bribed senior officers in the prison service and attempted to influence politicians, including the president, to grant him a pardon. The web of accusations also related to the period after his release from prison, forming a picture whereby Nimrodi was busy for years deal-ing with the various ramifications of the affair, even to the extent of try-ing to hire killers to murder the state witness.

Due to the severity of the accusations, Nimrodi was kept in custody for the entire period of the investigation, which lasted almost a year. The ramified investigation exposed the intricate network of connections of the Nimrodi family with the upper echelons of government, which he had tried to exploit in order to extricate himself from the original indictments and to attain pardon after the sentence. Even when it emerged that the attorney general did not intend to accuse Nimrodi of all the clauses in the indictment — the murder attempt, for example, was omitted quite early on in the investigation — the entire affair still left a very nasty taste. *Maariv* went on defending its proprietor, and in 2001 even fired Moshe Negbi, its legal affairs analyst and one of Israel's outstanding fighters for freedom of the press. In October 2001 the prosecution made a deal with the defendant, whereby some of the heavier charges were dropped in exchange for a plea of guilty on some of the lesser charges. Though the case is officially settled, the entire affair and its repercussions continue to have a lasting impact on the media in Israel.

The fact that Nimrodi was an outsider in Israel's media community, a businessman who did not emerge from within the press but had joined the community because of his wealth, enabled many to see his case as an exception. However, the scandal exposed some of the fundamental prob-lems of the Israeli media at the dawn of its commercial era. Furthermore, it revealed the danger that stems from another phenomenon of the 1990s: the process of media consolidation.

CHAPTER TWO

Television and Popular Culture

CONSOLIDATION AND GLOBALIZATION

The development of multichannel commercial television transformed Israel's entire media environment in the 1990s. As in many other countries, the proliferation of channels was accompanied by a swift process of consolidation, with a sharp decrease in the number of owners of news organizations. Family-owned newspapers were replaced by a handful of private commercial corporations, resulting in an oligopolistic structure of the print and electronic media. Whereas in 1950, seventeen national dailies served a population of fewer than one million, in 1999 there were only four national Hebrew dailies, with *Yediot Ahronot* cornering 70 percent of the market. This was the paper's justification for calling itself "the national newspaper," ironically rendered by its rivals as "the newspaper that has a nation."[1]

Toward the end of the 1990s, the Israeli media world was a changed one. At the beginning of the decade, it was controlled by three corporations that were identified with the Moses, Schocken, and Nimrodi families, which were later joined by tycoon Eliezer Fishman. By the late 1990s, these had become huge corporations that controlled a wealth of media-related activities, but were still run by the four media magnate families. The largest corporation is that of *Yediot Ahronot*, including a ramified concern, *Yediot Tikshoret*, that publishes sixteen local weeklies, six national journals, several foreign-language papers including the largest Russian daily, and Ynet, an on-line newspaper. The conglomerate also owns a book-publishing house and a nationwide distribution network. In addition, it owns one-third of the shares of Arutzei Zahav, which has the concession for cable TV broadcasting in Jerusalem, as well as Ramat Gan, Petach Tikva, and Herzliya, and is a partner in Idan, which has a similar concession in other parts of Israel. Furthermore, it recently held 24 percent of the shares of Reshet, one of the three Channel 2 concessionaires.

It is a partner in EMI music and Nur outdoor advertising. This financial empire also extends to other areas of activity, from printing presses to real estate. In volume of sales *Yediot Ahronot* was graded thirty-six among Israel's one hundred leading industrial companies in 1997, with annual revenue estimated at a quarter of a billion dollars.[2]

The Hachsharat Hayishuv corporation, a significant portion of whose shares are controlled by the Nimrodi family, acquired *Maariv* in 1992. The corporation floated *Maariv*'s shares on the stock market in 1994 and sold another block to big investors, including Russian tycoon Vladimir Gusinsky. *Maariv* is also involved in a variety of fields in the media as well as in other corporate sectors. It has a large business network, including several local papers, three magazines, foreign-language papers, a book-publishing firm, the Hed Artzi music company, and Rapid outdoor advertising company. The corporation was also involved in the electronic media as a partner in Tel-Ad, one of the Channel 2 concessionaires, in MTV, a company that broadcasts on cable TV, and in a company that operates international telephone services and cellular phones. It is involved in other financial spheres, including hotels, tourism, real estate, and health. The volume of its sales is about half that of *Yediot Ahronot*.

The corporation identified with the Schocken family is smaller. It owns the daily *Haaretz*, the quality paper that is considered to be Israel's *New York Times*. It also operates a chain of local papers with fourteen weeklies, as well as other media organizations, including local radio stations, a book-publishing firm, and an on-line information network. In the late 1990s, the annual sales volume of this company, which is rated seventy-third in the one hundred largest companies, is about U.S.$100 million a year.

In the second half of the 1990s, a new star rose in Israel's media world — Eliezer Fishman. This media magnate holds approximately one-third of the shares of the Monitin-Globus group, owners of the financial paper *Globes* — the smallest of Israel's four national newspapers. In 1998, Fishman acquired about one-quarter of the shares in *Yediot Ahronot*. The corporation he heads also has cable and satellite TV, as well as other media outlets.[3]

The development of commercial television in the 1990s led large financial concerns, particularly banks, investment companies, insurance companies, and food firms, to form partnership ventures in the media. Discount Investment, which belongs to the Discount Bank, both directly and indirectly had large investments in the media. Among other investments, this financial concern holds half of the shares of the cable TV station Tevel. The government, seeking to prevent the concentration of power, divided the broadcasting time of Channel 2, Israel's only commercial channel at that time, between three concessionaires, and legislated that each of the corporations, Keshet, Reshet, and Tel-Ad, would incorporate newspapers, banks, private investors, foreign investors, food firms, and others as partners. This model was used again when the second commercial channel, Channel 10, was launched in 2001. However, in this case there were only two concessionaries, particularly due to market pressures to merge the concessions of each channel into one. Some of these bodies were also partners in cable TV corporations. At first there were seven companies, which later merged into five and then three. In 2002, these firms requested the government to allow them to merge into one massive conglomerate. For example, *Yediot Ahronot* owns 24 percent of the Channel 2 concessionaire, Reshet, and of Channel 2's News Company, as well as 30 percent of the cable TV company, Arutzei Zahav.

The involvement of financial bodies in media companies created a completely new situation. First, newspapers and media outlets became partners of financial organizations, which they were supposed to cover and, if necessary, criticize. Second, news organizations themselves became bodies with financial interests. Deputy Attorney General Davida "Didi" Lachman-Maser commented on this: "The integration of industrial bodies, investment companies, banks, private investors, and press organizations, in the cable TV companies and in Channel 2 is designed to ensure commitment to the public interest, but what mainly guides them is their commitment to bringing revenue to their shareholders."[4]

Lachman-Maser also observed:

The shareholders in these new media organizations are the very same that the press is supposed to monitor. The press is supposed to see whether they are fulfilling their role in the media appropriately and ensure that they do not use broadcasting as a means to cover up and hide their interests. However, now the press is intertwined with these companies. . . . Now what we need to ask is not what is in the paper, but what is not in the paper, and why?[5]

Five years later she could bring proof of her words: various events and topics that were not covered by Channel 2 because of its owners' financial interests. Above all, there was no program on Channel 2 dealing with economics and the business world.

One grave example was the issue of bank managers' salaries in 1997–98. Following the privatization of the banks in the second half of the 1990s, the bank managers' salaries jumped by several hundred percent, rising to tens and hundreds of thousands of dollars per month. Although this fact was publicized in the media and was the topic of the day, scarcely any critical op-ed articles about this matter appeared in the newspapers. Anyone listening to the candid conversations in the offices of newspaper editors would have no trouble understanding the reason: banks were among the largest-spending advertisers. They had now also become major shareholders in the various news organizations and TV companies. Whether it was a question of private interests, business contacts, or social relationships, the fact is that the decision makers in the media preferred not to reflect the mood of the readers and viewers and avoided dealing with the issue.

Scholars who examined the effect of consolidation and cartelization in other countries identified several resulting negative effects, among them: restriction of free competition; price-fixing; obstructing the entrance of new actors into the game; homogenization of political contents and values; and lowered journalistic standards.[6] Nevertheless, only a few Israeli politicians were disturbed by these issues. Was there any reason to think that the results would be different in Israel? Yet the media were not concerned with these issues, even with the status of the writer. The only topic that came up for public discussion prior to the establishment of Channel 2 was the subject of "cross-ownership." The legislators' fear of the concentration of political power that might be turned against them led to the decision to divide the week's broadcasts among three concessionaires and required that each be a public partnership and include a newspaper, a bank, and other groups of investors. This same fear brought about the division of Israel into different broadcasting zones, each with their own group of concessionary companies. Furthermore, the government also forbade these firms from broadcasting national news.

In particular, fears were expressed concerning the power of the newspaper owners in the new partnerships. They envisaged Arnon Moses of *Yediot Ahronot* or Ofer Nimrodi of *Maariv* deciding to support certain business projects, or deciding to promote or destroy a certain politician, doing so by subtly intimating their positions to the editor of the popular newspaper, to the managing editor of a chain of widely read local papers, and to the editor of the Channel 2 News Company. Therefore, they proposed restricting the publishers' shares in the news companies to 10 percent. The publishers, meanwhile, demanded the right to acquire up to 50 percent of the shares in these companies, arguing that they would lose revenue from advertising in their newspapers once commercial television broadcasts were introduced. In the end a compromise was reached — the publishers managed to raise the upper limit of their share in the partnerships to 24 percent.

Although the law forbade a newspaper that was a partner in the operation of Channel 2 or cable TV from holding more than 5 percent ownership in a concession to run a local radio station, the final result was success for the press moguls, who succeeded in preventing the total prohibition on cross-ownership. Their success was proof that in Israel of the media revolution, very few politicians would dare to risk opposing the vital interests of those who control the media — it would be tantamount to political suicide.

In 1977, the minister of justice and the minister of the interior appointed a public commission to investigate the press laws, headed by former justice minister and president of the Press Council at that time, Haim Zadok. The commission warned of cross-ownership and the concentration of power in the media, as well as the creation of a media monopoly and called for "safeguarding citizens' rights against any power . . . the modern state has to practice the appropriate arrangements to prevent the dangers of concentration of power in the media."[7]

The issue was raised again in 1999 when the Knesset and government began discussing both the establishment of an additional commercial channel and the expansion of the communications infrastructure. Again, a compromise was reached between those who were worried about mergers and those who had vested economic interests in consolidation (including certain politicians who supported the media moguls). At the first stage of deliberations in the Knesset Finance Committee on January 21, 2000, *Yediot Ahronot* publisher Arnon Moses proposed that the concession of the new commercial channel be given to only one corporation. One argument against the concentration of the flow of information is utterly false, Moses said, "because today the internet gives everyone the opportunity to access multiple sources of information." The final decision was to give the new channel to two concessionaires, on condition that these bodies would not be those who had concessions on Channel 2, cable television, or satellite, unless they controlled fewer than 10 percent of the shares. Even in the latter case, the concessionaires would have to sell their shares on the other channels.[8]

The tensions regarding the control over the sources of information and political and economic power did not evaporate. On the contrary, they intensified by early 2002, as new channels were established, and market pressures for the media conglomerates to further consolidate continued. The dismissal of Moshe Negbi from the editorial board of *Maariv*, in 2001, as a result of his unwillingness to defend his publisher in the Nimrodi affair, was an illustration of the potential danger of such consolidation. Davida Lachman-Maser commented:

Negbi's case teaches us that the jobs of journalists and investigators are not secure. . . . If you control a number of forums — such as a newspaper, some cable channels and internet sites — and you also hold both the media infrastructure and the internet companies that is very significant political power. If a journalist confronts an owner who possesses this amount of holdings in Israel's media market, it is doubtful whether he can find a job in any of the bodies controlled by that owner.[9]

The concerns that some legislators had raised in Jerusalem while drafting the Channel 2 Law in the early 1990s resurfaced in February 1999, after the Likud primaries, when there was a struggle at the top of the party for the appointment of finance minister. One of the candidates was Knesset member Silvan Shalom, whose wife, Judy Moses, was a major shareholder in *Yediot Ahronot*. The newspaper had helped Shalom a great deal in his campaign for the role, Arie Caspi of *Haaretz* commented. "Huge pictures on the front page, as well as interpretive articles, turned the newspaper into a kind of election poster for a family member. Shalom's actual success in the primaries was preceded by extensive media coverage and testified that he has no enemies."[10]

Caspi continued:

Yediot Ahronot is a partner in the TV concessionaire, Reshet. Shalom's sister-in-law, Tami Moses, is married into the Borovitz family, which controls Arkia [a local airline] and Sonol [an Israeli gasoline company]. One of the partners in *Yediot Ahronot* is Eliezer Fishman, and both of them, together with Orek, are partners in the cable TV concessionaire, Arutzei Zahav. Orek, the parent company of Dapei Zahav and Amerox, is registered as an American company but is regarded as a vast Israeli concern. Its shares are traded at the rate of almost 5 billion dollars on the American stock exchange and it employs over two thousand workers in Israel. Even if Shalom were one of the archangels he could not sever himself from this reservoir of money and power. The appointment of a member of the Moses family to the role of finance minister is opposed to the interests of the state. There is a danger that instead of "the newspaper of the nation" we will become "the nation of the newspaper."

Indeed, in February 2001 Shalom was appointed finance minister in Ariel Sharon's government. Soon afterward, Shalom's wife, who is a journalist, was given her own show on public service radio at prime time. In 2003, Shalom moved to the Foreign Ministry.

Another dimension of the media revolution in Israel of the 1990s was the penetration of foreign capital into the Israeli media organizations, which had previously been under exclusive Israeli ownership. This began in 1989, when Hollinger, an international media corporation, acquired the English-language daily, *Jerusalem Post*, a newspaper that had once been owned by the Labor Party and later by the Jewish Agency. Two years later press baron Robert Maxwell bought *Maariv* (which, as mentioned, was sold to Nimrodi in 1992). Another international media tycoon, Rupert Murdoch, financed an abortive attempt to launch a weekly in Tel Aviv.[11]

European and American companies entered communication industries in cable TV (for instance, the Shamrock Investment Company bought into the cable company MTV). Prime Minister Netanyahu's political ally, American billionaire Ron Lauder, bought shares in a Jerusalem TV studio, negotiated for the purchase of shares in the Israeli media, and even considered suggestions by Netanyahu to acquire the Israel Broadcasting Authority after it became privatized. Netanyahu suggested similar ideas to other business tycoons among his political friends in the United States. In 1999, the Russian Jewish tycoon Vladimir Gusinsky purchased a 25 percent stake in *Maariv*. This was immediately reflected in the profile done on him in *Maariv* and in the paper's attitude toward the Russian economy, the Russian oligarchs, and Russian mafia.[12]

The Israeli economy, which underwent processes of privatization, liberalization, and deregulation in the 1990s, opened up to the flow of international capital into its leading branches. Approximately half of the ownership of Israel's twenty largest concerns, including high-tech and communication companies — whose aggregate value totals about 37.5 billion dollars — is held by foreign investors.[13] Foreign capital has also been invested in other branches of Israel's telecommunications. In the 1990s foreign companies entered into partnerships with all the leading Israeli companies in the fields of advertising and public relations. In the ten largest companies, whose budgets in 1998 were in the range of half a billion dollars, foreign partners hold between one- and two-thirds of the shares, particularly in the new high-tech companies.[14]

The Israeli media's integration into the international and U.S. communication systems, in addition to the "open skies" policies and the growing use of the internet, generated several unanticipated changes. One of these has been the change in wage structure and the abolishment of the principle of tenure in the press, but changes are also perceptible in the sphere of ethics and modus operandi, such as the coverage of IDF injuries in military operations. In the past, the Israeli press did not publish information about casualties in military actions or terrorist attacks until the families had been notified by the IDF manpower division. This was a practice that Israeli journalists had initiated out of social responsibility without any pressure from the military censor.

Israel's integration into the world market and the intensified competition in the 1990s led to the fact that Israeli journalists working for foreign networks broadcast these stories before the Israeli media permitted themselves to do so. As long as the information was broadcast only to the outside world, it did not disturb Israelis, but as soon as Israel's skies were opened in the multichannel era and viewers in Tel Aviv could see what was happening in southern Lebanon by watching CNN and BBC or by surfing on the internet, the Israeli media felt that it was losing in the competition. In the past, social responsibility had overcome considerations of ratings and profits, but now the balance had changed. As a result, Israeli newspaper editors put pressure on the military to allow the Israeli media to publish the occurrence of casualties. In the end, the military was forced to accept this change in the rules of the game (although journalists still do not publish the names of the victims until after their families have been notified).

The introduction of multichannel commercial television also altered the face of Channel 1. During the twenty years of monopolistic public service television — in Umberto Eco's terms, the "paleo-television era" (Eco 1990) — Israel, in fact, still remained in the era of print journalism. The era of visual culture, the "neotelevision era," began with the commencement of broadcasting by Channel 2, the commercial channel.

A comparison of the journalistic working style and the character of the television news in the 1970s and those of the 1990s illustrates the difference between the two eras. The television news product of the earlier period was a kind of broadcast newspaper. Initially, reporters on television acted as narrators, an approach long common in print. The newscasters read their reports live in the manner of radio, supplemented by film segments. For almost twenty years the visual news style amounted to a series of moderate shots of talking heads on a bland background. Film was inserted in the visual equivalent of lengthy textual quotations. Reports were patterned as a string of mostly hard-news actualities.

After the 1990s, the image acquired much higher news value than the spoken text. For this reason, more and more use was made of archival visual materials or graphic displays in cases of vital news without a visual dimension. In this new model, words provide the narrative bond for the images. Where previously journalists had acted as newsreaders on the air, using the old structure based on radio-news-with-pictures, they now adopted the unique television pattern: a chain of images overlaid onto a fast-paced narrative.

While many years passed in the United States before the image bite was added to the popular sound bite (Barnhurst and Steele 1997), in Israel the two arrived together within a relatively short period. Right from the start, neotelevision broadcasting adopted the rapid, segmented style: the sound bites of Channel 2 newscasters were much swifter — six syllables to eight — than was customary in Channel 1.[15] The new image bite was also shorter: more imagery of shorter duration with increasing motion, or an increasing flow of images squeezed into a shorter time span.

As a result, the number of items appearing in the newscasts increased.

The same thing happened with documentary programs; like the news-casts, they adopted cinematic principles and integrated visual images with the narrative structure, sometimes to the extent that journalists were "so busy with cinematic effects that they forgot the good old journalistic prin-ciples, particularly the investigation that exposes new information."[16]

The neotelevision principles that were imported to Israel by the com-mercial channel soon influenced the public service channel. Within a short time, both the sound bites and image bites on this channel began to change, although not as fast as occurred on the commercial channel. At first, each news story was still longer; therefore, the news broadcasts took longer. The Channel 1 photographers continued using film throughout the 1980s, despite the fact that new video equipment was waiting in the storerooms. A labor dispute between the management and the crews on this issue was not resolved, and the national channel went on broadcast-ing with the old equipment. It was the challenge posed by the commercial channel that finally induced them to end the dispute and start using video equipment.

A few years later, however, the programs became quite similar in many respects. In 2000, the number of news items on each newsreel was simi-lar (fifteen on Channel 1 and seventeen on Channel 2). The average time of each story was 1 minute, 58 seconds on the first and 1 minute, 49 sec-onds on the second. The positions of the items in the lineup were also identical, with little variation in the issues themselves. The same applied to the two channels' presentation style. On the commercial channel, there was more news on location (thirteen on Channel 1 and nine on Channel 2), but most items were nevertheless prepared in advance (85 and 80 per-cent, respectively). Channel 2 used slightly more visualization techniques, and the presentation style was more personal (Weiman and Goren 2001).

Channel 1 News Coordinator Yael Chen illustrated how convergence works when she openly admitted:

What did the competition with Channel 2 news do? A lot. To some extent we had to learn our job all over again after they came on the air, in terms of change of emphases, more pace, more color, as against less depth. It isn't easy for people who grew up with national televi-sion, very square and establishment, to change their way of thinking. . . . When they started broadcasting there was a big gap, since then we have caught up.[17]

However, the transition from the old style of print journalism applied to the audio-visual medium, to the new style of television journalism was much more than just a question of pace. "Television journalism is organ-ized in time whereas print journalism is organized in space. For this rea-son, viewers of television news must be carried out by narrative, they cannot leaf from page to page, from item to item, lose interest in the material. They have to be led through the whole newscast. Consequently, there is a need for a theme or story line throughout the broadcast" (Weaver 1975). Daniel Hallin claims that the difference between print and TV journalism explains the difference between Italian and American television (Hallin 1994a: 127–32). This is highly relevant to the Israeli case; it is exactly the difference between paleo-television and neotelevision.

Significant changes also occurred in the roles played by journalists in the television narrative. In the era of "print television" they were passive, linking the parts of the story, presenting matters "from the outside." Since the 1990s, they have acquired a more active and central role, their personality plays an important part in the story itself, and they are more critical and interpretive. It is not surprising, therefore, that the neotelevision era brought about a change in the status of the journalist or anchorperson. Their status has risen considerably, as evidenced by the screen time they receive compared with their interviewees, the nature of the frame in which they are shown, and their position on the front-screen.

The television narrative also changed from that of a broadcast newspaper. Television narrative requires a hero in the story, which is one reason why communication scholars frequently assert that television personalizes the news story and politics in general (Esslin 1982: 61). Indeed, the transition from paleo-television to neotelevision was one of the major causes of the personification and personalization of Israeli politics.

The other side of the coin is the change that occurred in television's attitude to its audience. In the period of the hegemonic party press, as well as in the early years of TV broadcasting, news departments bore in mind primarily politicians when preparing their newscasts. In the neotelevision era journalists' main reference group is the viewers. The fact that most of the paleo-television staffers had previously worked in the print press or state radio explains their respectful attitude toward politicians.

In contrast, the Channel 2 staffers of the 1990s and today are mostly young people of the generation of neotelevision, profits, and ratings, whose primary consideration is the consumer. In this respect, Israel's media revolution of the 1990s was a transition from the dominant European tradition of political journalism to the American tradition of commercial media. This geographical change in professional patterns was accompanied by a change in the style of politics itself, from the style of the old continent to the "New World." In this light, we can also examine whether the adoption of the new broadcasting principles entailed a change in the content of the political messages, their influence on the audience, the meaning they ascribe to these messages, and finally in their political behavior.

THE "TELEVISIONIZATION" OF THE PRESS

The introduction of commercial television had far-reaching effects on print journalism. The print media often write about television-related issues. Even quality papers discuss TV programs, the goings-on in TV companies, and the public and private lives of the TV stars. Issues that are raised on television receive extensive coverage. The business columns deal extensively with television companies, and the style articles closely monitor TV stars. "Receiving the daily press cuttings, I am amazed anew every day by the amount of coverage of TV. Instead of dealing with reality, the press deals with television. This is really obsessive," said Uzi Peled, who was director of Channel 1 television when it was established in 1968 and who later became head of Tel-Ad, one of the three Channel 2 concessionaires.[18]

Television's influence on the media, however, is far greater than simply on its coverage of television. The press itself has undergone a process of "televisionization"; first, with the establishment of a new daily paper that took the name *Hadashot* (News), designed as a TV-paper like *USA Today*, and later, with television's impact on the two tabloids, *Yediot Ahronot* and *Maariv*. The television influence was discernible in the visualization and their content: the use of color, significantly larger photographs, new layouts, huge headlines, the introduction of graphic elements, as well as changes in the content — shorter texts, the increase of space on the page, the increase of soft news, style, sports, and leisure columns, and so on. So powerful was television's impact on the press that it even led to the tabloidization of the highbrow newspapers. Even *Haaretz* changed the balance between its serious and light-news stories, added color, shortened its articles, and shrank the average length of its sentences in the second half of the 1990s.

The principles of "television journalism" also influenced other aspects of the press, such as the treatment of issues, the narrative form, and the use of journalistic rhetoric. The oral culture of television began to penetrate the printed press, introducing interpretive reporting to journalism. Although interpretive reporting is nearly as old as journalism itself, it has only recently become the dominant model of news coverage, which is largely a result of the impact of television.

"The inverted pyramid from the traditional newspaper story was not well-suited to television. . . . It gave the appearance of a news story that had lost its punch. Network executives sought a more dramatic style reporting that was built around storylines rather than facts." The result was interpretive reporting. "Today, facts and interpretation are freely intermixed in news reporting. Interpretation provides the theme, and facts illuminate it" (Patterson 2000: 250). The print press followed suit.

Additional examples further illustrate the impact of television on the Israeli print press. The language of the old Israeli journalism was characterized by a monologic style, and that was also the style of paleo-television. It is not, however, the language of neotelevision, which is characterized by dialogue. Yitzhak Roeh, who examined the presentation styles of Israeli radio broadcasters, found a shift from a cold, distant, neutral monologue to a warm dialogue, similar to the earlier broadcasting style transition (Roeh 1994). This style is increasingly prevalent in the printed press.

The term "tabloidization," the adoption of the style, techniques, rhetoric, and journalistic values of the popular press by quality newspapers (Sparks and Tulloch 2000), is misleading because it presupposes that it was the tabloids that transformed the highbrow papers, while the actual source of the change was television and the growth of the visual dimension in culture. Whereas the quality papers tended to tell a story from a distance, the TV close-up created a semblance of reality because of its photogenic nature. Whereas the Israeli press prior to the television era mainly used the technique of "telling," after the arrival of neotelevision it began to prefer the technique of "showing," not only in the prominence given to pictures in the papers but also in the writing style.

Television language emphasizes close-shot, in contrast to the old journalistic style, which preferred long-shot. Today, the close-shot style is typical not only of the tabloids but also of highbrow papers. This change can be identified even among political commentators. The style of the younger writers differs from that of the generation who reached maturity before the television era; their approach to the text is more visual, with enhanced imagery, and so forth.

Another example of the infiltration of television patterns into the written press is television's confrontational style. Television prefers competition and opposition. It generally deals with issues by presenting two opposing views and conducts interviews with people whose style is confrontational. This rhetorical structure now dominates print journalism. At the end of the 1990s, but not before that, one could occasionally see the front page of *Yediot Ahronot* or *Maariv* composed as follows: one big news item at the top, accompanied by a huge photograph, and two conflicting interpretations on either side, facing each other. Journalists' new approach to politics has not only been manifested in the contents of the page, but also in the fact that controversy and conflict have become the real issues of politics (Patterson 2000: 255). The television style is even expressed in the graphic design of newspapers.

The dominance of television culture, with its personalization and visualization, generated additional changes in some of the classic characteristics of print journalism. Some of these are the weakening of the editorial voice, the personalization of broadsheet writing, and the increase in personality journalism. The era of print journalism in Israel was characterized by the dominant weight attributed to editorials and the anonymous nature of the writing in the paper, particularly in the quality papers. "Anonymity had been a force for consistency and collectivity, an affirmation that facts and arguments mattered regardless of their authorship," writes Colin Seymour-Ure, referring to similar changes occurring in the British press (1998: 44).

All of this changed under the influence of television. Anonymous writing is disappearing. In contrast to previous decades in Israel, today every cub reporter can see his or her byline in the paper as soon as he or she starts work. Newspapers allocate more and more space to personal columns, with portraits appearing beside the writers' names. In the mid-1990s, *Maariv* completely eliminated the editorial, replacing it with an opinion piece by a different writer each day. All of these developments were the results of television influence on the press.

The increased personalization and personification is also evident in the content of the material published. Journalistic styles changed dramatically toward the end of the twentieth century. People, rather than issues, now became the pivot of the text in articles and reports. This development began with the tabloids but soon spread to the broadsheets and to radio. That said, Sparks's observation that the personification of political coverage caused "the personal [to] obliterate[s] the political as a factor of human behavior" did not apply to Israel (Sparks 1992: 40). The intensity of political coverage has not changed — what has been transformed is the nature of how politics is dealt with and the way it is presented. With the emphasis on the personal story as the center of the news, the boundary between the personal and public spheres has also changed.[19]

As several media researchers have indicated, television brought about a change in the conception of space and time, making it possible to leap over distances and move backward and forward in time. In addition to this, what had previously occurred backstage has now moved to the front stage (Meyrowitz 1985). To the extent that the backstage has remained, it has shrunk tremendously.

The new era ushered in by commercial television, as well as competition between the two television channels and between the two evening papers, generated important changes in the normative system with regard to the media's right to invade politicians' and individuals' private space. This transformation began with the shots of terror victims. Since the establishment of the State of Israel, the norm that had existed in the

Israeli press was that it was permissible to publish close-ups of enemy casualties, but not of Israeli casualties. Channel 1 adopted the same norm.

As soon as Channel 2 started broadcasting, and as a result of the growing competition between the two channels, the rules began to change. However, during the wave of massive terrorist attacks in Tel Aviv in 1995, the Channel 2 cameras went much further than they had ever done before, showing close-ups of the dead and wounded, even body parts that were scattered in all directions by the explosions. The fierce competition between *Yediot* and *Maariv*, with its new publisher, turned the front pages of these two papers themselves into battle arenas as well.

This time, however, they were met with harsh public criticism — in the form of letters to the editor, articles in the newspapers, listeners' calls to phone-in programs, and debates in talk shows. The directors of the two channels understood that they had gone too far and decided to restrain the cameras somewhat, although it was clearly impossible to restore the pre–1990 public-private boundaries. Indeed, the assassination of Prime Minister Yitzhak Rabin in 1995 was followed by a further breakdown of the old rules, again by Channel 2.

According to Jewish tradition, the bereaved family "sits in mourning" for a week, meaning that they stay at home, sitting on the floor or on low stools, receiving condolences from guests. However, in November 1995 a precedent was set and the rule changed: a Channel 2 crew visited the home of the prime minister's widow and interviewed her with her consent. Many conservative viewers expressed discomfort with this transgression, but the event did end up pushing back the boundary, and since then it has been pushed back even further.

TV crews interview mourners in their homes and take close-up shots of wounded soldiers arriving at hospitals and in the hospitals themselves, patently invading their private space. In one case in 1998, TV reporter Haim Yavin joined a police team that came to notify a family on the death of their son in an accident. The meeting was photographed without Yavin asking for the family's consent. As with the terrorist attacks of 1995, this invasion of people's privacy at such a moment provoked a hostile public reaction, and a private bill was proposed in the Knesset by Moshe Gafni of the Yahadut Hatora faction, forbidding the publication of the name or photograph of anyone injured in an attack or accident without their consent or that of their family.

A few months later, Justice Menachem Ne'eman was attacked by a criminal while leaving the courtroom and required hospitalization. The TV crew shot him lying partly uncovered on the operating table. Media critic Adam Baruch wrote:

Did you see District Judge Menachem Ne'eman on television, lying on a bed in the emergency room with bare shoulders, after being beaten up by a thug who was disappointed with his verdict? Did you hear Judge Ne'eman, photographed from above, describing the blows? Well, this was the first time in the history of Israeli television's invasion of private space that the person photographed (weak, injured, half burnt) belonged to the elite, which has always been out of bounds. Hitherto, whenever I saw a judge on television, I saw a well-dressed, authoritative, distinguished personage. When the photographed intrusion into the private sphere invaded only suspects, minorities, and women you did not think they would invade victims of terrorist attacks or soldiers. Now that they have reached the judge the invasion is complete: our entire private space is open to the TV camera.[20]

It is interesting to note, however, that one field was not affected by tabloidization — the sex lives and sexual preferences of politicians. In dealing with these issues, the Israeli press resembles the German tabloid press (Esser 1999) more than the British genre. Esser attributes the relative lack of coverage of these issues in Germany to the low level of competition between media outlets, but in Israel the cause might be deeper cultural values, rather than the economy. The Israeli public is more tolerant of extramarital affairs, and in the most famous case, that of former Defense Minister Moshe Dayan in the 1970s, this only added to his popularity. Similarly, a Knesset member's homosexuality would not receive coverage in the press.

THE TABLOIDIZATION OF CULTURE

The media revolution of the 1990s had an impact far beyond simply media culture — it in fact had a great influence on the entire Israeli cultural space. Such a widespread impact follows the theories of Bourdieu and others, who assert that in contemporary society, the entire field of cultural production is subordinate to the institutional constraints of the journalistic field (Bourdieu 1999: 62). This is a broad issue, which goes beyond the topics dealt with here, whose focus is media and politics. Nevertheless, it is important to position this issue as the background because this is the social and cultural environment within which political communication has developed.

The advent of independent commercial television has changed the position of popular journalism in Israel from a small and limited cultural phenomenon to a major one. This type of journalism, which is in constant search of a mass audience, mixes entertainment and news, slants toward the visual, emotional, and sensational, privileges the personal experience of ordinary people (Hallin 2000), and has become the dominant style of all of Israeli culture.

First, Israeli paleo-television, was almost "visual radio," speaking in the name of the elite and representing their point of view while relating to the public in a paternalistic manner. It knew better than the public what it needed and generally presented the points of view of political and cultural leaders. Neotelevision, by contrast, promoted — as cultural studies scholars like Raymond Williams and postmodernists like Jean-Francois Lyotard have argued — the democratization of culture, softened the pedagogic style of the media messages, broke the educational monopoly of the old elites, and undermined the hegemony of the experts.

Neotelevision, by contrast, is a loyal ally of popular culture in the latter's struggle to limit the weight of high, canonic culture. New popular culture was fashioned out of the predominance of the visual media with their dramatic, episodic, dynamic, active, metaphoric, dialectic, and rhetorical character — the opposite of the continuous, linear, abstract, stable, logical, or metonymic mode of the literati. Those familiar with the relevant literature will rightly surmise that I am using John Fiske's distinction between oral and literary modes (Fiske 1987: 105).

More than a few media scholars argue that the transformation from one mode to another has had a major impact on many facets of life. In the learning process, for example, the television mode of processing information is heuristic, while that of the newspaper is systematic. The latter mode also incorporates active processing. Thus, in contrast to television viewing, studying by reading enables the reader to exploit his entire cognitive potential (Iyengar 1991). These notions were not examined empirically in the Israeli case, but there are other fields in which the change of mode led to a visible change in the culture.

The changes in language and literature that occurred in the 1990s provide one example of such a transformation. Contemporary Hebrew is the product of an ongoing battle between two schools of thought. The former believes that one should speak as one writes, following a canon of set rules; therefore, the language has to be dictated from above. The Hebrew Language Academy was founded with the establishment of the State of Israel. Over the years it has invented thousands of new Hebrew words and has granted approval to some words for use and rejected others. This school of thought was opposed by another, subversive, school, which believed that we should write in the same way as we speak, and that language should reflect the dynamism and fluidity of modern life.

The history of the Hebrew language in the past fifty years is the history of this battle. In literature, the first school of thought prevailed. Prominent writers of the following generation (such as Amos Oz and A. B. Yehoshua) continued writing in standard, canonical Hebrew, whereas the early representatives of the subversive school, the generation of 1948 (writers like Amos Keinan and Dan Ben Amotz) did not achieve influential status in the mainstream culture. However, in the 1990s a linguistic revolution took place, when writers began writing in the language of everyday speech. The school advocating a "high-language" approach lost its canonical position. The key to the development of the language is the street. Usages that do not "catch on" in the street do not survive in the language, as testified by the thousands of words invented by the Hebrew Language Academy that are not used by anyone.

The new spoken Hebrew is much thinner, flatter, and shallower. The sentences are shorter, incomplete. "There is a process of shrinkage of speech, a process of minimization to the point of disappearance. Anyone who utters a full, rounded sentence is considered a nerd," wrote journalist and linguist Rubik Rozental in *Hazira Haleshonit*, a book describing these developments (2000). This language, with its low linguistic register and short sentences reflecting an MTV rhythm, was introduced into the press and literature by the young writers of the 1990s. Orly Kastel-Blum and Etgar Keret are two conspicuous examples of this phenomenon. But how did this happen? Rozental asserts that television was a major agent of change: "What happens in television is that anyone who writes a sitcom wants first of all to imitate the way people speak. Then they show the sitcom on TV and a kind of vicious circle is formed whereby the people who are influenced by television adopt the language of the sitcom."[21]

The old canonical school fought against the new spoken language, but literature was not a strong enough weapon to win this battle. The school that supported everyday language was able to expand its influence through television until it finally conquered literature. It is not mere coincidence that many of those who set the tone in Israel's culture today — in cinema and music, literature and art — are media professionals, mainly from television.

Advertising was another manifestation of television's impact on culture. A critical analysis of ads marked the second half of the 1990s as a period in which "Israeli popular culture penetrated the field of advertising, which had previously been regarded as elitist. The dominant image in advertisements [during that time] was not arrogant and condescending, but rather spoke to its consumers as equals. For example, the Mizrahi (Jews of Asian-African origin, particularly North African) cultural genre that characterized the lower classes was introduced, and some of the outstanding campaigns that year were defined as popular or as targeting the general public."[22]

However, advertisements are not only a cultural product that reflects aesthetic norms or cultural perceptions. The television product, of which advertisements are a major element, is also a significant force that influences the social construction of reality and shapes the cultural value system or *Weltanschauung*. TV news broadcasts, like other television products, routinely present encounters between people and suggest definitions of the meaning of these encounters to the television viewer. TV news orders and organizes reality through the use of interpretive schemes; it is a means by which society tells itself about itself.

Furthermore, by using language discourse, images, sounds, voices, and rhetoric, the news distributes significance and symbols regarding the collective social identity, particularly in terms of defining the factors that connect members of a certain group and divides them from members of other groups (Bhabha 1990: 3). This is expressed by the definition of social boundaries, by the updating of narratives that emphasize the mutual destiny of a group and its past, and by constructing representations of the physical space and the human body. The television representation participates in the constitution of the collective identity because it is routine, because it is accepted as natural, and because it infiltrates everyday lives.

In a retrospective analysis, film and TV critic Meir Shnitzer referred to the first week of commercial TV broadcasting in November 1993 in terms of a revolution, comparing it to the week in which the Bastille fell in Paris and the old order collapsed. The gap between the old television style and what viewers saw on the new channel was immense, in the subjects dealt with (for example, the attitude to sex), in genres (for example, games), in the linguistic texts, in the language of the camera, and above all in the social contents expressed.[23]

The picture that appeared on the Channel 2 screen did not emerge out of the blue: it reflected and accelerated the crystallization of the new culture in Israel at the turn of the century. The emphasis on style was part of the consumer revolution (Ewen 1988). From the culture of austerity of the 1950s, Israel became an affluent society (Ram 1999). This new society was a reflection of American society, as imported products and brands became very popular among Israeli consumers and chain stores and malls began popping up all over the country.

These economic developments also brought about significant cultural and political change. Indeed, researchers of culture had identified numerous changes in the patterns of cultural activity in Israel. Participation in highbrow canonical activities and public cultural events such as the theatrical arts began to drop in favor of participatory activities such as sports and entertainment. One researcher called it the " 'tabloidization' of culture" (Katz et al. 1999). Another change was in the deepened level of the most basic values. From national collectivism, Israeli society moved toward the opposite pole of individualism (Ezrahi 1997), as postmaterialistic expectations took the place of asceticism, pioneerism, and the readiness to sacrifice for the collective (Almog 2000). Furthermore, post-Zionism took root where Zionism had been the only civil religion in the past.

In September 1998, five years after Channel 2 first went on the air, Broadcasting Authority Director and veteran TV professional Motti Kirshenbaum was asked about the link between television broadcasts and social and cultural processes occurring in Israeli society. In his reply he referred to the beginning of the commercial channel's broadcasting as "a milestone in the process of disintegration, collapse and severance of Israeli society from its old values. I have no doubt that this channel played an important part in the glorification of trivia and of the insignificant, and the sanctification of the rating as a supreme value that concerns only the number of heads, not the brain cells inside them. The number of heads became the thing itself."[24] Kirshenbaum continued:

This is part of the famous privatization, part of Israeli society's abandonment of its ideological values, part of the decline of academic status as a central factor in society. Everything has become appearance, the "look." The advertisers are, in fact, the prophets of the Jewish state. You and I were raised on proverbs such as don't judge a book by its cover. That was our bible. Today it is the opposite. Today they say: What does it matter what's inside the cover? Just look at the cover. Take, for example, the deification of models. In no country in the world is there such worship of models as in our press. Every editor knows that he has to bring three pages of models. What is this?

Thus, neotelevision both reflected and, more than that, shaped the nature of Israel's cultural landscape at the end of the twentieth century. Against the backdrop of this new scenery, changes no less profound have occurred in the Israeli political sphere.

CHAPTER THREE

The Political Revolution of the 1990s

ISRAELI DEMOCRACY'S LEGITIMACY CRISIS

Toward the end of the twentieth century, a feeling of malaise prevailed among scholars of democracy throughout the world. Precisely at this juncture, when so many emerging democracies in Asia, Africa, Latin America, and Eastern Europe had joined the democratic club, the debate heightened about the crisis of legitimacy in mature democracies. This discussion began a quarter of a century ago when a report of the Trilateral Commission on the state of health of industrial democracies argued that the states in North America, Europe, and Japan confronted a "crisis of democracy." The scholars who wrote this report forecasted "a bleak future for democratic governments . . . disintegration of civil order, the breakdown of social discipline, the debility of leaders, and the alienation of citizens" (Crozier, Huntington, and Joji 1975).

In the same period, Habermas introduced another, more clear-cut concept — the "legitimacy crisis" (1976). This refers mainly to the conflict between the obligation of every democratic government in late capitalism to supply all the needs of the electorate, including those of the poor who do not pay high taxes, and the reluctance of the wealthier citizens to finance the welfare of the poor with their taxes. This conflict, says Habermas, is insoluble; as a result, the state fails to create a sufficient level of commitment and involvement among its citizens.

The crisis of legitimacy is expressed in many ways, the most outstanding of which is the reduction in the level of participation in elections. The common view is that the "public turns off, knows little, cares less, and stays home" (Norris 2000). However, the crisis is made up of much more than low turnout. Further symptoms include the reduction of public trust in political processes and institutions, general cynicism, dissatisfaction with the government, antagonism toward politicians, reduction in political efficacy, vanishing social capital (Putnam 1995), political disengagement, uncivic culture, intergenerational decline in levels of social trust, knowledge, and national identification, and political alienation (Bennett 1998). Toward the end of the second millennium, a veritable cottage industry has developed to try to explain these phenomena (Pharr et al. 2000).

One of the more interesting explanations — "video malaise" — is related to the media. This is the argument that the mass media, particularly television, are responsible for the decline in the public's dissipated democratic behavior and, eventually, the crisis for democracy. Other explanations attribute the crisis to other social causes, such as changing cultural values or the failure of government performance and problems of institutional effectiveness (Norris 1999).

Two explanations are particularly relevant to the Israeli case. One is reduction in the level of its stateness, and the other is the "colonial situation" in which Israel has existed for more than a generation. An example of the first explanation is the "state overload" theory (Nordhaus 1975), according to which the government breaks its promises to voters, thus creating apathy and mistrust among citizens. Indeed, the point of departure for the now generally accepted concept of a crisis of legitimacy is that the government assumes too many tasks, resulting in what Anthony Giddens describes as "the failure of the political order to generate a sufficient level of commitment and involvement on the part of its citizens to be able to govern them" (Giddens 1990: 742).

Some scholars go beyond this pessimistic description and see contemporary society as "a society that is endlessly fragmented, without memory and without solidarity, a society that recovers its unity only in the succession of images that the media return to it every week. It is a society without citizens, and ultimately, a non-society" (Castells 1997: 310). The legitimacy crisis has intensified because of the impact of globalization on the state. This cultural and technological process is transforming democracies into "powerless states."

What is specific to the capitalist state is that it absorbs social time and space, sets up the matrices of time and space, and monopolizes the organization of time and space that become, by the action of the state, networks of domination and power. This is how the modern nation is the product of the state. Not any longer. State control over space and time is increasingly bypassed by global flows of capital, goods, services, technology, communication, and information. (Castells 1997: 243)

The contemporary nation-state is losing the power of surveillance mechanisms, which were previously the secret of its strength, weakened on the one hand by internal forces (such as regional powers, identity groups, new political organizations working for its deconstruction), and on the other hand by transnational and supranational forces. Thus, an interesting international system is developing that, although containing nation-states, is in a hybrid condition with plural authority structures (Held 1991). The blurring of nation-states' boundaries and the globalization of production and investment have also damaged the welfare state, a key element in the politics of all industrialized countries since the 1950s and probably a central building block of its legitimacy. Because democratic institutions had developed within the nation-state, the weakening of the structure of the state had a direct impact on the weakening of democracy.

The voice of those who disagree with the "powerless state" thesis has been increasingly heard recently. These scholars support their case with considerable evidence on the state's continued power.[1] However, they can hardly rebut the argument that there has indeed been a recent decline in the stateness in most democracies (that is, the position of the state on the social institutions' list and how much it is in the focus of individual and public reference). In other words, if we see that "stateness" is not a dichotomous but rather a sequential concept, we may argue that there has been a relative decline in the level of stateness in all advanced democracies (Peri 2000).

The sense of this crisis is also evident in Israel. Despite the fact that it is a relatively young country embroiled in constant war, the state's power is still greater than in late-capitalist countries. By contrast, the damage caused by globalization processes is much worse because the founding fathers of Israel did not agree to settle for a "night watch" state, but rather sought to make it a republican visionary state. Its constituent ethos was social-democratic, whereby considerable power was invested in the state from the beginning. As a result, its weakening is more palpable. Furthermore, these processes occurred much more rapidly in Israel than in other nation-states. In the mid-1970s, the power of the political center was markedly eroded. Historically, the political center had been the main defining source of the collective identity, regulating internal struggles and allocating authority and resources. "The government stopped being the dominant definer of the collective identity and the main source of legitimacy and became one of the interested parties in the internal division over the definition of the symbolic order" (Ha-Ilan 1999: 184).

Economic developments and ideological transformations were among the major causes of the weakening of the center. The proportion of the private sector within GNP has increased significantly since the 1980s, and deregulation, liberalization, and privatization have expressed the decreasing involvement of government in the economy as owner, supervisor, and regulator. In addition, there was the development of a new consumption society. Other dimensions of globalization further lessened the influence of the state, such as the strengthening of personal communication between Israelis and the rest of the world, the 100 percent increase in Israelis who travel abroad, improved telephone and internet connections; the selling of stocks of Israeli companies on Wall Street, an increase in foreign investments in Israel, and many other indications of economic integration.

However, Israel is distinguished by an additional factor that does not exist elsewhere: it is the only democracy at the beginning of the twenty-first century that is still in a "colonial situation," a condition in which it has been entangled since the Six-Day War of 1967. This situation also increased the size and influence of significant groups in the population who lack deep democratic convictions. The combination of these factors led to a situation whereby, unlike the late-capitalist societies whose citizens no longer believe in the government's ability to implement its policy as promised, in Israel since the early 1990s many people question the legitimacy of the government to govern. This calls for elucidation.

At the beginning of the twenty-first century, Israel as a democracy is in the anomalous situation of controlling a population of more than two million people by oppressive military rule. What appeared to be the "fruits of victory" at the end of the justified war of June 1967 soon became a heavy burden bending Israel's back and distorting its image and soul. The internal division over the future of the occupied territories, which has intensified since the 1980s, is not just a political debate over Israel's borders, its security interests, or its relations with its neighbors. It is also a cultural battle over what writers call the soul of Israeli society and sociologists define as its collective identity. In the period following the Six-Day War it was thought that the territories would be a bargaining chip in the political negotiations that would begin a year or two afterward. Meanwhile a generation of Israelis and Palestinians has grown up with the situation of occupation as their formative experience, and this group is beginning to raise the next generation. The Oslo Accords and the establishment of the Palestinian Authority (PA) did not fundamentally change this situation, and the continued occupation has become the reference point in culture and art as well as in politics and everyday life. In the end, as the Algerian philosopher Frantz Fanon aptly expressed it, every conquest captures the conquerors more than the conquered.

Israel's political body was unable to cope with the colonial situation and its harmful social impact. It could not swallow it — adjusting, as it tried doing by constituting an "enlightened occupation" — nor could it spew out and part with the occupied territories, because of the increased power of almost 300,000 settlers and their political allies. When a serious attempt was made to solve the conflict by mutual recognition, and the acceptance of the "land for peace" formula, the Oslo Accords were signed. However, opposition to this policy grew to the extent of questioning the government's actual right to govern and the legitimacy of the democratic values and procedures themselves. The combination of nationalistic attitudes with regard to the territories, and religious extremism — which since the 1980s has been the socioeconomic variable most highly correlated with opposition to the peace process — has become a factor that is potentially fatal to Israeli democracy. Indeed, religious extremism is the cause of Israel's low place in the international index of democracies.[2]

Some religious leaders actually declared that the government, and even the Knesset, had no right to decide on withdrawal from the territories and that it was permissible to oppose such "illegal" decisions. Furthermore, rabbis and leaders of the settlers called on soldiers to disobey orders if they were commanded to evacuate settlements or army camps in the territories. In this atmosphere it is not surprising that more than 7 percent of the religious orthodox (as opposed to an average of 2.5 percent in the general population) replied in 1997 that they supported taking illegal, even violent, action against the government (Herman and Yuchtman-Yaar 1999: 319).

Thus, the colonial situation brought Israel to the verge of a "crisis of regime," the highest state of crisis in the political order. According to a model developed by Ian Lustick, dispute over the definition of the state borders — annexation or de-annexation of territories — may generate minimal changes in the political order without endangering the national institutions or shaking the beliefs and identities of its citizens, threatening only the stability of the incumbent government. However, if this dispute crosses certain critical thresholds, in the absence of a hegemonic view of the territories or of the collective identity, it is liable to lead to a battle over the rules of the political game and the very stability of the regime (Lustick 1993).

The colonial situation thus engendered a state of political indecision and immobility, with the political center unable to decide on the borders of the state and the nature of its relations with the neighboring countries or define Israeli citizenship (and thus mitigate the core of the dispute over the collective identity of the population, which is torn between the liberal-civil and the ethno-nationalist Jewish pole) (Kimmerling 1985; Peri 1988).

This situation weakens the state's ability to cope with other challenges it faces, such as the need to absorb large numbers of immigrants; to ensure continued growth and reduce the social damage created by globalization; to strengthen the integrative mechanisms of society to counter such different perceptions of identity among different groups; and to resolve deep conflicts between secular and religious, between Jews and Arabs, between "northerners" and "southerners," and between the haves and have-nots.

Israeli social scientists have described the inadequate functioning of the political body, using terms such as "overload" (Lissak and Horovitz 1989) or "ungovernability" (Barzilai and Shain 1991). The political system has been defined as suffering from "steering pathology" (Galnoor 1996), "the decreased ability of the administration, in the broad sense of the term, to guide society towards the achievement of its aims, while overcoming crises and preserving stability" (Galnoor 1998: 195). In Israel instead of consociational democracy, which aims to prevent deep social division and contain conflicts, a crisis democracy has developed "whose essence is evident deterioration of the public atmosphere and dangerous growth of the potential for the outbreak of cumulative divisions, to the extent of a deep and dangerous cleavage, threatening the stability and cohesiveness of society and the state" (Zisser and Cohen 1999: 10, 27).

The legitimacy crisis is manifested in many ways, one of which is government instability. Since the 1980s, every party in power has fallen in every election. Ariel Sharon, elected in January 2003, was the seventh prime minister in eleven years. Even more severe is the recurrent undermining of the democratic game rules and the violation of the rule of law (Galnoor 1996: 157–60). Israelis are disappointed with politics and politicians, and unlike the Supreme Court and the military, which enjoy the trust of 90 percent of the public, the political parties are trusted by no more than 21 percent (Peres and Yuchtman-Yaar 1998: 59). Eighty-one percent of the public believes that corruption is prevalent, and some two-thirds think that there is more corruption in Israel than in the past. A similar percentage estimates that there is more corruption in politics than in all other spheres. The institutions considered most corrupt by 70 percent of Israelis are the political parties, and the Knesset does not fall far behind with 56 percent.[3]

The most powerful manifestation of the crisis occurred on the night of November 4, 1995. Then, at the end of a mass rally in Tel Aviv's city square under the slogan, "Yes to peace, no to violence," Yigal Amir, a young protégé of the clericalist-nationalist movement, came within one step of Prime Minister Yitzhak Rabin. Firing three pistol shots to Rabin's back, Amir murdered the man whose private body symbolized the collective political body (Peri 2000).

A few years earlier people sensitive to the rule of law had already warned that systematic violations of the law by extremist settlers in the territories, while the authorities were oblivious to them and to the actions of their supporters, were liable to destroy the social and political order. But these warnings were interpreted as part of the rhetoric of the Left, intended to besmirch the good name of the nationalist camp. After Prime Minister Yitzhak Rabin was assassinated in the heart of Tel Aviv, Attorney General Michael Ben-Yair admitted to the existence of a real threat to the Israeli democracy and the rule of law.

We find that some of us have developed attitudes of disdain for the behavioral rules of the democratic process and justify any means to achieve the fulfillment of our beliefs. It is evident that this readiness to use any means, violating the democratic rules of behavior and distorting the fundamental values of Judaism, stems from a fanatic worldview that is dangerous to an enlightened society. The meaning of these phenomena is that the fundamental principles in which we believe, which are the foundations of the democratic regime and which it is designed to uphold, have not permeated all the strata of Israeli society. This means that the Israeli democracy is more fragile than might have been thought a year ago.[4]

The fear of civil war that prevailed in the first hours after Rabin's assassination turned out to be exaggerated. The political system settled down after the assassination; Shimon Peres was immediately installed as interim prime minister; six months later, democratic elections were held, won by opposition leader Benjamin Netanyahu. In May 1999, there were elections again, before the government's full term was completed, and again the change of government took place without disruption. But the legitimacy crisis is not over and the Israeli democracy still manifests its pathological condition. When all is said and done, no democracy at the beginning of the twenty-first century, and particularly not one whose fate is so dependent on international support, can maintain an occupation against the will of the occupied nation indefinitely. So long as this "colonial situation" remains as is, it will continue to erode the living fibers of Israeli society.

THE DECLINE OF THE "PARTY STATE"

The political crisis struck hardest at what had been the very heart of the body politic since its formative years — the political parties. As with the legitimacy crisis in general, the crisis of the parties in Israel was severe because it compounded the processes occurring in most Western democracies with the problems peculiar to Israel.

Dean E. Alger wrote in the late 1980s, "In America, the parties have declined notably during the past 25 years or so as forces in the organization and guidance of peoples' political behavior: the public relies on parties far less than it used to as sources of information and for cues on voting. . . . At virtually every point associated with the recruitment and election of public officials, the party organizations have suffered an erosion of power" (1989: 5). Israel's political system is closer to the European parliamentary democracies than to the political order in the United States, where parties have always been relatively weak. But in Europe, too, most political scientists agree that a "decline of the parties" has been occurring since the 1980s. The old parties are no longer capable of performing various functions that they did in the past, and they are being replaced by alternative organizations. This is reflected in the decreasing rate of party membership, the loosening of the parties' links with social organizations such as trade unions or religious associations, voters' tendency to disengage themselves from parties and shift from "membership voting" to voting on issues, and the general drop in the voter turn-out. The parties' organizational structure and internal cohesion were vitiated, the various parties lost their distinct social profile and ideology, becoming more and more alike, so that now it is hard to distinguish one from another. "The parties in Western Europe today are losing their distinctness," write observers of Western Europe (Koren 1998: 28). Consequently, coalitions are becoming more permissive, and government alliances that would have been unthinkable in the past have become possible. The policies of various governments no longer reflect the classic European differences between Left and Right.[5]

The decline in the parties' functioning and status led some of the politologists to a radical conclusion: we are now facing a new phase in the history of democracy. The familiar political parties representing social movements and groups have become a thing of the past, to such an extent that some argue that a certain stage in Western Europe's political history has come to an end. "Strong parties with well-defined platforms and a consolidated membership are a passing phenomenon . . . characteristic of the first, 'formative' phase [of pluralism], in which large collective actors are admitted to the representative system as powerful partners" (Pizzoreno 1981: 272).

There is also another school of thought, which does not agree with the "decline" thesis, but rather describes the changes that parties undergo as "adjustment." Even those who share this softer view agree that parties are changing and adapting themselves to the new conditions and they do not ignore the radical changes.[6] In the end, parties stopped performing the variety of social and political functions that they performed in the past, such as consolidating and mobilizing the citizen body, aggregating its demands and representing its interests, and formulating public policy. The parties are left with only two of their classic functions — choosing leaders and forming the government.

The change in the parties' status in Israel was especially extreme because they had previously filled additional roles to those of Western European parties, not to mention the United States. Since the 1920s and 1930s, they had been the cornerstone of the political body: they preceded and in fact established the state. The parties were "the central cause of high steering ability in the Israeli political system" (Galnoor 1996: 171).

In contrast to Western Europe, most Israeli parties were social-cultural enclaves, creating and representing communities that were fairly autonomous (Lissak 1998: 131). They provided services to their members in their employment bureaus, housing companies, and independent health services. They owned trade unions and banks, administered schools, controlled a socialization system, newspapers and publishing houses, youth organizations, and even sports clubs and financial enterprises. Beyond all this, they were responsible for supplying symbols of identity, serving their members not only as political organizations but also as a real home. It was not for nothing that Benjamin Akzin called Israel a "party state" (Akzin 1970).

Another unique feature of the Israeli case was the fact that since 1933 a dominant party, Mapai, which later became the Labor Party, had controlled its political body. The fact that this party, which had the plurality if not the majority, was at the center of the party map and remained in power for thirty-four years ensured the stability of the political system. However, in the early 1960s the weaknesses of the dominant party began to appear. It began to lose its unique ideological-cultural identity, stopped supplying social services, and above all failed both to adapt itself to the new social makeup of Israeli society and to integrate the large numbers of immigrants who had arrived during the previous decade from Islamic countries, mainly in North Africa.

After 1967 the Labor Party also lost another ability that is a necessary condition for a dominant party: that its ethos reflects the ethos of the period (Duverger 1963). The dramatic encounter with parts of the homeland in 1967 led to the creation of a new ethos that was better reflected by the nationalist camp, formed around the Herut Party. In 1977, ten years after the Six-Day War, a historic upheaval took place. The Labor Party, world champion in length of staying in power in a democratic multiparty system, fell.[7] This was not just the defeat of the ruling party, but the collapse of the old party structure, based on one dominant party and its replacement by a new competitive, bipolar structure, also described as polarized pluralism.[8]

The Likud did not succeed in building itself as a dominant party, or even in preventing the decline of the large parties. It merely postponed it for a period of time. Above all, the incompatibility between the old party map and the new needs and social forces was not resolved. The parties that had arisen in an earlier period, in the context of previous interests, needs, and reality, continued to exist but did not manage to adapt themselves to the new situation. On the face of it, the two major parties were distinguished by their different ideologies and conflicting political perceptions on the issue of the territories. In fact, the two parties had become supermarkets of ideas even on this central issue, not to mention their attitudes on other topics, for instance, the economy, where there was almost complete convergence between the two parties.

During the 1980s the character of the two main parties changed: both Labor and Likud became catchall parties. Otto Kircheimer, a social scientist from the critical Frankfort school, described the Americanization of the European political system, which in fact is applicable to subsequent developments in Israel. The catchall parties are the political equivalent of a supermarket. The purpose of such a party is to draw in as many voters as possible, and it does so by appealing to the lowest common electoral denominators, losing its social, ideological, or programmatic identity in the process. The way to attract "clients," as in the commodity market, is by adopting an image, a trademark, a label, that has drawing power (Kircheimer 1966, 1969). But, says Kircheimer, when such superficial and random factors as the leader's style and looks, random events, and passing moods are what dictate the voters' behavior, the party stops serving as an intervening link between society and the administration (Kircheimer 1966: 200).

Gradually, the parties stopped being membership parties, or ideological mass parties, and became skeleton parties. In the 1960s 18 percent of the voters in Israel were registered as party members. Toward the 1996 elections the number dropped to 10 percent, but only 7 percent admitted that they were really party members. The others registered only for the primaries (Rahat and Sar-Hadar 1999: 208), and they regarded even these as more symbolic than political, a kind of media event (Arian 1998). In the Likud, for example, of the 170,000 registered as members prior to the elections of 1999, only 100,000 renewed their membership after the elections.[9]

The scope of the parties' activities continued to shrink, as did their involvement in citizens' lives. They were no longer so assiduous in rewarding party activists with posts in public institutions or representing the demands of interest groups or individuals, and they were less involved in the everyday life of the population and community activities. The party machinery and the leadership became less dominant, the links between leaders and the led became tenuous, and ideological activity diminished (Horowitz and Lissak 1989: 223–30). In fact, the major parties had lost their important functions in the democratic regime, functions such as aggregating and articulating interests, being agents of social coordination, setting the social agenda and the public discourse, mobilizing support for the political center, obtaining backing for its policy, and, finally, strengthening and enhancing its steering ability (Galnoor 1996: 172; 1998: 198–202).

After becoming catchall parties in the 1970s, and declining further in the 1980s, the two major parties reached another stage and became cartel parties. This process, too, had occurred earlier in some Western Europe countries and was described by political sociologists as the process whereby parties lose their role as links between society and politics. Having lost their hold on society, they focus on the state.[10]

The explanation is that the party leaders functioning as legislators systematically exploit the state in order to strengthen themselves and repel new rivals from outside. The parties, instead of serving as mediators between the state and social groups, are themselves incorporated into the state. The party leaders stop being trustees (as in skeleton parties), or representatives (as in mass parties), or even entrepreneurs (as in catchall parties), and instead they become functionaries in seminational bodies (Arian 1998: 152). Thus a cartel is formed composed of all the existing parties, sharing the national resources among themselves, mainly for their own continued existence. The purpose of these parties is to maintain power and control the allocation of resources in order to ensure their survival; representing society is of secondary importance. Hence, the public reaction to them is understandable. The people feel betrayed and cheated, and they react accordingly, with dissatisfaction, disappointment, avoidance, and anger.

The decline of the Labor Party preceded that of the Likud, but the latter, too, could not withstand the process of "decline of the parties," even though it was in power from 1977 at the head of a right-wing clericalist coalition (between the years 1977–84, 1990–92, 1996–99) and together with Labor in a National Unity Government (1984–90). In the 1990s the Likud lost its raison d'être, which stood on two legs. The nationalist ideology of Greater Israel that strictly forbade ceding the territories occupied in 1967 was one of these. The other was a social-electoral base wherein the Likud was the focus of identification for the lower socioeconomic strata, particularly the Mizrahim.

The Likud failed on both these counts. Its ideological purity was tainted by being a catchall party. When it withdrew from Sinai in the early 1980s, after signing a peace treaty with Egypt, and when it began peace talks with the Palestinians at the Madrid Conference in 1991, it aroused the wrath of the ideological extremists, who left the party and outflanked it from the Right. But Netanyahu, political grandchild of Jabotinsky (his father, Professor Ben-Zion Netanyahu, had actually been the secretary of the Revisionist movement's founder), went further still. Whereas Begin had withdrawn from the Sinai, Netanyahu was the first Likud leader to sign an agreement involving withdrawal from part of the West Bank. In the Hebron Treaty of 1997, he agreed to Israel's withdrawal from the city which he himself had defined as the heart of the Jewish people. When all is said and done, the sixty-year-long debate between Labor and the Likud was for or against the partition of the Land of Israel, and with the withdrawal from Hebron the essential difference between the two historical movements collapsed.[11] The remaining differences — over exactly where the new borders would lie, or what the character of relations with the Palestinians would be — are secondary to that essential difference.

In the course of the 1990s the Likud cartel party also lost its social base. Its electoral success in the 1960s had sprung from the fact that its historical leader, Menachem Begin, was able to recruit the immigrants from Asian-African countries, who had begun to blame the dominant party for their inferior position in Israeli society. Between the years 1969 and 1977 a process of de-alignment and realignment occurred, when the Mizrahim, more than two-thirds of whom had supported Labor and fewer than one-third Likud, switched loyalties. At the beginning of the 1980s the proportion of Mizrahim who voted Likud rose even higher, reaching approximately 80 percent.

If the 1977 elections marked the first revolt of the Mizrahim — severing themselves from Labor and allying themselves with the Likud — the 1999 elections were the second revolt. When the Likud became a cartel party it could not satisfy the needs of the Mizrahim, neither on the symbolic nor on the practical level. The Netanyahu government's neoliberal policy hurt them economically (for example, the number of unemployed rose during those years from 4 to almost 8 percent). The "melting-pot" policy could not withstand the pressures from the Mizrahim to express their separate and distinct identity.

The Likud leadership acted as a cartel party and not as a mediating body between society and the state. The fact that the heads of that party belonged to the global side of the digital split alienated the Mizrahim, or as I prefer to call them, the "southerners," who were mostly to be found on the opposite side, the local side. The Likud was no longer the kind of party needed by the Mizrahi cultural group — the party of a camp, a party that represented a community. The evolution of new politics, and within this context the consolidation of the Mizrahim under the new party, gave birth to the Shas Party.

THE FAILURE OF POLITICAL REFORM

The weakened status of the major parties at the end of the 1980s resulted in attempts to resolve the political crisis through structural governmental reform. Commentators blamed the extreme form of proportional representation (with a qualifying threshold of only 1 percent) for encouraging the proliferation of parties. The public blamed the coalition structure for encouraging the small parties to use extortion against the large parties that needed them to form a majority in the Knesset. The political class protested against the government's inability to govern, particularly the major party, because of its dependence on its coalition partners, and against the prime minister for his helplessness vis-à-vis his colleagues in the government.

There were repeated complaints about the internal behavior inside the parties, along with demands to democratize them, to open them to the public and allow a free flow of new representatives, to increase the representatives' accountability to the voters, and to enhance the voters' power in the political process (Peri 1989). But in the end it was the two large cartel parties that initiated and even implemented electoral reform. Their common interest was not so much to enhance representation or to increase accountability, but rather to strengthen the prime minister and his power base, improving his ability to govern. The result of these reforms, however, was just the opposite. Rather than slowing down the collapse of the old politics, they created a new political reality that merely aggravated the political crisis.

Dissatisfaction with the government and the entire political game reached a peak in the coalition crisis of 1990, which came to be known as the "dirty trick." The disintegration of the national unity government and the abortive attempt to set up an alternative coalition headed by the Labor Party and without the Likud, brought thousands out into the streets against the politicians with the slogan, "Enough of your corruption!" Following this, the legislation of some new constitutional laws, described as a "constitutional revolution" (Hazan 1997), was speeded up. Among these were changes in the Party Law, in 1992 and 1993, giving the parties legal status and imposing financial supervision on them (Avnon 1993). But the principal changes were the introduction of primaries to choose the parties' candidates for the Knesset and the new Basic Law for direct election of the prime minister.

Until the 1990s voters in the general elections put one slip in the ballot box, bearing the name of the party. Each party's list was voted on by the party's appointments committee, or by a broader party forum after being handed down by the party leaders and political bosses. During the

1980s the number of people involved in composing the list of candidates grew until almost all the parties adopted the primary system whereby all the members of the party share in choosing the candidates. The Labor Party introduced this method in 1992, and after the elections of that same year it was adopted by the Likud. Consequently, by 1996 two-thirds of the Knesset members were elected through primaries.

The advocates of primaries had high hopes that giving the party members a share in choosing their Knesset candidates would cure some of the weaknesses of the old political system, but these hopes soon proved futile. The expansion of the circle of participation in party politics was revealed as artificial; many people registered for two parties, in contravention of the law. A survey conducted by the Registrar of Parties in March 1996 found that 11.2 percent of those listed had registered for two parties and some had registered for even more (Rahat and Sar-Hadar 1999b: 164). In a survey conducted prior to the 1996 elections a gap of 4 percent was found between those who said they had voted in their party primaries (13 percent) and those who declared they were party members (9 percent) (Arian and Shamir 1999). After the primaries there was mass desertion by registered members, and there were some places where the number of registered members of the Labor Party, for example, exceeded the number who voted for it in the elections (Rahat and Sar-Hadar 1999a: 304).

By contrast, giving equal rights to people who joined the parties just for the primaries was detrimental to the parties themselves. A systematic examination of the advantages and disadvantages of the method showed that the damage outweighed the benefits (Avnon 1998). The results of the reform "yielded rotten fruit." The main profit derived from it was the "democratic ritual, largely symbolic, of massive participation," but "the implementation of procedures that were ostensibly more democratic was more destructive than beneficial" (Rahat and Sar-Hadar 1999: 22–28).

The second reform, which was even more radical, ended up being more harmful than the first. This was the Law of Direct Election of the Prime Minister, which was passed in 1992 and first implemented in the 1996 elections. As a parliamentary democracy in which no party has an absolute majority, the practice in Israel was that the president would invite the head of the party that won the most Knesset seats to form a coalition. The coalition had to achieve the confidence of the majority of Knesset members and was dependent on this confidence throughout its term. The new legislation split the voting in the general elections into two. With one slip the people voted for their chosen party, as in the past, according to the Israeli system of proportional representation, where the whole country is one voting district, with the qualifying threshold now set at 1.5 percent. With the second ballot the voters directly elected the prime minister — as in Russia and in France — by a system of "winner takes all," with two voting rounds if necessary.

The method of direct election of the prime minister engendered a constitutional hybrid. Israel was no longer a purely parliamentary regime because the head of its executive was elected directly by the voters. But it had not become a purely presidential regime because its executive body and the individual heading it were still accountable to the legislature. Rather it was now a model that might be called a semipresidential, semi-parliamentary, or presidential-parliamentary regime (Hazan 1998).

The advocates of the new law had great expectations. They argued that it would replace the party hacks and improve the quality of the national leadership. They promised that it would strengthen the link between the public and the prime minister and promote more moderate and representative leaders. They predicted that it would weaken the small parties' bargaining power and eliminate extortion, reinforce the leadership ability both of the prime minister toward his government and of the government toward the Knesset, and stabilize the political system as a whole. But reality dashed these high hopes. The results of the reform turned out to be far removed from what its proponents had envisaged.

The elections to the 14th Knesset, in 1996, the first elections to be conducted according to the new law, immediately revealed the major defect of the electoral reform: it did not resolve the crisis of the parties but exacerbated it, thus hastening their decline. The possibility of voting with two separate ballots led directly to the disintegration of the two major parties. Likud and Labor, which together had held 84 of the 120 Knesset seats in 1992, now won only 66 (Labor 34 and the Likud 32). Since 1949 the two leading parties together had never received such a small number of votes. It was the first time in Israel's history that the biggest party had such a small representation in the Knesset. This process did not stop in 1996. In the 1999 elections for the 15th Knesset the combined seats gained by the two major parties dropped to 45: 26 for Labor and 19 for the Likud.

The decline in the weight of the major parties was accompanied by fragmentation of the party map and a dramatic increase in the total number of parties, all of them relatively small. Twenty parties competed in the 1996 elections to the 14th Knesset, of which eleven were elected, compared with ten in the 13th Knesset. By 1999, when the Knesset was dissolved, these eleven parties had splintered into nineteen factions, some of them consisting of only one member. This splintering process continued, and in the 1999 elections, the number of competing parties was thirty-three, sixteen of which won Knesset seats, eight of them small factions with five members or less. Thus, the electoral reform, instead of stabilizing the party map, made it more fragmented than ever.

The party primaries led to the proliferation of straw candidates, who ran not in order to win a Knesset seat but to decrease the chances of rival candidates. In addition, splitting the Knesset vote led to the rise of "pseudoparties," namely, parties "that are not a concrete organizational framework of people and ideas attempting to convince the voters of the rightness of their way and recruit their support, but a strategy designed to improve the status of their leaders compared with other parties" (Doron 1998: 223). The parties of the past, which had filled an integrative function, were now replaced by political organizations that were actually interest groups disguised as parties.

The fact that the Knesset candidates representing the various parties were chosen in primaries open to all party members weakened the status of the parties' central committees and decreased their influence over the party representatives, who now became much less dependent on the party and its leadership. The collective responsibility of members in the parliamentary faction, and even in the cabinet coalition, had lost a great deal of its meaning. This hindered the working ability of the parliamentary faction and the cabinet. Breaches of party discipline became a commonplace affair.

"That was the Knesset in which the term 'coalition discipline' died," as *Yediot Ahronot*'s parliamentary correspondent summed up the 14th Knesset. "It was catch-as-catch-can for the candidates and their sectors. Every vote was a deal, reached by negotiation." It was also an unstable Knesset, whose members flouted party and coalition discipline many times, even on critical issues such as the budget or votes of no confidence in the government (Rahat and Sar-Hadar 1999b). "In the 14th Knesset people could be both in and out at the same time."[12]

In the new era of the parties' decline, their significant role in formulating public policy also diminished. Setting the public agenda is an important stage in which alternative policy options are developed and consolidated (Nahmias 1998: 244–45). This was particularly salient in the Labor Party, whose representatives in the various national institutions, including the government, had previously maintained a preliminary decision-making party forum, *sareinu* (our ministers) and *chavereinu* (our members). When Golda Meir was prime minister she used to convene this advisory forum every Saturday night in her home, which is how it acquired the nickname of "Golda's kitchen," where they prepared "precooked" proposals to bring to the cabinet meeting on Sunday morning.

As the major parties declined, the remaining party members gradually lost their contact with their leaders. In the 1960s, and to a lesser extent even in the 1970s, the branches of the large parties still served as weekly meeting places where the party rank and file could meet with the party leaders and activists, receive inside information, and express their opinions on topical issues. However, in the 1980s the branches stood empty, and in the 1990s the major parties sold their offices, drastically cut the permanent apparatus, and fired many employees in the party headquarters.

The extent to which the major parties had lost their position is illustrated by the following fact, verging on the absurd. One hundred days before the 1999 elections, a new, unknown party joined the thirty competing in the elections. Its name was New Leadership, and its leader, Motty Karpel, was an unknown figure. Like every party, it was eligible to receive free airtime on radio and television, which Karpel used in order to wage a negative campaign against the Labor Party. One week before the elections, the party announced that it had decided not to run for the Knesset, and then the secret was exposed: this was a virtual party set up by the Likud in order to gain more air and screen time to attack Labor. In the past, parties got airtime for political campaigns. Airtime *was* now the campaign, and the party — or pseudoparty — was only a tool, a pretext for getting airtime.

THE DAMAGE TO THE KNESSET

The Knesset itself also suffered from the reforms. Because of its new fragmentation, the Knesset became ineffective as an integrative body and turned into a battleground for special-interest groups. This was most evident in the budget debate, when Knesset members did not question the budget proposal out of an overall view of the needs of the economy or the general good, but rather thought only of increasing funding for projects benefiting their particular sector and the specific interest groups they represented. Even worse were private bills that allocated subsidies without specifying funding sources. In 2000, the overall sum divided in response to private members' bills reached more than half a billion dollars, although it was obvious that the government could not follow through with these decisions, lacking the necessary funds.

The direct election of the prime minister, along with the primaries, also changed the relationship between the executive and the legislative branches. The direct election rendered the government less dependent on the Knesset, and hence weakened the Knesset's control over the executive. The primaries weakened the government's ability to control parliamentary activity and legislation. No more than three years had passed since the reform, when a minority government with an oppositional parliament began to govern as had been forecast by opponents of the original reform. This was when Ehud Barak's (Labor) government continued to govern without a parliamentary majority, a situation that had been inconceivable before the electoral reform. It was no surprise, then, that the prime minister was forced to call elections within a few months.

Even when the government enjoyed a parliamentary majority, relations between the two institutions deteriorated. Nissim Zvili, former secretary-general of the Labor Party, explained, "The real problem is the tension between Knesset members and ministers, which becomes explosive as we approach the primaries. The Knesset members know that if they support government policy they will disappear from the political map. This makes them want to be different and compete for headlines."[13] Zvili referred to the second important result of the reform — it accelerated the personalization of politics. With the enfeeblement of their authority and discipline, the parties lost their ability to determine policy, present a cohesive ideological image, and act effectively. The Knesset was one of the sites where the personalization of politics was most distinctly manifested, since the faction members no longer needed the party committees in order to be elected. As a result, they acted primarily according to their own individual considerations. The Knesset had become "a convention of 120 ambassadors."

If one compares the patterns of action of the 13th Knesset, when many members were elected through primaries, with the 12th Knesset, one can easily witness the privatization of politics syndrome. The number of questions in the house rose by more than 20 percent, motions to get an issue on the agenda rose by 45 percent, private bills rose by 139 percent, and the number of private bills that were approved reached 46 percent. More than half of the bills submitted and approved were private bills, compared with an average of fifteen in every Knesset since the establishment of the state.[14]

These figures relating to the intensified activity of Knesset members ostensibly indicate improvement in their work, but they themselves admit that there is no connection between quantity and quality. In many cases, in fact, the opposite is true. In a debate held in the Knesset constitution committee on the effect of primaries on the work of legislation, Knesset member Yitzhak Levy, who later became the leader of the National Religious Party (NRP), admitted that the heavy load of bills submitted placed a burden on the committees and obstructed their work.[15]

"In the past, the Knesset was an institution with inspirational power, it was a source of normative decisions (for example, the discussion as to whether or not Israel should accept the Holocaust reparation payments from Germany). Today, such decisions are taken in other places, including the Supreme Court, and the Knesset has lost its status as the setter of norms," said Knesset Speaker Avraham Burg. He also described the

Knesset's enfeeblement in two other spheres, legislation and control: "The Cabinet has become the main legislating body while the role of State Comptroller has grown in scope and strength."[16] Benny Begin, a former Knesset member and a minister in the Likud government, asserted, "The new system has caused Knesset members to neglect their basic work that is hidden from the limelight and to focus instead on superficial public activity designed to draw attention to themselves. Private bills, like motions for the agenda, are an expression of this phenomenon" (Begin 1996).

The personalization process was also manifested in other political institutions outside the Knesset. In the 1998 municipal elections, 40 percent of the mayoral candidates were independent candidates who did not represent parties. When the election results emerged, commentators in all the papers defined them as "the collapse of the large parties." Those most seriously affected were Labor and Likud, which had previously controlled most of the local authorities and now lost to sectarian parties like those representing immigrant ethnic groups and those that were independent political actors who set up pseudoparties.

It appears, then, that the direct election of the prime minister and the primaries weakened the commitment to the party platform and party discipline while strengthening individualistic politics in both arms of government. "It is clear that the phenomenon of separate tickets and the resultant enfeeblement of the major parties has eroded the representative model of political parties. The primaries are hastening the destruction of the party institutions in Israel, which began with the direct election of the prime minister, but now the destruction comes from within" (Hazan 1998: 88).

The reform did not end the political crisis; on the contrary, it exacerbated it. The new bill, whereby political parties would now be funded by the state, in fact served to strengthen their cartel nature and caused further anger against and alienation of voters from the parties. The fragmentation of the "party state," the decline in the state's effectiveness, the unpredictability of the political system, and the strengthening of the personal dimension of political action, all intensified the need for other political mechanisms.

Some saw the root of the problem in Israel's adoption of a semipresidential instead of a parliamentary regime, since the academic literature reveals general agreement that parliamentary regimes are more stable than presidential ones (Hazan 1998: 109). Dan Avnon accused the Israeli Knesset of entrusting a substantial part of its authority to the prime minister and asserted that the legislature had abrogated its representative and deliberative functions by imposing on the judiciary the responsibility for resolving issues of principle and essence on controversial subjects in society that should be discussed and decided in the Knesset. Thus, said Avnon, parliamentary democracy was enfeebled and the authoritarian character of the new regime was strengthened (Avnon 1998).

Indeed, just before Benjamin Netanyahu, the first Israeli prime minister to be elected in direct elections, came to power, weaknesses were exposed in the new political structure that eventually led to his fall after a very short period in office. During that period it seemed that the source of the defects and weaknesses of the system was the personality of the figure who headed the system. Yet the fact that the problems continued during the premiership of Ehud Barak, the second prime minister elected directly, should make it clear that the faults were rooted in the system itself. During Barak's term, coalition Knesset members voted against their own government, in total contravention of the government's bylaws. This was also the first time that a government ruled without a parliamentary majority: it faced an oppositional Knesset and was supported by only thirty Knesset members.

The intensity of the crisis was manifested in the fact that although only a quarter of the people's representatives supported him at the end of 2000, Barak continued to negotiate with the Palestinians over the future peace agreement and for the first time expressed a willingness to concede most of the occupied territories, including parts of East Jerusalem. When he was confronted with the argument that he should not negotiate over such a critical issue without a parliamentary majority, Barak replied, "I was elected by the people and I am not dependent on the Knesset." Barak was accused of acting undemocratically and was nicknamed "Bonaparte." Whether or not his claim was just, it is clear that an unprecedented and dangerous constitutional crisis had broken out. The public debate raged not only over the prime minister's authority to sign state agreements but also over the basic rules of the democratic game.

Barak's readiness to call early elections after only twenty months in office prevented the further deterioration of the political crisis. Nevertheless, public pressure snowballed, and within a few months after the elections the Knesset decided to reverse the new system. In early 2001, a majority in the Knesset voted to repeal the Law of Direct Election of the Prime Minister and revert to the old parliamentary system with a few modifications.

One negative effect of the prime ministerial government was that all the ills of the political system and the political crisis were attributed to it. This was clearly exaggerated; after all, parliamentary democracies that did not adopt a semipresidential system are also undergoing a democracy crisis. The Israeli crisis and the fragmentation of the political system

resembled that of other liberal democracies as described so well by
Manuel Castells: "The new institutional, cultural and technological conditions of democratic exercise have made obsolete the existing party system, and the current regime of competitive politics, as adequate mechanisms of political representation in the network society" (1997: 309–10).

Moreover, the Israeli parties have not completely lost their power. In
this respect they more closely resemble their European rather than their
American counterparts. This is evident, for example, in elections. In the
U.S. system, a candidate can run for office virtually independent of the
party and is totally dependent on support by mass media. The situation in
Europe is different. Although political leaders may run independently of
the traditional party system, as the Berlusconi case demonstrated in a
spectacular way, the usual pattern is still that candidates are nominated
by party organizations and that the campaign depends to a large degree
on the party organization (Mazzoleni and Schultz 1999: 256). This was
demonstrated in June 2001. Barak's control of the party machinery and
institutions was strong enough not to be challenged by any other candidate, and he remained the Labor Party candidate for prime minister
opposite Ariel Sharon, who had been a minister in Netanyahu's government and replaced him as Likud leader when he resigned. But, in fact,
Barak had lost the trust of Labor voters. On election day, it was clear that
Barak could not win without this support. Indeed he sustained a heavier
defeat than he had inflicted on Netanyahu eighteen months earlier. It was
a historic landslide in Israel.

Politics does not exist in a vacuum. Out of the ruins of the old party
system, something new emerged: mediapolitik, or media-centered democracy. But that new phenomenon is better understood in the context of the
changing relationship between the media and politics in Israel.

CHAPTER FOUR

The History of Media-Politics Relations in Israel

THE GOLDEN AGE OF THE PARTISAN PRESS

Israelis often cite their media as evidence of the democratic nature of Israeli society. Indeed, from its formative years in the 1920s and 1930s, Israeli society was a multiparty society with free elections. However, Israeli democracy during that time, as well as in the early years of statehood, was a formal rather than a liberal democracy, the kind that emphasizes elections and majority rule rather than the rights of individuals and minorities (Shapiro 1978). The press, too, reflected this brand of democracy, which was at a relatively low stage in Dahl's "polyarchy" system that measures democratic development (Dahl 1989). On the one hand, there was pluralism, with a great variety of newspapers and open debate among them. On the other hand, the political culture set limits on freedom of speech, and this was accepted by politicians and journalists alike. As a result, the Israeli legislative branch failed to adopt a bill to secure the freedom of the press as the U.S. Constitution does. Israeli political culture was thus closer to the European style, where the typical pattern is of pliability of the media to party institutions.

Since 1949, the pattern of relations between the media and the political body has changed enormously, and no simplistic model can describe it. A classification of the period from the establishment of the state to the present day, even at the risk of schematization of history, reveals three distinct periods (see chart on next page).

During Israel's first fifty years, its political structure, media structure, and political-media culture underwent far-reaching changes, which had a profound effect on "news management" (Pfetsch 1998), or, more broadly, on the nature of the relationship between the media and politics.

During the pre-state period, and decreasingly over the first two decades of statehood, the Israeli pattern was very similar to the model of "press-party parallelism." Seymour-Ure enumerates three criteria for this

Period	Political Structure	Media Structure	Political Media Culture
1950s & 1960s	A party state with a dominant party	State and partisan ownership and supervision of the media	The parallel model, party logic
1970s & 1980s	Polarized competitive party structure	Political control of public broadcasting plus private media	Collateral model
1990s	Prime ministerial government (presidential-parliamentary)	Combined model: commercial plus little broadcasting and sectarian media	Media logic

model: party involvement in mass-media ownership and management; the newspapers' editorial policies; and the readers' party affiliation (Seymour-Ure 1974). The Israeli case matches the highest of the five levels discerned in the parallel pattern: "The highest degree of partisan involvement exists when the parties are directly associated with running of media enterprises via ownership, provision of financial subsidy, or membership on management and editorial boards" (Blumler and Gurevitch 1995: 65).

Although there were private commercial newspapers both during the pre-state period and after the establishment of the state, notably *Haaretz*, Israel's media environment was largely characterized by party newspapers. When the state was established in 1948, there were twelve party newspapers (seven morning and five evening papers) compared with six unaffiliated papers (two dailies and four evening papers, respectively). Out of the 220 journalists in Israel during that period, approximately two-thirds worked for party papers and only one-third for unaffiliated papers.[1] Although the papers differed in the extent of their ties with their respective parties, they all ultimately matched up with Blumler and Gurevitch's criteria.

The parties subsidized the papers, which could not have survived without this support. The readers were primarily party members, and the party encouraged its members to read the papers. In addition, there were direct links to the parties in the newspapers' management and editorial board. For example, Mapam Party leaders Meir Ya'ari and Ya'akov Hazan shared in running the editorial board of *Al Hamishmar*. Yisrael Galili, one of the leaders of the Ahdut Ha'avoda Party and later a senior member of Prime Minister Golda Meir's "kitchen cabinet" (1969–74), was on the editorial board of the party paper *Lamerhav*; the paper's editor, Moshe Carmel, was a Knesset member and later a government minister. The leader of the General Zionist Party, Peretz Bernstein, was the editor of the party paper, *Haboker*. The founder and editor in chief of *Hatzofe* was Rabbi Meir Bar-Ilan (Berlin), one of the leaders of Mizrahi, the forerunner of the National Religious Party. The same is true of Labor's *Davar*, whose editorial board and management included the founding father of Israel's social-democracy, Berl Katzenelson, as well as others who moved on to occupy senior positions in the new state, such as President Zalman Shazar and Prime Minister and Foreign Minister Moshe Sharett.[2]

The privately owned papers, those that were not owned by political parties in the first period, nevertheless had a distinctly political character. For example, the evening tabloid *Maariv* was established by a group of journalists associated with the Revisionist movement, some of whom had even worked with the founder of the movement, Ze'ev Jabotinsky and supported the right-wing nationalist camp. Similarly, *Haaretz*, although independent, had a distinctly liberal (though nonpartisan) character. It is not surprising that its editor, Gershon Schocken, was a representative of the Progressive Party in the third Knesset in the years 1955–59.[3]

The conception of parallelism was influenced primarily by the political tradition of the pre-state society, brought by the founding fathers and mothers from Eastern Europe who saw the party as the cornerstone of political life. Ben Gurion used to cite Lenin, who said that his paper, *Iskra*, which he edited from his country of exile, Switzerland, had a decisive role in preparing the Bolshevik Revolution in Russia. "A newspaper is essential for a party," said Ben Gurion when the Mapai secretariat discussed the party's media policy on June 30, 1949. "A party cannot exist without a paper of its own. We must get our word out every day." In this respect, Ben Gurion compared the newspaper to the military arm, which he also saw as a tool that should be under the strict control of the party leadership.[4]

The politicians' supremacy over the media was also manifested in their ownership and control of the electronic media, namely the radio. Before the establishment of the state the radio was under the jurisdiction of the "national institutions," and later of the government, with the prime minister's office being responsible for Kol Israel (Voice of Israel). The broadcasts were of somewhat narrow scope — Kol Israel did not have many channels — but it played an important role as the official voice of the national leadership. During the War of Independence a new channel was established, the IDF Channel, Galei Zahal, which broadcast just a few hours in the evening, relaying news from Kol Israel (Mann and Gon-

Gross 1991) and then later expanded. Kol Israel confined itself to being the almost official mouthpiece of the government and was far from acting as an independent or critical news organization. Both the public and politicians focused their attention on what newspapers published because the "real action" in the media took place on those pages.

A symbolic expression of the spirit of the mobilized press could be seen on the day that independence was declared, when the five major newspapers published the exact same newspaper. However, the parallel model persisted after the establishment of the state, which assumed the powers, the functions, and even the aura possessed by the political parties in the pre-state period. The symbolic standing of the state was promoted as part of the new civil religion constituted by Ben Gurion, *mamlachtiut*, or the Israeli version of etatism. This was an ideology similar to those that characterized many national movements in the postcolonial era, according to which the political elite entrusted intellectuals and cultural and educational elites with the mission of helping in nation- and state-building.

Ben Gurion, appearing at the annual convention of the Journalists Association in Tel Aviv on March 13, 1953, described journalists' role as he saw it. "You must foster in the nation those qualities and attributes that are necessary to improve their ability for productive work for the good of the economy, raise the youths' cultural level and pioneering zeal, and enhance the strength, courage and loyalty of the IDF. If you do that you will fulfill your true mission to Israel and to the entire Jewish people" (Ben Gurion 1953: 193–95).[5]

The Israeli media during that period adopted elements of the developmental press model as states and societies in the third world had done. This model, according to McQuail, "Correlates 'nation building' as an overriding objective. To this end, certain freedoms of the media and of journalists are subordinated to their responsibility for helping in this purpose. At the same time, collective ends, rather than individual freedoms, are emphasized" (McQuail 1989: 121). This pattern includes not only overt principles such as limiting the freedom of the press, but also covert principles whereby the mass media were supposed to serve the needs of modernization.[6]

A salient manifestation of the statist conception was the supervision of public broadcasting, which at that time was only radio. Newspapers were directly controlled by the parties. Public broadcasting was, by contrast, officially under state control, but, in fact, it was controlled by the dominant party. Kol Israel was established in the 1930s as a department in the British Mandatory Government, and after Israel's establishment in 1948 it was annexed as a department in the prime minister's office. Therefore, it is not surprising that broadcasting policy was, in fact, determined by the director-general of the office, Teddy Kollek (later the mayor of Jerusalem), and Ben Gurion's secretary, Yitzhak Navon (later the president of Israel). This state of affairs "made the directors toe the government line."[7]

The justification for this model derived from the situation in which Israel was mired from the moment of its establishment, namely the ongoing conflict with its Arab neighbors. The prolonged state of war juxtaposed the needs of national security against the enlightened principles of an "open society"; it legitimized the political-military elite's defining Israel as a "fighting democracy" that had to place limitations on the fulfillment of liberal democratic values (Hofnung 1991; Barzilai 1992). During this time, without overt criticism from the media, Ben Gurion was able to make statements such as: "Discipline and public responsibility are required of the entire public, and above all, the press" (Ben Gurion 1953: 172).

The supremacy of the politicians in this period was manifest both in external and in internal controls. Externally, the state's supervisory mechanisms over the broadcasting authority included appointments, budgeting, and auditing, as well as supervision of contents. The political parties possessed similar supervisory mechanisms over the newspapers: the papers were published, funded, and budgeted by the parties; managers and editors were appointed by the parties; and the editorial line reflected the official attitudes of the party leaderships.

The state also supervised the newspapers, although less directly, through formal measures such as rules and regulations, for example, the Press Act, which stipulated that anyone wishing to publish a newspaper must have a state license. Other indirect methods of supervision were financial arrangements, such as the publishers' need to receive a foreign-currency allowance from the treasury in order to import printing paper. The most prominent supervision in this period was in the sphere of security, through military censorship and other restrictive measures (Caspi and Limor 1992).

Internal supervision — journalists' own awareness and willingness to accept politicians' hegemony — is, however, more efficient than external supervision. During the British Mandate the major cause of journalists' willingness to place themselves at the service of the national political leadership was the national struggle to achieve independence. After 1948, the perceived threat to Israel's security strengthened the position of the state vis-à-vis civil society, enhanced people's willingness to be called to the flag, stifled criticism of policies, and prevented change of the old order. In this political tradition with its two constraints — a limited conception of democracy due to the needs of nation-building, and the effect of the Israeli-

Arab dispute on the culture of criticism — there was no room for the development of an awareness of professional independence, which is a necessary condition for a democratic press (Blumler and Gurevitch 1995: 65).

Nevertheless, it would be incorrect to describe the Israeli case as monochromatic, homogeneous, or static. Even in the 1950s, there were expressions of criticism of the government in journals that did not belong to political parties. One of these was the subversive weekly *Ha'olam Hazeh*; its editor, Uri Avneri, presented a different conception of journalism — independent, investigative, subversive — and expressed political attitudes outside the consensus, advocating Israel's integration into the "Semitic region." Furthermore, *Haaretz*, Israel's quality newspaper that is comparable to the *New York Times*, operated in the spirit of its publisher and editor, Gershon Schocken, and attempted to fill an independent critical role. It occasionally drew swords with the government not only over its policies but also over the freedom of the press (Katzman 1999).

THE LAVON AFFAIR AND "UNITED PERES"

The first cracks in the power structure of the dominant party, Mapai, appeared in the early 1960s, in connection with the events that came to be called the "Lavon affair." This was the most turbulent political scandal that had occurred in the young state, and it constituted a milestone in the history of political communication. The core of the affair was the struggle between two subelites in the party over the inheritance of the founding father, Ben Gurion. On one side were the Mapai old guard (notably, Levi Eshkol, Golda Meir, Pinchas Sapir, Zalman Aran, and Mordecai Namir) reinforced by a political alliance with the leaders of Ahdut Ha'avoda (headed by Israel Galili, Yigal Allon, and Yitzhak Ben Aharon). On the other side were the "young Mapai" group (whose outstanding leaders were Moshe Dayan, Shimon Peres, Teddy Kollek, and Yitzhak Navon), who had established the Rafi Party in 1965, but returned to Mapai in 1968.

The affair began in 1954, with the failure of a sabotage operation carried out by a unit of the Mossad in Egypt. This botched operation came to be known as the "mishap," and debate arose as to who had given the order, Defense Minister Lavon or Chief of Intelligence, Major-General Benjamin Gibli, without the minister's knowledge. This question became the focus of political battles in the party leadership and the hub of political processes for twenty years. From a political communication perspective it was the first time that politicians from the same governing party had used the press as a battleground for their jousting.

Because the old guard controlled the party machine, the young group sought an alternative weapon, and they found it in something that had not hitherto been involved in internal party struggles — the press. With a constant flow of leaks to the press, they managed not only to present their case to the public but also to gain the explicit support of political columnists and commentators. At the same time, the internal division and the loosening of internal constraints in the inner circles of the ruling party helped to strengthen the media. For the first time, journalists became aware that they could play a significant critical role vis-à-vis the government and the political establishment generally.

The old guard was helpless in face of this change in the rules of the political game and had a hard time battling against the new weapon. They were used to internal party feuds that took place in closed, smoke-filled rooms and never reached the light of day. For example, the citizens of Israel did not know the true reason for Defense Minister Pinchas Lavon's resignation in 1954, or what led to the resignation of Foreign Minister Moshe Sharett the same year. In those cases, as in others, the public announcement concealed the truth, which became known to the general public only after some years. How strongly the old guard felt that this new game was illegitimate can be gathered from the sharp reaction of one of their leaders, Zalman Shazar, later president of Israel, who attacked the young group and Dayan in particular, in *Davar*, for "emphasizing the personal element rather than the ideology" and for using the press as a political tool, "putting announcements in the papers every day, and daily speculating on the pages of the newspapers, instead of discussing issues inside the party forums."[8]

The most interesting political figure of that period for those interested in media-politics relations was one of the leaders of the young Mapai group, Shimon Peres, Ben Gurion's protégé and a figure whose influence has been dominant in Israeli politics longer than any other politician, from the end of the 1940s and into the twenty-first century. At the time of the Lavon affair Peres was director-general of the Ministry of Defense (a position to which he was appointed at the age of twenty-nine); later he became a member of Knesset and deputy defense minister. From the beginning of his political career, Peres established close contacts with young journalists in all newspapers, relations he fostered when he was a deputy minister. So close were these ties that the group — which included the cream of the political journalists of that period, people like Shabtai Tevet and Abraham Schweitzer from *Haaretz*, Yeshayahu Ben Porat from *Yediot Ahronot*, and others — was labeled "United Peres" by his opponents (Ben Porat 1997). This was a new style of political activity, using journalists and the media as much as the party machine and developing relationships with journalists based not on shared ideological attitudes but on exchange relations, supplying inside information in exchange for political assistance.

The Lavon affair was a landmark in the history of the relations between the media and Israel's political body. For the first time since the establishment of the state the press dared to deal critically with security affairs, which had previously been taboo. The harsh criticism of Ben Gurion that appeared in several papers showed the press's ability to attack the revered leader. The unaffiliated papers — particularly *Maariv* and *Haaretz*, which published many details about the affair — proved their advantage over the party papers. This also gave a boost to the circulation of the two evening papers, which had previously been considered yellow and now acquired legitimacy.

At the same time, a reading of the papers of the period shows that, rather than serving as a mediating link between the general public and the political leadership, the press acted as a player in the power game within the political class itself, in a form of court palace journalism. The military censorship prevented the exposure of details, and the oblique language used in writing about the affair, which was obscure to the general public ("the third man," "the fighter," "the mishap," or "the high-ranking officer") was perfectly clear to the members of this class, who understood the codes.

The success of the Mapai young guard in using the press as an ally in the political feud against the old guard in the early 1960s led them to adopt this pattern and use it in the next crisis, on the eve of the Six-Day War in May–June 1967. This time it was not merely an internal crisis among the leadership of the ruling party, but a national and international crisis. As mentioned, the young guard had split off from Mapai in 1965 and founded Rafi, with limited parliamentary success; they gained only ten seats and found themselves on the opposition benches. When Egyptian President Abdel Nasser moved his army into the Sinai Desert in the summer of 1967, the resultant military and political pressure on Israel led to a political crisis. The government, headed by Levi Eshkol, who also held the defense portfolio, was perceived as being slow to respond to the threat to Israel's existence and hesitant to launch a preemptive military strike. The fear of a war initiated by the Arab states shook the public's trust in the government and strengthened the voices clamoring to take the defense portfolio away from Levi Eshkol and form a national coalition government together with the opposition parties.

This campaign was conducted by the Rafi leaders, who saw the crisis as an opportunity to weaken Mapai and return to the positions of power they had lost in the elections two years earlier. They argued that the government was incapable of resolving the crisis and that the only solution was to establish a National Unity Government and to transfer the defense portfolio to Moshe Dayan. The delegitimization campaign against the government was inflamed and inflated by the media to an unprecedented extent, encouraged by the young Mapai group. This was a bitter lesson for the Mapai old guard, who found it hard to digest the growing power of the unaffiliated press to mobilize public opinion, in the hands of those who knew how to use it.

THE COLLATERAL MODEL IN THE SECOND PERIOD

The first period, which was sometimes called the "golden age" of parties, lasted until the 1970s, when the transition to the second period began and the party press was replaced by commercial journalism.[9] The papers of the major parties were closed: *Herut*, the paper of the right-wing nationalist Herut Party; *Haboker*, organ of the General Zionists (later the Liberal Party, which joined Herut in 1965 to create the Likud); *Hayom*, a daily of the Likud (the bloc established by Herut and the Liberal Party in 1966); *Hakol*, belonging to the ultraorthodox Poalei Agudat Israel; *Lamerhav*, the paper of Ahdut Ha'avoda (which joined with Mapai in 1968 to form the Labor Party); *Kol Ha'am*, the Communist Party daily. The Mapai weekly, *Ot*, and the Rafi weekly, *Mabat Hadash*, were also shut down. Of all the party papers that existed before the establishment of the state, only one remained, the National Religious Party's *Hatzofe*, established in 1937.

Although party papers had also closed before the 1960s (among the most important of them were Mapai's *Hador* and the Progressive Party's *Zmanim*), this process reached a peak in the second period, with the closing of prominent papers identified with major parties. The process continued, until the closing of the last papers, Mapam's *Al Hamishmar*, in 1994, and the organ of the Histadrut (the Trade Union Federation), *Davar*, in 1996, which had been the voice of Mapai since its establishment in 1925.

Concurrently, the three independent commercial papers — *Haaretz* and the two evening tabloids, *Yediot Ahronot* and *Maariv* — were gaining strength. In the third period, these would become Israel's major newspapers. The diminished readership, lack of revenue from advertising, excessive political indoctrination, and a rigid writing and editorial style placed the party press at a severe disadvantage compared with the privately owned newspapers. The latter provided richer political coverage and offered the readers a wider range of topics. They also adopted the spirit of the period, both in graphic display and writing style. Instead of the flow-ery language and elevated style characteristic of the party papers, the evening papers used the direct simple language of everyday speech. This was a transformation from product-oriented marketing to consumer-ori-ented marketing. Whereas the party papers had specifically addressed a limited audience, the three commercial papers addressed the public at large. Thus their circulation grew, and with it, their influence. These papers' growing circulation attracted the attention of politicians, who chose to give interviews to them rather than to the party papers (Wolfen-son 1975). This led in turn to the private papers' increased involvement in major political controversies.

Contemporaneous with the change that took place in print journalism toward the 1970s, an important change also occurred in the electronic media. Throughout the first period, radio was owned by the government and was administered as a department in the prime minister's office. This is similar to the French television model, which has been described as "a theatre on whose stage the government performed every evening. The role of the journalists was the same as that of technicians in a theatre: to ensure the smooth running of the performance" (Chalaby 1998: 51).

According to the system practiced in France the broadcasting media belong to the state, which manages them directly, supervises budgets, dic-tates information, and practices censorship. State television broadcasts did not present the news from an independent viewpoint, but rather from that of the government. In Kol Israel, politicians appointed the CEO, and there was also political involvement of senior editors and directors. Directives were transmitted directly from the director-general of the prime minister's office to the CEO of the radio.

Levi Eshkol's inauguration as prime minister in 1963 marked the end of Ben Gurion's political era and the beginning of policies of decentral-ization and liberalization. This was also reflected in media policy. Before Ben Gurion's resignation, after the elections of 1961, the "club of four" was formed by four opposition parties, which sought to take advantage of Mapai's enfeeblement, and jointly presented it with several conditions for joining the coalition government. One of the demands was to remove Kol Israel from the supervision of the prime minister's office. The club broke up, and a few of the parties joined the government coalition, but some of the original demands were fulfilled by Levi Eshkol when he became prime minister in 1963.

A few years later in 1965, the Israel Broadcasting Authority Law was passed, transferring the radio from government to public ownership, headed by a public council and financed by license fees. The British Broadcasting Corporation (BBC) model was adopted, and the public council was supposed to include representatives of different groups and public organizations that had interests in culture, such as teachers, journalists, and writers. Ostensibly, public broadcasting was supposed to be more pluralistic than state broadcasting. However, despite the fact that the radio was freed of direct administrative subordination to the government, the ruling party did not lose its de facto control. This, in the end, is what characterizes a dominant party regime: that despite the formal pluralistic structure, the power, in fact, is concentrated in the hands of the hegemonic party.[10]

When television was introduced in 1968, it was incorporated into the Broadcasting Authority as a branch parallel to radio, with a similar pattern of news management. Because of the awesome power of the new medium, however, political supervision by the ruling party was stricter than in radio. The chairman of the Broadcasting Authority, a public figure, was appointed by the government, but so was the director-general, who was supposed to be a professional. The budget was still financed by licensing fees, but the size of the budget was determined by the Knesset finance committee, where Mapai had a majority. The governing party retained its political supervision over radio and television, although the pattern of its influence changed from direct and overt control to indirect and increasingly covert influence (Shilon 1999).

The hyperpoliticized character of Israeli society impeded the implementation of the BBC model in practice. The attempt to fill the Broadcasting Authority council with unaffiliated public figures did not succeed. It soon emerged that the new council members were in fact party delegates, and that the council was really only one more political arena, similar to the parliamentary one. Indeed, in the following years changes of government would also lead to changes in the council, when the new ruling party appointed its representatives to the role of chairperson or director-general of the Broadcasting Authority.

Journalists shared the political class's attitude toward the role of the media in the first period. However, there was often tension between the newspaper and the political party, and there were different nuances among the various party papers. The extreme doctrinaire attitude was expressed in an editorial in *Al Hamishmar*, befitting the paper of a socialist party that was pro-Soviet, even pro-Stalinist, until it became disillusioned: "The party paper has to educate and guide its readers in one direction. A revolutionary party and its paper cannot become a forum for endless discussion that does not lead to decisions and disciplined action."[11] In contrast, a more flexible line was revealed by the managing editor of *Davar*, Haim Isaac, who said that in his paper "there was freedom of expression where this was reasonable, but within certain limits."[12]

Even more liberal papers behaved this way. Moshe Sharett, who served as prime minister and foreign minister in the 1950s, recounts in his diary that one day he had delivered an important speech in the Knesset. Hearing it reported on the radio, he regretted some of his remarks, telephoned *Jerusalem Post* editor, Gershon Agron, and dictated a different text to him. The fact that his speech had been recorded in the Knesset chronicles and broadcast in Hebrew throughout the country did not deter him from rewriting it after the event. However, the most interesting aspect of this story was the newspaper editor's response. He agreed to the foreign minister's request without hesitation. After all, who would know better than the minister himself what was good for the country, and who was Agron, a newspaper editor, to argue with the minister?

Needless to say, in security matters and in foreign affairs the editors agreed to hide the truth or even to distort it when instructed by the government, for raison d'état, that is, in order to protect what they perceived as the state's vital interests.[13] But during this period they did the same for less vital reasons, such as to avoid hurting the country's leaders. When Nehemia Argov, Prime Minister David Ben Gurion's popular military aide, died in a road accident while he was riding a bicycle, there was some talk of suicide. The editor of *Davar* printed one copy of the paper without the news of the death, so as not to upset the adored leader, who was sick that day (the "old man" used to read *Davar* first thing in the morning). The news of the death appeared in all of the other copies.

An expression of Israeli journalists' sense of an educational mission may be seen in a resolution passed at the annual convention of the Journalists Association in July 1958. The resolution stated: "The assembly emphasizes the importance of writers, journalists in Israel, to social integration and fraternity among all its citizens, to the fortification of independence and cultural autonomy, freedom of the spirit and democracy in the state, to the promotion of peace and understanding between nations. . . . The journalist will show the light in our renascence enterprise and continue educating for good citizenship and loyalty to the State of Israel." The preamble to the professional ethical code that was drawn up the same year included the statement: "The journalist's role is to serve the public by supplying verified reliable information, responding to it and interpreting it in the spirit of public education for good citizenship and respect between people."[14]

If one compares this text with the new version of the code that was passed in 1973, one can easily observe the journalistic ethos of the first period. In the new code, the concept of education is completely absent, while the three opening paragraphs deal with the importance of a free press and of free speech as a basic right and cornerstone of human freedom and rights in a democracy, as well as with the journalists' need to see themselves as public servants. The text also states, "The mission of the journalist and the newspaper is to supply the public with verified information and interpretations that match the facts."[15]

THE LESSONS OF THE "DEBACLE"

Relations between the media and politics in the second period were characterized by the collateral model. This model allowed broader scope for criticism of the government than in the previous period. In the end, however, journalists willingly accepted many restrictions. In the collateral model, the main idea is the compatibility of goals between the politicians and media professionals. The media do not act primarily as antagonists of politics, as a watchdog or fourth estate. Rather, they embrace the political visions of the political forces and act as paladins of certain stances and opinions asserted by them. They still maintain a reverent approach to political institutions, reveal more commitment to the interests of the national leadership than to those of the general public, and are prepared to respond to its demands and allow it to set their media frames.[16]

Such behavior can be witnessed in the attitude of *Maariv* in the Bus 300 affair. This event took place in 1986, and the fact that the editor, Ido Dissenchik, behaved differently from his colleagues, who had already begun to abandon the old journalistic pattern, highlights the collateral model in a sharper light. Dissenchik received anonymous information of the greatest importance, not only in terms of newsworthiness but also in terms of its significance for the character and fate of the Israeli democracy. He verified the facts with the attorney general, but nevertheless chose to consult Prime Minister Shimon Peres and followed his advice not to publish the matter. When the story broke a short time later, published by other media outlets, it turned out to be the biggest scandal to rock the secret services and the government since the Lavon affair.

The story began in April 1984, when members of the General Security Service (GSS) murdered two Palestinian terrorists caught alive after hijacking a bus. The attempt to expose the murder opened a Pandora's box and revealed a whole string of illegal GSS activities in its relations with both the civil echelon (to which it was subordinate) and the judicial system. Matters even reached the stage of an attempt by top GSS people to place the blame for the murder on a senior army officer, then Brigadier-General Yitzhak Mordecai (who was later appointed defense minister). It was Attorney General Yitzhak Zamir (later president of the Press Council and a justice in the Supreme Court) who decided to fight the GSS, which in turn did not hesitate to deceive an internal judicial commission of inquiry. But Zamir had to face not only the top ranks of the secret services but also the top political echelon, which attempted to cover up the affair. This acrimonious struggle cost Zamir his position: he was dismissed by Prime Minister Shimon Peres.

The affair, which was conducted in the innermost chambers of government, leaked out to the press. As was the case with the Lavon affair, such leaks soon stopped the whitewashing. In the end, the scandal led to dramatic purges in the top ranks of the GSS and also to the president's controversial decision to pardon those accused of serious crimes — even of the murder itself. The journalistic treatment in assisting the attorney general created the momentum that forced the political leaders to act, both by the actual exposure of the various stages of the affair, and in cleaning out the stables. This was an example of a deviation from the collateral model that characterized the media in the second period, which the editor of *Maariv* wished to continue.[17]

The collateral model naturally had different nuances. Some newspapers continued to behave as in the first period. The editor of *Hatzofe* explained, "Israel, as a country at war, has to take upon itself censorial restrictions, imposed both by law and by the conscience."[18] *Haaretz*, by contrast, followed working patterns closer to the adversarial model. The public media pursued the old line, mainly because they were still under close government supervision, but the evening papers also largely followed the same line.

They did so because they wished to maintain comfortable relations with the government, both out of financial considerations (*Yediot Ahronot* was granted a concession for partnership in the football lottery) and out of *Maariv* editor Arie Dissenchik's sense of shared responsibility with the government. This sense was passed on to his son Ido, although the latter belonged to a generation of more critical journalists. In a television debate on the role of the press in the war in Lebanon during the summer of 1982, he said, "I am first of all an Israeli, then an officer in the reserves, and only after that a journalist and an editor."

The critical event that led the press to abandon the mobilized journalism model at the beginning of the second period was the "debacle," the term used in Israel to describe the Yom Kippur War of 1973. This war did to Israeli journalism what the Vietnam War did to the American press. Journalists began to recognize that their modus operandi and the principles of an "objective press" were a betrayal of their professional mission (Hallin 1994). The fact that Israeli journalists were not critical of the government and submitted to the directives of the military establishment had caused them to hide from the public the preparations of the Syrian and

Egyptian armies for the surprise attack, although they had known about the matter.

In his book *Blinded at the Top*, Shimshon Ofer, *Davar*'s military correspondent in the years before that war, angrily described the ways in which journalists had served as tools of the political establishment. In particular, he accused the IDF Intelligence Branch not only of feeding the government with misinformation and false assessments, but also of willfully manipulating the public. The IDF, said Ofer, considered it a duty to preserve the citizens' morale. It conducted psychological warfare against the enemy as well as the Israeli public, carefully manipulating the Israeli press (Zelinger 1990: 35).[19]

He referred to the term that became popular at the time, "the conception." The prevalent conception in inner political and military circles had been that Israel's power would deter Egypt and Syria from attacking. Israel could keep control of the territories as long as it wanted. Since it was the norm to accept the attitudes of national leaders as divine truth, even the facts on the ground did not cause journalists to question the preparations in Egypt and Syria for the war that they saw with their own eyes.

The collective conclusion reached by journalists following the debacle was that one must not assume that leaders know better than ordinary citizens what is good for the country; therefore, the role of the press is to expose information, give the government a hard time, ask questions, investigate independently, and bring the truth to light in all spheres of life, including the sphere of national security. Danny Bloch wrote in *Davar*, in the context of moral stocktaking after the Yom Kippur War, "I don't accept the idea that the role of the press is to keep up morale. Its major role is to deliver accurate information, expose the truth, criticize and sound warnings. The role of the press today is to make every effort to open additional paths to independent sources of information, so that we will not be dependent on one source that is not prepared to reveal everything" (Bloch 1990: 73).[20] In March 1974, the Press Council discussed the professional crisis engendered by the war and called on the Editors' Committee and the Journalists Association "to formulate proposals for the creation of conditions that will enable journalists to perform their duty to their readers on security matters."

This professional crisis led many journalists to adopt the principles of adversarial journalism, which they followed during the war in Lebanon in 1982. At the beginning of the war, all the Israeli media rallied around the flag. In later stages, however, they expressed critical attitudes toward the war and the government. In the end, media criticism of Defense Minister Sharon and his policies was one of the factors that led to the termination of his ministership and induced the military and the government to withdraw from Lebanon in 1985.

Israeli journalists' and politicians' increasing exposure to the professional culture of the Western media had a profound influence on their approach, with age playing an important part. At the beginning of the 1980s, many Israeli journalists were young people who knew and identified more with Woodward and Bernstein of the Watergate affair than with the old-party style that was practiced in Tel Aviv and Jerusalem. In the late 1980s and early 1990s, a group of young professionals who were around forty years old acquired top positions in the media, including chief editors and heads of news organizations. Their cultural approach had been formed in the student revolution of the 1960s; almost all of them were products of the American media culture of the post–Vietnam War period.[21] "Our role is to abhor the government," said Ilana Dayan, a leading Israeli television journalist, giving somewhat extreme expression to this group's approach.[22]

THE THIRD PERIOD: FROM AN ADVERSARIAL

TO A COMPETITIVE MODEL

The media revolution that took place in the third period, namely the development of a culturally hegemonic multichannel television system, created a more complex pattern of relationships between the government and the media. Whereas in the transition to the second period the government had retained its dominant position vis-à-vis the electronic media even when its control of the print press and partisanship came to an end, in the third period a mixed model (McQuail 1990) emerged in the national media, the major change being in journalists' professional perception.

The third period, which has not yet come to an end, is characterized by communication abundance, with diverse types of relationships. At one extreme there are still government media outlets: the educational TV channel broadcasts news and current events while remaining subordinate to the Ministry of Education. The IDF station also deals with public affairs but is subordinate to the military chief of general staff. Between these are TV Channel 1 and Kol Israel — the two departments of the Broadcasting Authority — which have the status of public channels. In the case of these two, there is a considerable gap between the formal legal structure and governmental control. At the opposite extreme lie commercial television (Channels 2 and 10) and cable TV. Their status is legally regulated, and they are subject to supervision by a public council appointed by the government. However, they are owned and controlled by financial conglomerates that possess vast wealth and power and also own the major national newspapers.

In the transition from the second to the third period, the structure of the media has changed, and new relationships evolved between them and the political institutions. First, there has been a decrease in both partisan and governmental control over managerial appointments in the media organizations. The second criterion is direct political control over media financing. Even the Broadcasting Authority's struggle to retain license fees was designed to prevent direct government intervention in its budget, although a degree of influence was still retained. Perhaps more important is the third criterion, which Blumler and Gurevitch call the degree of partisan commitment exhibited by mass-media outlets: there was a clear drop in this commitment as a result of journalists' newly changed political and professional convictions.

This brings us to the internal dimension of political supervision. Here, a fundamental change occurred in journalists' self-perceptions, self-awareness, and self-image. In short, the definition of their role as journalists — generally defined as their "level of professionalism." Israeli journalists have moved along a spectrum that began in a journalistic model subservient to political authority and then to the adversarial journalism model. At one pole of this sequence, the press sees itself as an educational tool at the service of the national leadership, disseminating the messages issuing from the political elite. At the opposite pole, it develops the self-perception of a profession that is supposed to provide checks and balances to the national leadership — the perception of the political media as representatives of the citizenry facing up to the government. In the two latter stages they adopt nonpartisan norms such as fairness, impartiality, and neutrality.

The journalists' changing attitudes toward political institutions, and especially toward politicians, at the end of the last century has been thoroughly investigated and described by media scholars. The works of Patterson (1996) and Cappella and Jamieson (1997) in the United States and Blumler and Gurevitch in Britain (1995), among others, supply a profusion of evidence and clarifications regarding the depth and consequences of the new attitude. Patterson, for example, found that "news reporting in the U.S. in the past few decades has changed from the traditional descriptive style to an interpretive style. This new approach to news reporting is filled with profound negativism and cynicism towards political personalities and institutions" (Patterson 1996).

So negative is this approach that journalists are characterized by general and unrestrained bias against all government institutions, including the presidency. The attitude of respect and admiration has disappeared, to be replaced by a critical, cynical, skeptical, and sarcastic approach. Politicians are suspected of acting out of self-seeking considerations rather than political conviction; journalists do not believe what they say consistently and criticize them to the point of undermining their legitimacy and that of the political institutions in which they hold office.

The critical and negative style of press reporting had penetrated Europe in the 1970s and spread to most developed countries; however, there are major cultural differences between states. In Sweden, for example, the assassination of Prime Minister Olof Palme in 1986 accelerated the change in press orientation and strengthened investigative journalism (Machill 1999). In Britain, media scholars refer to a more respectful and credulous attitude toward politicians and even more so toward political institutions, while in Germany observers even criticized political journalism as obsequious to government announcements and official statements.[23]

The change in the Israeli journalists' approach to politicians and political institutions in the third period may be described simply as a shift from the approach prevalent in Europe (Germany or Britain) to the approach more common in the United States. This should not surprise us in view of the Central and Eastern European origins of Israeli journalism and the growing Americanization of Israeli culture in general in the last few decades. In the current period, the critical, even cynical, style has become more prevalent, particularly among journalists who are in their twenties and thirties. They deal more with strategies than with issues, examining politicians' tactics rather than ideological discussion, openly express disdain toward politicians, and are skeptical of the information they supply.[24]

Emanuel Rosen, political editor of Channel 2 News and formerly military correspondent of *Maariv*, summed up this phenomenon best in speaking about the military sphere, where the change in journalists' approach came later and more slowly, and where a more socially responsible approach still exists to some extent. Nevertheless, Rosen said:

Many times, at symposia and in academic panels, people ask: "Is there confrontation between the military and the media, and if so, how can it be prevented?" without understanding that such confrontation exists just as the sun rises in the morning and the moon at night; without understanding that this confrontation is part of the foundation of a democratic state; without understanding that this is a question you don't ask, just as you don't ask, for example, whether there is confrontation between the thief and the policeman, and whether it can be prevented.[25]

Today, these words reflect the opinions of the majority of media scholars. Twenty-five years ago, they would have sounded almost treasonous.

The adaptation of the interpretive journalism style (Patterson 2000) and the transition from the view of the journalist's role as a "neutral transmitter" disseminating to the general public the party/political message dictated by the political leadership — to the role of "qualified interpreter," who adopts an adversarial, critical, even aggressive approach, was most evident in Israel in the Broadcasting Authority, on radio and later on television. This was precisely because journalists in the Broadcasting Authority had in the past claimed for themselves very little freedom, much less than in the press.

Until the 1990s the Authority's explicit instructions forbade broadcasters to express their personal opinions or engage in political interpretation. This was one of the major directives in the "Nakdi Paper," a handbook of do's and don'ts written by Nakdimon Rogel, one of the senior staff in the Broadcasting Authority, after the Broadcasting Authority Law was passed in 1965, in order to ensure the apolitical, neutral, and objective character (meaning, in fact, reflecting only government attitudes) of the new Authority which had just been released from direct dependence on the prime minister's office.

Here, too, it was the Yom Kippur War that generated the change in the journalists' professional awareness. In a book, *The Debacle*, published by seven journalists after the war, they poured out their bitterness at the political establishment. Under the heading, "The Huge Brainwash," they wrote:

Television has become [a tool of] hypnosis and deception for the establishment . . . because television, like you and me, is the private property of the government. In the free world a revolution is taking place, giving people freedom of speech in the McLuhan media era. . . . But with us the media are still a toy of the ruling party, they do not supply information but just deliver the party line. . . . As with television, the same is true of radio and the press, the "educational information" line dominates. (Ben-Porat et al. 1974: 301–2)

Despite the deep shock to Israeli society caused by the 1973 war, and although it aroused some professional soul-searching among journalists, leading many of them to adopt the confrontational approach, the old style still largely persisted on television and to some extent also on radio, where they continued to operate according to the "impartiality doctrine" and the ban on editorializing, which were part of the culture maintained from the past.

The real change in the media, however, occurred only during the media revolution of the 1990s. One of the early manifestations of the transformation in radio was the journalistic style of Hanan Kristal, a political commentator who began his professional career in the short-lived newspaper *Hadashot*, which had introduced the new style of journalistic discourse to Israel. Kristal almost completely ignored the issues that had occupied the old school of political commentators, who dealt with ideology and policy analysis. He concentrated on the analysis of political tactics, focusing exclusively on the politicians' personal considerations motivated by power seeking, ambition, and self-interests.

This was such a radical innovation that Kristal could not introduce it directly at first. He started out, instead, by role-playing as if various politicians were being interviewed by the host of the program in a semihumorous tone. At the beginning of the 1990s, he adopted a more direct and open political analysis that exposed the personal interests of public figures. The private became public, backstage became front stage.

Immediately preceding the elections of 1996, the style of interpretive, or opinion journalism was also adopted by television, at first on the commercial channel and then on Channel 1. After the elections, the main political broadcast summarizing the events of the week, *News of the Week*, aired at peak viewing time on Friday evening and began to feature a journalist in the role of political pundit. This was the first time in the history of public broadcasting in Israel that a political journalist had presumed to express personal opinions and evaluate the politicians' behavior and actions on a news program. The journalist involved was the highly gifted and professional Amnon Abramovitch, who had left the staff of *Maariv* because of the wiretapping affair. He enjoyed an excellent reputation with the viewers, so when he started to appear on television there were only a few complaints from angry Knesset members who were hurt by the new practice.

When Prime Minister Benjamin Netanyahu appointed a new director of the Broadcasting Authority in 1998, in order to "correct the professional defects in the Authority," in other words, to strengthen government control of broadcasts and curb the radio and television staffers' independence and criticism, the director general, Uri Porat, attempted to reintroduce the "Nakdi Paper," resurrecting the old prohibition on expressing political attitudes. But at the end of the 1990s these clauses seemed anachronistic and aroused mockery and scorn in the journalist community. It was too late to turn back the clock.

Despite the fact that the professional conception and working patterns of adversarial journalism took root in the third period, it would be a mistake to generalize that the entire Israeli press has adopted this approach. In fields such as security, or in certain situations, such as terrorist attacks, the media reverts to rallying around the flag, as it has done in the past and most recently with the eruption of the Intifada El Aksa in September 2000.

At the same time, in all other matters not related to security the media move beyond the adversarial approach to the competitive approach. As Mazzoleni has observed:

According to this model, the news media plays a role, which is antagonistic toward politicians. Such a role is enacted by means of criticism and scrutiny of government policies, political persons, party activities, election candidates, political movements, and political misuse of power. The underlying concept of the adversarial model is distance and incompatibility of the respective logics, goals, and interests of the media and political actors.

The competition model builds on the concept of confrontation and challenge, mostly on the media's part, toward their political interlocutors, but, unlike in the adversarial model, within the context of a search by the media of a power (of political influence) alternative to that exerted by political institutions in certain political contexts there exist strong news reporting traditions characterized by a high degree of politicization: several news machines "do politics," stepping into the same terrain in which political actors "play their game," so contending for news space with politics. At stake here are the same goals: leadership of public opinion, public consent for political actions, and social legitimation.

Mazzoleni cites the German magazine *Der Spiegel* and the Italian *L'Espresso* as instances of the competitive model. The political and media revolutions in Israel in the 1990s made this model more prevalent. This is because the synergy of the two revolutions in the 1990s created a new type of political system, which functions according to media logic and which should be called "mediapolitik."

CHAPTER FIVE

The Fusionist Character of "Mediapolitik"

MEDIA LOGIC

"By the end of the twentieth century," Bennett and Entman argued, "virtually every country (democratic and otherwise) had seen a shift in the locus of influential political communication to the mass media" (2001: 9). Blumler and Gurevitch observed:

The media have gradually moved from the role of reporting on and about politics, "from the outside" as it were, to that of being an active participant in, shaping influence upon, indeed an integral part of, the political process. . . . Taken together these developments have resulted in the increased dependency of both politicians and voters on the media and the messages they provide. Nowadays more than ever, politics cannot exist without communication. (1995: 3)

This statement concerning the growing importance of the media in politics is common among scholars of contemporary media, politics, and society. Even those with reservations, who claim that "politics of substance" is still practiced behind the scenes, away from media spotlights, admit that sooner or later it must go through the publicity stage. "The center of the new political system appears to be the media" (McLeod, Kosicki, and McLeod 1994). Gurevitch adds:

The enhancement of the roles, and the powers, of television can be traced to its emergence, in the era of instant global communication, as an active participant in the events it purportedly "covers." Television can no longer be regarded as mere observer and reporter of events. It is inextricably locked into these events, and has clearly become an integral part of the reality it reports. . . . The "norm of apartness" is clearly flawed, both empirically and conceptually. Journalists cannot extricate themselves from their societal context. . . . They cannot therefore claim . . . to be able to observe the social world as if they were not part of it. . . . They became part of the environment which they observe and of the event they report. (Gurevitch 1993: 189)

This recognition of the centrality of the media in politics has spawned numerous concepts that attempt to describe this development: "an age of press politics" (Kalb 1991); "packaging politics" (Franklin 1995); "video-politique" (Landi 1994); a "political-media complex" (Swanson 1997); "videocracy" (Mazzoleni 1995); "la democratie virtuelle" or "telecratie" (Scheer 1994); "informational politics" or "mediacracy" (Castells 1996); "televisual politics" (Statham 1996); "government by publicity" (Cook 1998); "media-driven democracy" or "media-driven republic," "talk show democracy" (Brokaw et al. 1997); "electronic democracy" (Bennett and Entman 2001); "teledemocracy"; and "mediapolitik" (Edwards 2001). It was also called "media centered democracy," "media democracy," "media-centered democracy," and "medialism" (Gilboa 2000).[1]

For a long period, scholars who dealt with the media's influence in democracy tended to focus mainly on election campaigns, because "in both symbolic and pragmatic terms, campaigns are a microcosm that reflects and shapes a nation's social, economic, cultural, and, of course, political life" (Swanson and Mancini 1996: 1). However, they soon shifted to analyzing the character of the new democracy in a broader context, beyond campaigns and electoral politics. After large quantities of information had been accumulated, it emerged that despite their agreement on the excessive intrusion of the media into the political arena, scholars were divided on the fundamental question: Who ultimately has the upper hand, the media or politics?

There were some media scholars who thought that the media with their institutions and agents had taken over the political institutions and processes. According to this view, those who set the agenda, who make political decisions, and who shape the fate of modern societies are the profit-driven news media. Some experts went even further, stating that the very legitimacy of the exercise of power lies in the ability of rulers to communicate through the media (Cotteret 1991). According to this description, politics have been transformed into media-driven politics.

In contrast, other scholars believe that it is a mistake to overestimate the importance of the media because in the end politicians make the decisions. A series of empirical studies supported this approach. Daniel Hallin, for example, who examined the attitudes of the American media toward the Vietnam War, showed that the media began to sharply criticize the war only when it found support for such criticism in the mood of those in the innermost political circles (Hallin 1994).

A similar argument has been voiced by other scholars, who emphasized journalists' dependence on their sources. A theory, based on empirical studies, was proposed by Bennett in his "indexing hypothesis," according to which journalists' and editors' critical attitudes do not express their independence but reflect the range of attitudes that prevail in the government. "Mass media professionals, from the boardroom to the beat, tend to 'index' the range of voices and viewpoints in both news and editorials according to the range of views in mainstream government debate about a given topic" (Bennett 1990: 106).[2] Despite the large number of studies and books that emphasize the growing weight of the media in contemporary politics, the opposing voice has also gained strength. Wolfsfeld, while agreeing that the relations between politics and the media are relations of competitive symbiosis, asserts that "the political process is more likely to have an influence on the news media than the news media are on the political process" (Wolfsfeld 1997: 3). Zaller goes further and states explicitly, "American politics tend to be driven more by political substance . . . than by the antics of media politics" (Zaller 1998: 187).

The debate between the two approaches was conducted both at the theoretical and macro levels and in empirical micro studies that examined specific relations between journalists and politicians. Here, too, scholars are divided between those who see journalists as masters or servants of politicians (Franklin 1994: 13), between those who describe the relationship in terms of conflict, and those who describe it in terms of cooperation. Some of the descriptions, in both schools, are quite picturesque. In the former case we find metaphors such as: "The relationship is essentially cannibalistic. They feed off each other but no-one knows who is next on the menu." The latter speak of politicians and journalists who are not in adversarial relations but "sleeping together, although the shifting balance of power within their relationship ensures that no-one ends up being constantly dominant" (Franklin 1994: 16).

Which of these descriptions is correct? Is the media the master or the servant? Blumler and Gurevitch offer a distinction that can explain the contradiction between the two schools. This stems from different points of departure in the research. Those who deal with relations between journalists and politicians in democratic regimes from a normative point of departure inevitably place the emphasis on their adversarial nature; those who deal with this subject from an operational level necessarily see the exchange relations and the interdependence that exist between them (Blumler and Gurevitch 1981).

The concept of mutual dependence, interdependence, or mutual interdependence has increasingly supplied an easy way out of the unsolved question. Journalists and politicians are inextricably linked. It is true that journalists can determine the fate of politicians for political life or death (in fact, there have been cases where stories published in the media have led to actual physical death, especially suicide). But it is equally true that politicians who are media savvy have become very skillful in handling the media, and so have various media experts, spin doctors, political advisers, and experts in image building and political marketing.[3] But doesn't the concept of mutual dependence in fact serve to evade the question as to who, in fact, influences whom?

The beginning of an answer can be found in the concept "media logic." The first use of this concept, by Altheide and Snow (1979), related basically to the professional needs and values of the media, to technology, working principles, interests, and norms accepted by media organizations and professionals. Media logic means "a way of looking at and inter-preting social affairs. . . . Elements of this form [of communication] include the various media and the formats used by these media. Formats consist, in part, in how material is organized, the style in which it is pre-sented, the focus or emphasis . . . and the grammar of media communi-cation" (Altheide and Snow 1991: 10). A similar concept is the media's "production values" (Cook 1998).

The television production values are known and familiar. Visualization is an important criterion of newsworthiness, and the result is that an important but not visual matter will give way to a less important matter that produces good pictures. Television does not like to deal with issues as abstract topics and prefers to personalize them. Therefore, it enters into the details of a candidate's personality rather than dealing with substan-tive issues such as the political or social organizations to which he or she belongs or his or her political outlooks or principles — factors that play much more critical roles in the political process. The media is interested in the personal characteristics and the private lives of the famous for the same reason — they prefer the political game and its actors to the actual purpose of the game. They are more interested in questions of political tactics and less in the content of the political field.

Other production values are that an item should be terse, colorful, and easily described. This affects the choice of topics to be presented in the news media and reduces the possibility of dealing with a social prob-lem that is complex or multidimensional. These production values pre-vent deep analysis of an issue, except in the case of a few special pro-grams, and reinforce the provocative and sensational dimension in the treatment of any topic, even a "serious" one. The timely principle averts treatment of a subject that may be very important if it does not suit the timetable and the agenda of the media.

Drama and, even more so, conflict are basic elements in television and determine both the choice of subjects and the way of presenting them.

Therefore, the negative dimension has become so dominant in news coverage, promoting a cynical approach to public affairs and a loss of trust in public figures. The tendency to present a multitude of media events and to lend the air of a spectacle to political events also stems from the same principles (Dayan and Katz 1992). The result is that shrewd politicians quickly learn to find "symbolic solutions" to problems in the political sphere, projecting a television solution without treating the roots of the problem in the real world. For example, the president visits a stricken area to demonstrate his identification with the residents' suffering and his sensitivity to their problems, and this may hide the fact that the government does nothing to alleviate their distress.

The media logic strengthens the tendency to deal with the unusual, the dramatic, the special, the different, and the deviant. Here we see an interesting contradiction. The more that a certain topic is unusual, special, or deviant, the more that television tends to deal with it and present it as such. But because the same thing already happened with the previous subject, and will happen with the next one, the unusual and deviant become, in fact, the usual and the norm. At the same time, matters that are really routine, even if they are more important to society, will clearly not receive the same level of coverage.

Television production values prefer the appeal to the emotional and the exciting; they prefer speed over reflection, which calls for time and silence. Therefore, says Bourdieu (1999), the producers cultivate articulate, fast-thinking interviewees, and this in the course of time distorts the social model of the thinking person. Media logic also stresses isolated events, or series of events, rather than processes; therefore, according to Bourdieu, "It is a view detached and detaching from any history." I found a rather depressing substantiation of this theoretical argument in a study examining the Israeli and Jordanian media's treatment of each other before and after the peace treaty between the two sides, signed in 1994.

After the euphoria of the peace treaty had passed, the media in each of the two states largely lost interest in what was happening across the border, and the amount of coverage dropped. The Israeli media, for example, barely covered the relations developing between the two countries and two societies, returning to the subject only when there were dramatic events of a negative character, such as anti-Israel demonstrations in Jordan, or when a Jordanian soldier shot schoolgirls who were visiting the border area. It is interesting that the Israeli media adopted this policy despite the fact that they supported the peace with Jordan. However, due to the dictates of media logic, the story of the developing relationships was ignored, while the accounts of isolated, particularly negative incidents were emphasized. The cumulative effect of this type of coverage was

not conducive to the growth of positive relations between the former enemies who were supposed to become friends (Wolfsfeld, Peri, and Khouri
2002).

Television's production values are intrinsically biased. This does not
refer to a liberal political bias, or in the Israeli case, to a left-wing bias,
that many impute to the media, but to a structural or situational bias.
This is reflected in the preference for covering a given political actor
because he understands the needs of the media, knows what attracts their
attention, knows that they "like timely, terse, clear-cut, easily described,
vivid, dramatic, colorful and visualized stories" (Cook 1998: 80). The
media also suffer from other biases, resulting not from journalists' political leanings but from the media's storytelling imperatives. One of these is
the preference for dealing with events, actions, plans, or opinions of powerful officials. The difficulty in reaching the TV screen or getting into the
papers for someone who is not at the top of the ladder is known to all
political novices and grassroots organizations struggling to get their message through to the public.

This bias leads politicians to adopt a certain style of behavior, which is
a sine qua non for reaching the media, creating a vicious circle of cause
and effect. Former U.S. Speaker of the House of Representatives Newt
Gingrich referred to this when asked in a newspaper interview why he
used such strong, brusque language: "Part of the reason I use strong language is because you all will pick it up. . . . You convince your colleagues
to cover me being calm and I'll be calm. You guys want to cover nine seconds; I'll give you nine seconds, because this is a competitive requirement.
. . . I've simply tried to learn myself half of your business."[4]

Media logic did not always reign in the media. In the past, when the
press was almost totally dependent on political directives, it operated
more according to other principles of political message production,
defined by Mazzoleni as "party logic." According to him:

"Media logic" is guided by the values and formats through which events and issues are
focused on, treated, and given meaning by media professionals and organizations. "Party
logic" draws on the structural and cultural assets that govern the communication and the
objectives of the political parties and the focus is to strengthen the parties as institutions and
to mobilize and integrate the voters within their sub-culture ties. (Mazzoleni 1987: 81–103)

THE THREE ACTORS OF THE NEW POLITICS

What distinguishes media-centered democracy is that television, the main
cultural arena, has penetrated into the field of politics, causing it to lose

its autonomy and control of its logic. Castells describes the change thus: "Not that the medium is the message, because political options do differ. But by entering the media space, politics and politicians are shaped according to a new set of rules" (Castells 1997: 321). Mazzoleni and Schultz also point to this direction, saying that mediatized politics, the politics of the third period in the history of political communication, in which we live today, "is politics that has lost its autonomy, has become dependent in its central functions on mass media, and is continuously shaped by interactions with mass media" (Mazzoleni and Schultz 1999: 250). However, they confine this analysis to the United States, arguing that in Europe "political forces still retain their monopoly of the political game" (258).

They reached this conclusion because, although they discern the convergence of media and politics, they still see them as two essentially separate spheres. Cook (1999) goes a step further. First, he says, we need to understand that the media are a social institution and should be analyzed as such and not as the behavior of individuals or even of other organizations. Second, they are essentially a political institution, since they deal with authoritative allocation of values, which is the essence of political action. The media can determine who will be authoritative, they share in deciding what are the important values of society, and they even participate in the process of allocating them.

Cook goes even further. The media, he says, are not just a political institution; they are part of the government. However, he does not agree with Carter's (1959) definition that they are the fourth branch of government (after the legislative, the executive, and the juridical) because they were constituted and are largely controlled by private corporations. Thus, he sees the media as much closer to two other political institutions: parties and interest groups, which act both inside and outside the government.[5]

After the big step taken in seeing the media as part of politics, recognition of the powerful influence of media logic must lead us another step forward. Many scholars, including those who recognize the political character of the media, nonetheless see the media as "outsiders on the inside," an agent mediating between the different branches of government, between different elite groups, and between the elite and the general public. But the fact that media logic has taken over the entire political sphere, that both the political structures and agents act according to media logic, requires us to recognize the fact that a media-centered democracy gives rise to a new political configuration. This is politics that is fundamentally constructed, in its substance, organization, process, and leadership, by the inherent logic of the media system.

What emerges is a symbiotic structure, in which the media, no longer an external factor, interact with politics. We can no longer speak of the media as an outside actor intruding into politics; it has become one integrated, fusionist system. Therefore the question as to who influences whom, the media the politicians or vice versa, is meaningless, just as the question as to who exerts more influence, the party or politics, is meaningless. The media are part of politics. Like the party, or the presidency, they have their own specific characteristics, but all are part of the political field.

This state of fusion between the media and politics develops only in a contemporary media-centered democracy. The special character of this new configuration is that the media are multifaceted. They still serve in their old role of mediator, but they also fulfill the role of an actor who has his own interest in the political process. They are the major arena in which politics takes place, but they also play an active part. They constitute a major actor in the production and distribution of information, as well as in shaping the symbolic order. They are the main disseminator of representations of the normative political order. They grant meaning to the social arrangements and constitute them, when the information that they disseminate — mainly, but not only, news — imposes order on reality through schemata of interpretation. The media are a tool of government in the hands of those with political power. Without images, sounds, and symbolic manipulation, there can be no successful exertion of power. The media both monitor and restrain government. They are privately owned and act according to financial interests, but at the same time they are a public institution and serve as a trustee of the public.

The news media's new active role in politics is also manifested in their changing professional approach. In the past the journalistic ideal was the descriptive style: objective journalism, with neutral coverage of facts, adhering to the classic 5 w's (what, when, where, who, and why). In today's media, the interpretive reporting style is dominant; this is a genre in which journalists have much more freedom of action and room to maneuver than before. Facts become the material with which the chosen theme is illustrated, journalists have much more control over news stories, and they don't hesitate to use it: in the latest presidential elections in the United States, for each minute that candidate spoke on the screen, journalists had no fewer than six minutes (Patterson 2000: 265).

Quite often, politicians and officials accuse journalists of "interfering in what is not their business," "overstepping the line," "dealing in politics instead of journalism." This is a natural reaction on the part of politicians; nobody wants competitors. But journalists themselves reject this accusation, pretending that they do not deal in politics and are not motivated by political calculations. Why do they react in this way, and why do they declare in general that all they want to do is report the facts, expose the truth, and therefore are innocent of political calculations concerning the results of what they publish?

The explanation to this self-deception is related to the essence of the legitimacy of the profession of journalism itself. During the long period when the press was dependent on the government, it vitally needed to preserve its independence in order to receive public legitimacy, and not be seen as a mouthpiece of the government. Objectivity, neutrality, impartiality of the press, all were designed to keep it separate from politics. Today, when the government is less capable of restricting the freedom of the press, journalists need to continue fostering the myth of objectivity in order to gain an advantage in their contest against the politicians. Listen to me, says a TV commentator; read me, says an editorial writer: we — not the politicians — will tell you the truth. We are objective, neutral, we don't take sides. We have no ax to grind. It is this very pseudo-objectivity that permits them to be what they really are — political.

But in the era of mediapolitik, now that the media have become part of politics and of government, is it not time for journalists to modify their conduct? Should they not be subject to the constraints imposed on other arms of government? Are the media included in the system of checks and balances that operates on other government bodies? Perhaps journalists' reluctance to admit that they are a political body is designed precisely to avoid having limitations imposed on them? These questions will be examined later. First, let me describe and analyze the fusionist character of mediapolitik, and particularly the way in which media logic has affected the political sphere and changed the political game in Israel. I begin with a concrete example to illustrate the character of the fusionist model — the Likud primaries in February 1999.

In the weeks preceding the Likud Party conference, at which primaries were to be held for members to elect their party list for the Knesset, the party power brokers cooked up deals between various groups. A few days before the conference the media held opinion polls among the delegates on the composition of the anticipated list and discovered the existence of these deals, which naturally received massive exposure. It was revealed, for example, that groups headed by former minister Tzachi Hanegbi and Israel Katz had managed to reach a high place in the list, and that the top echelon of the party would include almost no candidates of Mizrahi origin.

The publication of this information affected the behavior of many delegates to the conference, and the result was that they voted differently from what they had promised to the power brokers. The role played by the media in this affair was most interesting. They used the methods of investigative journalism to disclose the deals, then served as mediators in revealing the important information, known only to a small group at the top, passing it on to the general public and particularly to the party members competing in the primaries. They also played a part as an independent political actor in expressing their opinions about the nature of the secret agreements. As such, they shared in the allocation of social values, expressing the opinion that it was not fitting for a party in power to deprive certain ethnic groups of representation. The media played an active role in generating change in the behavior of other actors and gave meaning to the development of the Knesset list. In doing all this, the media operated according to media logic. They supplied a dramatic story that included conflict and personalized the abstract political discussion on representation. The media presented the timely story as a narrative depicting a problem and ending in a positive solution. It was no surprise, then, that this action of the media elicited a response from a Knesset member from another party (Meretz), Dedi Zucker, in a television interview, who said, turning to the journalists, "You must be very careful what you do now, as you have changed from reporters into full partners with a great deal of influence."[6]

Three groups of actors operate in mediapolitik. In addition to (1) journalists and media professionals and (2) politicians, there is now a third group: media experts. A review of election campaigns during the past decade reveals an interesting power play between the three groups. In the distant past the politicians were the stars who dominated the game, but later their luster declined while that of journalists grew. The state of affairs that existed in the 1980s, when politicians dominated screen time, was replaced by a situation whereby the candidates were little more than scenery for the show of journalists. As noted above, in 1992, journalists in the United States spoke on television six minutes for every minute of the candidates. Effectively, they were doing the talking for the candidates (Alger 1989: 114).

However, at the end of that decade the third group, which in the distant past had been small and uninfluential, became the dominant group with the decisive influence: the media experts and the specialists on persuasive communication. These are the experts in marketing and voter research techniques, message development, advertising, image building, speechwriters, pollsters, and particularly political strategists and consultants whose expertise lies in media manipulation. They are the ones who tell politicians what position to take and which policies to follow. Their centrality in the system, especially during elections, increasingly drew the attention of journalists, who were aware of their manipulation, appreciated their skills, but were wary of them. Therefore, more and more of the election coverage today deals not with policy issues or even with candidates, but rather concentrates on media experts.

In the United States, Jo McGinnis, in his book *The Selling of the President* (1968, not to be confused with Theodore White's *The Making of the President,* 1960, referring to President Kennedy) started the demystification of politics in the television era and showed how public relations experts marketed the president like a pack of cigarettes or soap. But twenty years later the media shifted the focus in the election campaign to the stage managers themselves, media gurus, handlers, and spin doctors (Adatto 1993: 43). Israel went though these two stages more quickly, in less than ten years. In Barak's election campaign in 1999, his campaign headquarters held receptions and initiated meetings for journalists with a team of American consultants — Carville, Shrum, and Greenberg. Veteran reporters were taken aback by this new phenomenon, saying that in the past, if there had been such experts every effort was made to hide them. And what started in the election campaign continued throughout the year.

The concept of media-centered democracy, like all social models, is an ideal type in the Weberian sense. In reality, the diverse national traditions and political cultures in different countries create different nuances. Just as there is a difference between Europe and the United States in the extent of state control of broadcasting, or differences in the degree of partisanship of various newspapers within the same country, there can be diverse styles of mediapolitik. Journalists may be more or less determined advocates of a certain position, may be more or less active in promoting it (Patterson 2000).

On the part of the politicians, too, there is a variety of possibilities, and some political actors might be determined to attain their goals by using the old political logic. But if a politician does not act according to media logic in a society in an advanced state of mediapolitik, if he does not "go public" (Kernell 1986) and "package his politics" (Franklin 1996), his prospects of success are minimal.

The dominant position of media logic explains why there is now more compatibility than in the past between the media agenda and the political agenda. The media does indeed have a decisive influence over the public agenda, but those who largely germinate and shape it are politicians (Wolfsfeld 2001). With the help of media experts, they operate the media to some extent, but their ability to manipulate finally depends on the degree of compatibility with media logic. This vicious circle is the meaning of the fusion in the media-political complex. When Max Weber, the father of modern sociology, in the winter of 1919 described politics as a profession and argued that journalism was a "political occupation" or "political art" (Weber 1961: 37), he did not know how prophetic he was. When Weber wrote those words he did not envisage the possibility that moving pictures accompanied by voices would be added to the printed characters on the newspaper, yet he already saw the political dimension of the journalist's work. In the new media era of the late twentieth and early twenty-first centuries the boundaries separating the media from politics collapsed. Journalism is politics.

The Brazilian television network Globo was one case in point. In the military dictatorship's battle for survival in the mid-1980s, Globo supported the old regime, but, pressured by the movement for democratization, it changed its position, particularly because its owners feared an advertising embargo. By joining the forces demanding change, Globo gave momentum to the democratic movement, which ultimately led to its victory in 1985. The democratic movements in Eastern Europe at the end of the 1980s can supply other examples of such interdependence, but in the Brazilian case there is a piquant addition. The victory celebration held for the new democratic president, Tancredo Neves, in 1985 did not take place in the party headquarters or in a hotel hall, and its stars were not professional politicians, the presidents' colleagues who headed the Alianca Democratica. The event took place in the Globo studios, and the star of the party was the TV company's owner (Porto 2001). In Israel on the morning after the 1999 elections, Barak phoned only six people, five of whom were journalists.

THE MEDIA DEFINE THE GAME

What are the characteristics of mediapolitik? In mediapolitik reality is determined primarily by the media. The actual publicity of an issue brings it to life and makes it real. Only what is published in the media is defined and considered part of the real world. News of events, ideas, problems, and topics for discussion, all gain public attention and above all the attention of the political class and the political apparatus only if they are publicized. A matter that is not covered by the media will not reach the policy sphere, which is a "subset of the public sphere where ideas and feelings explicitly connect with — are communicated to, from, or about — government officials, parties, or candidates for office who may decide the outcome of issues and conflicts facing society" (Bennett and Entman 2001: 4).

It is worth paying attention to this argument. First, most of the public acquires its political information from the mass media, especially from television (in the United States this includes about three-quarters of the population; Castells 1997: 313). Second, this is more than just a return to the classical theory concerning the social construction of reality. When this theory was propounded it was innovative in showing the media's ability not only to report reality but also to shape it (Gamson and Modigliani 1989). Now — and here is the main point — we say that reality is only what the media cover. What is not reported doesn't exist. This is true both of issues and of people. With regard to the latter it is more than status conferral, it may be their actual political and symbolic existence. To paraphrase Descartes's well-known dictum, in the age of mediapolitik, *videor ergo sum*: "I am seen, therefore I exist."

Since political existence is so dependent on media visibility, journalists in a media-centered democracy have a virtual monopoly on entrance to the political space, not only for people but also for ideas, opinions, or concepts, as well as for perceptions and for what Max Weber called *Problemstellung*, the way problems are presented or problem solving. Sometimes there may even be media existence without existence in reality, as is the case with pseudoevents or with Fiske's idea of media events. "In the postmodern world we can no longer work with the idea that the 'real' is more important, significant, or even 'true' than the representation. A media event then is not a mere representation of what happened, but it has its own reality, which gathers up into itself the reality of the event that may or may not have preceded it" (Fiske 1996: 2). Hence also the additional influences of the media on the political reality: the media determine the nature of the thing itself through its framing and position every matter relative to others by agenda building and setting. The chairman of the Knesset Constitution, Law, and Justice Committee, MK Uriel Linn, admitted that when he said "what is not published does not exist," he referred, surprisingly, not only to the parliament but to the entire administration, including the judiciary.[7]

The importance of publicity, the fact that there is no political existence outside the media space, explains the widespread phenomenon of leaks. Leaking has always existed; political actors in the past used it to advance a political agenda, to spoil their rivals' agenda. By leaking information a politician can accumulate credit with journalists, which he can use in the future. In mediapolitik leaks have acquired meaning beyond this. Today, leaking an issue to the media means placing it on the agenda and in the policy sphere.

That the media have become *the* arena where the political game is played is expressed in the fact that during election campaigns other types of communication that still exist — politicians' face-to-face meetings with the general public, going from door to door, soapbox speeches in the street, or town hall meetings — have lost their meaning and become merely spectacles. They are designed mainly to serve as a backdrop for TV shots, with the text written by persuasion experts and spin masters. The public, too, understand today that the media are the best channel for raising demands before the national leadership. Among respondents in Israel who were asked about the most effective ways of influencing government policy, almost twice as many replied approaching the media as acting at the party level.[8]

Politicians recognized this phenomenon and soon adjusted to it, as shown by the way they now allocate their time to the media. In 1999 Knesset members and ministers spent an average of two hours a day listening to the radio, reading newspapers, and watching television. The least time spent was half an hour and the most over three hours. In a survey I conducted, Knesset members reported that they spent half an hour every day on average talking or meeting with journalists. Many of them spent double that amount of time, and many veteran politicians said that they used to "devote far less time to the media in the past." There is a correlation between the amount of time spent and the political level of the individual. Those with higher-ranking roles, such as chairs of Knesset committees, devote as much as an hour a day more to the media than do backbenchers.

Officials also build their schedule largely according to the media agenda. Knesset members, ministers, mayors, and also directors of public institutions admit that their schedules and that of the executive bodies that they head are influenced by the media. The news media become significant agents not only in establishing officials' agenda but also in accelerating the pace of decision making. "In Western democracies, the politics of time is increasingly the politics of news time, often with adverse consequences for policy and opinion" (Patterson 1998: 65). Moreover, press releases carry considerable weight in determining the direction of political meetings.

The most surprising of many testimonies to this was the story of one senior IDF officer, who admitted to me that when military professionals sometimes have difficulty persuading politicians of the importance of a certain matter, they discreetly leak the information on the issue to the media. While an internal document might lie on the official's desk without arousing his attention, the publicity almost always guarantees that the official's attention will not be long in coming.

Even the sphere of security, an area previously closed to the media in the past, became open to media scrutiny with the beginning of media-centered democracy. In the middle of the 1950s, the defense establishment could be involved in long preparations for a preemptive war against Egypt without a hint of it being published in the newspapers. And in

1970, there was a bitter dispute in the IDF general staff concerning defense strategy in the Sinai Desert. During this conflict, one school of thought supported mobile defense, based on the movement of armored forces in the open space of the desert, and another school favored static defense based on a line of outposts along the Suez Canal. This dispute had historic significance, since the decision to build the "Barlev line" determined the nature of the Yom Kippur War of 1973. However, this important debate remained within the confines of the top military echelons and was not covered at all by the media.

In contrast, in the second half of the 1990s a dispute in the general staff on how to defend the north of the country against Hizbullah attacks from Lebanon — by continuing to hold onto the security zone in southern Lebanon, or from the international border — was also conducted in the pages of the newspapers and on the airwaves. This open debate in the media intensified the professional discussion within the political-military establishment. In the end, the desire to respond to the public attitude, which increasingly opposed remaining in the security strip, led prime ministerial candidate Ehud Barak to adopt one of the most important decisions in his election campaign. During the first year of his term as prime minister he implemented the decision and pulled back the IDF to the international border. In the 1990s, media and political-marketing considerations were regularly included in the planning of IDF campaigns, and when the Intifada El Aksa broke out at the end of 2000, more than a few IDF soldiers were equipped with cameras in order to document the Palestinians' violent actions and disseminate them throughout the world. The camera had become no less important than the assault rifle.

Another example of the media's transformation into the political arena deals with appointments to public office. In the past such appointments were made by the political leaders in closed rooms and reached the media only after the fact. Nowadays, the intention to appoint anyone to a given position is announced in the media before the final decision is made, and in many cases opposition and criticism have prevented the appointment. Disclosure of intended appointments has become such a routine matter that it would be a mistake to go on thinking of it as a "leak," a deviation from the proper democratic process, as it was regarded by the party logic of the past. On the contrary, it should be seen as an integral part of the new system, with the media discussion fulfilling the function of advice and consent, as performed by committees in the U.S. Senate.

This system, whereby the appointing authorities use information leaks as feelers to see whether there is no opposition to the proposed appointment, has penetrated areas that were not previously exposed to the public eye, such as the IDF. In one case, in 1996, an item was published concerning the chief of general staff's intention to appoint to the post of head of manpower an air force major-general who had been accused in the past of improper behavior. When the CGS saw that the publication did not arouse serious public opposition, he appointed the man to the post.[9]

The coalitional structure of Israeli governments had led to their being riddled with leaks in the past, as well. Former U.S. Secretary of State Henry Kissinger, who knew Israeli political culture well, complained of this a great deal during the period of his shuttle diplomacy in the 1970s. Government leaks were always an effective weapon in political battles, designed to damage adversaries, sabotage moves, or advance initiatives. However, in the 1990s the leaks acquired a different character: they became the norm, and the demand to curtail them stemmed from failure to understand the new game rules. While in the 1980s ministers could be seen running straight from a cabinet meeting to the TV cameras in order to gain some valuable publicity, in the 1990s it was not uncommon to see ministers, even generals, coming out in the middle of a cabinet meeting to make themselves heard over the airwaves. This is a graphic illustration of the fact that the media have become a political arena no less than the cabinet itself.

When Ehud Barak became prime minister in July 1999, he attempted to restrict media involvement in cabinet meetings. At his first cabinet session he announced that he was introducing a new policy — he would not reply to ministers' questions during question time if the minister publicly announced the matter to the media beforehand. Cynics recalled that ten years earlier, when he was chief of general staff, Barak had tried to increase his influence over the general staff by ordering IDF officers to limit their contacts with journalists. In the summer of 1999 the newspapers correctly predicted that the fate of his new initiative as prime minister would fail just as its antecedent had failed when he was chief of staff.

MEDIA INFLUENCE ON CIVIC ENGAGEMENT

Media logic's domination of politics was a catalyst in one of the major changes occurring in the character of politics in our period. What happened in established democracies was not only that the parties' status declined and they lost their traditional roles, but that the existing parties lost their social bases. Unlike parties in the older Western democracies, parties in the new electoral democracies are not linked to deep-rooted sources of cleavages.

The most important among these sources of conflicting interests and different ideologies, was class. This is not the situation today, neither in many of the new democracies that emerged out of the collapse of communist regimes, nor in the mature democracies, where the political struggle is over postmaterialist issues, such as the environment, equality for women, education and health, permissive morality like abortion, gun control, or mercy killing. In none of these cases do the parties represent social cleavages based on class differences. Indeed, in some third-wave democracies with weak party systems that emerged in the 1970s in Latin America, personalism or elite interests rather than cleavages, form the basis of most so-called parties, further weakening these fledgling democracies (Lipset 2000). However, in the mature democracies, parties representing cleavages and conflicts based on long-standing social divisions have been replaced by social organizations or single-issue movements. Loyalty to these groups is not continuous and stable, the movements have a fairly fluid structure, and what their members have in common is agreement on values, or a certain value, and issues, or one particular issue. Even the issues themselves change, just as the issues on the public agenda change. These are ad hoc coalitions around specific issues rather than relations based on ongoing, stable, and largely institutionalized social links.

The phenomenon identified by social critics reached the public awareness in the United States during the last elections of the twentieth century. "Political party is no longer dictated by class status" was the title of an article by Thomas B. Edsall, published in the *Washington Post* after the 2000 elections: "Once it was possible to make a strong prediction of a voter's loyalty to the Democratic or Republican Party on the basis of their income and education, two basic measures of class status. The 2000 elections, however have underlined the diminishing significance of these indicators and the rise of a new set of patterns of party loyalty based on more subtle social and moral matters."[10] The changes in the character of electoral politics are one expression of a more profound change in the politics of mature democracies. Another expression, no less significant, is the change in the patterns of involvement in organized civic life. In the United States, for example, this change was manifested in the shift from large organizations like the old membership associations or national federations of the 1950s, and the social movements of the 1960s, to associations of a different kind — advocacy groups, largely run by advocates and managers without members. In the United States, the shift from a system of membership associations to one of advocacy organizations took place on a large scale and was described as the advocacy explosion, but similar phenomena occurred in Europe. These organizations do not need large numbers of grassroots members and do not maintain extensive activities in the periphery. Instead, they were staff-heavy and focused on lobbying and media projects. They are also managed from the top.

In a large study on civic involvement in the United States, Theda Skocpol writes:

Classic American association-builders took it for granted that the best way to gain national influence, moral or political, was to knit together national, state, and local groups that met regularly and engaged in a degree of representative government. . . . Today, nationally ambitious civic entrepreneurs process in quite different ways. . . . New routes to civic influence opened. . . . Patron grants, direct mail techniques, and the capacity to convey images and messages through the mass media all changed the realities of organization-building and maintenance. . . . No longer do civic entrepreneurs think of constructing vast federations and recruiting interactive citizen-members. When a new cause arises, activists envisage opening a national office and managing association-building as well as national projects from the center. Members, if any, are likely to be seen not as fellow citizens but as consumers with policy preferences. (Skocpol et al. 1999: 491–92)

Although this development in the nature of civic organizations in the United States stems, according to Skocpol, from profound social and political changes, she is aware of the fact that developments in the media also played a part: on the one hand, the need of national media outlets to stage debates among polarized spokespersons, and on the other hand, the need of organizations to keep their causes and accomplishments visible. "By dramatizing causes through the national media, advocates enhance their legitimacy and keep contributions flowing from patrons and direct-mail adherents. In short, all sorts of new organization-building techniques encourage contemporary citizens' groups to concentrate their efforts in efficiently managed headquarters located close to the federal government and the national media" (Skocpol et al. 1999: 491–92). Various explanations have been offered for this new political and social phenomenon. However, insufficient attention has been paid to the decisive weight of the media. The news, particularly on television, deals with events rather than processes, exploits the public interest in a certain subject while constantly seeking new topics with which to hold the audience's attention; in other words, it does exactly the opposite of what parties did in the past. Instead of expressing ongoing interests or values and cultivating a stable social base, it gives prominence to ad hoc organizations around a specific issue, flutters like a bee from flower to flower in order to suck the nectar, directing attention to one flower for a short time and then hurrying on to the next.

In addition to television, the print press also exhibits this phenomenon. In Britain, for example, the press has lost its party identification and become independent. "Unhinged papers are losing their fixed attachment in politics, they are likely to become increasingly changeable, unpredictable, expediential, inconsistent." The connection is that "in the textbook truism, groups stress particular interests, parties the general interest.

Papers speaking in a multitude of voices better reflect the politics of an interest group culture than do party papers" (Seymour-Ure 1998: 49).

THE CHANGE IN THE LEADERSHIP PATTERN

"In the same way that the media select and frame events, they select which actors will receive attention, and frame those actors' public images" (Mazzoleni and Schultz 1999: 251). In democratic regimes the public chooses its representatives; also in a media-centered democracy the formal act of elections still determines who will be the leaders. However, in practice the center of gravity in the election process has shifted to a small group of people with a monopoly of public visibility. They are the ones who decide what will be publicized, where and how. Even the advocates of rational choice, who believe that when the moment of choice arrives the voters use their judgment, have to admit that before the voters are presented with the choice the media have already done the preliminary screening. By the very fact of devoting time or space to coverage, or by ignoring certain candidates, they decide who is worthy of participating in the game and who is not. And just as the media have the power to shape the issues presented in the policy sphere, they also mold the players, build their image, construct their persona, and even force them to behave in a certain way.

Since television entered the homes of the modern audience, it has wrought a tremendous change in the point of reference to public affairs, as a result of the medium's singular characteristics, which distinguish it from the newspaper. This has special significance for the political field, in relation to the learning process. A large body of research has marshaled evidence showing that newspapers enhance information gain and political knowledge, while television appears to have an "inhibiting effect" to learning (Guo and Moy 1997). Television news deters conceptual learning because it concentrates on conveying the essence of personalities and vistas of places and events, while print media are better at imparting abstract information (Graber 1989; Stone 1987). Unlike the print news, television news has been found to lead to "incidental learning," as opposed to motivated or intentional learning. The print media allow readers to take full advantage of their cognitive potential (for example, making use of schemata, memory, imagination, ongoing thought process, and anticipation), while television is a medium where these political information-processing activities are unlikely to occur or are impossible to execute (Singer 1980).

Because television is an extremely poor medium for conveying abstract or analytical information, its coverage of public affairs has increasingly been reduced to the level of human-interest stories. Nothing is of more interest than people themselves. Hence the argument, familiar among media scholars, that television has led to personalization of events and personification of news. Politicians, not politics, are the actors in the drama. Because there is no longer ideological consistency and politicians tend to change their attitudes frequently, the attention focuses more and more on their maneuvers and their personal motives. What is remembered is the impression of their personality. "The messenger becomes the message" (Castells 1997: 322). All this naturally has an extremely negative effect on the perception and understanding of politics. "The personalized view of politics gives people little, if any, grasp of political processes or power structures. . . . The world of personalized politics is thus a fantasy world" (Bennett 1983: 13).

In order to attract television's attention, in order to pass the entrance test to the screen, in order to wrest from the media the chance of visibility and recognition, a public figure today needs other qualities than those that characterized the politician of yesterday. In the past, when a considerable part of the political game took place behind the scenes, in the corridors of power and in secret chambers, the ability to twist arms was more important than rhetorical skills. Today, when the main political game takes place on center stage, the politician needs other skills: acting ability, stage presence, persuasive skills, eloquence, and presentation. Politics of spectacles need actors.

Meyrowitz, who studied the effect of personalization of the public sphere on the change in patterns of leadership, stated that television has increasingly fostered the use of "dating criteria" over "resume criteria" in the public sphere (Meyrowitz 1985, 1992). In private interactions we judge people by appearance, gestures, and vocalization: "What is this person like?" By contrast, in public life in the past a leader was judged in a more abstract manner, by his words and actions. This has changed in the television era. Today, a candidate for the presidency, like the prime minister or an elected member of parliament, is judged by the extent of personal sympathy he or she arouses. Many citizens today are prepared to elect a candidate with whom they disagree because they like him personally. This degree of seemingly intimate acquaintance with a candidate did not exist before television, and it is what makes television democracy so different.

The personalization that is fostered by the television culture affects public life in general. The commercial pressures of the media intensified the modern "cult of the personality." The central place that was once occupied by party platforms, values, and ideologies, and especially the candidates' political plans, was replaced by the personal characteristics of the political actors. But it is not a question of their characteristics so much as their representation, their external reflection on the screen. In a society where 42 percent relate mainly to the speaker's appearance, 50 percent to the way he or she speaks, and only 8 percent of the viewers listen to the contents of a speech, the image management and the style factor are all-important (Ewen 1988: 261). What matters is not the actual person but the persona. Image building, image maintenance, and image promotion have become decisive factors in fostering a political career, and in the course of time this art has been perfected. It is no longer enough to say that "the personality counts more than the issue." Long-term research and accumulated experience have shown which specific qualities the candidate should project, wisdom or likeability, decision-making ability or ability to identify with the other and project empathy.

Focusing on the personality instead of on the issue and fostering a personality cult have led the public figure to be confused with the celebrity. More and more politicians reach a senior position because of their celebrity characteristics. In the United States this led to film stars becoming governors of states and reaching the White House. In Israel it is one of the reasons for the large number of retired generals in politics. They come to the political arena by virtue of the recognition and symbolic capital they accumulated when in uniform. Having received coverage not only in the news media but also in entertainment programs, talk shows, and gossip columns, they are the talk of the town. Simply put, they are celebrities.

Mediapolitik changed the relations between the leader, the party activists, and the members, especially the kind of relationships between the leader and the members. The party members' support of their leader is different from the past, when the members identified with the leader's and ideological and cultural commitment as representing a social movement. Now the identification is much more personal and emotional (Mancini 1999: 233).

In Israel's bureaucratic politics the party functionaries — the apparatchiks — were the link between the leadership and the members. They administered the party; they were the power brokers. Many of them even reached the summit of the political pyramid — the Knesset and the government. The disintegration of the party state decreased the need for those people. In the Israel of the 1990s, the title of party functionary acquires a derogatory connotation, which could only harm anyone with ambitions for public life.

Panebianco described this change in European parties at the end of the twentieth century, and his description exactly matched what happened in Israel. In his book, published in 1982, he called the new type of party a "professional-electoral party." In this party, he said, the cadre of functionaries is replaced by professionals with various skills, who hire out their services, primarily for management of election campaigns. These are the media experts, political strategists and consultants, public relations experts, pollsters, spin doctors, and other political savvies. Their expertise is in techniques of the world of persuasive media, mass media and marketing, such as the permanent campaign, the negative campaign, or the attack campaign (Blumler and Kavanagh 1999). With them, the content of political discourse has changed. "The language of politics has been married with that of advertising, public relations, and show business" (Mazzoleni and Schultz 1999: 241).

A second group of professionals who have gained importance are the policy experts, those who sit in research institutes and think tanks and supply the decision makers with position papers, policy analyses, and recommendations for action. This phenomenon first appeared in the United States, partly because the role of the parties there was limited to begin with. It spread to Europe in the 1980s, with the weakening of the parties, and arrived in Israel in the 1990s.

Media logic influences both the contents of political action and the political discourse. The practice of the mass parties was constructing processes and structures of political socialization or ideological identification, as was the practice of the mass, whereas the main aim of the party that Panebianco calls professional-electoral party is to win the elections and put its leaders in power. Victory in the elections is the major criterion.

Indeed, the two leaders of the era of mediapolitik in Israel in the 1990s, Benjamin Netanyahu of Likud and Ehud Barak of Labor, boasted that they were winner types. This consideration — "I win in everything I do; therefore I will bring the party to victory" — became more important to leadership than earlier criteria such as ideological loyalty or a defined political program. "The future battle will not be over ideology but over leadership," declared the head of Ehud Barak's campaign team, Defense Minister Binyamin Ben-Eliezer.[11] He himself was elected to head the Labor Party in 2001. The Hebrew language has yet to come up with a word to express the concept of electability, but the idea has already become a major factor in the new politics and is used ad absurdum.

POLITICAL FUNDING
AND THE POLITICS OF SCANDALS

The shift from a party based on an apparatus, functionaries, and political bureaucrats, on the one hand, and masses of members, volunteers, and activists, on the other, to a skeleton party whose leaders employ the services of professional experts and rely on modern marketing technologies significantly increased the importance of money in politics. The political process, especially the elections, which in the past were labor intensive, now became capital intensive. The activists and volunteers participating in rallies and conventions, going from door to door, filling the party branches, and working on the campaigns were now replaced by professional agencies hiring out their services.

In the 1950s and 1960s, citizens of Tel Aviv and other Israeli towns used to hang placards with their candidates' photos and party logos from the balconies of their apartments and in the main streets. In the 1990s huge billboards took the place of these placards. In the past, members of youth movements used to take to the streets with banners and slogans. Today, the manpower agencies hire out paid demonstrators to stand at city intersections with huge posters. In the past volunteers filled the party branches. Today, professionals run the campaign from the "war room," which is not necessarily located at party headquarters.

The need for funding grew due to the increased use of expensive television, despite the fact that broadcasting time is not very expensive and is allocated to the parties by the state both on public television and on the commercial channel. In addition, the frequent polls, outdoor advertising, and other means of political persuasion all swallow big budgets. As more international companies, particularly American ones, entered the Israeli market, prices rose to match the American standards.

This increased expenditure had radical results. Party funding in Israel, both throughout the year and during campaigns, comes from the government budget by decision of the Knesset and is subject to inspection by the state comptroller. But the growth in expenditure makes this allocation insufficient. Accordingly, in the 1990s a ramified system of gray-and-black funding developed. Soft money from associations working for various social causes flows into the party coffers to fund candidates and parties. Other illegal monies reach the campaign unseen by the state comptroller or the state attorney. No candidate for the premiership in the 1990s would dare to begin planning his campaign without first raising the funding, a large part of it from American Jews. The political implications of this involvement for Israel's society, economy, and politics have yet to be thoroughly investigated.[12]

PACs (political action committees) — overt associations and covert organizations — weakened the parties still further. Whereas in the past, before the primaries and direct elections of the prime minister, the party machinery ran the elections and all the individual candidate had to do was to make sure of his or her popularity with the party activists, the candidates now needed independent funding. This strengthened the leader's status vis-à-vis his party and its functionaries, but it strengthened even more the donors with interests vis-à-vis the decision makers. In the United States, says Jamieson (2000), the infusion of money in elections has transformed the nature of the process itself, from an evaluation of known candidates and parties, to the saturation of the communication environment with often misleading and emotional issue campaigns funded by obscure cause groups.

Something of this is beginning to be seen in Israel. In the old bureaucratic politics, and especially when the hegemonic ideology was social-democratic, economists, industrialists, financiers, and the business community were dependent on the politicians' decisions. In the media-centered democracy the politicians' dependence on their funding sources has grown. The politicians' agenda and decisions are influenced by these sources. Thus, Peres was persuaded to support the proposed reforms in the electoral system, Netanyahu was funded by nationalist Jewish millionaires who bought land to settle Jews in the midst of Palestinian-populated areas, and Barak was supported by liberal Jewish organizations pressing, among other things, to reduce the dominance of the religious orthodox in Israel.

The personification of politics combined with the growing importance of funding in the era of mediapolitik led to the development of politics of scandals. Central figures in public life have always been the focus of public interest, and their actions or omissions were the subject of gossip, debate, and public reaction. But it is only in mediapolitik that the leaders' private morality occupies such a central place in the public discourse, especially personal corruption in the context of sexual behavior or financial matters.

The explanation for this is straightforward. In the old party politics ideological issues and differences of opinion over policy were at the center of the public debate. In the new politics the actors' personality is the focus of public attention. That is why they are chosen, and that is how they are judged. Since this personal dimension is central and attracts the attention of the media, political rivals shoot their arrows at their adversaries' personal behavior and character. Because media logic leads to a constant flow of scandals and crises, the competition between the various media outlets leads them to intensify their treatment of these topics. Thus, media logic shapes the political discourse and the political praxes.

Indeed, quantitative examination of this phenomenon in some countries reveals a significant rise in the coverage of political scandals. In Britain, for example, this happened even in the quality papers. Between the years 1990 and 1994 the number of general articles on the British

Parliament in these papers dropped by 20 percent, while the number of reports on scandals was five times higher (Esser 1999). A similar situation exists in Israel (Liebes 2001), mostly in connection with financial corruption. The new politics is expensive, thus requiring extensive fundraising, much of which is done by illegal means. Thus, financial maneuvering, which was seen in the past as a weakness of those in power, is today an existential need, and the political battle focuses on exposing such corruption, as the examples of French President Valerie Giscard d'Estaing and the German Chancellor Helmut Kohl, among others, have shown.

MEDIA INFLUENCE ON THE POLICY PROCESS

In a media-centered democracy the media play a major part in shaping, consolidating, and implementing public policy. Here, too, we can see the nature of the symbiotic structure of mediapolitik. Although the government is the final decision maker on most public policies, other bodies are involved at each stage of this process, such as interest groups outside the government and even competing subgroups within the government. The media are highly involved in every stage of the public policy process, and their influence may often be decisive. This refers not only to their weight vis-à-vis the elected decision makers, who are concerned with considerations of political survival, image maintenance, and the like (Blumler and Kavanagh 1999: 216), but also to the bureaucrats and public administrators.

David Paletz (1998) demonstrated the media's contribution to the policy process and discerned six different stages, beginning with the policy formation stage, when the media bring events and issues to public and policymakers' attention. He showed how labeling treatment of women as sexual harassment or wife abuse had the effect of transforming private misfortunes into failure of public policy. The ways an issue is defined at the various stages of the policy process can be crucial. The most recognizable influence of the media found in the study is at the agenda-setting stage. The policy agenda consists of issues commonly perceived by public officials as meriting governmental attention and those actively being considered by them for action. An interesting finding in this context is that *New York Times* coverage (in contrast to local newspapers) led political activities even more than it followed them.

Once an issue is on the agenda, policymakers have to decide what to do about it. Because of their limited time and resources to cover many issues, the media are most effective in producing symbolic response by policymakers and have a limited impact on formulation of policy alternatives. However, they do influence decision makers in the limiting-choice stage because they, especially those elected to office, usually try to respond to policy issues in ways that appeal to the public.

The next stage, which Paletz calls the "legitimation and adoption stage," was referred to here in the discussion on the Knesset. At this stage, the prospects of any policy being adopted, changed, or dying are very much conditional on the amount and type of coverage they receive in the media. Finally, the media also have a role in the stages of implementation, administration, and evaluation of the policy. The media can be a significant force at these stages in policy process, by reporting whether and how policies are being administered and implemented and by holding government officials accountable for their actions. Media coverage can cause policies to be reappraised, changed, and even abandoned. A dramatic example of this latter point is President Reagan's decision to demand that Israel stop bombing Beirut in the summer of 1982, following the horrific sights he saw on the TV screen.

The media play a part in each of these stages of the public policy process. Every attempt to measure the weight of their influence is doomed to failure. They play a part like the other actors in the political body, the various units of government, power groups and pressure groups, civic groups and think tanks. The relative weight of the media differs at each stage and is dependent on a long list of variables. The important point is that we need to see the policy process as one in which various actors are involved. True, the politicians make the formal decisions, but this formal stage is influenced by a long list of factors whose weight is often greater than the actual formal decision. In this complex "subterranean" game the media play a distinguished part. However, more than media institutions, media logic is most effective, as politicians and officials operate by "governing with the news."

CHAPTER SIX

Israel's Media-Centered Democracy

INTENSIFICATION OF POLITICS

When television came to Israel in 1968, we, "the boys on the bus," a group of young political journalists covering the election campaign who were fascinated by the American media, became convinced that television would irrevocably transform Israeli politics. We were sure that many older-generation politicians would not be reelected, despite their status and abilities, simply because they were not telegenic. The test case for our hypothesis was Tourism Minister Moshe Kol, then leader of the Liberal Party, who was an amiable man but completely lacked any telegenic quality. On election night, our prediction was proven wrong, and Moshe Kol served another ten years as an Israeli government minister. So what was all this talk about magic effects of television in elections? We asked ourselves but could not find an answer.

In the following elections in 1974, television campaigns were conducted with improved technical skills, but there was still no change in the nature of the political game. Even the critical elections of 1977, when the Labor Party fell from power for the first time and Menachem Begin became prime minister, did not reflect any change in the Israeli media culture. Begin had run as the head of his party in no fewer than eight elections since 1948 and had failed each time, until his day finally came on the ninth attempt. This victory, however, cannot be attributed to the advent of television. His personality and leadership style had not changed over the years — he remained a populist leader of the old type, and his main strength lay mainly in his gifts as an orator, haranguing the crowds in city squares.

It took more than two decades, during which time neotelevision arrived, until the Israeli political sphere assumed the pattern of media-centered democracy. The first signs appeared during the 1994 elections to the Histadrut, Israel's federation of trade unions. Unlike other trade unions, the Histadrut fulfills a broader range of functions and includes representatives of all the political parties. The number of Israelis eligible to vote in Histadrut elections was approximately half the number with the right to vote for the Knesset. In the 1994 elections to the Histadrut the Labor Party fought yesterday's battle. It set up an elaborate campaign machinery, and its leaders rushed around the country to speak at rallies attended by a handful of bored voters. Labor's rival was Knesset member Haim Ramon, one of the prominent young leaders of the Labor Party, who had left the party a few weeks before the elections and established a new party without an apparatus. Ramon followed the rules of the new politics. His campaign focused on television and he appeared alone, preferably on entertainment programs and talk shows, where he mocked and attacked the old functionaries and sold mainly himself. His spectacular success not only destroyed the old establishment in the Histadrut but also dealt a deathblow to the old campaigning style. The Histadrut elections in 1994 were what the Spanish Civil War was to World War II, a "dress rehearsal" before the big show. When the general elections were held two years later, they were won by Israel's top expert in media-centered politics, Benjamin Netanyahu.[1]

In the mid-1990s the characteristics of mediapolitik in Israel became clearly visible — a combination of the ideal model with elements specific to Israel's political culture and traditions. To mention some of the most outstanding: expansion of the political space; the emergence of infotainment; changes in the patterns of political leadership; professionalization of political marketing; the modification of both the way that Knesset representatives operate and the government's modus operandi; and the growing importance of polls. In none of these topics is the Israeli case unique. What distinguished it was the rapidity and intensity with which the change took place, as well as its results.

Israeli society is distinguished by its hyperpoliticized culture. Israelis are simply always talking, writing, and thinking about politics. Politics is not restricted to its own arena — it intrudes into many spheres of life and social action, and the preoccupation with it is intensive. This is "total" politics, similar to Alessandro Pizzoreno's (1981) concept of "absolute politics," which "dictates the rules of behavior in all important areas of social activity." But more than that, in contrast with liberal politics, which is grounded in a pluralism of worldviews, absolute politics has a central transcendental component that includes an element of sacredness. It presumes one and only truth and sets absolute moral criteria.

Politics in Israel is "total politics" because it deals with existential questions of life and death, war and peace, setting state boundaries and determining the collective identity. Underlying this setting, however, is a history and a collective memory of thousands of years involving God. Philosopher Michael Walzer, who coined this phrase, sees the nonseparation of religion and state in Israel as one of the major factors in its extreme and fanatical character (Walzer 1998). One should not overlook as well, though, the contribution of the radical character of Israel's founding fathers, which came from Eastern Europe with revolutionary socialist zeal.

This Israeli political arena did not change with the introduction of paleo-television and the beginning of media-centered democracy. On the contrary, neotelevision led to the intensification of politics. News broadcasts are main prime-time programs on the three television channels, with viewing rates of almost half the total population (Akiba Cohen 1998). In addition to the usual public-affairs programs or political interviews, politics has also penetrated other television programs and genres and even created new types of political talk shows.

These programs join a large number of others that deal with current events, interviews, news, and discussions, forming a considerable part of the media diet on both channels. And when the six weekdays were not enough, politics invaded the sabbath broadcasts. Since the mid-1990s, more political broadcasts have been added on the commercial channel and, in its wake, on the public channel. Some of these were imitations of American programs such as *Meet the Press*, while others were original, like *The Saturday Game*.

While in the past, Israel's high rate of political participation was measured by rates of active membership in the parties, measures typical of party culture (Arian 1998), the continued high level of political participation in the 1990s was expressed in measures characteristic of the media culture, namely, the high rate of viewing political broadcasts. According to a summary of the first five years of Channel 2 broadcasting, two of the ten most popular programs belong to this genre, and this on top of the news broadcasts, each of which reaches about 25 percent of the exposure.[2] In contrast to the claim that the displacement of public service television by commercial channels has impoverished the public space (Dahlgren 1995), the opposite happened in Israel. The number of consumers of political communication, both in the press and on television and radio, has grown considerably, as has the number of channels and broadcasting hours.

THE POLITICAL BROADCASTING SCHEDULE

The political media day starts before six in the morning, when the newspapers, *Haaretz*, *Yediot Ahronot*, *Maariv*, and some other small papers are placed on the doorsteps of more than 250,000 homes, totaling almost 20 percent of Israeli households. The two tabloids, which started off as evening papers and were sold only on the streets in the 1950s, became midday papers in the 1960s and were sold in newsstands. In the 1980s, they were published in the morning, and in the 1990s, when fierce competition broke out between them, they both developed subscription services.

These newspapers are also placed on the desks of the producers of the major morning programs on the two main radio stations, Kol Israel Reshet Bet and Galei Zahal, providing the basis for news and current-events programs. Although these two are not devoted solely to news, but are, rather, diverse "supermarket channels," they nevertheless carry huge quantities of political material and their ratings are high. The newscasts start at 6 am, followed by the newsmagazines *This Morning* and *Good Morning, Israel*, each two hours long. The average viewing rates of these news programs are quite high, close to four out of every ten Israelis (39.6) listen to Kol Israel Reshet Bet, and approximately three out of ten (26.7) listen to Galei Zahal.

From the morning till the late hours of the night, the two stations broadcast newsmagazines and current-affairs programs. News programs are broadcast every hour, and the headlines every half-hour. In between, there are updates.

The first television news programs are broadcast at 5 o'clock in the afternoon on all channels — only a tiny percentage of people watch the morning news on TV — and this is the time that the majority of Israelis switch from radio to television.[3] Prime-time television viewing in Israel occurs between eight and ten in the evening and centers around the main news broadcasts. In 1999 the Channel 1 newscast lasted for one and a half hours, starting at 7:30 PM. In fact, the Israeli viewer can zip between the channels and see the news for most of the prime time. All this was true even before the second commercial channel (Channel 10) started to broadcast in January 2002 and subsequently added more news programs.

The news broadcasts on both channels in the 1990s were among the five programs with the highest viewing rates, with the commercial channel enjoying an average share of nearly 40 percent of all households, and the public channel 20 percent (Tokatly 2000: 201). The political talk shows are among the ten programs with the highest ratings, averaging more than 20 percent.

However, this does not end the list of political programs. Unlike the daily talk shows in the United States, which are broadcast late at night, in Israel talk shows like *Popolitika, Hakol politika* (It's all politics), and others are broadcast at peak viewing hours. Channel 1 ends its broadcasts at midnight with another half-hour news magazine.

During the 1990s, live broadcasts, direct broadcasts, and special broadcasts became common, even in response to political events that were not exceptional. The peace process, the continued fighting on the Lebanese border, and Palestinian terrorist attacks in Israel have all naturally provided material of special interest and received extensive treatment.

Additionally, all the other radio stations, local and pirate radios, broadcast news as well. In the 1990s, political programs became increasingly interactive: not only their listeners but also politicians and other public figures called in to the studio. They would call the host while the program was on the air and would react on the spot to the issues reported. This occurred during talk shows as well as during the more formal news broadcasts. In fact, such call-ins have become routine during news broadcasts, with the officials responding to what has just been presented. The increasingly interactive character of the political news channels in the 1990s is also expressed in the proliferation of phone-in programs that enable listeners to express their opinions. These are broadcast every afternoon on the two main radio channels, and their listening rates are very high. Other stations carry similar programs, but with lower listening rates.

THE DEVELOPMENT OF INFOTAINMENT

Scholars of media and culture have long made a clear distinction between two genres: news, or public affairs, and entertainment. Although this distinction, which was perceived for many years as self-evident, appeared more and more complicated and, some argued, socially constructed (Carpini and Williams 2000), it is now common knowledge that the walls that separated the news, with its civic function, from entertainment, with its diversionary or amusing function, have collapsed.

The changes that occurred in the media, the takeover of neotelevision, and the news media's transformation into market-driven journalism led to the convergence of these two modes, as defined by the concept "infotainment."[4] The two genres, political information and entertainment "draw on the same narrative forms and consequently transmit the same message" (Dayan and Katz 1992: 31). Various scholars emphasize different components of this syndrome while sharing the basic definition, whose essence is that politics, instead of being a serious business of popular discourse, is becoming politics as popular culture. Both advertisers and journalists share the assumptions that the discussions of "political heads" are boring, and that media consumers have a short attention span. These assumptions, together with the television industry's basic principles that the way to maximize profits is to provide large amounts of entertainment, are the source of television's way of treating political materials: presenting politics as a game, emphasizing its personal dimension, and accentuating human interest and the sensational. Thus emerge the popularization of political issues and their shallow treatment as delivered in an exciting, entertaining manner.

This blurring led Brants (1998) to relate to information and entertainment not as dichotomous but as ideal types at two ends of a continuum, when informative programs are considered to have content conducive to rational participation in the political process, and entertainment programs are for distraction and pleasure. Between these two extremes there is a broad range of possibilities, in which elements of the first code penetrate the second and vice versa.

The Israeli case demonstrates that even in a society where politics is wrapped in an aura of sanctity, absolute politics may nevertheless turn into entertainment when broadcast on television. In the paleo-television era, nothing changed in the original character of Israeli politics. For the twenty-five years of Channel 1's existence as photographed radio, it had the same heavy, deadly serious character that it had before television arrived in Israel. But all of this changed with the advent of neotelevision. Knowing how much the Israelis love and need politics, television editors did not hasten to remove political material from the screen but turned it into entertainment, first in the commercial channel and soon after in the public channel. This forced the politicians to adapt themselves to the new game, to change their rhetoric, to increase the amount of humorous material, to adjust to the use of easy sound bites, to perfect the art of the punch line. They soon discovered that only those with such skills are invited to the studio a second time.[5]

If at first the news acquired entertainment value, in the course of the 1990s, there was also movement in the opposite direction, and issues relating to public affairs were introduced into purely entertainment programs. In essence, entertainment is the opposite of information about the "real" world. It is designed to avoid realism by lowering cognitive activity or by reconstructing reality in a fantastic form. And in the 1990s, entertainment began to make more and more use of reality. In the United States it was done with the proliferation of reality shows, and in Israel, with the introduction of political issues and politicians into entertainment programs.

Most scholars who analyze infotainment refer to it with concern related to the video malaise syndrome, the fear that infotainment will create marginalization of political news and eventually depoliticization. The reverse has happened in Israel, though at the same time, the process has affected the nature of public discourse. At all events, those politicians who knew how to ride the wave and become celebrities had learned how to interweave political and nonpolitical material.

The program *Popolitika* is a salient example of news as entertainment. This is a roundtable discussion with many participants, with an active audience, with a regular host, and with a panel of three journalists. The program's density, both in the number of issues and participants, and above all in its pace and style, generates an emotional, provocative, tense, and extremely aggressive atmosphere. The most common television genre is contest, say Dayan and Katz in their book *Media Events*, and indeed in *Popolitika*, at the basis of the intellectual dispute insofar as this exists, is the contest to win the microphone and the eye of the camera and then speak without interruption. The success of the program spawned several imitations.

The program is designed ostensibly to serve as a platform for political debate, but in fact it is a duel, a contest between the participants, who happen to be using political arguments as their weapons. Those who do not understand this entertainment element are not invited to more than one program, but those who grasp what the producer really wants become superstars. The success of one of the three panel members, journalist Yosef (Tommy) Lapid, was so great that he used it as a springboard for the Knesset elections in 1999 at the head of the Shinui Party. Not only did he succeed in averting the demise of this small party, but he also increased its representation in the Knesset to five seats. In 2003 Shinui won 15 seats, and Lapid became justice minister.

If *Popolitika* expresses the divisions in Israeli society, the political fervor, and the intolerance and impatience of total politics, *Dan Shilon Live* was the expression of social solidarity round the tribal bonfire. The participants in this talk show sat in a circle on a raised platform in a huge studio with a large audience, while the host held a conversation of the type people conduct with their friends when they get together on Friday evenings, which is the most common form of entertainment and socializing in the country. What made this program different was the mix of people who would not normally be found together, but who appeared to be a microcosm of Israeli society. Sitting side-by-side one could see a singer and a politician, a model and a senior IDF officer, a celebrity and a released murderer, an outstanding sportsman and a prostitute. They all sat together, talking about themselves and discussing current events, politics and sports, crime and economics, fashion and security. The diversionary element was stronger than in *Popolitika* and the discussion was of a personal nature, but in Israeli total politics the personal is also political. This program's success also spawned imitations. Using Brant's distinction, *Popolitika* may be defined as an inter-mediate pattern of EI (entertainment-information), and the group in the circle as IE.

Another interesting reflection of the transformation of politics into infotainment can be seen in the images and metaphors used by the media. Until the 1990s, campaigns in Israel were described in military terms. In a society that goes to war almost every decade, in which there is hardly a family that does not have a son or daughter serving in the military, and former generals occupy almost 20 percent of the seats in the cabinet, it does not take a great deal of imagination to understand how the world of military images and metaphors has permeated many spheres of civilian life. Reports of election campaigns are rife with military expressions such as attack, outflanking, battles, blitz, retreat and offensive, duel, conquest, and the like.

In 1992, but even more in 1996, there was a change in the language. The use of the military vocabulary was largely replaced by concepts taken from the world of sports. The confrontation between the prime ministe-rial candidates was described in terms taken from the boxing ring. Coverage of the Knesset elections included many terms used in football or basketball games. Channel 1 launched a new political program prior to the elections of 1996, called *The Saturday Game*, which was shot in the workout room of a health club. Since politics had become infotainment, no viewer expressed surprise that the participants in the program exchanged opinions while walking a treadmill, sitting on exercise bikes, or in front of weights. After the primaries in 1999, when the parties had chosen their lists of candidates, one of the tabloids published the two lists in a photomontage of two soccer teams dressed for the match, standing face to face, each team with twelve players.

The change in the character of politics is also evidenced by the politi-cians' willingness to submit to the flogging of satirical programs. When the first attempt was made to introduce political satire on television in the mid-1970s in the program *Cleaning the Head*, it met with sharp criticism from the government, and Prime Minister Rabin even imposed sanctions against the program and its editors. Twenty years later a much more scathing satirical program appeared, *Hahartzufim*, with dolls caricaturing politicians, in the style of *Spitting Image*. This time, even the politicians who were most sharply lampooned had to join in the general laughter, though their stomachs were twisted with shame and pain; they couldn't afford any other reaction. Although the causal relation was not measured empirically, it is commonly believed in Israel's political community, and it is probably true, that the popularity of some of the politicians rose or fell according to the image that was attached to their doll.

THE CHANGE IN LEADERSHIP PATTERNS:
FROM APPARATCHIK TO CINCINNATUS

Media-centered politics brought about a change in the dominant pattern of political leadership in Israel. The old model of the politician was that of a bureaucrat or a functionary. This was the party hack who rose through the ranks, often as a paid employee. He or she maintained unwavering loyalty to the party, even when its leaders changed. The party hack was an expert at internal power games, spent hours sitting in meetings that ran well into the night or in internal forums, usually in smoke-filled rooms, maneuvering and twisting arms. The founding fathers and mothers of Israeli politics, who formed the skeleton of the apparatus parties, came from Eastern Europe, from regimes where this model of leadership, called the apparatchik, prevailed (Brzezinski and Huntington 1963).

In contrast, in the United States a different pattern of leadership can be seen, that of Cincinnatus, a leader acting in an open forum, in the city square, whose major skills are his oratorical talent, his ability to enthuse and carry away the masses (Brzezinski and Huntington 1963). These two types of politicians differ in the forms of their mobility. The apparatchik is promoted by leaders who pull him up in exchange for loyalty and political services provided. The Cincinnatus, by contrast, is able to win the hearts of the masses and gain their support. This is the source of his mobility; he is pushed up by the public due to his popularity.

In Israel's old party system, the apparatchik was the dominant pattern, although apparatchiks sometimes co-opted other types of leaders, writers, and academics (such as authors S. Yizhar and Dov Sadan), people from the public sphere (like Zeev Scherf and Y. S. Shapiro), retired senior IDF officers (Moshe Dayan, Yitzhak Rabin, Ariel Sharon, and Ezer Weizman, as well as dozens of others), but in the final analysis the apparatchiks were still the ones who pulled the strings.

With the decline of the parties, the apparatchiks, power brokers, and political bosses lost a great deal of their power. In the era of media-centered politics, the potential ability of leaders with other advantages — mainly television appeal — rose. The change in the pattern of election of prime ministers in Israel illustrates this revolution.

Israel's earliest prime ministers — all from the Labor Party — were chosen by a very small group of power brokers, who then brought their decision for approval to the party's central committee, which numbered fewer than one hundred members, but this approval was no more than a predetermined ritual. This is how Moshe Sharett was elected after the temporary resignation of Prime Minister David Ben Gurion in 1954, and

Levi Eshkol in 1963 after Ben Gurion's final resignation. In the same way that leaders of the Labor Party decided in 1969 that Golda Meir would succeed Eshkol, despite the fact that she had gained only 5 percent in public opinion polls.

With the weakening of the party apparatus, a new competition was sparked between Shimon Peres and Yitzhak Rabin for premiership after Golda Meir's resignation in 1974. For the first time two candidates presented themselves to the four-hundred-member central committee, who chose Rabin by a majority of forty votes. Three and a half years later, the same pair competed again, but this time the decision was made by a larger party forum, the party convention, with fourteen hundred members (where Rabin won again, by the same margin of forty votes). In the elections of 1992, however, five candidates competed for the leadership (Yitzhak Rabin, Shimon Peres, Yisrael Keissar, Ora Namir, and Gad Ya'akobi), and the elections were held in primaries with all the party members taking part.

The expansion of the body that elected the party's candidate for prime minister gave an advantage to the candidate whose power did not come from the internal apparatus and his bureaucratic abilities but from public recognition and popularity among the general public, both because of his telegenic qualities and the fact that the public felt that he had electability potential. Just as studies on President Reagan had shown in the United States, in Israel as well television made the candidate's personal characteristics more important than his political attitudes. Labor's election campaign in 1992 was personal, placing all the emphasis on the candidate, "Rabin at the head of Labor." For this reason, Labor also won the votes of traditional right-wing and religious voters. They could identify with Rabin's authoritative, fatherly, clear-headed, and confidence-inspiring image, even though his views were more dovish than theirs.

Things went a step further in the 1996 elections. By that time media-centered politics was already established, and the contender was a Cincinnatus, well-versed in American political television, Benjamin Netanyahu. Therefore, it was not hard for him to defeat the incumbent, Shimon Peres, an experienced senior politician who had grown up in the old school and was not aware of the changes that had been happening around him. The pattern created in 1996 was repeated in the next elections, in 1999. Like Netanyahu, Barak was popular although he lacked a party base and political experience. Though he lacked Netanyahu's command of television skills, Barak, like Netanyahu, was elected to head his party mainly because of his electability — the party members knew that he alone had a chance of leading them to power.[6]

THE PROFESSIONALIZATION
OF POLITICAL MARKETING

With the disappearance of the old-style functionaries — the full-time, tenured staff at the parties' headquarters — a need arose for alternative experts in political organization. Out of this need grew a new breed of politico-media strategists, with professions that were unknown in Israel before the 1980s. Parties had begun using the services of independent advertising agencies in their election campaigns since the mid-1960s, but these experts mainly prepared and placed campaign ads in the newspapers, while the actual campaign policy was determined solely by the politicians. In the late 1970s the experts began to take a larger part in policy setting, often accompanied by tension and even disputes with the politicians. However, it was only at the beginning of the 1990s that the professionals began to set the tone in the strategic planning of election campaigns, and political consultants also began to work with politicians during periods between elections.

Professionalism is the antithesis of amateurism. Waging publicity competition through the media, messaging journalists' news values, putting the best spin possible on significant stories, fashioning political advertising, designing opinion polls and interpreting their results — all these require the skills of experts, who are single-mindedly dedicated to the goal of victory in such competition, and for whom all other goals, including policy and politically educative ones, are subordinate if not irrelevant. (Blumler and Gurevitch 1995: 207)

Indeed, what distinguishes the professionals from their predecessors is the following element: their identification is primarily with their profession — political marketing — and not with the ideology or political attitudes of the people for whom they work. Their loyalty is like that of lawyers, tax consultants, or similar professionals: today they work with one candidate, tomorrow with another, sometimes even their former clients' archrivals. Their expertise is in the political media market, and their sole aim is victory in the elections.

In the second half of the 1990s, political marketing underwent a process of differentiation and specialization, a process characteristic of advanced stages of professionalization. This stemmed from the fact that the Israeli professionals adopted working methods practiced abroad, and it was accelerated with the arrival of American advisers in Israel.

Netanyahu's election campaign at the head of the Likud in 1996 was the first in which the rules of political packaging were followed by the book. The use of American experts, with Arthur Finkelstein at their head, and techniques that had been proven in American election campaigns, gave Netanyahu and the Likud a tactical advantage over Shimon Peres with

Labor's clumsy old election machinery. Peres's successor, Ehud Barak, learned the lesson, and in the 1999 elections he confronted the two Finkelstein brothers (most of the work this time was done by the young brother, Ronny, who remained anonymous) with James Carville, Stanley Greenberg, and Bob Shrum, the team that had helped President Clinton to be elected in the United States, Tony Blair in Britain, and the social-democratic Chancellor Schroeder in Germany. It is not surprising that this election campaign was labeled: "And tonight: Finkelstein versus Carville."[7]

The introduction of direct elections, along with Netanyahu's prestige as an expert in political marketing, led his colleagues at the top of the party to leave the running of the 1996 election campaign to him and his professional team. When Ehud Barak tried to do the same, he faced much stronger opposition in the Labor Party. Due to the long-standing bureaucratic party tradition, the party's organizational headquarters was not happy with Barak's decision in 1999 to entrust the running of the campaign to external professionals. A sharp dispute arose between him and the party secretary-general, Knesset member Ra'anan Cohen, a veteran politician with experience in election campaigns. However, when Barak announced that the professional team would be the Americans famed for the victories of Clinton, Blair, and Schroeder, the old-time functionaries were silenced.

The foreign advisers' contribution was mainly in using polls and in preventing digression from the preplanned strategy (past election strategy tended to change constantly during the course of the campaign, and there was a great deal of improvisation). However, their principal contribution was that they gave Barak an excuse to keep the functionaries out of the election HQ and run the campaign by himself with his professional Israeli team.[8]

In the 1999 campaign headquarters one could see for the first time the full range of political professions. In addition to the political advisers, there were copywriters, public relations experts, publicity experts for both television and newspapers, specialists in timing and positioning of advertisements, spin doctors, sound-bite writers, experts in various kinds of polls and focus groups, and other professionals in political marketing. The growing professionalization of political marketing was manifested in the manner in which the campaign was conducted, similar to what had happened in Britain two years earlier (Norris et al. 1999).

The 1999 election campaign was marked by systematic use of spin doctors; press conferences became election rallies, attended by the candidates' supporters; the candidates' campaign tours were not designed, as in the past, to reach out to the public, but were used as media events if not pseudoevents for the purpose of the campaign. The political packaging

also affected the contents of the package. Traditionally, the party manifesto had been drawn up with great effort and then presented to the party
convention for approval, not without discussion, sometimes very stormy
ones. This time it was completely marginal. True, even in the past these
party conventions had a ritual dimension of symbolic politics, but they
also dealt with substantial issues, providing a forum for ideological
debate and policy decisions. In 1999 they were pure carnivals, staged by
a theatrical director, orchestrated according to the needs of the media,
timed so that the leader would appear live and unedited in the main
evening news broadcast. The television impact was also the major consideration in deciding which of the participants would be allowed to
speak to the delegate.

The innovative nature of these methods in the 1996 elections also
caused the media to fall in love with the new game. Although a very few
were aware of the manipulative impact of political marketing, most of the
political reporters "played the game" that was prepared for them by the
election experts. The result was that in covering these elections the Israeli
media fell into all the traps that are only too familiar to media scholars.
They referred to the candidates in a style appropriate to a horse race,
focused on the front runners in the prime ministerial elections, ignoring
the Knesset elections, and dealt with election tactics instead of discussing
the pressing political issues (Patterson 1994).

THE KNESSET:

FROM WORKHORSES TO SHOW HORSES

Mediapolitik brought changes not only in the party system, leadership
styles, elections, and electoral politics, but also in the legislature and the
executive. In the past the press had some influence over the parliamentary
agenda: a certain percent of the motions for the agenda submitted by
Knesset members originated in material that they had taken from the
press (Caspi 1982; Kadman 1998). In the end, however, the Knesset
agenda was determined by the political elite, particularly cabinet ministers. This was not the case in the 1990s. During that period the parliamentary agenda was largely determined by the media agenda (Shabat
2001).

Knesset members' endeavors to adapt the Knesset agenda to that of the
media stem from their understanding that their political success, even
their very political existence, depends on the media. But what guarantees
the individual Knesset members success in the media? What will ensure
favorable media attention? There are two dimensions to the competition

for the media's selective attention. One is competition over access to the media, that is, actually receiving media attention; the other is competition over the media framing, over who will succeed in dictating to the media his version of reality (Wolfsfeld 1997). Surely the answer should be that in this contest the Knesset member who does his job best will win. Isn't it self-evident that the member who is more active and effective in legislation, oversees the work of the executive branch, represents the voters' interests, in fact, does the work he was elected to do, will succeed in dictating his version of reality?

The answer, without any trace of cynicism, is of course not. The distinction between "workhorses" and "show horses" (Payne 1980) is enlightening. The former are the ones whose main interest is the "gray" parliamentary work. They never miss a plenary session and they submit many private members' bills as well as propose motions for the agenda and questions in the house. These members are active in committees and also prepare for debates and deal both with legislation and with monitoring the government. While the "workhorses" believe that these activities will win them the appreciation of the voters, such efforts are considered "gray work" and useless as a way to achieve recognition and appreciation by the "show horses." To them, exposure, recognition, and publicity bring fame. Marketing considerations are the prime motivation for their work and thus precede other considerations. Therefore, they devote time to the plenum only when they are sure of media coverage, deal mainly with subjects that they know the media are interested in, and use a variety of methods in order to gain media attention. In sum, they act according to media logic rather than political logic.

Looking at the U.S. Congress, Payne found that congressmen are either high in publicity and low in legislative work ("show horses"), or low in publicity and high in legislative work ("workhorses"), and that no member is high on both." The same distinction was also found to obtain in the Knesset, as shown both in interviews that I conducted with Knesset members and journalists in 1997–98, as well as in a quantitative study by Tamir Sheafer (2001). Sheafer writes: "Investing one's creativity, initiative and energy in parliamentary activity may help in making laws, but not at all in making the news. . . . Those actors who invest their creativity, initiative and energy in parliamentary activity were somewhat less successful in promoting their media frames than the average." In contrast, those who possessed the skills suitable for mediapolitik achieved success in the media, in the form of media exposure and dictation of their chosen media frames. These skills, says Sheafer, are "the ability to adapt to the routines and formats of news organizations; deep understanding of the 'good story' structure; demonstrated rhetorical abilities that fit the sound-bite requirements; a flair for dramatic performance; know-how in creating and promoting media events; and ability to develop working relations with journalists." Discerning observers saw these things back at the beginning of the 1990s and warned that government reform would exacerbate the problem: "Candidates with stage presence and self-marketing ability will naturally have an advantage. Others will have to resort to cheap media gimmicks in order to achieve exposure, and the addition of gimmicks will lower still further the Knesset members' status," said Knesset member Uzi Baram (1996: 218). He could have never imagined how right he would be.

Indeed, some Knesset members are prepared to sink very low just so long as they can draw the media's attention. They invent gimmicks and tricks, sometimes even violating the code of parliamentary work, coordinating in advance with journalists, especially television cameramen. Aggressive and raucous tones of speech, heckling, and disruptions, almost to the point of physical violence, have also become the order of the day, forcing members to summon all their creativity in order to draw the attention of the camera. In the 1990s a Knesset member standing on the podium pulled a handheld fan out of his pocket (to demonstrate hot air), one ate a sandwich, and others initiated various media events in order to reach the headlines and hopefully to get their pictures in the papers. Likud Knesset member Moshe Nissim, who for years was a minister in rightist governments, mourned what he called a decline in the culture of parliamentary life, "adopting gimmicks and shows in order to stand out" (Nissim 1996).

The press coverage of the Knesset changed considerably over the years. In the 1950s, Dr. James Jacob Rosental of *Haaretz* was an exemplary figure of a parliamentary correspondent. He covered the plenary debates accurately, analyzed and explained the bills proposed, and described in detail the legislation processes in the committees, the parliamentary policy setting, and the parliamentary supervision of government authorities. The other newspapers, which were party papers, covered the Knesset debates through the party prism, giving extensive favorable coverage to the representatives of their parties and little coverage, and that more critical, of the others.

The narrow and distorted character of the parliamentary coverage in the party papers is illustrated by a story that became a legend in the Israeli press. In 1945, when the newspapers learned of the nuclear attack on Hiroshima and Nagasaki, *Hatsofe*, the National Religious Party's paper, covered it in a two-column item at the bottom of page one. The main headline dealt with an unimportant parliamentary debate. When asked about his decision, the editor replied, "I knew that nobody would telephone me complaining about the small headline, but can you imagine what an earful I would have got from the party if I had printed the speech at the bottom of the page?"

The disappearance of the party papers, the removal of many constraints on print and broadcast journalists, and the new profit-orientation of the profession, led journalists to operate new, more independent, journalistic criteria. The party papers' criterion for covering an issue was partisan and ideological. They quoted at length the speeches of the Knesset members that belonged to the "right" party or supported the "correct" attitudes. The news value of the stories reported by the commercial media was based on other considerations, primarily the consumers' interest. Interest superseded importance. This was precisely the shift from the sacerdotal orientation to the pragmatic approach as described by Blumler and Gurevitch (1987).

The sacerdotal treatment is the typical form of journalism sensitive to the demands of the political leaders, while the pragmatic approach selects and produces news according to media logic. According to the former approach, parliamentary reporting has to be factual, regular, and ongoing regardless of the inherent news value of the events on a given day, whereas according to the pragmatic approach, only if something of special journalistic interest happens is it worthwhile to devote space to it in the paper or over the airwaves. What happened in Israel was similar to what occurred in European countries such as Germany (Esser 1999).

When the new newspaper *Hadashot* (meaning news) was founded in 1984, it adopted a pathbreaking style of coverage, completely ignoring the existing practice of preferring political news to soft news. Its approach to the legislators was critical, even cynical, and it often completely ignored debates in the plenary and committees, concentrating instead on the goings-on in the political corridors and the gossip in the Knesset lounge. In a sense, this revolution recalls Michael Schudson's comment on the revolutionary stage undergone by the American press much earlier: "With the establishment of the summary lead as newspaper convention, it became clear that journalists began to move from being stenographers, or recorders, to interpreters" (Schudson 1982: 102). With the end of the old-style press coverage, stenographic reporting was replaced by a much more impressionistic reporting style. Journalists felt free to use texts from the Knesset as raw materials in order to express their opinions and attitudes. The reporter's role became that of interpreter.

The third-floor Knesset lounge thus became one of the most important institutions of the new politics. Unlike the British Parliament, where the politicians meet at the bar, the Knesset cafeteria has the atmosphere of a social club. Knesset members, journalists, senior officials, and others from the political class mingle, move from table to table, and join in conversations that go on all day, especially on Mondays, Tuesdays, and Wednesdays, when the Knesset is in session. There the political information flows, rumors are floated and quashed, canards are invented, and deals are made. There the Knesset members' advisers and spokespersons grab journalists and thrust press releases into their hands; there items are leaked from closed discussions of committees. This is the big pond where the analysts fish material for their weekend columns.

Knesset spokesperson Sara Yitzhaki-Kaplan commented:

A look at the media coverage of the Knesset shows that the print press has reached new peaks in dealing with cafeteria gossip instead of political news reporting. Just one example: On the day when the Knesset plenary debated a motion of no confidence, a senior reporter for the "national newspaper" [*Yediot Ahronot*] chose to stage the robbery of a painting from the collection displayed in the Knesset, in order to illustrate his point and create a good story. The no-confidence motion was dwarfed. The fabricated story got a full page, naturally with its producer's photograph.[9]

In an attempt to soften the effect of the independent critical media coverage of its work, the Knesset decided in the mid-1990s to introduce direct TV broadcasting of plenary sessions, through a new public service channel. In order to prevent journalistic interpretation and editing, the Knesset decided that the broadcast would be static, with a camera fixed in one place shooting only the speaker, or a long shot of the chamber, without zooming in to incidents occurring in the house. The broadcasts enable those who are interested to view the Knesset debates, but the viewing ratings are very low, as most viewers are more interested in the edited newscasts and news magazines. The latter formats have had a detrimental effect on the Knesset's public standing. Since the deterioration of the debating culture during the 1990s hotheaded rhetoric, aggressive speech, shouting, disruptions, and verbal battles now mark parliamentary debates.

Knesset members accuse the media of biased reporting. In particular, they criticize television for forcing them to adapt to its needs. Professor Shevach Weiss, Knesset Speaker from 1992 to 1996, said, "The Knesset members think mainly how they can attract the eye of the camera. They have become experts in provocative tricks, allowing the political extremists to celebrate at the expense of the moderate majority. This is a system that legitimizes trivia instead of dealing with the big issues."[10] There is almost unanimous agreement among Knesset members that the media coverage of the Knesset's work makes the debates more sensational, encourages the theatrical mannerisms of their parliamentary appearance, especially their use of extreme language and an aggressive style. Above all they accuse the media of exploiting their ability to promote or destroy Knesset members, regardless of the quality of their parliamentary work. "In mediatized politics there is no need to attack a politician, ignoring him can kill him politically. That is control by disregard," said former Knesset member and minister Benny Begin from the Right (Likud). An identical opinion was expressed by a former Knesset member and minister from the Left (Meretz), Yair Tsaban, who added, "If you are a Knesset member who knows how to work the media — you are a manipulator like Yossi Sarid or Yossi Beilin, but if you don't know how to do that, you are lost. The journalists will settle your fate."[11]

THE GOVERNMENT:
FROM WEAVING A FUTURE TO BLOWING BUBBLES

The shift to media-centered politics has also been evident in the output of the political system, in the executive arm's modus operandi, as well as in policy making and implementation. As in the case of electoral politics, it was the United States that heralded the advent of the new era. President Jimmy Carter and later Ronald Reagan used the method of "going public" — "a strategy whereby a president promotes himself and his policies in Washington by appealing to the American public for support" (Kernell 1986: 1).

Compared with the old method, which he called "institutionalized pluralism" or bargaining, Kernell defined individualized pluralism as the appeal to the public at large via the media, in order to recruit support in battles against Congress and the Senate or for other needs. Ostensibly this is an act of democratization, and the president turned the public into an actor in the political game. But does the public really participate, or is it merely used and manipulated? Whatever one thinks, it is clear that in this direct democracy the media have become stronger than ever.

The growing use of political marketing methods for the purpose of implementing government policy recurs in all the descriptions of contemporary democracies. We find it, for example, in descriptions of Canada (Siegel 1966) and Britain (Franklin 1994). The chapter headings in Franklin's book speak for themselves: "Central Government: Managing the News"; "Central Government: Selling Policies like Cornflakes"; "Local Government Communications: Propaganda or Promoting Democracy?" and so forth. In the end, it is not merely a question of more professional marketing of government policy by expanding the sphere of political media and using proactive news management, but also of integrating the principles of political marketing even at the stage of policy making (Blumler and

Kavanagh 1999: 215). This has led to a fundamental change in the role and status of the political leadership in shaping the future.

In policy making, as in other aspects of the political process, Israel joined the club of media-centered democracies in the 1990s. The preference for short-term considerations for the purpose of image building today, over long-term considerations, for the purpose of creating political realities in the future, is an inevitable result of membership in this club. "All politics and government," wrote Yehezkel Dror (1998), "deals with blowing bubbles, putting out fires, distributing favors [but also] weaving the future." Dror used Plato's metaphor concerning the actions of a statesman — weaving the future constitutes the decisions and actions that can meaningfully and intentionally affect the future, as opposed to "blowing bubbles," which is "doing actions that are conspicuous but lack real meaning." Dror adds:

The relative weight of these actions, in terms of the ideal and the reality, depends on the political culture and the structure of the political system, on the one hand, and the challenges posed by the environment on the other — and these differ from country to country. However, what characterizes all the democracies that have been established in the last twenty years is that the shift to "television-guided mass democracy" has intensified the occupation with blowing bubbles at the expense of weaving the future. (Dror 1998: 61)

There were some who were dumbfounded when they saw the government's working modes up-close. One of these was Brigadier-General Rafi Noy, who served as bureau chief of Defense Minister Yitzhak Mordechai from 1996 to 1998. Noy was a close, loyal, and devoted friend of Mordechai during their military service. When Mordechai was appointed minister of defense in the summer of 1996, he asked his friend to run his bureau. Noy agreed, but within a short time he discovered that Mordechai the politician was not Mordechai the officer with whom he had worked for so many years in the military. In a revealing newspaper interview Noy bared his pain in speaking about his long-time colleague: "It's impossible to work with him; ratings have become everything to Mordechai. It's not important what you do but how you look. The result is obsessive occupation with the media. He wants to be popular, loved, every day, all the time. He seeks instant gratification."

Noy illustrated this with several examples. One of them was the number of meetings that Mordechai held on working days. Noy wanted to squeeze a lot of meetings into the minister's working day, as they had done in the past, but Mordechai asked to leave him several hours free every day, so that he could devote them to dealing with the media. In trying to persuade his minister, Noy checked the schedules of previous defense ministers Shimon Peres and Yitzhak Rabin and found that they had held an average of eighteen meetings a day, while Mordechai held only six on average. When Noy reached the conclusion that Mordechai's main endeavor ended up being the media, and not doing anything "real," Noy resigned in November 1999.[12]

"WEATHER VANE POLITICS"—
THE POLITICAL POLLS

The domination of ascending political marketing values within the policy-making process reinforced Israeli political leaders' need for an alternative tool to monitor the sentiment of the public — the citizens who had now become political consumers. Political polls became the alternative tool developed for the purpose of monitoring and surveillance of public opinion. Until the 1970s parties did not use public opinion polls except during the short periods of elections, in order to measure their popularity. In the 1980s the use of polls expanded, though were still only used during election periods, and they included evaluation of the effectiveness of political messages during the campaign. The changes that occurred in the politicians' attitude to such polls were clearly reflected in the transition undergone by Yitzhak Rabin.

During his first period as prime minister, in the years 1974–77, Rabin related to polls solely as a tool for election periods and rejected a suggestion to establish a special survey unit in the prime minister's office.[13] However, when he was elected for the second time in 1992, he asked his chief pollster in the Labor Party, Kalman Gayer, to continue providing him with information, as he had done during the election campaign, and to set up a special polling unit in the prime minister's office for this purpose.

Gayer reported weekly to Rabin on public attitudes toward government policy, but polls were more for the purpose of self-assessment than for actual policy making. "A leader's role," Rabin often said, "is to lead the people in the way that seems right to the leader, but he should not be a captive to public opinion."[14] Rabin treated polls as a partial and fairly marginal factor in the entire range of inputs required for policy planning. In the end, this disdainful attitude to public opinion polls cost him his life.

In the summer of 1995, Gayer examined the public attitudes to the plan to withdraw from the occupied territories following the Oslo Accords. "I told Rabin that there was a hard core of opponents, comprising a few thousand people, who were prepared to use physical violence against him in order to stop the withdrawal," said Gayer. This information was supported by reports from the security services, and the head of the GSS (General Security Services) even asked Rabin to wear a bulletproof vest in his public appearances and to use an armored car that had been brought from the United States specifically for this purpose. Rabin resisted and even opposed increasing his protection. "These polls," Gayer quoted him as saying, "will not affect my decisions." If he had behaved differently and had worn a bulletproof vest, perhaps he would not have been killed by the assassin who shot him in the back at point-blank range.

As opposed to the sparse and marginal use of polls by Rabin and his "Generation of 1948," public opinion polls became an extremely important working tool for policy-making purposes among politicians of the younger generation. Bibi Netanyahu was a typical example: he began frequently using polls in the primaries, when he was elected to the leadership of his party, and he continued using them in the general elections of 1996. For example, Netanyahu chose his main campaign slogan based on a poll. Examining the various slogans, a poll showed that the phrase "Peres will divide Jerusalem" (that is, the Labor Party is prepared to cede the eastern part of the city to the Palestinians), was the easiest to absorb and would create the strongest political effect for the Likud. When the Likud began to use this slogan, the Labor Party and Peres ignored it completely. Dividing Jerusalem was not his policy, and furthermore, the very issue was not on the agenda. While Peres had relied on his gut feelings, Netanyahu had already read voters' cognitive maps. By the time Labor realized that the Likud's slogan had been thoroughly absorbed, that the public believed it and was even influenced by it, it was too late.

In the municipal elections held in the summer of 1998, a quantum leap occurred in the use of polls for the setting of policy. In the past, the candidates of the major parties for heads of local authorities were chosen after a battle between power brokers of the party's local branch. In 1998, however, electability became the most important criterion. Parties in many locations, including cities like Jerusalem and Tel Aviv, decided to choose their candidates on the basis of popularity polls.

The absurdity of this method was exposed by the case of Ron Huldai, who was elected mayor of Tel Aviv in 1998. Huldai, a retired air force commander, and principal of Herzliya High School, sought to run for mayor of Tel Aviv on behalf of the Labor Party, but was rejected by the head of the Labor branch on the grounds that a public opinion poll had shown that he had no chance of defeating the incumbent mayor, Ronny Milo. Huldai then decided to run as an independent candidate. It soon appeared that his determination and the campaign that he ran increased his recognition and popularity. Close to the actual election date, when his victory was almost certain, Labor agreed to support him, and he indeed ended up winning the election. If he had submitted to the judgment of the polls that predicted failure and decided not to compete, he would not have come to sit in the mayor's chair.

Huldai's story exposed some of the shortcomings of the polls as a decisive tool in making political decisions, but the use of polls did not decrease. On the contrary, in the 1999 elections it grew, rising to a peak in the extraordinary affair of the Center Party, a party that was born, rose meteorically, and crashed one year after the general elections. This party was established by four politicians, both new and old, who were united in their wish to bring down Netanyahu's government. Each of the four saw himself as the most worthy candidate for prime minister. In the absence of some binding factor, such as a common ideology or many years of shared experience in politics, public opinion polls served as the tool for making decisions. The four leaders agreed that whichever of them received the highest popularity in a poll would lead the movement and would be the party's candidate for prime minister.

The Center Party was born with Tel Aviv Mayor Ronny Milo's decision to run for prime minister, following polls showing that there was public support for this step. The next stage was when retiring Chief of General Staff Amnon Lipkin-Shahak decided to enter politics in order to defeat Prime Minister Netanyahu. Ehud Barak, the Labor Party leader, invited Shahak, who had been his deputy when Barak was chief of general staff, to join Labor. Shahak, however, declined the invitation, explaining that "the polls show that Barak has no chance of defeating Bibi." The same polls revealed that Israelis were hungry for a new figure in politics and predicted that the likeable and telegenic officer had a good chance of defeating Netanyahu in the second round, if there was no decisive victory for Netanyahu or Barak in the first round.

The other two who joined the Center Party's "gang of four" were Dan Meridor, who was finance minister in Netanyahu's government but left the government after a long period of friction with Netanyahu, and Yitzhak Mordechai, who was minister of defense in the same government but took the same path as Meridor one year later. All four accepted the main rule of the game: the victor in the poll would be the party's candidate for prime minister. Thus, late one evening in January 1999, a telephone poll of a national sample of five hundred respondents determined that Mordechai was the most popular by a margin of less than 1 percent (with a statistical error of 4 percent!). Yitzhak Mordechai would lead the Center Party in its quest for power.

Former Knesset Speaker Shevach Weiss, who had opposed the extensive use of polls, used to say, "Polls have become the emperors of the new politics." This was a wordplay based on the similarity between the words *sekarim* (polls) and *kesarim* (emperors).[15] But even he, a professor of political science, could not have envisaged what later occurred in the Center Party. It was no surprise that journalists and politicians called it "the mood-swing party" or "the poll party."

Nachum Barnea, an astute critic of Israeli politics, remarked in *Yediot Ahronot*:

> Imagine, 50 or 100 people, part of a random sample, responding over the phone to the question of a polling institute, decide who will be the Center Party's candidate for prime minister, and perhaps will be the next prime minister. Until today, political polls photographed situations. For the first time a political poll decides them. It is so easy, so efficient, that it obviates the need for elections. Why bother to go to the polling booth, when Mina Tzemach [head of the Dahaf Institute, which ran the poll] can determine the election results for us.[16]

The party, however, came to a sad end. As the election campaign advanced, support for Mordechai declined. In the end, he dropped out of the prime ministerial race in order to try and save the party in the Knesset elections, but it was too late. In contrast to the polls' prediction of more than 10 percent for the party, they ended up winning only 5 percent in the elections. Within a year, a split had already emerged among the Knesset faction, who had been at odds with each other from day one. Some of them resigned, the party dissolved, and Mordechai himself was forced to leave the Knesset after he was found guilty of sexual harassment.

Despite the Center Party's demise, the popularity of polls in the new political culture has not declined. They have been adopted enthusiastically by the Israeli media. Week after week, newspapers measure the popularity of the government and its ministers, as well as the public attitudes toward government policies and current events. Television stations conduct polls at the end of programs in order to receive the viewers' reactions to the discussion, and radio stations are not far behind. It is little wonder that the number of polling institutes has grown. In contrast to the four institutes that existed in Israel in the 1970s, there were more than twenty companies in the 1990s, although some of them were rather unprofessional.

As media exposure increasingly brought the leaders' broad use of polls to public attention, the public perceived this not as an expression of the leaders' desire to consider their voters' wishes, but rather as marketing manipulation of the political consumer audience. The media thus called Netanyahu a "mollusk," and his policies "weather vane policies."

Although Barak used this criticism of Netanyahu, he too employed the same techniques. While he was holding peace talks with Yasser Arafat at Camp David in the summer of 2000, he operated his polling system in Israel by "remote control" to examine the public's reaction to various proposals that he had raised in the talks. The results of these unpublished polls gave him the courage to decide on exceptional positions, such as the willingness to divide Jerusalem and cede the eastern part to the future Palestinian state.[17] Just as ratings provide the market's judgment of cultural products, so too public opinion polls have become an arbiter for political decisions; they express the leaders' surrender to the demands and needs of the general public, and to populist pressures.

CHAPTER SEVEN

Symbolic Politics

DOES MEDIA MALAISE EXIST?

A list of "the hundred words that made the century" was published in the *London Times* in early 1998, each word accompanied by a short explanation of its original meaning. The choice for 1926 was "television," and the *Times* commented that the very word was "terrible barbarism." The inventor of the word had made a crude hybrid of classical Greek and Latin. If he had wanted to correctly use the classic languages, he should have named the new invention "teleophais" (Greek) or "procolovisia" (Latin). "Television" was simply linguistically inaccurate.

The "barbaric term" was not, however, the only thing criticized. Since the beginning of media studies, scholars had criticized the negative influence of television on contemporary culture and society, and over time their voices reached the pitch of a crusade. Already in 1985, a compilation of social science literature identified more than 1,000 (to be precise, 1,043) effects, mostly not flattering, of television on social behavior (Herold 1986). It would be interesting to see how high the number would reach if it were done today.

The same applies, perhaps especially, to the particular area dealt with in this book: television and politics. The harsh criticism of television's destructive influence on public life first appeared under the heading "videomalaise" (Robinson 1975) and later "media malaise." Kurt and Gladys Lang were the first to suggest a connection between the rise of the network news and broader feelings of disenchantment with American politics. Michael Robinson popularized the term "videomalaise" to describe the link between reliance on American television journalism and feelings of political cynicism, social mistrust, and lack of political efficacy. Greater exposure to television news, he argued, with its high "negativism," conflicting frames, and anti-institutional themes, generated political disaffection, frustration, cynicism, self-doubt, and malaise. In the

1990s, criticism of television's effect on political life reached the dimensions of a deluge.[1] Thus, in 1995, Robert Putnam, roused a new debate when he argued that television was the root cause of vanishing social capital that left television-drenched citizens diminished in their feelings of social and civic responsibility (Putnam 1995).

Although this wave of criticism started in the United States, it soon reached Europe, where public television's traditional status was being eroded. European critics have a strong backing to lean on: the critical tradition of French thinkers such as Bourdieu, or the followers of the Frankfurt school such as Habermas and his associates. In Israel, a fierce indictment of commercial television was published in 2001, based on ideas taken from the workshop of the "culture industry" school à la Adorno (Yuran 2001).

The major argument of the media malaise thesis is that the overall character of television — its production values, or its media logic, to use concepts mentioned earlier — cause civic disengagement. Roderick Hart (1994) contends that enabling average Americans to bring images of the world into their living rooms misleads them into believing that they are powerful when, in reality, they are passive observers.

The television product that deals with politics is infotainment, a shallow, flat, basically negative product. It distorts the perceptions and awareness of political events, as well as creating a distorted image of political reality. It causes the public sphere to become consumed with personal communication, while the policy sphere becomes negative and intrusive. It weakens public trust in governmental institutions and decreases social trust and human capital. Thus, it makes citizens passive, depoliticizes them, and generates disaffection and disengagement from government — a "great retreat into enclave consciousness" (Slater 2001).

A cursory glance at the titles of the many books dealing with this subject in recent years reveals the major argument that the media are negatively influencing politics and democracy. Fallows, for example, titled his book, *Breaking the News: How the Media Undermine American Democracy* (1997a). What is developing is a situation of *Rich Media, Poor Democracy* (McChesney 1999), thus creating *The Sound Bite Society* (Scheuer 1999) or a *Republic of Denial* (Janeway 1999). In fact, the most touching laments were heard almost twenty years ago from Neil Postman, who wrote that if only television had never been invented, we would all be living in an enlightened democracy instead of this age of entertainment, where public discourse has decayed into a circus of pseudodebate and commercial staging (Postman 1986).

Naturally, among media scholars, now as in the past, there are some who extol television's contribution, not only to culture in general but even to democracy. Scholars like Fiske (1987) see it as a democratizing force. Meyrowitz argues that the text of the print era limited the number of people exposed to political information, while the spread of television expanded the circle of those sharing information. He goes on to say that even if this does not deepen their political understanding it gives a broad frame of knowledge to groups who had no access to it in the past (Meyrowitz 1985). Furthermore, television likes discussion and encourages debate, teaches that for every attitude there is an opposing one, and thus promotes critical thinking, encourages pluralism, and legitimizes oppositional views. To all this we should add the important social functions of television as a social institution that promotes national integration and social cohesiveness, as a tool that creates a sense of belonging to some social category (Calhoun 1988).

There has recently been a more crystallized reaction to the media malaise theory, as the books of Pippa Norris (2000) and Doris Graber (2001) testify. These are based both on theoretical arguments and empirical studies that refute the claim that extensive television viewing is detrimental to democratic involvement. Others take a less extreme position, but still cast doubt on the existence of a causal link between the two phenomena.

The growing disaffection with government and the decline in trust in the media both express a change in the citizens' attitude to public institutions in general, and they come from the same source. This is a phenomenon that characterizes established democracies. What is clear is that those who refute the idea of media malaise are on firm ground in their critique of the Americanization thesis, namely, that media malaise spreads in the world the more the style and structure of the American media are adopted by the media organizations and the professional communities beyond the Atlantic and Pacific Oceans.

In Germany, for example, it was found that the rise in television viewing following the proliferation of channels led, in fact, to a rise in political engagement. Mere exposure to television is positively associated with interest in politics, even though television viewing caused a decline in the level of trust in politicians, as happened in other countries. Trust in politics even rises the more people attend to newspaper information, though interest in politics and internal efficacy seem to benefit more from reading newspapers and listening to the radio than from watching television. However, the prevalent assumption that television viewing has negative effects on political interest and participation is not correct as a general rule (Schultz 1999).

The case of Germany is not the only one in Western Europe. On the contrary, it indicates a fairly widespread phenomenon in Europe, where in most countries commercial television has not marginalized political news. And in eight Western European countries, almost 6 of an average of 13.3 items per newscast in the early 1990s were about politics (Brants 1998).

The Israeli case, too, refutes the media malaise hypothesis, as well as its concomitant Americanization thesis. In Israel, there has in fact been no decline in interest and engagement in politics. The political news has not lost its centrality, and the public has not become less interested than in the past. The public space has expanded, penetrating into the various genres of television, and the circle of participants in the political discourse has grown. Media-centered democracy has not made the public passive or politically alienated, has not eroded the citizens' commitment and active character, or made them consumers. There are no signs of civic disengagement or of detachment. Participation in extraparliamentary activity even rose during the years of the media revolution, the voluntary sector acquired greater weight, and the number of organizations in the third sector grew by a considerable proportion (Gidron 2000). The case most like that of Israel is perhaps the Italian one, where political information has not decreased, but rather almost doubled between 1976 and 1998 (Brants 1998).

THE WEAKNESSES OF MEDIAPOLITIK

Even if Israel was not affected by media malaise, its entrance into the era of television-centered politics nevertheless generated a series of other transformations in the political sphere, some of which have been negative. In terms of input, the media has acquired increasing weight in the election process and in influencing the nature of political alignments. This has led to a change in the character of Israeli political leadership, as well as in the patterns of political mobility. There have been changes in the style of formulating and presenting demands, addressing them to the institution where authoritative allocations of resources are made. These demands will become more focused on single issues and will be ad hoc, fluid, and not based on a permanent and stable social base.

In terms of output, there has been a change in the government's working patterns. Media logic now has more influence than in the past in shaping the public agenda, the decision-making processes, and the implementation of public policy. Beyond this, there has also been a change in the country's political culture. This is particularly true with regard to the media construct that Max Weber called the *Problemstellung*. The media now influence the formation of Israeli political culture and the political discourse, both its content and style.

The shift to the new politics caused profound changes in the party system. Traditional democratic institutions of representation were undermined and were made less relevant by the electronic communication between voters and officials, particularly the prime minister. The consolidation of the media-centered democracy in Israel accelerated the deterioration in the status of the parties, which lost their functions as cultural institutions mediating between the people and the government. Their detachment from the general public deepened, and their membership and internal apparatus shrank. Furthermore, the volunteers that had worked for the party were replaced by experts — salaried professionals without ideological or community commitment to the party and its supporters.

Other changes occurred in the party system as well. First, the relations between the party leadership and its members was transformed. There was a growing trend of concentrating all power in the hands of the party leader, and for the first time the principle of "sole command" was practiced, as was particularly evident in the election campaigns. Breaking away from the tradition of collective management of the campaign by the party leadership, the campaign was now conducted from a functional headquarters close to the party leader. Netanyahu, in 1996, and Barak, in 1999, did exactly as Tony Blair had done in Britain and Gerhard Schroeder in Germany, to the disgust of the old-party activists.

The Israeli media-centered democracy changed the nature and style of political leadership. The apparatchiks gave way to the Cincinnatuses; image and persona became preeminent at the expense of the ideological message and political content; the personality cult took root; the distinction between political leaders and celebrities became blurred; and electability became a vital condition for national leadership. The new leadership style, and particularly the new management of news, facilitates the use of manipulation and shrewd political marketing by cynical and opportunistic politicians.

In Israel's new politics of the 1990s, political funding became a necessity and a driving force. Incompatibility between the political needs and the constitutional reality led to systematic violations of the law and encouraged a politics of scandals. In the 1990s the police investigated top officials, including the prime minister himself, more than ever before. Some may see this as improved efficiency of the law enforcement agencies, or even as a sign of democratization, but the fact that Israel's three prime ministers in the second half of the 1990s, Netanyahu, Barak, and Sharon, were all accused of similar offenses related to political funding indicates an immanent structural flaw in the new system.

The media are interested in and promote the politics of scandals, as the latter are so well suited to television's production values. In many cases, they play the role of investigator, prosecutor, and judge all in one and provide the popular consumer goods of infotainment. In the end, however, this boomeranged on the media, which the public perceives as not acting impartially, but out of political motives and interests. The public's criticism and mistrust of the media grew to such an extent that it undermined their base of legitimacy.

A series of political institutions were affected by mediapolitik. The Knesset lost status, parliamentary factions were weakened, and Knesset members' modus operandi changed for the worse. Mediapolitik also affected public policy procedures. Various phenomena, such as the use of political packaging, frequent changes of policy, emphasis on style and image management, and overdependence on public opinion polls, which seemed idiosyncratic to Netanyahu, are simply the result of the new political method that he was the first to employ.

The weakness of media-centered democracy stems, in part, from the visualization of politics. The availability of relevant visuals is a major criterion of news value. This led to distorted selection of the issues raised for discussion in the policy sphere. Important matters that would not make good stories on television — particularly social and economic issues — are often pushed aside in favor of marginal issues that would have better visual impact.

Research over many years casts doubt on the ability of television news to achieve the major aim for which it was created: to provide clear information to the public (Akiba Cohen 1998). The adoption of the image-bite style certainly did not increase the viewer's ability to learn from the material presented in it (Graber 1996). The culture of disputation encouraged by the media fell on fertile ground in Israel. Television was not the cause of the deep divisions in society, but television logic fosters conflict. It prefers fast talkers and people with extreme attitudes and brusque speech to more moderate people. All of this turned discourse into dispute.

Television's presentation style initially drew sharp public criticism. Both talking heads and program producers were accused of lowering the rhetoric and standards of public discourse. At the same time, this style of discussion became a model for imitation, and thus a vicious circle was created between what was represented and its representation. The final result was that existing political divisions and social tensions were exacerbated by the screen, inflaming public debate at a time when the traditional mechanisms for regulating and containing such tensions were weakened. The end result was damage to social integration and national solidarity.

Although Israelis' interest and involvement in politics did not decrease, something no less deep changed: the nature of public discourse. The critique of the new political culture stems from the democratic theory of the media, whereby the democratic system has to include collective decision making through deliberative communication and debate among the members of the public. "A prerequisite for a well-functioning democracy in this theory is an actively and rationally participating citizenry that has access to a free market-place of ideas and is fed by relevant information and that knows something about the actual issues in the political agenda" (Brants 1998). Beyond the formal-esthetic-rhetorical dimension of public discussion, the nature of such discourse also changed radically. Habermas's distinction between discursive communication and instrumental or strategic communication can help in describing what happened.

Habermas's model sees democratic debate as a rational dialogue between people relating to each other as subjects equal in value and status, trying together to reach agreement and understanding concerning the best possible conclusion. It may be argued that the domination of media logic over politics removed the political discourse from the Habermas ideal of rational discourse. The political discourse of mediapolitik is of a totally different kind: instrumental, or strategic. It is a discourse of force, in which each side relates to the other as an object, uses manipulation to persuade or coerce him or her to accept the attitude rejected at the beginning of the discourse.[2]

According to Habermas, the domination by individuals' egoistic interests, or states' aggressive ideas, over the public sphere that developed in the modern era, the era of rationality, has robbed this sphere of its meaning, destroyed its character as a free autonomous space, which is a necessary condition for the existence of rational, reasoned, and pertinent debate on the alternatives for achieving the highest social aims. The public sphere turns into public space. And while in the public sphere one exchanges ideas, in the public space one exchanges blows.

This new discourse was largely created by the media, which seek to draw the attention of media consumers and raise media consumption. Instead of encouraging rational argumentation, they deal with passionate emotional debate. Instead of showing the complexity of the issues, they present a pattern of two protagonists, and instead of trying to reach a solution, they stir up the debate for the purpose of show and leave it open. The program *Popolitika* became a symbol of the political culture and media culture of the 1990s in Israel for good reason: it is a symbolic synthesis of the two spheres, media and politics.

To sum up, in addition to causing severe damage to the quality of the public debate and public discourse, media-centered politics has many other defects that stem from its very nature, which obstruct its achievement of the goals of democratic theory. One salient defect of the new politics is that its major practices lead to de-institutionalization of the entire realm of politics. It is in this element of the new politics — whereby people speak of what they see — that presentation replaces representation, and the media serve as the main mechanism of contact between the various political agents. This is a mercurial system that encourages volatility of the electorate. Without the ability for ongoing aggregation and articulation of interests, there is a lack of political loyalty grounded in a deep social basis, as well as a decline in both political leaders' ability to navigate and the overall damage to political stability (Galnoor 1998: 197). In sum, the political field has become much more fragmented than in the past.

The system's fluidity also leads to the creation of overnight stars, new candidates racing for the top, usually riding on one issue, achieving huge exposure and arousing high hopes, only to disappear as quickly as they appeared. This is also the reason why in most countries where this system of government has taken root in recent years the public tendency is to change the incumbent party or candidate rather than to support them (Castells 1997: 348).

The question is: What do these radical changes mean for the nature and the stability of the entire political body? How will the representative political system — on which every democratic government is based — function effectively? Who will do the job of aggregating increasingly segmented, individualized political demands and channel them into coherent, legitimate public policies? And what will guarantee the stability of this fluid system? This situation is particularly difficult because of the media's negative influence on the parties, which since the birth of modern democracy have formed the basis for the stability of this sensitive political structure. "Political parties created democracy and modern democracy is unthinkable save in terms of parties," as theoreticians of democracy have repeated often since the days of Alexis de Tocqueville. And as yet, no better mechanism has been found which both allows for changes of government and permits "the largest possible part of the population to influence major decisions by choosing among contenders for political office" (Lipset 2000).

The weakness of the new political system stems from the fact that the press is not suitable to serve as a tool of government. It was never meant for this purpose. The news may indeed raise issues for public discussion that lead to decisions, but it is not the best route to public policy. The news only reflects a small portion of the entire range of important social problems. Certain issues often reach the news columns because of the constraints and needs of the market-driven news organizations, and not because they are issues relevant to public policy. The range of news coverage is narrow and insufficient for gaining political insight, particularly into international affairs (Graber 1996). And television is deceitful in general (Graber 2001: 82–86). The visual imagery unavoidably alters the spatial and temporal dimensions of reality, creating mediated versions of people, places, and events that are fundamentally different from unmediated experience (Griffin 1992: 121–41).[3] "The media provide a narrow and biased version of political reality" and in fact harm the relations between the public and the political leadership and institutions (Patterson 2000: 264). There are even some who argue that television harms politics in that its close look at the leaders is apt "to destroy the majesty and mystery of government" (Hart 1987).

Finally, another serious problem of media-centered democracy is that the media, the new component in the government system, have, in fact, no responsibility (Mazzoleni 1995: 315). Democratic theory has devoted a great deal of thought to ensuring the responsibility of the institutions of government toward the citizens. Separation of power, the rule of law, mechanisms of checks and balances, federal or consociational arrangements, even freedom of the press itself — all of these and other principles are designed to safeguard against the abuse of power by elected officials. In a media-centered democracy the media acquire the ability to share in government without there being any effective means of control over them. Except in the case of their breaking the law, there are no real public sanctions that can be used systematically against the behavior of the media.

Journalists, by contrast, are fond of arguing that the reverse is true, that there is more control over them than over elected representatives. "The politicians," they say, "run for election once every few years, while we do so every day." However, there is a demagogic element in this argument. It is rare for consumers to embargo a news organization. Public consumption patterns are affected not by the extent to which the media function to fulfill democratic ideals and values, but by the extent to which they supply the consumers with the commercial product they seek. This is a commodities market, not a market of democratic values.

THE SHIFT TO POLITICS OF IDENTITY
AND RECOGNITION

Another significant social process occurred that shaped Israeli politics at the end of the twentieth century. Since the 1950s, Israeli society has been divided along five major cleavages: nationally, between Jews and non-Jews, or Palestinians; ethnically, between Ashkenazim and Mizrahim; religiously, between religious and secular Jews; politically, between the Right ("the national camp") and the Left (the "peace camp"); and economically, between the haves and have-nots. The relative prominence of each of these cleavages has changed over the years, and with them the Israelis' subjective sense of the political system's ability to regulate them (Smooha 1993).

Globalization, the technological revolution, and the transformation to an information society added a new cleavage: the divide between the wired and the unwired. The crisis of democracy and the inability of the political body to contain and manage the old conflicts, further deepened with the formation of the new cleavage, the digital divide.

During the course of the 1990s, the Israeli economy underwent a process of restructuring, marked by unequal development of the new and the old economies. High-tech industry leaped forward in a very short period, with 100,000 workers, comprising about 5 percent of the workforce, manufacturing 25 percent of Israel's exports, and the export of high-tech rose four times higher than low-tech exports (Kop 2000). This economic growth led to the fact that the International Monetary Fund for the first time included Israel in the club of industrialized states.[4] In 2000, the gross domestic product per capita was approximately $17,000, and Israel was eighteenth in the world in the globalization index.[5]

Globalization, however, has far-reaching implications for the social structure and results in growing social polarization between the rich and poor, on both an international and a national level. In Israel, a small but powerful social class has developed, connected to the new information economies. These were company directors who began to receive huge salaries or senior employees in high-tech industries and in the financial markets. One example of this phenomenon was the dramatic rise in the salaries of senior management in the business sector — the 530 companies trading on the Tel Aviv stock market. In 1994, this figure was thirteen times higher than the average wage, while in 1999 it was twenty-nine times higher.

Below this group of senior directors, whose wage level is higher than that of their counterparts in the United Kingdom, Japan, or Germany, there are media people and professionals, celebrities in all star-studded walks of life, popular music, sports, and entertainment. This class enjoys real economic advantages. It has developed life patterns shared by what Ralf Dahrendorf has defined as the "global class" (2000). It travels abroad very often, surfs the Internet, reads the *International Herald Tribune*, watches CNN, and buys books on Amazon.com. It subscribes to the "third way" worldview and shares similar patterns of cultural consumption. Dahrendorf estimates that the new "global class" comprises 1 percent of the population, but in Israel one may assume that it includes a larger part of the top decile (Israel's top centile includes 25,000 families).

Compared with this class, the accelerated economic development left behind broad strata of society that were not partners to globalization processes and were even hurt by them. The growth of high-tech industry severely hurt more traditional economic sectors in Israel, and in the course of the 1990s factories, mostly textile plants, closed down one after the other. Furthermore, other industries such as carpentry and agriculture that had been established in the 1950s in development areas in the North and South in order to provide employment for masses of unskilled immigrants also suffered. The poor stratum in Israel grew throughout the 1990s, and by the end of the decade included 210,000 families, comprising more than 1 million people (1.6 million in 2000), one-sixth of the population. The poverty line is defined as a level of income equal to 50 percent of the median available income, that is, half of the income level that is below what half of the population earns. The average income of poor families in Israel was 26 percent below the poverty line in 1998 (Kop 2000).

Unemployment rose from 4 percent in the 1980s to more than 8 percent in the late 1990s, while unemployment in the development towns (towns established in the 1950s to accommodate new immigrants) reached a whopping 20 percent, reflecting the chronic crisis in this sector. The shrinkage of the national welfare mechanisms aggravated this situation and led to a further growth of poverty. Without massive help from the state, the percentage of families living below the poverty line would be 35 percent, and it is only this intervention, through income supplements, that brings it down to 16 percent.

As opposed to the improvement in the two top deciles of the national income (a 4.4 percent rise in the top decile, and 0.6 percent in the second), the situation of all the other deciles deteriorated. As a result, Israel, which had been one of the most egalitarian societies in the West, rose quickly in the scale of inequality in income. In 1988 the top decile earned 8.6 times as much as the lowest decile. Exactly ten years later, it received 11.8 times more. According to the Gini index, which measures the level of inequality in income, the level of inequality when the state was established was 0.284, which rose to 0.43 in 1980, and reached 0.51 in 1998.[6]

The poor class in Israel includes many families who were there in the past, with an overrepresentation of old people, ultraorthodox who are not in the labor market because they study in religious colleges, and Israeli Palestinians. The high birthrate of the two latter groups adds to their poverty levels. In the 1990s, however, many new families joined the ranks of the poor, and many others, even if they did not fall below the poverty line, experienced negative mobility and a drop in social status. Added to these was a large group of immigrants. Within an extremely short period — about ten years — close to one million immigrants arrived in Israel from the former Soviet Union, approximately one-fifth of the local population.

Many members of this new group experienced the cultural and economic shocks of migration and suffered status incongruency — unemployed academics and professionals who had to work as laborers in primary or service occupations. The picture, previously unfamiliar in Israel, was of immigrants with advanced degrees working as street sweepers and of accomplished musicians playing in the streets. All of these changes led to an accelerated mobility of many people — both upward and downward — and created status anxiety for a broad stratum of the populace.

The social groups most affected by the shock sought an alternative to their inferior situation. They expressed protest against the existing social order and the groups that benefited from it. They rebelled against the dominant concept of Israeliness and against the hegemonic status of the groups that constructed it. This protest acquired two salient expressions, the first of which was these groups' attitude toward the peace process. The new class, acting as it does beyond the boundaries of states and nations, in Israel became a natural and ardent supporter of the peace process, which it saw as part of Israel's integration into the international system. Since the 1990s the political elite, headed by Rabin and Peres, estimated that the peace process would improve Israel's overall economic situation and thus help all strata of society. Therefore, they believed that the lower social levels would also back the peace process. There was thus great surprise when it emerged that the opposite was true. After Rabin's assassination, when these classes ended up supporting Netanyahu's policies, the strength of the connection between low socioeconomic status and opposition to the peace process was fully revealed.[7]

The second expression of the protest had deeper structural significance. The new political system, media-centered democracy, was perceived by the disadvantaged as benefiting the ruling classes and especially the economic, political, and media elite. The sense of deprivation and exclusion led to the "revolt of the periphery against the State of Israel" (Ben Ami 1998), a revolt that was formulated in the terms and language of the politics of identity. "Identity is a process of construction of meaning based on cultural attributes, or related sets of attributes, that are given priority over other sources of meaning. Identities are sources of meaning for the actors themselves, and by themselves, constructed through a process of individuation" (Castells 1997: 6; based on Giddens 1991). The collective identities that were constructed toward the end of the century were of the type that Castells calls "identities of resistance." These are the identities that arise out of a sense of alienation, on the one hand, and resentment against unfair exclusion, whether political, economic, or social, on the other. The reaction of the victims of globalization to their condition was to formulate an alternative to the new order: identity groups of resistance that formed around communes or communities.

The bases of this collective identity were different from the bases of identity in the past. The politics that had prevailed in Israel since its formative years, the 1920s and 1930s, was "politics of status," that is, politics "in which parties and political groups care for the material interests of groups in the population" (Shapiro 1989: 13). The nature of the Zionist project — the leadership of a national movement that implemented a campaign of mass immigration and construction of a new society — resulted in the fact that politics (namely, power, rather than money or social prestige) was the predominant field from the start. This society was organized by political entrepreneurs who headed political organizations and fought over the allocation of the dominant resource of this society: power.

The centralized character of the new social system, the dominance of the social-democratic ideology, and life in a physically and politically hostile environment, all strengthened the dependence of the various social fields, including the economic one, on the political field and increased the dependence of the periphery on the decisions of the politicians at the center. Absolute politics was what dictated the rules of behavior in most areas of social activity. Whoever controlled the resources of power determined the distribution of the other resources — money and status.

The processes that occurred in the 1980s and 1990s, above all globalization, eroded the predominance of the political resource. In the politics of identity, loyalty and political identity are not based on class or on an ideology whose basis is the power relations between classes, but rather on identification with cultural groups based on other factors, such as ethnicity, religion, or gender. These are cultural groups characterized by a common lifestyle. The process of constituting these identities naturally has political and economic aspects, but it is important to see that this is fundamentally a cultural phenomenon. In the politics of identity, unlike the politics of status, the dominant resource is not political power but prestige. The conflict centers around the individual or group's social status.

Indeed, the groups that pursue the "politics of identity" are first and foremost groups located on the low rungs of the social ladder seeking to improve their status; "minority groups," Diaspora groups, or subversive groups. It is also no coincidence that in the past groups demanded senior social status in recognition of their achievements and successes and used their contributions to society as a legitimate support for their demands. This is what the Labor movement did by virtue of its contribution to agriculture through the kibbutzim and later to security. Now, in the era of politics of identity and recognition, the demand for enlarged social rewards and improved status is justified by its references to past discrimination.

Whereas the "politics of status" operated within the political order and its dominant resource was power, "politics of identity" operates in the symbolic-cultural order, and the major resource in this order is status. Thus we can see the reasons behind the identity groups' battle against exclusion and their struggle to raise the prestige and status of their way of life.

Status, respect, and prestige are all symbolic in essence. The politics of status emanates less from the motivation to satisfy basically economic interests, or from psychological expressivism, that is to say, it is not behavior designed solely to release emotions. Status politics, which strives for prestige, is essentially semiotic action, playing with symbols (Gusfield 1963). That is why it suits the era of television-centered politics, in which the symbolic dimension is salient. Television reality by its very nature is a set of signs and symbols, the reality of representation.

There is an interesting conjunction in the Israel of the 1990s. Media-centered democracy emerged concurrently with the transformation from the politics of status to the politics of identity. Both in media-centered democracy and in the politics of identity, the symbolic dimension, that dimension in which the media and particularly television play such a decisive role, is of the greatest importance. Thus, the politics of identity assisted the media, and the media, in turn, helped and encouraged the politics of identity. These developments can be witnessed in the two new social trends that were sweeping across Israeli society during that time — populism and communitarianism.

THE POPULIST
AND COMMUNITARIANIST ALTERNATIVES

The shift from party politics to the new mediapolitik did not harm the old elites. They utilized their economic advantages; they held on to positions of power in the new political-media complex; they still controlled the mechanisms of symbolization and representation and remained the "gate-keepers" of the national culture. The peripheral groups, meanwhile, remained excluded from decision-making loci and living with a sense of detachment and alienation from the new system. They sought political frameworks in which to integrate, express themselves, attain legitimacy, and influence the formation of the symbolic social order.[8] They found this possibility in two alternative options: neopopulism on the one hand, and communitarianism on the other.

Despite the fact that the Israeli political system was highly institution-alized from its formative years and was characterized as the politics of status with apparatus parties, populist trends also existed. Populism could be found mainly in the Herut Party and was largely due to the lead-ership style of Menachem Begin, the party's founder. Begin preferred not to create a party with an established apparatus, but rather to build Herut around his personal leadership and the direct link he cultivated with the masses. Every attempt to institutionalize party bodies was regarded by Begin as a threat to his special personal status and as an attempt to secure a share of political power. He therefore fought these initiatives and did not hesitate to dismiss their "perpetrators" from their positions and even expel them from the movement. In this way he was able to maintain a "leader's party."

When the State of Israel was established, Herut began as a small party of European immigrants. Its historical success resulted from Begin's pro-found understanding that he could create an alternative to Mapai only by establishing an antihegemonic group that would aggregate the strata not happy with the existing social order. He succeeded in drawing to his party the Mizrahim, residents of peripheral communities, who were on the lower rungs of the social ladder. They had immigrated to Israel in the 1950s, and by the mid-1960s they were beginning to break free of their dependence on the establishment that had absorbed them. At the end of that decade, they finally supported Begin and his party en masse. The realignment process was swift: in the 1969 elections, for every two Mizrahim who voted for Labor, one voted for the Likud. In the 1974 elec-tions the rate was one to one, and four years later the rate was reversed — two voted Likud for every one who voted Labor.

Begin's party possessed many of the features of populist movements, beyond the external style, the leader's rhetoric, and the method of politi-cal recruitment. There were mass rallies in city squares, including a motor-cycle cavalcade in 1953 that drew criticism for its fascist overtones. Begin's populism was based on integral nationalism mixed with a close link to religious tradition, and fostered collective memory fed by ancient histori-cal myths ("the whole world is against us," or "we are the few against the many") so aptly described by Nurith Gertz (1995). He revealed many of the classic characteristics of populist outlooks: he extolled the nation and the lower classes, which were authentic and expressed the spirit of the nation — its culture and tradition. He emphasized the direct link between the leader and the nation. He attacked the ruling elites and their treacher-ous connections with elements external to the collective (gentiles, Western culture, the international community, and so forth).

Begin understood that he could not compete with Mapai's ability, as the party that controlled the political economy, to grant material resources to the masses. However, with his sharp political intuition he understood what his supporters from the lower classes, the Mizrahim living under the domination of the Ashkenazi culture, really wanted. They wanted inclusion; they wanted to be partners in setting the social agenda; they wanted prestige; they were hungry for recognition. They felt that they were worthy of respect just like the mainstream groups. This non-material resource can be supplied in unlimited amounts, even by those who have no control of material resources. Indeed, Begin knew better than any other political leader how to exploit the symbolic dimension of the politics of identity.

The key word that summed up all these demands was respect. This word was reiterated constantly as the Mizrahi consciousness began to rise in the early 1970s, after the War of Attrition. The first to bring this matter to the public awareness were the "Black Panthers," young people of Mizrahi origin living in the slums of big cities. The concept "respect" then took root in the politics of identity after Begin's election victory in 1977, and even more so after the elections of 1981, when the Mizrahi ethnic rhetoric reached a peak, as can be seen in the political slogans of the 1980s and afterward.

The first abortive attempt at organization on a Mizrahi ethnic basis was that of young people from the NRP (National Religious Party), who broke away and established the Tami Party. Its slogan was "Stand Upright." The Shas Party was established in the mid-1980s, rallying to the slogan "Return to Our Former Glory," meaning to restore lost honor to the ultraorthodox Mizrahi cultural group. And when the cultural groups who adored Begin and raised him to power were asked what was his main contribution as prime minister, the usual answer was honor or self-respect. "Begin restored the honor of the Mizrahim." Ten years later, when the first party of immigrants from Russian-speaking countries was established, it also played on the same theme. Yisrael Be'aliya, a party of immigrants from Russia headed by Natan Sharansky, chose as its campaign slogan "Security for Israel — Respect for Immigrants."

The survival of a populist party depends on the existence of a populist leader, and when Begin disappeared from the political scene after the war in Lebanon in 1984, there was a decline in the Likud's populist style. The top level of the party was split between various young pretenders to the throne; thus, the compromise candidate, Yitzhak Shamir, who was a veteran ally of Begin, was elected as leader, even though he was a gray bureaucratic type. Under his leadership, especially during the period of National Unity governments, the major parties, especially the Likud, lost their historical role. Meanwhile, there was a growing dissatisfaction with the social order during this period — disappointment not only with the political leadership but also with the political order itself. There was thus a rapidly growing body of people who could no longer find a warm home in the large parties, and they were ripe for recruitment by a populist leader.

Such a leader appeared at the beginning of the 1990s. Bibi Netanyahu, who returned from the United States in 1989, was a devoted student of media-centered politics and had the appropriate worldview, as well as the neopopulist leadership skills. He had a rare ability to use the mass media, especially television, to consolidate such a movement. The social and political situation was suitable, the mood of his potential followers was ready, and the new leader finally arrived. The dissatisfied classes, the members of the various cultural groups that were far from the center, the rejected, the seekers of identity, recognition, and respect, found a political alternative in the figure of the new movement consolidated by Netanyahu. They united under the flag of this telepopulist leader.

Neopopulism was a convenient solution for the distressed members of the cultural groups outside the old center. It was not, however, the only one. The second solution was communitarianism. With the weakening of the old political structure in the 1990s, the political alliance that Menachem Begin and the Likud had formed with the Mizrahim, and especially with those from North Africa, began to unravel. When the Likud became a catchall party, and later a cartel party, it could no longer meet their needs or give them respect, a sense of belonging, or a home.

Moreover, the fault line of the new split, the digital divide, made many of them feel that the Likud leaders were in fact just like the Labor leaders and belonged to the elite and not to the antihegemonic bloc. As the welfare state shrank and retreated from its role as the supplier of social services, with the two major parties supporting this policy, the need for an alternative home grew. This disaffected population needed a home that would give them what the old parties had given in the past. They needed a party that would provide social services that had been provided by the state in the past, that would mediate between society and the state, that would establish a social order with which they could identify, and that would promote a sense of inclusion, partnership, and belonging. In other words, there was a need for a different type of solution for the purpose of identity building in the new era of late modernity. This solution was communalism.

The construction of collective identities, combining elements of religious fundamentalism and ethnic components, became common toward the end of the twentieth century in various parts of the world, among both Muslims and Christians. It mixed religious tradition with social innovation, creating an "invented tradition," while the name "fundamentalist movements" in fact hid the modern entrepreneurial power of these movements. This solution, which was so successful in other places, including the Middle East, also suited Jews in Israel. It combined a traditional religious lifestyle together with complex and effective mechanisms of social support and presented a clear and harmonious worldview that could give meaning to life, especially to those deprived by the social order. Out of this Shas was born.

The story of Shas is the best illustration of the success of innovative-traditional communalism based on the politics of identity. The party began in the early 1980s, when ultraorthodox Moroccan immigrants, the largest community in the Mizrahi population, split away from the Ashkenazi ultraorthodox. Shas, headed by its leader, Rabbi Ovadia Yosef, entered parliamentary politics in the 1984 elections and won four seats. From then on there was a continuous and intensive process of political recruitment and institutionalization, leading to the steady growth of the new movement. Shas's success stemmed from a special cooperation of the spiritual leadership of Rabbi Ovadia Yosef and the political organizational ability of a group of young politicians headed by a talented political entrepreneur, Arie Deri. Together they built the new ultraorthodox Mizrahi party, at last giving the Mizrahim a home in the sense that the historical parties in Israel had once given.

Shas, indeed, built itself in the style and according to the model by which the Labor Party had operated in the pre-state period. It supplied broad social services to the lower classes who were hurt by the shrinkage of the welfare state and neoliberal policy; promoted an ideology and a cultural order that reflected the spirit of the Mizrahi tradition; organized a social movement, and built a community. The success of Shas resulted in the fact that after the first period, when the emphasis was placed on the religious dimension, it also began to attract Mizrahim who were not ultraorthodox, who were estranged from the Likud and were attracted to its unique symbols of Jewish Mizrahi identity.

The electoral reform of 1996 that separated the vote for the prime minister and the party, enabled the Mizrahim to support Likud candidate Netanyahu while fostering their separate communal identity under the framework of Shas. Indeed, in the 1999 elections Shas succeeded in replacing the Likud among Mizrahim, religious and secular alike, particularly in the peripheral communities in the south of the country, which had been the traditional province of the Likud since the realignment of Israeli politics in the early 1970s. Beginning its way with four seats in the 1984 elections, Shas grew to six in 1988, and ten in 1996. And in 1999, when seventeen Shas representatives sat in the upholstered seats of the

Knesset chamber, it was now the third-largest party, hot on the heels of the Likud, which had only nineteen seats.[9]

The communal solution also suited another large group in the Israeli society of the 1980s, the new Russian-speaking immigrants. These broke the Zionist tradition that had seen immigration to Israel as a kind of ascent (which is the meaning of *Aliya*, the Hebrew word for immigration to the Holy Land), namely, spiritual and moral elevation. They, instead, saw themselves as emigrants who had come to Israel mainly in order to escape from the old world. They were highly critical of Israeli society and culture and refused to turn their backs on their past, as immigrants were supposed to do according to the old Zionist ideology of the "melting pot." They resisted being assimilated into the new society and insisted on joining it as equals, while fostering a "hybrid identity," namely, preserving the Russian component of their cultural identity, as well as adopting many elements of the new Israeli identity. The immensity of this body of immigrants brought an end to the melting-pot approach that had dominated Israeli society until the end of the 1990s, making room for an alternative approach, for a certain kind of multiculturalism (Sikron and Leshem 1999).

The Russian immigrants first achieved parliamentary representation following the 1996 elections. Contrary to the assessments that this would be a short and ephemeral phenomenon, the political organization of the immigrants from the former Soviet Union grew stronger and enjoyed considerable success in the municipal elections of 1998. One year later, there were already two parties of Russian-speaking immigrants in the Knesset. The process of political establishment and institutionalization continued to gather strength.

The fact that contemporary democracies have become media-centered has drawn attention, including research attention, to the national media. However, to many cultural groups the national media is part of the problem; they reflect the social order to which these groups are antagonized. Their detachment from the national media is part of their antagonism toward the power structure. It is impossible to understand the overall social, cultural, and political scene without seeing the role played by the separate media of these groups. But before we examine this solution, let us first look more closely at the neopopulist phenomenon.

PART TWO

Netanyahu's Telepopulism

CHAPTER EIGHT

Populism and Neopopulism

THE RETURN OF POPULISM

Contemporary democracies' reactions toward the crisis of democracy and toward the dramatic challenges and conflicting forces operating on them have been extensively described by political and social scientists, and a large body of knowledge about this topic has been accumulated.

Another phenomenon that emerged against the background of this crisis was the emergence of radical right-wing movements, along with the growth of a new brand of populism, labeled "new populism," "neo-populism," or "postpopulism" (Betz and Immerfeld 1998; Taggart 2000). While scholars dealt extensively with these new political movements, "surprisingly the scholarly literature about populism has paid less attention to the contribution of the media, especially the news media, to populism" (Mazzoleni et al. 2003: 2).[1] This was a significant oversight, since the media influenced not only populism's surge but indeed the whole course of its development. There is no more dramatic expression of the fusion of politics and the media than these cases of neopopulism. Thus, the use of a new term "telepopulism" is justified (Taguieff 1995).[2]

The most well-known example of such telepopulism, is that of Silvio Berlusconi in Italy (Mazzoleni 1995; Statham 1996), but there are many others: Carlos Menem in Argentina (De la Torre 1998), Fernando Collor de Mello in Brazil (Porto 2000), Abdala Bucaram in Ecuador, Compadre Palenque in Bolivia (Castells 1997), Alberto Fujimori in Peru (Protzel 1996), and Hugo Chavez in Venezuela. The same phenomenon has appeared, in different forms, among neopopulist leaders in Europe — such as Jean-Marie Le Pen and Bernard Tapie in France and Jörg Haider in Austria — and in other continents. In the United States, Ross Perot's presidential candidacy exhibited some telepopulist traits, but the phenomenon was given its most quintessential expression in Israel, in the form of Benjamin Netanyahu's political career. The Israeli case study is interesting in itself, but it is also important in that it enables us to form general theoretical conclusions regarding telepopulism in contemporary politics.

Populism was explained, mainly by functionalist scholars, as a response to modernization — a mobilization of the masses for involvement in political life by independent organizations and autonomous groups before the people were ready for it (Di Tella 1965). Therefore, populism was of great interest to scholars studying developing societies in the 1960s, who later, when the phenomenon appeared to have faded, lost interest in it. However, toward the end of the twentieth century it reappeared, this time in a new form, and strikingly, in the developed European countries. Neopopulism is "a direct response to the transition from industrial welfare capitalism to post-industrialized capitalism" (Betz 1994). And neopopulist movements propagate "a radical transformation of the socioeconomic and sociocultural status quo," and have as their most important political targets the social welfare system and multicultural drifts in society (Betz and Immerfall 1998: 4).

Habermas probes further in his analysis of the conditions that led to the growth of neopopulism in contemporary societies. In his opinion, populist policy develops against the background of the growing alienation and dichotomy between the state — a remote, abstract, and cold institution — and the immediate environment, the everyday life of the citizens. In Habermas's terms, this is the gap and the contrast between the "world system" and the "lifeworld" (Habermas 1984). Neopopulism thus expresses these strong antistate trends and poses a postmodernist communitarian alternative to the alienation that results from liberal democracy.

Scholars of populism frequently mention the polysemic and elusive, chameleonlike nature of the concept. They agree that "populism is a notoriously vague term" (Canovan 1999; Trautman 1997; Betz and Immerfall 1998). In 1967 it was defined as an ideology, a doctrine, or a movement. There were some who saw it as a mentality, or a political psychology, while others analyzed it as a system of ideas, a number of discrete historical phenomena, or as a product of a certain type of social institution (Stewart 1969: 180).[3] Today, it is variously defined as a movement, a critique, and a discourse (Kazin 1998).[4] Thus, Taguieff (1995) was right in suggesting that one should speak of populism in the plural as populisms and should examine each concrete case individually.

Due to the difficulty in defining populism, scholars chose to classify it according to its different types (see, for example, Canovan 1981). The most popular classification was based on geography, and it is easy to see why. It is not difficult to distinguish between the *Narodnichestvo* of agrarian Russia and the *populismo* of the Argentinean *descamisados*, the "shirtless people," or between the American populism that "leads to the strengthening of democracy" and the populism that sprang up in Europe and caused the collapse of democracy (Urbinati 1998).

In all circumstances populism is "an appeal to 'the people' against both the established structure of power and the dominant ideas and values of society. Populism challenges not only established powers but also elite values" (Canovan 1999: 3). Today, just like forty years ago, the debate is still raging over whether populism is essentially a negative phenomenon, or whether there is positive populism that deserves the support of lovers of justice and progress (Canovan 1999). An analysis of the Israeli case may contribute to this debate.

The terms "populism" and "populist" have become very common in the public discourse since the end of the twentieth century.[5] In many cases, the meaning ascribed to it in Israel is not relevant to our discussion. One use of the term relates to the linguistic aspect, to a popular rhetorical style, adopting a folk style of language. As Kazin said regarding the United States, "Populism is the supposed discourse of ordinary, apolitical Americans" (Kazin 1995: 272).

A phrase that is common in this context is "talking at eye level," meaning speaking to people as equals. A tendency that developed in Israel during the 1990s was to adopt low linguistic registers, even among higher cultural levels. The supporters of this populism see it as a healthy reaction to the stiff, formal language, to speech that is arrogant and condescending, while the critics of linguistic populism see it as "speaking from the gut" or "from the heart," as opposed to rational speech, which is "speaking from the head." The audience that becomes accustomed to this kind of discourse is prompted by emotional stimuli rather than by rational considerations and is therefore apt to be led astray by leaders who use a populist approach, who use cheap rhetoric and demagogy for manipulative purposes.

The second prevalent use of the term "populism" is broader than the linguistic aspect and relates to the change that took place in the balance of power between high culture and mass culture in favor of the latter, with the masses occupying the bastions of power that were traditionally controlled by the cultural elite.[6] For example, Education Minister Yitzhak Levy decided in 1998 to reduce his ministry's subsidy of the Israeli opera and gave it instead to an orchestra that plays the popular music favored by immigrants from North Africa.

Because of the congruence that exists in Israel between class structure and ethnic background, the change in the relative power of the "high" Ashkenazi and the "low" Mizrahi culture is described by the Mizrahim as a positive process of democratization. This process is also supported by a small intellectual group, that makes the postmodernist argument that it is impossible to draw a value-based distinction between "high" and "low" culture. In contrast, the Ashkenazi population, who are the devotees of Western culture, fear that the Mizrahi culture's penetration will lead to devaluation of the mainstream culture and produce Levantinism (the term mostly used in the past), or "Mediterranean culture" (the more politically correct term used today). They thus warn of the dangers of cultural populism.

The third and most dominant aspect of populism in the public discourse today relates to the economic sphere, particularly the competition for the allocation of national resources. Those who advocate limiting state intervention in the economy and cutting the national budget, reducing government debt, and curtailing welfare services are opposed by those who claim to speak in the name of the middle and lower classes. The latter groups call for strengthening the mechanisms of differential allocation in order to increase equality in incomes and, more specifically, in order to increase welfare budgets designed for low-income groups and the needy. This school of thought is described in a derogatory manner in Israel as "populist."

The conflict between these two approaches is evident in the dispute between Ministry of Finance economists and Knesset members with neoliberal views on one hand, and what was called in the 1990s the "social lobby" — the parliamentary representatives of economically depressed, peripheral communities, trade unions, and the lower classes on the other. The former group claims that they speak in the name of economic truths, and that they consider only the general interest. They accuse the latter group of caring only about the particularist interest of narrow groups and "speaking from the gut." By contrast, neo-Marxists and radical intellectuals justify the social lobby in the name of democratic values and oppose the intellectual elite with the argument that what they call "rationalism" is not a neutral, ahistorical essence, but rather "implies a type of thought which is the result of an unending cultural/political struggle" (Filk 1996: 225).

What all these uses of the concept populism have in common is the sense that the term refers to a subversive act of invasion and conquest of the social and cultural systems by the masses, the "street," the "common man," or the "simple people," and their culture and interests. Keren (1996), who analyzed the Israeli society of the 1980s, argued that during that period two opposing cocultures stood face to face: "one of war, the other of peace; a messianic versus a pragmatic culture; one populist, the other rational." One was composed largely of members of the intelligentsia from the Left, and the other of right-wing supporters, "who see themselves as underdogs and on the outside looking in." According to

Keren, the intense need to counterbalance the growing strength of populism and the "politics of the street" was what led National Unity Prime Minister Shimon Peres to take the intellectual elite under his wing — scientists and technocrats, the intelligentsia, academics, and professional managers in the public and private sectors. The positive influence of this group was one of the secrets of Peres's success as prime minister during that crisis period, argued Keren (1996: 9).

In contrast to these prevalent uses of the term populism, I wish to emphasize here the political meaning of the phenomenon. Populism is a model of direct democracy. It is a reaction to the power structure of representative liberal democracy. It speaks in the name of "the people," which is the source of its legitimacy. Populism is based on the axis of leader-people relations, in which the people are the antihegemonic bloc and are perceived as the source of the "good." The leader embodies this good of the nation in his personality; therefore, the intervention of bodies mediating between the people and the leader — such as parliamentary institutions — is perceived as detrimental to this positive link.

Today's neopopulism differs from the old populism. Unlike the old, with its radical or left-wing stances, neopopulism "migrated from Left to Right" (Kazin 1995: 4). It adopts neoliberal economic patterns, which populism opposed in its previous stage (see Urbinati 1998). The old populism regarded banks and capitalists, especially those from abroad, as the enemies of the people, presented them as demons and directed the anger of the masses against them. Today's capitalists and financiers, by contrast, are perceived as allies. "Populism has almost always demanded an expansionary monetary policy" (Wiles 1969) and had an etatist character (De la Torre 1998: 89), while neopopulism believes in a small government and supports the shrinking of the state. It prefers a conservative monetary policy, propagates a radical transformation of the socioeconomic and sociocultural status quo, and has as its most important political targets the social welfare system and multicultural drift in society (Betz 1994: 4).

Indeed, neopopulism revolts against the hegemonic values of the liberal elites in the late democracies, against individualism, liberalism, multiculturalism, and progress. A comprehensive summary of the characteristics of neopopulism was recently done by de la Torre:

Populism is simultaneously a rhetoric and a style of political mobilization. Populist rhetoric radicalizes the emotional element common to all political discourse. It is rhetoric, which contrasts politics as the moral and ethical struggle between *el pueblo* and the oligarchy. The *pueblo* is negatively defined as all who are not the oligarchy. Given their suffering, the *pueblo* is the incarnation of the authentic Nation — the good, the just, and the moral. The *pueblo* confronts the oligarchy, which represents the unauthentic, the foreign, the evil, the unjust, and the immoral.

Populist discourse transmutes politics into a struggle for moral values without accepting compromise or dialogue with the opponent. Populism thus has ambiguous relations to liberal democratic procedures. While it incorporates people previously excluded from the political system, the moralism, personalism, and authoritarianism inherent in populism simultaneously run counter to liberal democratic institutions. [It] rejects parliamentary government and representative institutions on behalf of a democracy of the masses in which the people govern directly. Populist politics are based on crowd action. Crowds directly occupy public spaces to demand political participation and incorporation. At the same time, these crowds are used by their leaders to intimidate adversaries. Mass meetings become political dramas where people feel themselves to be true participants in the political scene.

The continuing inability of liberal democratic institutions to provide a sense of participation and belonging to the political community have contrasted with symbolic political participation through populist, non-parliamentary politics. The main legacy of populism, then, has been to create a style of political mobilization and a rhetoric that links the state and civil society through mechanisms that do not correspond to the rule of law or to respect for liberal democratic procedures. (De la Torre 1998: 88–89)

The one behind the neopopulist movement, the one who practices this style of political mobilization, is the leader, whose role and status are critical to the very existence of the movement. He expresses the nation and embodies its spirit, he represents all that is good and beautiful in the nation; therefore, he is qualified to maintain a more autocratic system of government than liberal democracy.

What makes contemporary neopopulism telepopulism is, as the term indicates, the new role that the media have taken on in modern politics. Thus, telepopulism is the neopopulist form in media-saturated societies. It is the political system in which the media, and particularly television, are the major forum for contacts between the leader and the nation. It is the principal tool used by the leader for political mobilization, creating and promoting the masses' identification with the leader. Therefore, communication skills are a sine qua non for leadership in this system. Just as charisma was essential for the old populist, the telepopulist leader must excel in telegenic qualities.

Extensive use of the media, particularly television, characterizes all contemporary political regimes. In telepopulism, however, the media is even more important because it serves as the major mediating body between the public and the political leadership. In modern societies, television replaces the public gathering in city squares. In the not-too-distant past, it was radio that enabled the authoritarian leader to establish a direct link with the public, while minimizing the importance of the parliament. Fascist leaders also used to spectacularize politics, expressing the direct link between the leader and the nation through spectacles and events with a conspicuous symbolic dimension.

The role previously played by radio for authoritarian leaders is now performed for neopopulist leaders by television. However, the addition of visuality and movement magnify the power of television immensely. This is what Statham (1996) calls "televisual populism." Thus, it is clear why it is so important for the populist leader to solidify his control of media outlets. Without power over this tool, he cannot maintain his political hold. This control can be acquired through private ownership (as in the case of Berlusconi), control in the name of the state (as with Collor), or by virtue of the admired leader's personal skill and status (for example, Compadre Palenque). All of them, however, share a deep understanding of media logic, that is, a knack for using the media and manipulating them for political ends.

There is also another reason for the importance of the media in tele-populist regimes. The populist fervor against the status quo is in fact directed at two groups: the politicians, who represent the political order; and the cultural elite, who represent the symbolic order. In contemporary society, media personalities are a central part of the second elite. They are the ones who give meaning to things, determine the symbolic order of society, and shape its outlook. Hence, it is not hard to understand why members of radical and populist movements voice such strong criticism, hatred, protest, and disgust at those who control the means of representation, the mass media and particularly the elite media.

Ironically, this very media culture also encourages populist trends. The appeal to, and in the name of, the common (wo)man; the engagement of emotions; the professed anti-intellectualism; the promotion of a popular culture and popular discourse: all serve to link the cultural and political phenomena. Media organizations are putting more stress on the accessibility of the language in which the news is written and on covering issues that matter most to people. The voiced opinions of men and women in the street are being taped more often than in the past (Blumler and Kavanagh 1999), and the more people rely on television for political knowledge, the more they are influenced by their populist approach (Mazzoleni and Schultz 1999).

In the case of Alberto Fujimori in Peru, "The language and the decision-making system of television fit the requirements of the antiparty ideology deployed by the neopopulist government" (Protzel 1996: 90). In Brazil of the 1990s the telenovella had a direct influence on political actions because these programs "blurred the lines between fiction and reality, becoming a central stage on which the national identity was negotiated" (Porto 2001).

We can thus conclude that telepopulism is a political system in which an authoritarian leader heads a neopopulist movement, either in opposition or government, using mass-communication outlets, particularly television, as a major tool for political mobilization and legitimization of his rule. The internal logic of the telepopulist method requires the leader to strive for hegemonic status vis-à-vis the national media, if not exclusive control of them. Neopopulism developed because of structural factors in the political system, changes in the economic and social environment, as well as ideological and other changes. However, it is clear that political communication and television culture were among the most important factors that shaped this new political phenomenon.

Just as television did not create video malaise but strengthened it considerably, it did not create telepopulism. However, it was television culture that, among other things, increased people's preoccupation with stylishness, image, presentation, and appropriate tastes, encouraged closer association of politics with popular culture, and fostered and encouraged populist trends. All these were combined with the antihegemonic bloc's political tendencies for ethnocentricity, xenophobia, and conservatism, and were exploited by mediagenic and manipulative political leaders, thus generating an integrated process that caused the phenomenon to become so widespread. The combination of tabloid television, sports, pop culture, and the cluster of values of the radical Right, makes Berlusconi's case particularly close to the ideal type of this political pattern (Mazzoleni 2003), but there were other similar cases as well.

BEGIN'S POPULISM

The sources of populism in Israel were first presented by sociologist Yonathan Shapiro, who correctly discerned the rise in populism as an expression of the weakening of the party mechanism, especially the dominant Mapai (Labor) Party. However, Shapiro (1989) erred in his overall analysis, particularly with regard to his perception of Israeli populism as belonging to the category that Canovan defined as "populism of politicians" (1981). It was thus that Shapiro related to Rafi leaders, headed by Shimon Peres and Moshe Dayan, who took advantage of the military crisis with Egypt preceding the Six-Day War in May 1967 to turn public opinion against the Eshkol government and in favor of going to war and bringing them (Peres and Dayan) into the government. Although it was true that Rafi leaders incited public opinion and enlisted the support of their friends in the media, this does not justify the definition of their activities as populist. First, not every mobilization of public support outside of the party structure is an expression of populism. Second, the main thrust of the Rafi leaders' activity was actually carried out within the bureaucratic political institutions.

Shapiro's error is compounded in his analysis of the populism of Herut and its leader, Menachem Begin. Herut under Begin's leadership was the closest case to populism in Israel. Whereas Mapai was the classic model of the party of the masses, an organized bureaucratic party with a strong, efficient apparatus, Herut was the model of a leader's party. Herut had no permanent apparatus, was clearly dominated by a powerful leader maintaining direct contacts with the members, had either very weak decision-making party institutions or the facade of such institutions, which merely carried out the wishes of the leader. Herut (which later became the Likud when it joined with the Liberal Party in 1965) expressed populist tendencies, and Begin was its populist leader.

As a skilled orator who knew how to use demagogy, who radiated charisma and could stir up the masses in the city squares, Begin nurtured the ideology of integral nationalism. He succeeded in mobilizing the masses by building an antihegemonic bloc that included the lower classes, the disadvantaged, the disenfranchised who felt alienated from the centers of power, as well as an elite group that aided him in leading the party. As with other cases of populism, the structure created by Begin continued to exist after he and his party rose to power in 1977. Even then, he did not develop a strong party apparatus or encourage party and parliamentary activity. The Likud bodies did not meet to set policy or guide their representatives in the government, and their parliamentary faction had little influence, either in guiding the government or in monitoring its activities. "The Likud," wrote the *Haaretz* parliamentary correspondent, "just like the government, shows its presence *through* public relations and feeding the journalists information that is window-dressing, because it presumes to show activity where none exists."[7]

Shapiro was right in describing Begin's demagogic rhetoric, but he was mistaken in explaining Begin's populism as pure manipulation and deception of the masses. Shapiro's analysis of populist politics as emotional and irrational, as opposed to party politics that judges policy by rational considerations, was what led him to the conclusion that the masses were deluded by the leader out of a false collective consciousness and failure to understand their own interests.

As a liberal elitist, Shapiro had difficulty viewing populism from the standpoint of the masses; therefore, he saw only the demagogic, manipulative dimension of the leader. If he had examined it from the other side, he would have seen that the lower strata preferred the populist system as a strategy for attaining their real needs. In this spirit, Laclau interpreted the populist movement of Latin America as a process of hegemonic rebalancing within the power bloc that was attained through the incorporation of the popular-democratic ideology of the masses (Laclau 1977). This explanation of populism also appears in other places. Even in the United States, for example, Kazin considers populism as the democratic expression of political life that is needed to rebalance the distribution of political power for the benefit of the majority (Kazin 1995).[8]

The theoretical contributions of Ernesto Laclau and Peter Rannis are helpful in discussing the Israeli case. Laclau's contribution is the important distinction of the axis: the power bloc versus the people. Despite his Marxist origins, Laclau sees the dominant polarization in the social-democratic formation not as being between classes, but between the ruling power bloc and the rest of the people, who have no access to positions of power. These constitute popular-democratic subjects as an opposing entity to the dominant ideology. They organize as a counterhegemonic bloc, which includes both opposing elite groups and broader groups whose social bases are not necessarily related to class. The common denominator of these groups is a sense of exclusion from the political game. From this point of view, it is hard to ignore the emancipatory nature of populism, and thus its democratic character. In fact, populism introduces groups who were previously forbidden entry into the political game (Laclau 1977).

Rannis examines the nature of the answers that populism supplies. In analyzing Peronism in Argentina, he claims that the Peronist movement represented a populist ideal that used Marxist terminology in a nonsocialist context. In contrast to the class consciousness of the Marxists and the individualistic consciousness of the liberals, Peron's populism offered an alternative, communitarian consciousness, through which the working class achieved both social status and access to political power it had hitherto been denied (Rannis 1992).

Nevertheless, there are substantial differences between Argentine and Israeli societies. The hegemonic ethos of the power bloc in Israel was essentially social-democratic. Over the years, this ethos eroded and was replaced by neoliberalism, which became the new ethos shared by center-Right and center-Left, the labor movement, and particularly the new class.

Instead of the social democratic ethos, which had sought to build social solidarity on a class basis, and the liberal ethos, which had tried to create social integration based on individualism, Begin offered the social groups that had been excluded from the political game a third option: national populism. This is what Rannis calls "social communitarian consciousness," a worldview of integral nationalism, which defines itself by sharp differentiation from the outside world and especially from the Arab enemy and sees the entire nation as one cohesive unit. The leader, who embodies the nation's unity and is directly linked to it, is the central element in this worldview.

Begin's brand of populism confronted the power-bloc with a counter-hegemonic coalition of the rejected that advocates a different social order. This was similar to European populism, in that it was not a strategy of the Left. Indeed, "the emergence of populism is coincident with the very decline of the Left, of its party organizations and the prominent role of intellectuals" (Urbinati 1995: 114).

Given the high level of democratic participation in Israel, populism was not expected to bring with it increased participation in the formal democratic process, as in Latin America, where there was an absence of basic civil, political, and social rights. Thus, in Argentina, for example, populism gave women the right to vote. In Israel, the inclusion of the marginalized classes was expressed not in a change in formal participation in elections, but rather in participation in decision-making concerning the symbolic social order. The symbolic expressions of participation were more important than the concrete ones; the images and consciousness were more important than the empirical facts.

In contrast with the Labor Party leaders, who were trained in "creating facts on the ground," Begin was a master of symbolic politics, an art that he had perfected during his many years in opposition. Using symbolic practices, he attempted to "restore the lost honor" to the classes that felt distanced, deprived, and diminished. However, he did not effect a real structural change in Israeli society, and no transformation occurred in the composition of the social and cultural elites. Furthermore, after his resignation, the hub of the populist alignment disappeared, just when the formal political body was undergoing processes of erosion and the populist potential was growing.

After Begin's resignation, the populist potential still remained in Herut, but the leadership that followed him and the internal struggles in the upper echelons of the party blurred this pattern. Yitzhak Shamir, who succeeded Begin, was a compromise candidate and lacked any kind of charisma. However, this fact did not eliminate the populist trends in Israeli culture. On the contrary, they gathered strength. What was needed in order to fulfill this populist potential was a leader, a telegenic tribune, of the new, telepopulist breed. In the Histadrut elections of 1994, this figure appeared in the person of the young Knesset member Haim Ramon.

Ramon belonged to the "octet," a group of eight members of the Labor Party who were more dovish than the rest of the party. In 1994 he left the Labor Party to run for the leadership of the Histadrut (the Trade Union Federation), which had been controlled until then by a conservative faction within the Labor Party. Ramon established an independent list of supporters and formed a coalition with groups outside this list.

Without party machinery but with very effective use of the media, particularly television and clamorous billboards, he won the street.

Ramon knew how to combine populist rhetoric and tactics, such as his slogan which in fact said nothing: "Ramon: New Life in the Histadrut" (his first name, Haim, means life in Hebrew), and a negative campaign, together with populist contents. Through his personal charisma, rhetorical skills, telegenic qualities, and manipulation of slogans and images, Ramon succeeded in ousting the old Labor Party leadership from the Histadrut. He was particularly popular with young journalists, many of whom could identify with "the young maverick running against the corrupt establishment." The old Labor leadership had continued to behave according to the "iron rule of oligarchy," conducting an election campaign of the old type with an utter lack of talent. They failed completely to understand that the old political system had collapsed and that a new one had arisen in its place (Peri 1996).

Ramon's success and the amorphous movement that he had established revealed a telepopulist working style of action and showed what a charismatic leader could do when he understood media logic and the new game rules. However, this phenomenon was short-lived. Ramon himself lacked the patience to nurture the movement. Less than two years later he resigned from his position as chairman of the Histadrut and returned to the bosom of his mother party. The potential for telepopulism had to wait for a leader who would know how to nurture it and ride on it. The time was ripe for Benjamin Netanyahu.

THE PERES – NETANYAHU DEBATE: THE NEW ERA BEGINS

The man who expressed more than any other the transition from the old politics to mediapolitik in Israel was Benjamin Netanyahu, who was elected prime minister in 1996, in the first direct elections for prime minister. Born in Israel in 1950, he had spent many years in the United States, where he absorbed the American television political culture that developed during the Reagan period. Netanyahu returned to Israel at a historic moment: the political order was suffering from a legitimacy crisis, latent processes in the various cocultures had ripened, the old political culture was collapsing. The old leaders, however, symbolized by Yitzhak Rabin and Shimon Peres, were unable to decipher the new picture and to digest its meaning. Netanyahu arrived equipped with all of the necessary skills for the new political game, first the contest for leadership of the Likud and then for the premiership.

If there was one event that could symbolically express the victory of the new politics over the old it was the televised debate between Peres, the incumbent prime minister, and Netanyahu, on May 26, 1996. Televised debates of candidates for the premiership have taken place in Israel since 1974, but this was the first that could truly be called a debate. Previously, the heads of the major parties had participated in these confrontations (Peres versus Begin, Peres versus Shamir, Rabin versus Shamir). These were all figures well known to the public, and they had appeared on television hundreds of times between elections. Therefore, the debates had no great significance, especially in a culture where television was not a major political actor.

In 1996, however, this was a new kind of duel. It was the first direct election of the prime minister, in a television-centered political system and a turbulent political atmosphere, a few months after the assassination of Prime Minister Rabin. Netanyahu entered the debate trailing Peres in public opinion polls. He used all of his skills in the debate, and they were not lost on the public. He was assertive, brief, direct, outspoken, incisive, and impressive. Peres looked old, tired, and weary. He expressed himself clumsily, and it was clear that the camera did not like him. In fact, this was the difference between the old politics, which emphasized the verbal message, and the new politics, which recognized the importance of visual imagery. Peres continued the old discursive campaign, based on the spoken and written word, while Netanyahu thought in terms of visual management and effective use of symbols in political communication to persuade his audience. Peres wanted to convince the viewers, but he did not realize what Netanyahu knew so well, that in television culture it is more important to impress them.[9]

Each candidate was allotted ninety seconds to answer each question. Netanyahu spoke more quickly. In the first ten minutes of the debate he uttered 576 words, compared with only 301 words uttered by Peres. Netanyahu was in control of his time, transmitted more messages, and managed to finish all of his answers; Peres got stuck in the middle of a sentence and was cut off by the moderator. Netanyahu also had control of his messages. He came ready with a clear message and used the questions he was asked as a springboard for marketing it, violating the conventional norms that require the answers to be relevant to the questions. In each of his answers he repeated the same message, formulated in simple sound bites, easy to absorb and easy to remember. Peres tied himself up in long, convoluted sentences.

Blum-Kulka and Liebes's analysis (1999) reveals the secret of Netanyahu's victory in the debate. With regard to modes of address, while Peres related to the debate as a press interview, looked at the interviewer, and used the rhetoric of a classic interview, Netanyahu used the debate as an opportunity to address the audience. He looked straight into the camera and spoke directly to the audience ten times, twice as many as Peres. Avoidance of eye contact in televised encounters is interpreted as a sign of dishonesty, whereas a straight look into the eye and camera and firm unhesitating response are interpreted as evidence of honesty (Graber 1984). Peres, who did not want to grant Netanyahu legitimacy as an equal, avoided direct verbal and eye contact with him and talked to the moderator, journalist Dan Margalit. Netanyahu addressed Peres directly no fewer than thirty-four times and referred to him another forty-four times, in a manner that was "systematically highly accusatory and challenging in tone and content" (Blum-Kulka and Liebes 1999).

The difference between the old and the new politics was also expressed in content. Peres spoke a great deal about his government and his party, and when asked personal questions he answered in the plural "we," out of modesty, and focused on policy. Netanyahu devoted his efforts to building his own persona, emphasized the personal dimension, spoke of himself in the first person "I," and used tactics of self-aggrandizement. As Blum-Kulka and Liebes wrote, "The difference in the style of the two candidates may be seen in terms of two major advertising strategies: the 'personalized' format, in which the product is associated with personal qualities, and the appeal to the public is through direct address, and the 'product-information' format, in which experts present argumentative reasons to convince us to purchase the product" (1999: 82). In the televised debate Netanyahu behaved like he did throughout his entire campaign, which was a sharply negative campaign. While Peres maintained a dignified appearance as an incumbent prime minister who was above conflicts, Netanyahu moved like a boxer in the ring, attacking his opponent again and again.

Netanyahu prepared thoroughly for his television appearances. Prior to the debate he took part in a series of simulations, and during the actual event he used many aids. For example, he stuck notes on his podium containing statistical information and reminders of how to behave. The journalists sitting in the studio saw the notes, but the camera did not catch them since it was fixed in one place according to the rules of the debate. Peres came without any real preparation, after a sleepless night. When the two entered the studio and Netanyahu raised the subject of seating, the gentlemanly elder statesman waved his arm and said "choose wherever you want." It later emerged that Netanyahu was determined not to be shot from the angle that showed the scar on his upper lip. He was ready to fight over the question of seating, but Peres concurred so easily without himself or his advisers being aware of the importance of the positions.

It is not surprising that this debate reminded analysts of that historic encounter in 1961 between the grim, perspiring professional politician, Nixon, and the charming telegenic representative of the younger generation, John F. Kennedy.

The result was unequivocal. *Yediot Ahronot* declared Netanyahu winner of the debate and the next morning the paper's senior columnist, Nachum Barnea, wrote "Netanyahu was more convincing." A poll conducted by the paper also found the audience thought that Netanyahu had won. On seeing the headlines, Netanyahu announced to his campaign staff, "We have won the elections" (Caspit et al. 1996). And he was right. His victory in the debate reversed the trend in the opinion polls. Only three days before the elections Netanyahu began to lead in the race.

When he assumed the office of prime minister, it emerged that Netanyahu was not just well versed in election campaigning in the television era, but that he also had a specific concept of government in the new political age. Television acquired a new role, becoming one of the prime minister's major working tools, in a way previously unknown in Israel. For a long period journalists, analysts, and political pundits had difficulty understanding Netanyahu's behavior as prime minister. It seemed strange and incomprehensible. Only after some time did its outlines become clear. It was not just his extreme exposure to the media, much more than any previous prime minister, but mainly the theatrical element in his appearance. His body language appeared somewhat unnatural. He seemed to be deliberately acting on a stage. "There are things about him that I strongly dislike," Nachum Barnea was to write. "The posing. The tendency to act. Once, in a frank conversation with him, I told him that and he answered that one sometimes has to be an actor. And I said yes, [but only] sometimes."[10]

Netanyahu's advantage over other politicians in using and exploiting television, his skill in controlling and using it for his needs, fostered the legend of the "media wizard." But if in his first months in office it seemed as if the television appearances were designed to explain, or complement, his political action, it later appeared that the many press conferences, photo-ops, political spectacles, and media events were designed to replace political action — that they themselves were the political action.

Those in the political community began to refer to Netanyahu's politics as "pseudopolitics" or "virtual politics." In fact, this was not "pseudo" or "virtual" at all: this was mediapolitik in its telepopulist manifestation, whose language, grammar, and logic were unfamiliar to the old actors and even to senior commentators in the media and academic scholars.

NETANYAHU'S PERSONAL
AND TELEVISION POLITICS

Netanyahu first decided to become prime minister when he was serving as public affairs officer at the Israeli embassy in Washington in the early 1980s. He knew that, as an outsider, he could not conquer the traditional loci of power in the Likud. He would be unable to topple his rivals, "the princes," sons of the previous generation of political leaders, who had inherited the aura of ideological torchbearers. Therefore, he aimed to erode their potential power inside the party by weakening the party system itself and taking the struggle out into the street. This was the reason for his ardent support of the initiative to institute direct elections for the premiership, which gathered momentum in the late 1980s and early 1990s.

While still in the United States, he began making thorough preparations for his accession to power by developing those skills that he considered necessary for the task — above all, a mastery of television. He studied how to appear on television, taking lessons with Lily Wielder, the best expert in New York, eventually establishing a reputation for being an expert performer on television. These efforts finally paid off, when Netanyahu was appointed as Israel's permanent representative to the UN. He inherited the role of "Israel's voice in the world" from Abba Eban, the most distinguished Israeli diplomat.

There was, however, a significant difference between the two figures. Abba Eban, who served as ambassador to the UN and United States and as foreign minister, was a European intellectual with broad horizons, a linguistic virtuoso, an orator of the kind that the English upper-class nurtures in the debating societies of Oxbridge. Bibi Netanyahu was a product of the American television culture, a child of the sound bite and CNN generation, with the persuasive powers of a salesman (he actually had worked as a furniture salesman in the past). He spoke in short sentences with middlebrow images familiar to every listener.

Netanyahu's talents as a popular television commentator made him a welcome guest on all of the American TV channels, a favorite of ABC's Ted Koppel and especially CNN's Larry King. He enjoyed a special status among groups of conservative analysts in the American media, such as E. M. Rosental of the *New York Times*, Charles Krauthammer of *Time*, and George Will of the *Washington Post*. He was careful to keep cultivating good contacts with media people when he was deputy foreign minister in Yitzhak Shamir's government. His major contribution in that role, as testified by his patron, former minister Moshe Arens, was less in policy making, and more in speech making.[11]

Netanyahu had learned from American politics that the road to political success required extensive fund-raising in addition to television skills. For this purpose, while serving as ambassador to the UN, he began to weave a web of ties with a group of millionaires, who funded his first campaign for the Likud leadership and helped him after he was elected, enjoying in exchange the proximity of the Israeli prime minister, social status, business rewards, and political influence. Ron Lauder (of Estée Lauder cosmetics), for example, funded Machon Shalem, the first Israeli think tank, modeled on the conservative think tanks established in the United States in the 1970s, and which prepared the ideological ground for neoconservativism (Ricci 1993). During Netanyahu's term in office, Lauder became chairman of the Council of Presidents of Major Jewish Organizations in the United States and even served as Netanyahu's special envoy to Syrian President Hafez el Assad.

As a student of the American political media, Netanyahu was well aware of the importance of the image and the persona for electoral success. As soon as he returned from the United States and entered the Israeli political arena, he started to plan his image-building strategy to create a persona for himself. "His press clipping files testify that Netanyahu saw exposure of his private life as a tool to promote his political image long before he competed (publicly) for the premiership," commented Anat Balint, who researched this period. The use of the leader's private life to build his public image was an innovation introduced by Netanyahu into Israeli politics.[12]

The construction of public-self "personae" in the media is a basic feature of modern consumer societies (Ewen 1988). The personae of politicians in our culture are constructed out of diverse public appearances and out of what is known of the private life of the person. This public self is cultivated and enhanced through practices of salesmanship and image management (Tolson 1996).

The authors of his two political biographies agree that Netanyahu professionally examined, certainly from the end of the 1980s, what personality traits were desirable in a candidate for the premiership in Israel. Then he cultivated these traits. "He used a sophisticated professional research system. Do the people want the figure of a family man? He will supply it. Bibi is a very professionally constructed product," says journalist Ronit Vardi, author of the book, *Bibi — Who Are You, Mr. Prime Minister?*[13]

At first, this emphasis on style and image positioning was alien to the Israeli political culture. For example, Israeli politicians, with the exception of government ministers, tended to dress informally in the summer and even dispensed with suit jackets. Netanyahu, as soon as he was elected leader of the Likud, while still in the opposition, wore a jacket even on hot summer days. In this way he not only placed himself on a par with government ministers but also distinguished himself from the veteran leaders at the head of the Likud. Whenever he appeared together with them he stood out not only for his height and broad shoulders but also for being the only one wearing a jacket.

Netanyahu continued his image maintenance after he was elected as head of the party, refining his image throughout his entire period in office as prime minister. When he left his office, one of his assistants would bring along a makeup kit, in case he happened to find himself near a television camera. Despite his love of cigars, he was careful never to be photographed with one because cigar smoking is perceived as elitist by some of the Israeli public. It was two years before this secret was revealed to the public when a shot of him smoking a cigar appeared in a newspaper. And although his height and broad shoulders gave him an impressive stage presence, Netanyahu made sure that in his public appearances an assistant would place a podium in front of the microphone and quickly remove it before the other speakers got up. This fact, too, was revealed only after three years, by an agile television reporter.[14]

When Netanyahu went on his annual vacation with his children and was photographed with them at the seaside, he was seen wearing a black t-shirt in the water. In Israel men do not go into the sea wearing a shirt, but the effect was dramatic. The picture radiated a masculine, sporting image because it recalled an image that was engraved in the Israeli collective memory. This was the photo of a young officer (who later became major-general) Yossi Ben-Hanan, bathing in the Suez Canal with his clothes on, a picture that became a visual symbol of the great victory in the Six-Day War of 1967. The black shirt both hid Netanyahu's spare tire and created the masculine and fatherly image he wanted to project.

Persona building and image management through television were only one aspect of the new politics: the other was Netanyahu's planned effort to destroy the old bureaucratic party politics. He was assisted in this endeavor by his closest ally, Avigdor Lieberman, an immigrant from Russia living in a settlement in the Judean Desert, who possessed significant organizational and political skills. When Netanyahu was elected as Likud candidate for prime minister, he appointed Lieberman as director-general of the party, and with his help gained control of the party machine. They established a central committee that was absolutely dominated by him, changed the internal constitution in order to strengthen his control (for example, the new constitution prohibited holding additional elections for the party leadership before the Knesset elections), and forestalled the growth of rival loci of power.

After this, Netanyahu began to empty the party organs of content and meaning, systematically ignored them, and used the party's central committee as an arena for carefully planned stylized spectacles. Protest banners were prepared in advance and waved at the appropriate moment, although they were made to appear spontaneous, activists were seated in different parts of the hall to boost outbursts of protest or praise for the correct speakers, rival politicians were shouted down, and the meetings of the central committee became virtual shows.

After forming his cabinet, in which he had to include his political rivals (such as Dan Meridor, "the highest prince"), at the end of 1996 he turned to Lieberman for help in destroying the internal opposition in the party. Together they aimed to weaken the status of ministers and to concentrate power in the prime minister's bureau. It was during this period that he also tried to engineer the dismissal of independent journalists or those identified with the Left in the senior ranks of the Broadcasting Authority.[15] Lieberman's coercive methods and rough style, together with his political views, did not improve his public image. His dummy in the satirical show *Hartzufim* (the Israeli equivalent of *Spitting Image*) portrayed him as a violent Russian bully, dangerous and frightening. The show also poked fun at his criticism of the media, having him announce, "There is a whole group of journalists that should be kicked out." This was part of his attack on the "Left," "the old regime," or "the rule of the elites," and it hardened his antidemocratic image. Following Lieberman's attempts to purge the Broadcasting Authority, *Haaretz* media columnist Ehud Ashri wrote, "Lieberman has shown the ministers and the public his strong-arm, distorted and dishonest working methods that do not match the rules of personal and public integrity."[16]

Criticisms of Lieberman in the media grew increasingly fierce, as Lieberman intensified his attacks on the institutions of Israeli democracy, the state attorney, the Supreme Court, the police, and the parliamentary regime in general. Lieberman's actions, words, and views largely reflected the attitudes of his political partner, Netanyahu. Of the police, for example, he said that they were not clever, acted dishonestly and unfairly, conducted witch-hunts, and persecuted pure and innocent public figures. He cast doubts on their motives, insinuating that they had "political motivation in very dangerous directions." These utterances, coming after he was questioned by the police several times on suspicion of committing various acts, led many, not only his political rivals but also impartial observers, to wonder, how can a director-general of the prime minister's bureau who attacks the very foundations of the regime remain in this role?[17]

When Lieberman became a liability to Netanyahu, the pair agreed that he would resign from his position as director-general of the prime minister's office. He left the Likud, and established a new party, addressing the immigrants from the former Soviet Union with right-wing nationalistic rhetoric and a manifesto resembling the radical right-wing parties in Europe.

The personalistic leadership nature of the telepopulist regime was evident in, among other things, Netanyahu's treatment of the Likud when he formed his government. In the coalition negotiations in 1996 the old Likud leaders discovered that Netanyahu was prepared to give significant government ministries to the coalition partners, the ultraorthodox Shas and the Russian immigrants' Yisrael Be'aliyah, at the expense of the Likud, breaking with the tradition of the past. Throughout his term of office, he severely weakened the party organization, almost paralyzed the internal life of the party, and finally, toward the 1999 elections, even encouraged Lieberman to establish his new party, although it was clear that this would result in a loss of votes for the Likud.

At the end of his term as prime minister, he took the last step that expressed the shift of emphasis from the party to the leader. When he began his election campaign in 1999, he decided that the campaign would focus on the elections for the premiership, ignoring the Knesset elections. Netanyahu conducted the campaign himself, to the great annoyance of the Likud leaders, who suspected that his own success in the elections was much more important to him than the success of the party. As it became increasingly clear in the course of the campaign that Netanyahu was falling behind Barak, there was growing pressure to put the emphasis on the party in order to save it and have at least some representation in the Knesset. But it was too late. Years of the party's systematic weakening led to a double failure in the elections. Netanyahu, who had won 1.5 million votes (50.5 percent) in 1996, now received 1.4 million votes, which was 43.9 percent. Likud got 468,000, which was only 14 percent of the votes, in contrast with the 770,000 votes (25 percent) it had won in 1996.

As prime minister, Netanyahu had attempted to establish a kind of presidential system of government, to concentrate all the power in the office of the prime minister and turn the ministers into "state secretaries." Barring constitutional reform, this is not possible in the Israeli coalitional regime, where ministers are chosen by their own parties and not by the prime minister. This caused a great deal of friction within the government, which became less stable than any previous government. There were constant disputes between Netanyahu and his ministers, four of whom resigned. Within three and a half years three finance ministers came and went, and in 1999, for the first time in Israel's history, the prime minister fired his defense minister. In the end, Netanyahu fell on a vote of no confidence (this, too, had happened only once before in more than fifty years). Finally, he was forced to call elections after three years, a year before his term was due to finish.

However, the personalistic character of Netanyahu's regime stemmed from his leadership style, and not necessarily from his telepopulist approach. It is a deep-rooted characteristic of media-centered politics, and therefore, the same pattern could be observed in the style of Ehud Barak as well. When he was elected prime minister in 1999, at the head of the Labor Party, Barak endeavored to stress the differences between them, both in policy and in the nature of his leadership. Nevertheless, his political management approach resembled that of Netanyahu, even if he did not possess the same telegenic qualities.

Barak behaved like Netanyahu as soon as he started preparing for his conquest of the position of party chairman and candidate for the premiership. Like Netanyahu, he raised large sums of money abroad and set up an independent campaign headquarters outside the party. He also constructed a central party committee of his loyalists, not in order to work with it but to neutralize it and let him conduct his own politics without having to resort to the party committees. He, too, did not include veteran party members in the coalition negotiations, breaking with the tradition of this apparatus party. In allocating the portfolios he diminished their status and established a government of the prime minister.

For this purpose he set up a strong staff in his office and placed his trusted old friends there, most of them from the military. He compartmentalized his ministers and kept them largely uninformed about the actions of his government, including on urgent matters related to the peace talks with Syria and the Palestinian Authority. He astonished senior party members with decisions that he had taken in the course of these talks, such as his readiness, contrary to the party manifesto, to cede parts of East Jerusalem to the future Palestinian state. And he also surprised them with political decisions, including his decisions to call early elections and to resign from the Knesset after his defeat in the elections. Barak was not a populist, however, but rather a typical leader of the mediapolitik era. To become a telepopulist something more fundamental is needed.

THE NETANYAHU–MORDECHAI DEBATE:
THE MAGIC FADES

The shifting of emphasis to the prime minister himself, his team, and his office, intensified the personalization of politics. The media encouraged this trend, and the younger generation of journalists knew no other style of journalism. They pushed it to its extreme, framing political issues only in terms of personal battles, ignoring political dilemmas such as the ideological collapse of the Greater Israel movement, as well as the weakening of the mechanisms of welfare policy, the social significance of globalization, and the neoliberal economy. They preferred to describe power struggles and personal stories. The "horse race" of which they were so fond, instead of only marking election days, became the major theme year round.

That is what happened with Netanyahu. The media focused almost entirely on his personality and paid little attention to anything else. This state of affairs was described in an article summarizing the Netanyahu period, written by Uzi Benziman, *Haaretz* columnist and editor of *Ha'ayin Hashevi'it*, a media affairs journal. He wrote, "It was not Netanyahu's policy that led to the disintegration of his government, but his personality. . . . He managed to make himself hated by the members of his government and his coalition partners until he found himself without a parliamentary majority."[18]

His personality became the talk of the day among the entire political class, as well as the general public. Even his battles with his ministers focused on his personality. However, Netanyahu was a leader with more television skills than any other political actor; he knew how to use the media better than others and succeeded in countless struggles for survival throughout his three years of office. His repeated successes strengthened his image as a winner — he was called "the magician."

It was not only his ability to control the media that aroused admiration ("A genius at propaganda," as characterized by analyst Joel Marcus in *Haaretz*, October 15, 1997), but also his political successes in holding onto his position despite the many battles waged against him. He bounced back time and again after being knocked down for his failures and mistakes. The image of the magician was so strong that prior to the elections of 1999, when polls showed that Barak had galloped ahead, there were still expectations that the magician would somehow pull a rabbit out of the hat at the last moment and win.

In a retrospective article in May 1998, *Maariv* political columnist Hemmi Shalev criticized the media that created Netanyahu's persona and built the image of the magician:

the winner, the man who always succeeds, who lands on his feet in every situation, the winner whom his rivals can only envy. . . . The rating culture that dominates and controls the media . . . determines media coverage. As soon as he was elected, the media devoted broadcasting hours and whole pages to Netanyahu's lifestyle, his family, his past, and his habits. The direct election system that justifies probing into the winner's personality, combined with the media's growing tabloid tendency to deal with persons rather than issues, made Netanyahu a hot and almost exclusive item, who overshadowed all other ministers and politicians. As with television, so with politics, ratings are everything, while the reasons for their growth are completely secondary.

Shalev goes on to describe important political issues that were on the agenda during Netanyahu's term, in which:

> The media revealed little interest because they focused almost exclusively on the prime minister's personality and his struggle for survival. In the last two years the media have devoted only a few lines to the collapse of the normalization process with the Gulf States and North Africa. To the television viewers and newspaper readers this destructive process remains a mystery. Israel's deteriorating relations with the Arab states do not interest the media because they are not filled with drama or sensation; there is no bottom line.

Similarly, with regard to the reasons for the resignation of the finance minister and the approval of the state budget, the collapse of tourism, the loss of support for Israel in world public opinion, and other matters: "This was a gradual process occurring more by default than by action. This story has no place on the front pages of the newspapers, because there is no battle between personalities, there is no clear-cut decision, no bloodshed." Above all, it did not deal with the political game, the campaign, and survival.[19]

The persona and the television screen, which was at the very heart of the new politics and led to Netanyahu's success, in the end also caused his downfall. By 1999 so many flaws in Netanyahu's persona had accumulated that the magic began to fade — both his magic command of television and his magical skill at political manipulation. Netanyahu was wounded in the very spot that was the cornerstone of his regime: personal leadership. He had tried to construct a political body based on personalization of the leader, using television for this purpose. His opponents used the same tools with which he had sought to govern and created his counterpersona of a liar and a man without credibility, with *Newsweek* even describing him as "Tricky Bibi."[20] These new image-destroying critiques shattered the persona that he had succeeded in constructing with such great effort.

Just as he had won the office of prime minister following the successful marketing of his persona in the historic debate of 1996, he was ousted in 1999 following a television confrontation that focused on his personality more than anything else. On the face of it, this should never have happened. Shortly before the 1999 elections, Netanyahu came face to face in a televised debate with the defense minister he had fired, Yitzhak Mordechai. Mordechai was usually clumsy of speech and slow of thought, sparing with words and speaking mostly in clichés — he lacked all telegenic ability. But at an early stage of the debate Mordechai scored a hit, pushing Netanyahu off balance. Netanyahu lost control of the situation, and by the time he recovered, it was too late.

Mordechai used strong tactics: direct frontal attack, face to face, and concentration on Netanyahu's personality traits. Mordechai neutralized Netanyahu's advantage by admitting that he himself was weak on television, but he turned this disadvantage into an advantage. "Everybody knows that no one can compete with you on television," he said, "but reality is not television." He portrayed him as mendacious and hinted at irresponsible decisions on security matters that Netanyahu could not debate publicly or deny. He responded to Netanyahu's counterattacks with a sarcastic smile that obviated the need for words.

Netanyahu started off by completely disregarding Mordechai. At that stage of the campaign, there were three candidates competing for prime minister, and Netanyahu knew that Barak was the real threat to his position, not Mordechai. However, Barak had taken the advice of his election advisors who had helped Tony Blair and the "New Labor" in Britain's 1999 elections (Norris et al. 1999). Aware of his weakness on television, he refused to compete with the "wizard" in that arena. As soon as the debate began, it became clear that Netanyahu intended to use Mordechai to attack Barak, and by the time he realized that he was being powerfully hit by his former defense minister, he had lost time and points. He continued shooting most of his arrows at Barak, "who had fled from the confrontation." Netanyahu then tried to deny Mordechai legitimacy as a rival worthy of consideration, by ignoring him and not speaking to him directly, just as Peres had done to Netanyahu three years earlier. Mordechai treated this as avoidance and attacked frontally, addressing him directly and personally again and again. This was almost a repetition of the 1996 debate, except that this time Mordechai was the one who made better use of the medium.

What Mordechai did in essence is familiar to scholars of symbolic politics. Symbols lose their effectiveness when the way in which they are used is exposed. When we see the strings that work the puppets, the magic of the puppet show fades. And Mordechai referred to these strings throughout the interview. He exposed and detailed more and more of Netanyahu's working methods, particularly his manipulative character. Mordechai did not win the debate, and his public standing did not improve. The one who profited from this evening was the absent candidate, Ehud Barak. But Mordechai showed that Netanyahu could be beaten on his own territory — television. The program reached a peak rating of more than 40 percent. It looked more like a street brawl than a debate of candidates for the premiership, and Netanyahu came out of it bruised and battered, his mask torn.

CHAPTER NINE

Netanyahu's Media Strategy

Netanyahu fell with a great splash. In the elections, the public showed that they could no longer stomach him, and he was defeated by an unprecedented margin of 12 percent. His opponent, Ehud Barak, although well known to the public as the chief of general staff (or, CGS), the most decorated soldier in the history of the IDF, and a popular figure, was completely lacking in television skills, and all of his efforts to acquire these skills had failed. On the screen Barak came across as cold and unable to radiate empathy, with a convoluted analytical-intellectual style of speech and stiff nontelegenic body language. He was so inept on television that his advisers decided to turn that liability into an asset. "I am not Mr. Television bluff, I am a real person, a leader who knows how to do things," he said, constructing a persona based primarily on his credibility.

In the end, however, Barak's political fate was the same as Netanyahu's, perhaps even worse. Netanyahu failed to complete three out of the four years of his term in office; Barak did not even complete two. The disappointment was great because he failed so miserably after having raised such high hopes. Barak had come to power after the stalemate in the peace talks with Syria and the Palestinian Authority (PA), and he led the talks almost to the point of signing a peace treaty, even at the risk of shrinking his coalition. Indeed, when he left Israel on his way to the Camp David summit in the summer of 2000, he had already lost the Knesset majority and could rely only on fifty-eight members of the Knesset (MKs), instead of the seventy-three he had when his term had started. The talks subsequently broke down, and in September of that year a new wave of violence swept over Israel and the occupied territories. The second Intifada had begun, Barak had lost the elections to Sharon, and the peace process had suffered a mortal blow.

The contents of Israeli foreign policy are beyond the range of this book, which deals with the political body. Neither is it my intention to discuss Barak's approach to politics at length. He is mentioned here only for comparison with Netanyahu's telepopulism. Indeed, an examination of the patterns of government of the two shows the fundamental difference between them. When Barak's leadership style began to unravel, there seemed to be no difference between the two. He was even called "Netanyahu II." Both Netanyahu and Barak were leaders in the era of new politics, and the similarity between them lay in the fact that they behaved according to the rules of the new media-centered democracy. Barak, like his predecessor, acted to weaken the party power base. He established a loose political framework of which the Labor Party was just one component. He ran a prime ministerial government, and in his second year of office even attempted to dismantle the Labor Party altogether. Nevertheless, only Netanyahu himself can rightly be called a telepopulist leader. He subscribed to neopopulism's belief system and conducted a telepopulist media strategy. These two elements were not present in the case of Barak, who belonged to the power bloc and expressed the values of the dominant cultural elite, the very group which had been the focus of criticism of Netanyahu and his supporters.

Barak's fall was no different from Netanyahu's. His support base gradually shrank, with the parties leaving the broad coalition that he had formed, internal opposition in the party growing, and the media's criticism swiftly and systematically destroying public trust in him. His parliamentary support slowly withered away during his last days, shrinking to only thirty-seven Knesset members in July 2000. Nevertheless, Barak and Netanyahu differed greatly in their news-management style. Barak tried to use the media for the purposes of political marketing — and was sometimes quite successful — but generally speaking, he had a cold and remote relationship with television.[1] Netanyahu, by contrast, understood the meaning of television politics, felt comfortable in the visual cultural space, and made extensive use of symbolic management.[2]

THE PERMANENT CAMPAIGN

The principles of modern political marketing were alien to the bureaucratic tradition of Israeli politics. This applies to election campaigns and to policy marketing by incumbent governments. The concept "permanent campaign" was first used by journalist Sidney Blumenthal (1982), who referred to "a combination of image making and strategic calculation that turns governing into a perpetual campaign and remakes government into an instrument designed to sustain an elected official's popularity" (Heclo 2000). The idea that an incumbent prime minister needs to conduct a campaign throughout his entire term of office, and not just during the elections — in other words, that he has to employ a strategy that permanently combines elements of political marketing, including polls, marketing, and planned recruitment of public support — was something completely new to Israeli political culture. Only in the 1990s did Israeli politicians begin to express ideas that echoed Hilary Clinton's words: "You have to run a campaign for policy just like you do for elections" (Woodward 1995: 392).

Even in the era of old politics, every government had to market its policy in order to muster public support. Governments in Israel did not appeal directly to the general public, but rather to power groups and various organizations such as the Histadrut (the Trade Union Federation), trade and business organizations, and a plethora of interest groups, as part of the style known in the American context as "power to bargain" (Kernell 1986: 3). The permanent campaign is "something different from government's perennial need for public support. In the permanent campaign every day is election day. Such campaigning is a nonstop process seeking to manipulate sources of public support to engage in the act of government itself" (Heclo 2000: 17). Furthermore, in Israel's old political culture there was a clear distinction between "doing" and "explaining." What was important was the implementation of policies, or "doing," and it included drumming up support for political action in the party, parliament, and the bureaucracy. Appealing to the public, by contrast, was regarded as "explaining," which had marginal importance. Golda Meir, a typical representative of the old bureaucratic leadership style of the Labor Party, was fond of repeating the saying, "Action is the best explanation," and even Yitzhak Rabin, of a younger generation, used to say, "Only one who does nothing needs to explain."[3]

Rabin held on to this conservative view even after he saw that public opinion was swayed by the opposition's massive propaganda campaign against the 1993 Oslo Accords, which included mutual recognition between the PLO and the State of Israel and an Israeli agreement to return occupied territories. Rallies, protests, and demonstrations against these government policies were held throughout the country; posters opposing him and his government were hung everywhere, and road intersections were blocked. Rabin was asked to initiate a public countercampaign expressing support for the government's policy. But his reply was, "There's no need. The opposition has nothing to do, so they demonstrate. The government has tools for real action. That is more effective."[4]

When more and more appeals came to him in the second half of 1995, he changed his mind and gave his consent to a rally in Tel Aviv's main square, in support of government policy under the heading, "No to violence — yes to peace." This was one of the largest demonstrations ever held in Israel and the massive attendance gave him great happiness. After many months he saw clearly that the peace camp was also capable of bringing hundreds of thousands out into the streets. However, Rabin's happiness was short-lived. At the end of the rally, Yigal Amir murdered him with three pistol shots at point-blank range.

Netanyahu, in contrast to Rabin and other predecessors, regarded the distinction between "doing" and "explaining" as fundamentally flawed and meaningless. "It might have been expected that Israel would recognize the fact that one cannot separate policy from explanation. But this is not the case," he wrote in a book that was designed to help him reach the apex of Israeli politics, adding, "In other countries it is taken for granted. U.S. presidents and most world leaders do not usually make important decisions without examining the probable reactions to these decisions in public opinion. . . . The decision-making process includes a detailed discussion of how the decision will affect the public, and what should be done to elicit a positive reaction" (Netanyahu 1995: 338). The veteran leaders' avoidance of marketing campaign methods was due not only to their bureaucratic attitude toward democracy, according to which the political process should take place in the corridors of power and not in the city square, but also to their conceptions of leadership and political representation. Since the beginning of democratic thought in Europe, there have been two main concepts of political representation, that of the agent and that of the trustee. On the one hand, the representative is expected to represent the voters and confine him- or herself to expressing their attitudes. On the other hand, the trustee is the one whom voters entrust with the right to make his or her own decisions, with the knowledge that he or she acts in the light of the principles presented during the campaign. In the end, the trustee is expected to report to them on his or her actions.

The approach prevalent in Israeli political culture was that of the trustee, particularly with regard to the national leader, who received broad scope for action, and who was entitled to take decisions in a process that was not necessarily revealed to the public, without having to please those represented or even report to them at any given moment. Ben Gurion gave expression to this approach in what became a classic statement: "I don't know, nor am I interested in what the public wants. I know what the public needs" (Bar-Zohar 1994: 546).

When Israel became a media-centered democracy, in which the government employed the strategy of the permanent campaign, the previous attitude was replaced by the approach that viewed the leader as an agent whose duty was solely to implement the policy of those he represented. In the permanent campaign, affairs of state are conducted like an election campaign. Public opinion is constantly examined through polls, focus groups, and similar techniques. The policy supported by the public is the one adopted; after it is chosen, persuasive media techniques are used to enlist maximum public support for it. The aim of the policy, however, throughout the entire term of office, is political survival, to ensure success in the next elections.

It is thus not surprising that the permanent campaign raises many questions regarding the nature of democracy and the meaning of democratic leadership. Is politics in contemporary democracies more about public satisfaction than about running a country? What kind of leadership is it when public support is the major criterion for determining the agenda and the policy? Is it not the leader's role also to set out for the public long-term objectives and goals that call for sacrifice and effort and are therefore unpopular in the short-term? On the other hand, if the leader is constantly campaigning, when will he or she stop pursuing party interests and assume the role of head of state, serving the interests of political opponents, as well as supporters? Is there no danger that the democratic discourse will, in fact, become total manipulation of public opinion?

The person who introduced and implemented the permanent campaign to Israel was Netanyahu. As an opposition leader he made extensive use of demonstrations against the government, and between 1993 and 1995 he placed himself at the head of a task force that organized demonstrations against Rabin's government and the Oslo Accords. Even after he was elected prime minister, he continued using the kind of methods that Rabin deemed "suitable for the opposition." He encouraged an ad campaign in support of his government and its policy, which appeared under the names of various organizations, so as to seem authentic and spontaneous. Furthermore, he encouraged mass rallies, demonstrations, and street posters expressing identification with the prime minister.

Netanyahu began to follow the practice of "going public" in the first months of his term of office, when he decided to cut the national budget by 7 billion shekels (about 2 billion U.S. dollars). He did this, however, only after testing the strategy according to the rules of the permanent campaign, addressing the public directly on television, over the heads of the ministers and Knesset members. Much of the public liked this innovation and the respect shown them by the prime minister, and they expressed support for his attitude. The ministers and the Knesset had to respond to this and to modify their positions accordingly.

Perhaps the most significant element of the permanent campaign is the use of polls. Netanyahu used them constantly. Before deciding to appoint a minister (such as Finance Minister Shetreet), or fire one (Defense Minister Mordechai), he monitored public opinion with a special poll.[5] However, the polls were intended not only to examine the public response to his actions but also to determine his agenda, and even the actual contents of his policy. "My instructions were to locate the subjects on which there was a national consensus and those over which there was deep public division," admitted Shay Reuveni, the prime minister's pollster, in an interview with a journalist, who concluded sarcastically, "Today, it appears, they no longer ask what is good for the country, but what will appeal to the public."[6]

Thus, when Netanyahu headed the Israeli delegation to the summit talks with the Palestinians at Wye Plantation in October 1998, he brought his pollster with him and instructed him to examine public opinion in Israel regarding the various positions that arose during the negotiations with President Clinton and Chairman Arafat. Israel's former ambassador to the UN, Abba Eban, writing in the 1980s on the new diplomacy, lamented the fact that the news media make it difficult for modern diplomats to conduct international negotiations. While engaged in the process, they are forced to maintain a dialogue with their constituency, and this puts constraints on their ability to maneuver in the negotiations. What would the elder statesman have written had he known that a day would come when the prime minister would conduct diplomatic negotiations based on instant public reaction to each step in the negotiations?[7]

The decision that eventually led to the collapse of Netanyahu's government — his decision not to implement his commitment to the Wye Agreement — also had its sources in a poll commissioned by the prime minister. The poll revealed that if he transferred additional territories to the Palestinian Authority, according to the agreement that he had signed with Arafat, Ariel Sharon would be likely to oppose this and to compete with him for the premiership, possibly winning as many as eighteen seats in the Knesset. Netanyahu therefore decided to renege on his commitment to implement the Wye Agreement.

Netanyahu's reliance on polls did not, however, increase his popularity. His leadership was damaged, and there was growing criticism of him by his ministers as "the zigzag man," an opportunist who changed his mind and his policies according to which way the wind was blowing. Knesset member Shlomo Ben Ami (later foreign minister in the Barak government) defined him in a Knesset speech on May 26, 1997 as a "media surfer, a man who rides the media waves as a substitute for policy." Even Eyal Arad, Netanyahu's close associate and political strategist for years, admitted, "It is true that Netanyahu tells the audience what it wants to hear, and as a consequence the public doubts his trustworthiness and determination. This style is not succeeding in strengthening his political position, but the opposite" (Preuss 1997).

THE NEGATIVE CAMPAIGN

The problematic nature of the permanent campaign stems from the fact that vital and irreducible differences exist between campaigning and governing because their purposes have an inherent difference. One of the major differences is that campaigning is fundamentally adversarial, while governing is predominantly collaborative (Heclo 2000). This difference becomes increasingly significant as the campaign becomes more and more negative.

The adoption of the permanent campaign method, and particularly of the negative campaign, intensified the opinion class's criticism of Netanyahu. In the past, attack campaign techniques had been used only during elections, and even then only to a limited extent and with restraint. His critics were particularly angered by the fact that the aggressive character of the campaign did not subside after the elections, but rather characterized Netanyahu's conduct throughout his term.

This was a critical decision on Netanyahu's part, which he came to regret later. Not only was he the first prime minister elected directly by the public, and half the public did not want him (his majority was only 14,740 votes, less than half of 1 percent of the electorate), but he came to this office while many regarded him as indirectly responsible for Rabin's assassination. In the negative campaign he had conducted against Rabin he had not flinched from challenging the very legitimacy of Rabin's government. "Anyone who prefers the welfare of our enemies to the security of our citizens cannot lead this nation," he said. "You [Rabin] have no ideological commitment to this country. For you it is not a homeland but a piece of territory that can be traded." And referring to the government's parliamentary majority, he said, "It is a non-Zionist majority, that includes five representatives of an Arab party that identifies with the PLO. I want to remind Yitzhak Rabin that Darawshe's children [an Arab Knesset member for the Labor Party] do not serve in the military, and yet he relies on them for his twisted majority."[8]

The deep division in Israeli society, which was widened even further by Rabin's assassination and the 1996 election results, made it harder than ever for a new prime minister to fulfill the central function of government — to generate national integration and strengthen social solidarity and cohesiveness. Even a leader of the "national healer" type would have found it difficult to cope with this task. For Netanyahu — the great believer in the negative campaign — it was ten times more difficult.

The principles of the negative campaign fit Netanyahu's personality, which not only his political rivals but also his partners recognized as suspicious, closed, aloof, competitive, power-driven, cold, and sparing of emotions. He made intensive use of these traits, not only against his political critics from the opposing camp, but also against any of his partners who criticized him for his policies.

He often used labels to castigate his rivals. A favorite, with the connotation of treachery to the country, was on the "Left" or a "leftist."[9] One of the victims of this label was Lieutenant-General Amnon Lipkin-Shahak, whose case is an illustration of Netanyahu's negative campaign tactics. Netanyahu knew that the distinguished and telegenic chief of general staff was very popular among the Israeli public, and he thus feared that Shahak would enter political life and run against him in the 2000 elections. Therefore, Netanyahu began sniping at his CGS while he was still serving in the military. He cancelled the weekly talks that had always been the practice between the prime minister and the CGS, appeared with him in public as little as possible, and unlike prime ministers in the past, even attacked him and the military top brass, accusing them — as he accused the media — of acting out of political motives and supporting the Labor Party and the Left.

So long as Shahak was chief of general staff, Netanyahu could not attack him directly and openly, but this he did immediately after the end of Shahak's term. In his usual manner, Netanyahu contrived to do so on television. During a routine visit to a hospital, surrounded by journalists and TV cameras, Netanyahu was asked by a radio reporter what he thought of Shahak's political plans. He referred to Shahak disparagingly, calling him a "leftist." The attack caused astonishment, especially in view of the fact that Shahak was on retirement leave but formally still in uniform and had not yet uttered even one political declaration. Soon it was discovered that the reporter's question was not innocent but had been planted. The prime minister's media advisors had asked the journalist in advance to pose the question.

Why was this message, that Shahak was a leftist and always had been, so important to Netanyahu? In Israel's total politics, everyone must belong to a political camp: subscribing to one camp's principles means that one is denied support by the other camp's members. A notable exception to this division is IDF officers. They are forbidden from expressing their political opinions during military service, which gives them the status of supraparty, all-national leaders, who enjoy admiration and prestige across the entire political spectrum. This is one of the reasons for the success of high-ranking officers who enter the political arena upon retirement from the military.

Therefore, Netanyahu wanted to strike Shahak at the source of his power. If Shahak were identified by the general public as a "leftist," he would at once lose his credit with the supporters of the Right. It was important to do this before Shahak began taking his first steps in politics. The timing was perfect: General Shahak, not yet a civilian, could not argue with his prime minister, so the label stuck. Shahak, who was hesitant about entering politics in the first place, was propelled into political life largely by Netanyahu's attacks. As soon as he announced that he was entering politics, he had to devote most of his efforts to removing this leftist image. He thus rejected Barak's invitation to take second place in his Knesset list and established a new party, calling it the Center Party.

The negative campaign also fit Netanyahu's worldview. The world, according to Netanyahu is analogous to a wild jungle, where only power relations prevail, and the strong survive. The test of a leader is foremost a test of his endurance. "There is no friendship in matters of policy. There is pressure," said Netanyahu, quoting something that Jabotinsky had written in 1929 (Netanyahu 1995: 385). Life is a constant battle in which there is no compromise and only two camps. Referring to the Middle East, Netanyahu reflected his perception of the world at-large, both between states and between people.

In my opinion the main motive for disputes [in the Middle East] is the clash between us and the Arab world [which sees us] as an alien element that has no right to exist in this place. . . . We tend to develop cycles of exaggerated hopes followed by moments of despair.

I, on the other hand, suggest that we look at our environment in a much more balanced and rational way, and understand that the basic hostility to Israel is still very widespread. . . . We are in the Middle East in an era of iron walls. . . . Contrary to what we were promised, Israel has not found peace and quiet. The conflicts in the Middle East will not stop, and history, of course, will not come to an end there. . . . Even if we achieve contractual peace with all our neighbors — these contracts will not guarantee that the security problem is over. . . . The Middle East is a region of shifting sands.[10]

The negative campaign concept was developed in the United States as an election strategy between rival candidates. For Netanyahu, the campaign fulfilled a broader role. It was part of his populist view, in which there were two camps, "we" and "they," the "good" and the "bad." Therefore, his campaign was directed against his personal rivals, the opposition parties, and all the cultural groups gathered under the label "the Left" or "the elite": the labor movement and the kibbutzim, the political Left, academia, the legal system, the civil servants, the culture and arts communities, with the media at their head, and all those who had belonged to the establishment, the old center, who had dominated Israeli society. Netanyahu bunched all of these groups together under the code word "elites." Facing this "other" were the Likud, the religious bloc with its various streams, the Russian-speaking immigrants, the Mizrahim on the periphery, the downtrodden, and the rejected, all gathered under the code word "the nation." This was an act in the best tradition of populist movements, the division between the power bloc and the antihegemonic camp.

Netanyahu went so far, at times, as to identify these "others" with Israel's enemies. This was the message of his main propaganda clip in the 1996 elections, showing Peres walking hand in hand with Arafat. The text "explained" the picture: Peres was being willingly led by Arafat, abandoning Israel to the interests of the enemy. Netanyahu accused the Left of relating to his government and to himself personally in a nonparliamentary manner that bordered on incitement. Indeed, the political discourse in the strife-torn Israel of the 1990s was far from being reminiscent of the gentlemen's debating society in Westminster. In content, this was a battle to delegitimize the opponent, using not rational arguments, but rather stinging personal insults, delivered in strident tones. It is not my intention to judge whether the behavior of one side was more gentlemanly than the other, but simply to highlight one fact — the introduction of a new political practice whereby the government deliberately and consistently employed negative campaign tactics, using the media, mainly television, for this purpose.

The aim of this practice was not so much to change the opponent's political attitudes as to strengthen the collective identity of the antihegemonic bloc — even when it was already in power; to increase its inner cohesion and mobilize it for political battle. This was politics of identity and recognition at its best. The other camp, the "Left," was portrayed as turning its back not only on patriotism but on everything Jewish, severing itself from the Jewish nation, even betraying it. Netanyahu continued this practice of binding together personal rivals, internal political opponents, and the external enemy even after he became prime minister. Appearing before an audience of his supporters, he said, "Why do you think the Left and the Arab world attack us?" Thus, as if unintentionally, he bound together the Arab world, the Palestinians, the Left, the elite, and the media on the one hand, and the Right as representing the entire Jewish people on the other.[11]

This method of battering political rivals uses familiar techniques of symbolic manipulation, externalization, and the technique of scapegoating (Alger 1989: 51). In the 1999 election campaign this was manifested in the use of the slogan "Either Bibi or Tibi." Ahmed Tibi, a Palestinian citizen of Israel, was Chairman Arafat's advisor in the 1990s, and in 1999 he ran for the Knesset and won a seat. The meaning of the slogan was that anyone who voted for Barak instead of supporting Netanyahu was in fact supporting Israel's external enemies.

However, his constant use of negative campaign tactics had a boomerang effect. This happened once when the method was exposed in an attack on Shahak. Another case was a comment that Netanyahu whispered into the ear of Rabbi Kadouri. The rabbi, over one hundred years old, is a revered Kabbalist with an aura of sanctity; people come to him pleading for a blessing. During one of Netanyahu's visits to his home, the microphone of a Channel 1 reporter picked up the prime minister whispering in Rabbi Kadouri's ear, "The Left are not Jews," and describing the Left's cooperation with the PLO as "compromising the security of the state." The disgusted reaction to this was evoked as much by the manner and style of the remarks as by their content: Netanyahu bending over the decrepit Rabbi, whispering in his ear.

The last time that Netanyahu was exposed planning a negative campaign was in the final stage of the 1999 elections. In May of that year an election rally was held in Tel Aviv in support of Ehud Barak and attended by actors and artists. In the weeks preceding this rally, the polls had shown repeatedly that Netanyahu was falling behind; only a blunder on Barak's part could save him from defeat. This blunder was supplied by actress Tiki Dayan at the rally, when she described the Likud voters as "rabble." Netanyahu, hoping to generate the energy needed to save the sinking ship, seized the opportunity to incite the Mizrahim against the arrogant Ashkenazim, the supporters of Labor. Not content with castigating Dayan, Netanyahu attacked Barak, who was standing near the actress when she spoke, for not disassociating himself from her words. This attack naturally included the entire Left camp, for secretly thinking what Dayan had said out loud. The negative campaign gained momentum when stickers saying "I am rabble and proud of it" began to appear all over the country.

Attempting to ride this wave, Netanyahu canceled his previous plans and went to make a special visit to the main Tel Aviv street market. There, in that stronghold of the Likud, the word "rabble" was likely to inflame many against the treacherous and arrogant Left. Still, someone would have to light the fire, and Netanyahu did not hesitate. Again the microphone of a television reporter caught the prime minister goading the stall-holders on, "They hate the people," he said. "They [the Labor Party, Barak, the Ashkenazim, the media, and the elites] hate the religious, the Russians, the Mizrahim, everybody." This time he had gone too far. The picture that appeared on the TV screen showed the prime minister attempting to fan the flames, to stir up the battle between the camps. Even some of his own supporters thought this was excessive.

In a society as deeply divided as Israel, and in a political body that is split almost entirely down the middle between Left and Right, a negative campaign is an effective device. As only a few in the opposing camp are likely to change their minds, the side that can maximum its own electoral potential wins. That was the secret of Netanyahu's success in the 1996 elections. In the areas where Labor traditionally had a large majority, such as north Tel Aviv, voter turnout was relatively low (60–70 percent), while in places where Netanyahu had an absolute majority, such as the ultraorthodox population centers, almost 100 percent of the electorate voted.

As his last appearance at the Tel Aviv street market indicated, however, Netanyahu had gone too far with his negative campaign. After three years of internal tension and deep splits, people began to tire of the mutual incitement. Increasing sections of the population wanted peace and quiet, and there was a growing desire for internal unity, evinced by the growing support for the establishment of a national unity government and the relatively high support for the new Center Party, which decried the internal division.

Ehud Barak identified this mood and quickly drew the right conclusions. When he first launched his election campaign, Barak was drawn into the negative campaign, and the first election posters that appeared early in 1999 played on the theme of "we" and "they." He attempted to arouse the public on the Left against the national-religious camp. "When we are in power, we will allocate money for education and not for settlements, budgets will be directed to development towns and not to religious colleges," said the posters. The "we" referred to was the moderate majority, and "they" were the extremists, the ultraorthodox, the settlers, the national-religious Right, with Netanyahu at their head.

However, when public opinion polls and focus groups identified the public's weariness with the internal strife and a growing desire for national unity, Barak at once abandoned the negative campaign and began to play on the feelings of fraternity and solidarity. And while Netanyahu tried to rescue his sinking campaign by fanning the flames of negativism, Barak's "we and they" posters disappeared and were replaced by a different theme — partnership. Barak's main election slogan was now, "I will be everyone's Prime Minister," with the emphasis on everyone. It appears that a negative campaign also has its disadvantages.

NETANYAHU'S NEWS MANAGEMENT

Israel's first prime ministers, David Ben Gurion, Moshe Sharett, Levi Eshkol, and Golda Meir, as well as Menachem Begin of the Likud, belonged to the era of the party press, and they knew how to use it for their own purposes. However, they regarded dealing with the media as secondary to the real work of government, which took place in bureaucratic frameworks. It is thus easy to understand why there was no full-time press officer in the prime minister's office until the 1970s. Every Sunday, the cabinet secretary would issue a laconic report on the weekly cabinet meeting, and the routine contacts between the prime minister's office and the press were handled by the prime minister's secretary or bureau chief, in the context of his other various tasks. "If there is a full-time spokesman he will have to talk to journalists all the time. When you fill this role among all your other tasks, I am sure that you will speak to them less, and the less the better," said Golda Meir to her bureau chief, Simcha Dinitz.[12]

The attitude toward the media began to change when Yitzhak Rabin became prime minister in 1974 and the office of prime minister passed from the founding generation to the 1948 generation (meaning those who were young adults during the War of Independence). "Rabin did not have much experience with the press, and during his term as ambassador in Washington he had become aware of its power, was aided by it, and began to understand the reciprocity between the establishment and the press," recalled the embassy spokesperson at the time, journalist Dan Pattir.[13] When he was elected in 1974, Rabin created a new position in his bureau, that of press advisor. A few special cases notwithstanding, however, he paid little attention to the press in the course of his daily routine. He glanced at *Haaretz* with his morning coffee, sometimes leafed through a newspaper while being driven to his office, but he did not follow the press closely. Others — his wife, Leah, his advisor, Eitan Haber, his assistant, Shimon Sheves, or his chauffeur, Yehezkel Sharabi — would tell him the news.

Menachem Begin and Yitzhak Shamir, although they came after Rabin, belonged to the founding generation. This was particularly evident in the case of Shamir. "The press was not among his chief interests. He was inner-directed, a bit closed, kept his thoughts to himself. Consideration of the media was foreign to him, and he would say, 'I'll do what I think is best for the country, and let the press write what it likes.'"[14] This reticent approach harmed Shamir during the Gulf War in 1991. The Israeli public, under attack by Scud missiles from Iraq, expected to see its leader and hear calming and encouraging words. Shamir did not deem it necessary to appear more than once a week, and his absence from the TV screen gave the impression that there was no leadership, arousing severe criticism of the prime minister.

Shimon Peres, who had known from the start how to work with the press, opened a new era in relations with the media when he became prime minister in 1995. He devoted quite a lot of time to journalists, and more than one of his advisors was charged with maintaining contact with the media. However, Netanyahu was the first one to enter the office of prime minister with a firm overall conception of the media as an integral part of the governing machinery. Once, when the director-general of the Foreign Ministry recommended a candidate for the post of ambassador in a certain country, describing his excellent qualities, Netanyahu interrupted him, saying, "But how does he get on with the media? After all, that is the most important thing."[15]

The media to Netanyahu meant primarily television. Rabin and Peres still related to the press as being more important, but Netanyahu changed the order of priorities. He definitely preferred meeting with TV crews to talking with print journalists. In planning political activity, the needs of television were considered first, and only afterward the needs of radio and newspapers. This included timing, and events were planned according to TV programming schedules. It also included adapting to the logic of television, with messages adapted to TV's visual language, and replacing classic political rhetoric with television rhetoric.

One political reporter explained:

Every time Bibi has a message to convey, he sets up an event to begin at 8 PM, in order to bring it directly to the general public in the evening news broadcast. Then, early the next morning, he gives lots of radio interviews to the morning news programs of Kol Israel and IDF Radio, and the transcript is sent to the press. At the same time, he receives international news crews. This is the pattern: television, radio the next morning, as well as the newspapers and representatives of the international media. (Elishar-Malca 1999)

The importance ascribed to the media was evident in the structure of the prime minister's bureau and its daily routine. Contacts with the media were no longer left to one spokesperson or press advisor; they became the work of the entire office. All the members of the inner circle of advisors (nicknamed "the submarine") were knowledgeable and experienced in the field of communication. The press advisor, Shai Bazak, was one of those closest to Netanyahu from his days in the opposition, and when Bazak left, Netanyahu appointed in his place the IDF radio political reporter, Aviv Bushinsky. Cabinet Secretary Danny Naveh had been press advisor to former Defense Minister Moshe Arens. The information section was headed by David Bar-Ilan, who was taken from his former position as editor of the *Jerusalem Post*. Bar-Ilan had been close to neoconservative circles in the United States, and after immigrating to Israel he collaborated in Rupert Murdoch's attempt to penetrate the Israeli media market and in 1988 edited the Tel Aviv local paper *La'inyan*. When Netanyahu's bureau chief left, Uri Elitzur, one of the leaders of the settlers' movement and editor of their magazine *Nekuda,* assumed the post. Added to these were others who were experienced and skilled in political communication and information.

Netanyahu often said that the newspapers didn't interest him at all. Once he said, "I don't read the papers. I've decided it's not worth the time." On another occasion he said, "The press has made itself irrelevant to me. Every morning I glance at the daily crop of stories in the papers, then I go on my way." When criticism increased, Netanyahu even claimed that he didn't read the papers at all: "I stopped paying attention a long time ago to articles about me. . . . *Yediot Ahronot* doesn't cross my threshold." The truth was just the opposite, and everyone knew it. Netanyahu followed the press closely and methodically, devoting much time and thought to it. "He was a compulsive consumer of the press, especially of what was published about him." Another political analyst added, "The totality of the media in Netanyahu's mind is astonishing and never ceased surprising me."[16]

His daily schedule reflected the media's news programming. He got up at 6:30 to listen to the headlines on Kol Israel and the IDF radio. "I know that right after the headlines I will start to receive phone calls from the prime minister's bureau, because the main report of the day is at 7:00 a.m., and whatever was broadcast at 6:30 titillates them, and they start trying to influence me. It is a regular morning ritual," said a Kol Israel political reporter (Elishar-Malca 1999). Naturally, this first message from one of the prime minister's aides was delivered to the newsroom of both radio stations, in order to have an impact on the main morning news broadcast at seven. When the prime minister arrived at his bureau in the government compound in Jerusalem, each workday began with a detailed discussion with his close circle of advisors on the media. This discussion lasted a long time, sometimes hours. "In the morning meetings, the media were the major issue," said one of the prime minister's advisors, "the atmosphere was that of an election campaign. What do the media say this morning and what shall we tell them, what is the main media topic and what will be today's spin?"[17]

This description underscores the essential difference between Netanyahu's workday and that of his predecessors. Unlike Golda Meir, who said that one should talk to journalists as little as possible, or Rabin with his favorite saying, "Only a failure needs to explain his actions," and Shamir, who would ask, "Must we comment on that?" Netanyahu's daily question was, "What shall we sell to the media today?" The basic conception behind this question was that statesmanship — namely, steering the affairs of state — means foremost setting the public agenda, and this is done through the media.

Netanyahu developed a set of principles to deal with the media, which I have compiled from a series of interviews with many journalists, members of his administration, and other politicians, in addition to a great deal of material published in the press during his term in office.

Always Take the Initiative

The first rule is: always be proactive. David Gergen, advisor to four American presidents, stated this simply to President Reagan: "To govern successfully the government has to set the agenda, it cannot allow the press to set the agenda for it" (Hertzgaard 1988). This was a radical innovation in Israeli political thinking. Philip Gould, the media expert of the British "New Labor," developed the idea that in a media-centered democracy you have to relate to the media as a rival to the politicians. Therefore, you have to apply the rule that was applied in the past to political rivals: "You must always seek to gain and keep momentum, or it will pass immediately to your opponents." And how does one gain momentum today? "Gaining momentum means dominating the news agenda, entering the news cycle at the earliest possible time, and repeatedly re-entering it, with stories and initiatives so that subsequent news coverage is set on your terms" (Gould 1998: 294).

Indeed, these ideas became the working assumptions of the daily morning meetings. Netanyahu always took care to be the initiator, introducing a system to distribute information to the public on every matter, even those of minor importance. He made sure to put his spin before and after events, at the end of political meetings, and particularly after talks with foreign leaders or diplomats on the Middle East crisis, sometimes even dragging them against their will to make press appearances with him.

The fact that he was the first and sometimes the only one to provide information on these discussions with heads of state enabled Netanyahu to dictate the media frame on this sensitive issue to the Israeli public. Over time, journalists discovered that there was often a wide gap between Netanyahu's spin on such meetings and what his interlocutors actually said. In 1996, when Netanyahu met in Lisbon with French President Jacques Chirac, Shai Bazak reported that during the conversation Netanyahu did most of the talking, while Chirac maintained silence. "It later transpired that most of the discussion consisted of Chirac protesting vigorously against the diplomatic deadlock," recalled *Haaretz* columnist Aluf Ben.

"It was the same after the Washington conference in November 1996, when the official announcement described the meeting between Netanyahu and King Hussein as an event that took place 'in a pleasant atmosphere,' when in fact the king took bitter issue with the prime minister over his policies."[18] Netanyahu made a point of reacting first, particularly to events that were personally significant to him. An especially dramatic example was the Bar-On affair, which occurred during the first months of 1997. On January 22, Channel 1 news reporter Ayala Hason threw a political bombshell, announcing that the appointment of the new attorney general, Jerusalem attorney Roni Bar-On, was carried out within what appeared to be a web of political conspiracy. Allegedly Shas had promised to vote in the cabinet in favor of the Hebron Agreement (whereby Israel would cede further parts of Hebron to the PA, as part of the withdrawal following the Oslo Accords), in return for an understanding that the prime minister would appoint as attorney general someone (Bar-On) who would remove a legal threat hanging over the head of Shas leader Arie Deri and stop the police investigation against him.

Bar-On's appointment was received with shock in Israeli legal circles. Previous appointees to this eminent position had always been jurists of high professional and public status. Hason's exposé explained why the prime minister had deviated so sharply from tradition and appointed an attorney with little standing in the legal community, who would have no independent status and would leave the prime minister free to act as he chose. Moreover, the affair was perceived in the media and in political circles as an attempt by elements involved in criminal activities to usurp the rule of law and take over the judicial system.

The exposure prevented the appointment and led to an investigation by the police and the state attorney. After the investigation, in the course of which the prime minister was questioned, the police recommended proffering charges against a number of people who were involved in various aspects of the affair, including the prime minister. However, Attorney General Elyakim Rubinstein and State Attorney Edna Arbel decided against it, although the police's conclusions clearly indicated that ethically questionable acts had been committed. They announced this decision at a dramatic press conference on April 20, 1997. Among other things, Arbel's statement contained the following:

The investigation revealed that many of the facts as they were reported in the media were true and that it is not a case of false information. . . . It can be stated that there are prima facie grounds for the suspicion that Knesset member Deri had an interest in Bar-On's appointment as Attorney General for reasons connected to his own criminal trial, and that Deri, together with others, worked to promote the appointment. In addition, there are grounds for the suspicion that Deri conveyed a message indicating a possible link between the appointment and the way Shas would vote on the Hebron Agreement.

Attorney General Rubinstein said at the same press conference, "In the final analysis, the media filled a positive role in exposing a grave and painful subject. . . . The public interest was served, even if not all of the details were reported with complete accuracy."

Even before this press conference was over, Netanyahu, who had prepared for it in advance, rushed to appear at a press conference in his office, stating proudly that the attorney general's investigation had found him innocent of any wrongdoing. "All the accusations that were made against me on Channel 1 were proven wrong," were his opening words, and then he immediately attacked:

Some journalists who are identified with the Left are happy to embrace any accusation of malicious intent, however fictitious and unfounded, so long as I am involved. They spread these fabricated accusations using all the tools at their disposal. . . . Some Channel 1 personnel are still unwilling to accept the decision of the electorate, and almost every evening they try to undermine the legitimacy of the government. . . . The elections are decided at the polls, not on Channel 1.

This was a very one-sided interpretation of the attorney general's conclusions, but the fact that Netanyahu was the first to comment on these conclusions achieved exactly what a spin is supposed to achieve. Netanyahu was the head spin doctor for the results of the investigation, and he shaped the public understanding of the attorney general's conclusions. His detractors' explanations already sounded trivial and argumentative in response to his words.

Netanyahu's rule of being first off the mark sometimes assumed the character of a preemptive strike, as in the case of the dismissal of Defense Minister Yitzhak Mordechai on January 23, 1999. Netanyahu understood that Mordechai had sent him a letter of resignation and did not want the public to hear his explanations. Therefore he forestalled him, assembled his ministers for a televised appearance, and announced that he was firing Mordechai, voicing bitter criticism of him. This was an unprecedented event, but this time, too, the rule proved itself. Mordechai's appearance on television was now a response to the prime minister's announcement. Mordechai, interviewed standing outside his front door, was shocked and speechless. *Haaretz* columnist Yossi Verter wrote:

With perfect timing, not a moment too soon or too late, Netanyahu took the situation into his own hands and left Mordechai gasping in front of the cameras, trying to explain himself, nearly in tears from the humiliation. . . . In the Netanyahu era, everything happens on TV, from confessions of adultery to firing a minister. Netanyahu is the first prime minister to fire a minister live on TV.[19]

However, the urge to appear all the time and always to be the first might sometimes be embarrassing. On the afternoon of Friday, February 6, 1999, Netanyahu arranged a press conference in hopes of making the main newscast of the week on Friday evening with a eulogy for King Hussein of Jordan. Nachum Barnea's sarcastic description captures the scene: "But the King refused to coordinate his death with the prime minister. Netanyahu waited, and the radio and TV crews waited, and the journalists, but the King tarried. Until the Sabbath had almost begun, and Netanyahu was forced to postpone his grief until Sunday."[20]

It's Not What You Did, but What You Say You Did that Is Important

One of the first rules taught to cadets in the Foreign Ministry training course in Jerusalem is a motto attributed to the founders of the ministry: "You did something and reported it — you did it. You did it and didn't report it — you didn't do it." Netanyahu, who had been deputy foreign minister and responsible for information, was familiar with this saying. According to his approach, however, and the approach of mediapolitik in general, media activity is the essence of political action, in the sense of: "You didn't do it but you reported it — you did it." The very fact of "going public," especially on television, creates political facts. It sets the agenda, frames the issues, creates images and expectations, evokes solidarity or criticism, and ultimately enhances or diminishes political power.

A television appearance enables one to convey a message through images. When a society transforms into a visual culture, visual imagery becomes a valuable political tool. It is therefore important to set up visuals to gain coverage, to stage spectacles that give meaning to things and project a certain symbolic order. A shot of the prime minister in a pilot's uniform in a fighter plane demonstrates commitment to the security of the state, and a visit to archeological sites in Jerusalem demonstrates the link to the holy places and to tradition. This combination of the political message with personal image building is what Murray Edelman calls "symbolic leadership," and it creates the feeling that the man behind the wheel is reliable. "As the world can be neither understood nor influenced, attachment to reassuring abstract symbols, rather than to one's own efforts, becomes chronic. And what symbol can be more reassuring than the incumbent of a high position who knows what to do and is willing to act, especially when others are bewildered and alone?" (Edelman 1974: 76). Clearly, by using image management it is also possible to fabricate facts — this is the meaning of visual demagogy.

An example of sophisticated image management creating the illusion of dealing with concrete problems was demonstrated in 1997, when it was announced that, despite promises of economic growth, unemployment rates in Israel had risen to 8 percent. How would prime ministers of the old school have reacted to this report? They would have summoned an emergency meeting in their office, inviting various of his advisors with business and labor leaders and then setting up an interministerial committee to prepare a plan to solve the problem. Throughout this period there would have been a growing feeling among the public that the government was not doing anything. How did Netanyahu choose to deal with the problem? He asked where the unemployment rates were highest, and the very next morning, together with some of his senior officials, went off to Ofakim (an economically depressed town in the South), where he announced a list of steps that would be taken immediately to improve the local employment situation.

The prime minister's visit to Ofakim was the headline story of the day. The media accompanied him there and described the hardship in the town, but emphasized the proposed solutions. Netanyahu showed his mastery of media logic. First of all, television likes to feature personal stories in a dramatic location. By focusing on Ofakim, the media made the audience forget that the problem was not local but national. Second, Netanyahu provided the media with news within a day. Unemployment was yesterday's story; today's story was job creation. By visiting the town and focusing on proposed solutions, Netanyahu replaced the existing media frame with one that was far more congenial to him.

Beyond this, in going to Ofakim Netanyahu played on one of the two main strings of persuasive communication: assurance (the other is arousal; Alger 1989: 49). He transmitted a message of identification with their suffering and created a sense that he cared for them. The visit generated a visual symbol of concern on the evening news program. This was a typical example of the "politics of quiescence", which symbolic leadership can use (Edelman 1971, 1974, 1985).

After many such television events, various critics of Netanyahu began to accuse him of empty talk, calling him "the virtual prime minister," and even "the walking hologram."[21] But with most of the public Netanyahu had achieved his goal. He looked like a head of state is supposed to look: like a problem-solver. After the story reached a "happy end" with the announcement of the plans to resolve the crisis at Ofakim, the media quickly put another issue at the top of their agenda. Indeed, TV generally prefers not to deal with economic matters, which do not photograph well on television. Two months after the event in Ofakim, a curious journalist decided to check on what had materialized from the plan that was pitched to the public during Netanyahu's visit. The results: unemployment in Ofakim remained at the same level as before the widely covered visit.

Use Both Sticks and Carrots When Dealing with the Media

Unlike previous prime ministers, who had limited contacts with the media, Netanyahu took care to maintain personally close contact with journalists and a constant presence in the media. He was seen, heard, and quoted almost daily on television, radio, and in the papers. He did not hesitate to inundate the media in places where past prime ministers had not usually appeared, such as magazines, local papers, nonpolitical programs, children's newspapers, and local TV channels. He also took part in an on-line discussion over the internet.

There were some who described this as inflation and thought that the excessive media appearances were not to his advantage. *Haaretz* commentator Joel Marcus defined it thus: "Bibi is talking himself to death."[22] However, Netanyahu was convinced that political news management should pursue the classic marketing principle of "the more the better." We can see how far this modern pattern of television use differed from the pattern in the old politics by comparing it with the strategy of the French President Charles de Gaulle. His television appearances were considered real political events, but throughout his term of office between May 1958 and April 1969 he appeared on TV only seventy-eight times. He made special appearances to the nation not more than twice a year. These appearances were very stylized, official, and pompous, and were designed to enhance his charisma and his prestige, which he thought could only be achieved if a leader knew how to guard one of the most important foundations of power — mystique (Chalaby 1998).

With the telepopulist leader the media are a daily tool, in order to be constantly in the electronic environment. In one instance, Netanyahu even broke the law. On election day May 17, 1999, he tried to influence the voters until the last possible moment, although election propaganda is forbidden on voting day. Therefore, Netanyahu appeared that day on the pirate radio stations of Shas, which joined together on this occasion for a joint broadcast. He called on his supporters to go and cast their vote. This was in fact a double violation of the law: both broadcasting election propaganda on election day and doing so on a pirate station, thus tacitly condoning pirate radio broadcasting. Only an explicit warning from the chairman of the Central Election Committee, a judge, stopped Netanyahu's continued appearance.

Netanyahu also made a point of devoting at least one hour a day to personal contacts with journalists, and both he and his bureau staff held frequent private meetings, interviews, briefings, and off-the-record talks with them. He would telephone journalists, compliment them on a certain article or take them to task about a critical one, rebuking them for lack of professionalism and objectivity or for relying on false information. "When Bibi spoke to Rabbi Kaduri and told him that the leftists had forgotten what it means to be Jewish, the Kol Israel reporter who taped his words got such angry phone calls from the prime minister's office that I sometimes feel that they are really trying to silence journalists" (Elishar-Malca 1999). Sometimes journalists would amuse themselves with humorous contests over the length of these conversations with the prime minister. "We sometimes asked ourselves whether he had time for any real work," they joked. However, this was not just publicity; the work with the media *was* the "real work."

When Criticized, Distract the Media's Attention with Another Issue

Netanyahu was skillful at staging media events to distract the media, and thereby moving public attention away from uncomfortable issues — a practice internationally known as "eliciting coverage" (Wolfsfeld 1991). One such example is an incident that took place on the day when President Ezer Weizmann was elected to his second term of office on March 4, 1998. Netanyahu had supported another candidate, Knesset member Shaul Amor of the Likud (the president is chosen by the Knesset every four years). When Netanyahu was informed that his candidate had lost, he sought to minimize the loss of prestige and the political damage that he would suffer when the fact was announced on the main TV news broadcast that evening. He did this by staging a media event to distract attention from the election of the president.

Netanyahu hastily called a press conference in his bureau to issue a special announcement, coincidentally taking place at 8 PM, the time of the evening news broadcast. At this dramatic press conference he announced to the nation the appointment of a new head of the General Security Services (GSS), Major-General (Reserves) Ami Ayalon. Until then it had never been the custom to publicize the name of the head of the GSS, and never had a prime minister personally announced the appointment, certainly not live on the evening news. But it worked. Weizmann's reelection was relegated to second place in the news lineup.

Another example of Netanyahu's use of the media to distract attention occurred on November 4, 1998. A memorial rally marking three years since Yitzhak Rabin's assassination was to be held in Tel Aviv's Rabin Square. Netanyahu, knowing that the rally would get significant TV coverage, summoned the press to an event at his bureau in Jerusalem. When the TV crews arrived, they discovered that the occasion was the renewal of Israel's defense agreement with the United States. In the past, this ratification ceremony had not been televised. The United States was represented at that year's ceremony only by its ambassador, a lower-key presence than before. Above all, such events had taken place on weekdays, never on a Saturday night. Thus the unflattering images from the Rabin memorial rally were balanced by positive images of Netanyahu bolstering Israel's security.

If You Repeat It Often Enough, It Becomes the Truth

In 1997, Netanyahu appeared before students at a Tel Aviv high school. As usual, he spoke a great deal about the media, and in reply to a complaint that the government had oppressed the lower classes, he said, "There's no such damage. That's a deception created by the media. You all know the media. They think that if they repeat something often enough, it becomes the truth."[23]

It was media advisor Arthur Finkelstein who introduced the "hammer principle" — a concise, thirty-second message repeated nightly — to Israel's political communication market. This was in the Likud campaign broadcasts in the 1996 elections. Until then, the parties would broadcast new campaign ads almost every night, showing most of them only once. At first, TV critics and political commentators reacted with scorn to this new marketing approach. They considered it unsuitable for political messages, deeming it crude, cheap, and insulting to the viewers' intelligence. After the elections, they all admitted the effectiveness of the technique. It was then adopted by Barak's team in their election campaign in 1999.

Netanyahu continued this practice of repeating messages after the elections. For example, in his battle against the PA, Netanyahu's psychological warfare machine took care to put out daily announcements designed to prove that the Authority was not keeping the agreement it had signed. Even if only a small part of this information was published in the media, the very fact that it reached the ears of journalists might influence them (Elishar-Malca 1999). The media was used not only for supplying information to the public, but also for political gain. Sometimes, Netanyahu would release information as a kind of weather balloon to check reactions. Other aims of such testing tools were influencing a third party to change his or her position in view of this information, or creating an advantageous mood for the next political move, checking for political backlash, and so forth. "Information leaks on the progress of the peace talks, followed by staunch denials and declarations of steadfastness, became a regular pattern with the prime minister and his advisors."[24]

Some of the media manipulation was designed to achieve goals within the journalistic community. The day before the Netanyahu–Peres TV debate in 1996, the headquarters of the two parties negotiated as to who would be the moderator. Netanyahu's headquarters leaked the names of certain journalists that the Likud ostensibly intended to propose. These were straw candidates who had never been offered the role. The purpose of this exercise was simple: since an invitation to serve as moderator in the debate grants considerable prestige to a journalist, the prospect of receiving such an invitation ensured that a whole group would avoid critical coverage of Netanyahu, at least until the selection was announced.[25]

Media manipulation is a familiar phenomenon in other mediapolitik, but Netanyahu's frequent use of this tool led journalists to the conclusion that during his term as prime minister, "all records were broken for manipulation of the media."[26] Blumler and Gurevitch describe journalists' reactions to this "packaging of politics." "Thus, in campaigns dominated by media-savvy politicians and consultants, journalists feel in danger of losing their independence" (1995: 210). They react in various ways, among them "inordinately heavy coverage of any blunders that the professionalized politicians may happen to commit, indulging in what has been called 'feeding frenzies' " (Sabato 1991).

Journalists' suspicions that they were being manipulated were so great that even in covering negotiations with the Palestinians or the United States, they began relying on foreign sources more than on the government. A few months after the elections, one of the members of Netanyahu's "psychological warfare" team admitted to the fact of the team's existence and to its working methods. He related that the team, called "the Uri team" after the name of bureau chief Uri Elitzur, engaged regularly in media spin. "If we wanted to get rid of unfavorable material we would leak it on a day that was replete with headlines. Our item would be pushed to the bottom of page 8, and no journalist would deal with it after it was published."[27]

The longer Netanyahu's media spin lasted the more angry journalists grew, and they intensified their attacks on him. He gradually lost his credibility among the entire opinion class. Netanyahu also lost credibility with the foreign reporters in Israel. *Newsweek* commented on this state of affairs with a piece headlined "Just Call Him Tricky Bibi." On the day that his government fell in the Knesset, things came to a grotesque head. Netanyahu tried to prevent a vote of no confidence, holding many talks with Knesset members, acceding generously to all their requests and scattering promises far and wide. But they no longer believed him. The situation was described by one journalist:

> In his office, flanked by Deri, Netanyahu began to lose control. Everyone who went in found the "magician" on edge, scared, pleading for his life. There were no more rabbits in his hat. People came out of the office and rushed to the radio reporters to report live what he had promised them and have a laugh at his expense. "He's become a laughing stock," remarked one senior Likud member as he passed down the corridor.[28]

Netanyahu sought to make one last-ditch effort to prevent the no-confidence vote, and together with his political ally, Arie Deri, cooked up a scheme. Deri took the Knesset podium and put forward a suggestion that had just occurred to him, so to speak. He proposed postponing the vote for two weeks in order to set up a National Unity Government during this time. When Deri finished, Netanyahu asked to respond to the suggestion, as if he was hearing it for the first time. "It had been my intention," Netanyahu said, "to support the proposal for early elections, but in light of what I have just heard, I am prepared to support Knesset member Deri's proposal." Netanyahu looked sincere, but the Knesset members could not control their outbursts of laughter. They knew that this was not a spontaneous reaction. Even as Netanyahu spoke, they did not stop laughing, mocking and joking, and the whole nation saw it all broadcast live. A majority of Knesset members returned a vote of no confidence.

Thus, the very politician who understood so well the new politics and the crucial role of the media managed to completely damage his relations with most of Israel's journalists, to shatter his persona that he had labored so hard to create, to destroy his own credibility, and to bring down more condemnation on himself than any of his predecessors. Netanyahu's exit from the arena on election night, May 17, 1999, demonstrated the political isolation into which he had fallen, as well as the special nature of his relationship with television.

That evening, he sat in his suite in the Tel Aviv Hilton with his wife and a small gathering of aides. As the hours passed and the pregnant sense of failure prevailed, the politicians gradually left, and the aides followed. Finally, the fateful moment arrived: the ten o'clock news, when both channels broadcast the results predicted on the basis of the exit polls. The result was dire for Netanyahu — a landslide in Barak's favor. Netanyahu asked the makeup artist to make him up and then he went down to the lobby where the journalists were waiting. Seventeen minutes after the announcement of the exit poll results, hours before the actual returns had started to come in, he conceded the election and announced his resignation as head of the Likud.

It was a moment that illustrated his fate. For the first time in Israel, a prime minister had watched the election results alone, not surrounded by friends. Facing the TV set in the hotel room he sat with his wife and a makeup artist. This was also the first time that a prime minister had admitted defeat so quickly. Yet, it was symbolic that the admission of defeat did not come after the broadcast of the actual returns. For Netanyahu a public opinion poll was enough. In his fall, as in his rise, television reality was what mattered.

CHAPTER TEN

The Characteristics of Israeli Telepopulism

NETANYAHU'S PERSONA
AND THE ISRAELI COLLECTIVE IDENTITY

Like many other telepopulist leaders, of whom Berlusconi, Collor de Mello, Menem, and Fujimori are just a few examples, Netanyahu's days in power were turbulent, rife with crises and drama, and he did not succeed in finishing his term of office. Nevertheless, in May 1999 1.4 million voters, 46.9 percent of the electorate, voted for him again. Although he resigned in shame, defamed and battered in a way that had never happened to any previous prime minister, before two years had passed he was again embraced by the Israeli public. If he had run in the 2000 elections, he would indeed have returned to the prime minister's office, according to all public opinion surveys, as he constantly received the highest results in polls for the role of prime minister. Netanyahu joined the Sharon government in 2002 and became finance minister in 2003, and his public standing has improved. Why was this happening? Why was Netanyahu so popular? What was his secret?

One possible answer lies in rational choice theory. Columnist Ari Shavit explains:

The source of Netanyahu's power is not in the advice he receives from Arthur Finkelstein, nor in his proven manipulative ability. Barak, Shahak, and Mordechai are also good at manipulation, but Netanyahu has a unique asset, which is not possessed by any of the retired generals who attempt to defeat him. And this strategic asset is the identification that he has created between himself and the endeavors of the Jewish national movement, between himself and the Zionist battle for survival.

According to Shavit, in contrast to the postnationalist politics of the Left and the dogmatic nationalism of the extreme Right, Netanyahu represents a rational policy for the nation. He describes Netanyahu as someone who understands the cruel laws of the Middle East conflict and knows how to maneuver within them, is motivated by a deep-rooted national ideology, but also has the ability to be a wolf among wolves, a predator among the predators of the jungle. . . . The national struggle in the history of the Middle East is not yet over; in fact it is approaching its critical moment. And at this moment Israel needs a national leadership that understands the outlines of the big story in which we are all trapped, that precisely for peace we have to wage a national battle.[1]

Those who question the validity of the rational choice theory may find a better answer to Israeli voter behavior in 1999 by focusing on a symbolic dimension, which increases in the era of mediapolitik. An analysis of Netanyahu's political behavior, rhetoric, body language, style, persona, image maintenance, and news management reveals that he well understood the importance of using symbols and representations. Politics always involves the use of symbols and representations, but in the politics of identity, and particularly in telepolitics, the symbolic dimension becomes more central, and symbolic management acquires significance. Netanyahu understood this and knew what to do. "He constructed the product Bibi professionally," writes his biographer Ronit Vardi (1997). The question that arises is: What is there in this public figure, this persona, that captures the hearts of half the Israeli public?

A semiotic analysis of his television appearances and of the hundreds of press clippings about him that appeared during the three years of his office in the three national newspapers in which his characteristics were mentioned shows how he succeeded in creating a persona that would reflect the Israeli collective identity, thus bringing as many of the pubic as possible to identify with him. The analysis shows how "Bibi" was transformed into the collective Bibi, thus becoming, as described by the astute observer of Israeli culture, Doron Rosenblum, "the only one who understands what really makes this nation tick."[2]

Netanyahu the persona is an attempt to present in aggregate the traits of "Israeliness." Its salient characteristic is power. Netanyahu the persona is a strong man who radiates power. This is manifested in his body language, the thrust-out chest and raised shoulders, the manner of speech, the gesticulations, and piercing glance. It is reflected in the way he constructed his personal history, his tendency to emphasize his past as an officer in the most prestigious IDF special force, Sayeret Matkal, and his expert knowledge of counter-terror warfare. It is also expressed in his belligerent worldview, particularly in his rhetoric.[3]

This emphasis on power was perceived by his critics as machismo, demonstrative and swaggering bellicosity. As described graphically by one of his admirers in the marketplace on a TV news broadcast, "Bibi has balls this big," drawing with his hands a circle bigger than a watermelon.

However, this bellicosity reflected a certain conception in the Zionist vision, which sought to turn the Jews from a weak people at the mercy of other nations into a nation able to defend itself and determine its own fate. This conception was further developed by the militaristic element of the Israeli civil religion (Lomsky-Feder and Ben-Ari 1999).

The belligerent motif in Zionism had been expressed by previous prime ministers, from Ben Gurion and Golda Meir to Begin and Rabin. Ironically, Netanyahu emphasized this aspect of the collective Zionist identity just when the Zionist ethos of heroism began to erode and Israeli culture had begun taking a more critical attitude toward the hundred-year-old myth of the hero. In the 1990s a process of demilitarization was underway that was expressed in many aspects of society and culture, in the military and the attitude toward military service, in literature, theater, and cinema.

The postwar era in the 1990s saw the beginning of an ideological transformation, which was embodied by Rabin: he was the figure of a soldier who became a warrior for peace. Netanyahu, by contrast, expressed the continuation of the old pattern. King Hussein referred to this matter, which was contrary to the new spirit of peace: "I warned him about his arrogance," Hussein of Jordan said in an interview with historian Avi Shlaim, "I spoke of the arrogance of power, the need to treat people equally."[4] Netanyahu knew, however, that most of the Israelis like this heroic stance.

The emphasis on the element of power in the collective image was expressed in the Likud slogan in the 1999 elections: "The Likud — strong leadership for Israel's future." This motif had appeared in different forms in past election campaigns, but against the background of the new climate in 1999 the slogan aroused impassioned public debate and was even labeled fascist. The very fervor of the debate indicated that Israeli society was in a state of transition with regard to power and domination.

Nevertheless, it is important to remember that the majority in Israel support Netanyahu's views (Bar-Tal, Jacobson, and Klieman 1999). Evidence of this can be seen in Barak's election campaign against Netanyahu in the 1999. Barak did not dare to present the new alternative myth but instead resorted to the same bellicose discourse. Barak's campaign preferred to undermine Bibi's image not by discrediting the concept of heroism and power, but rather by claiming that Bibi was not what he claimed to be, and that in fact he, Barak, was the strong one. To counter the Likud's negative campaign slogan, "Barak will buckle under," Barak's campaign placed great emphasis on the power and heroism of "the most highly decorated soldier in the IDF." The main slogan was "Barak fights for Israel," and the picture most displayed was one showing Barak as commander of the General Staff commando unit, with gun in hand, seizing control of a Sabena airplane in a well-known operation to release hostages.

Another component of the "collective Netanyahu" was the Jewish element. This element illustrates how far symbolic reality is more meaningful than empirical facts. Netanyahu does not radiate Jewishness in the traditional sense; he does not wear a skullcap or observe religious tradition. He does not observe the rules of *kashrut* (dietary laws), was once married to a non-Jewish woman, and was the only public figure in Israel who admitted publicly that he was an adulterer. In spite of all this, he was still supported by the religious cultural groups and projected Jewishness. This was his discourse — these were the symbols he used.

In the difficult days when he was being questioned by the police regarding the attempted illegal appointment of the attorney general (the Bar-On affair), he chose to respond by being photographed not in his office or official home but during a private visit to some archaeological excavations in Jerusalem, where he spoke about the sacred values of Judaism. On another occasion, when he took part in the ceremonial March of the Living to the Treblinka death camp, he chose to walk wrapped in a prayer shawl and carrying a huge Israeli flag. Rabin, too, had participated in such a march, but it would have been inconceivable for him to be seen in a prayer shawl. To the *sabra*s of his generation, this act of Netanyahu's seemed unnatural, but this scene resonated in the hearts of most Israelis, both religious and traditionally oriented, who together form the majority in Israeli society.

The reason for this is that the Israeli Right identifies more with the Jewish element in the collective identity, while the Left feels more closely linked to its Israeli component (Shamir and Shamir 1995). Netanyahu was in the habit of visiting rabbis, expressing his deep admiration for them, both in words and gestures, and he spoke a great deal about Jewish values. "I estimate that the vast majority of the Israeli public are united around a few basic questions that are expressed in the wish to preserve the Jewish identity and in the understanding that there is both a religious and a national dimension to being Jewish," he said in an interview with Ari Shavit.[5]

A third component in Netanyahu's cluster of symbols is his Americanism. More than any other politician, he expressed the Israeli aspiration to be American. Here, too, his behavior is comparable to Rabin, who also had an American element as one of his sources of popularity. And if this was the case with Rabin, who had lived in the United States for only a few years as ambassador, these pro-American feelings were much stronger in the case of Netanyahu, who was raised and educated in America, whose

English is better than his Hebrew, and who has as many American cultural traits as Israeli ones. While Rabin had an American thread woven into his Israeli sabra character, Netanyahu's Americanism was more deep-rooted, so much so that his critics saw it as an expression of foreignness and alienation from the Israeli experience. To his supporters, on the other hand, which included most of the Israeli public during his reign as prime minister, such Americanism was in fact a point in his favor.

Another trait that Netanyahu projected, difficult to define in a word, is expressed in Hebrew slang as "not being a *freier* [a sucker]." This expression encompasses the ability to wheel and deal, to improvise, to get along, to land on one's feet. It is a survival skill perfected over hundreds of years by Jews in the Diaspora in order to live in a hostile environment, combined with the sabra qualities of roughness and pragmatism. It is constant suspicion and fear of being exploited, while not hesitating to exploit others; jealously guarding one's rights at the cost of violating the rights of others. Israeli society is divided in its view of this survival trait: liberals, intellectuals, humanists, and those with Western universalistic orientation are critical and contemptuous of it, while the popular culture praises it as a worthy trait.[6]

Ron Meiberg and Amnon Dankner referred to this trait when they chose Netanyahu as "Man of the Year" in December 1997:

The prime minister, who symbolized this year, is the frightening reflection of the people who elected him, as well as those who did not vote for him and are gnashing their teeth under his yoke. Someone once said that every nation gets the government it deserves, and it appears that every nation gets the prime minister who reflects important threads in its national character. Could it be that the anger and the opposition, the mockery and criticism which Benjamin Netanyahu arouses anew every morning, stem from the fact that this man, the big "fixer," the manipulator, the braggart, the whitewasher, the improviser, who compromises himself but manages to survive against all odds . . . is a reflection of ourselves?

Not being a "sucker" is related to being a "winner," another highly valued characteristic in Israeli society. It expresses personal achievement, marking the transition in recent years from a collective to an individualistic orientation in Israeli society (Katz and Haas 1997), as part of the penetration of American values. In the past, individual success was measured in terms of its contribution to the group; today, it is perceived in terms of self-fulfillment. In the past, recognition of success was granted to "pioneers," who fulfilled a collective mission. Today, individual success is manifested largely in terms of wealth and fame; this goes a long way to explain why Netanyahu spoke a great deal of his need to succeed and of the fact that he succeeded in everything he did.

Finally, Netanyahu made great efforts to emphasize that he was an exemplary family man. His emphasis on this trait is particularly interesting. While family is a highly regarded value in Israeli society, it finds little expression in the political arena, neither in politicians' behavior nor as a trope in Israeli political symbolism. So strongly emphasized by American politicians, family values have never been an issue in Israeli elections. On the contrary, some politicians who were known for their predilection for philandering, such as Moshe Dayan, were considered glamorous by the public. Netanyahu's emphasis on family values was considered an odd innovation. Was it an attempt to copy the American model? Perhaps it was part of an attempt to overcome his image as young and inexperienced and make him appear more seasoned and respectable. Or was he trying to live down the affair of the "red-hot tape" and his numerous (by Israeli standards) marriages?

Whatever the reason, Netanyahu, more than any other Israeli politician, went out of his way to present the picture of his happy family life, his loving relationship with his wife, and his deep involvement as a caring father. To symbolize this idyllic family scene, whenever he appeared in public with his family, he held hands with his wife. This was unusual in Israeli public life, and it looked unnatural. The demonstrative emphasis on the image of the devoted husband and father created the impression referred to by Nachum Barnea, that he was posing for the cameras.

By virtue of his mastery of the game of representations and his ability to stage many symbolic media events, Netanyahu expressed, in essence, the cluster of components of Israeli collective identity. Because such a fierce battle is continuously fought in Israel over this identity, no Israeli could be neutral toward him. His supporters adored him; his opponents could not bear what he represented. However, the extent of his enormous success is indicated by the fact that part of the criticism of him was not of the ontological meaning of the symbols he expressed and represented, but of the fact that he wore borrowed feathers, that he was not an authentic representative. In other words, some of the criticism of Netanyahu indirectly supported those values and identity components that he manifested.

These elements of Netanyahu's persona explain his attractiveness to his voters. They recognized his theatrical personality, and the question as to whether it reflected his backstage personality is irrelevant. However, the persona alone does not suffice to explain his success. Just as the political phenomenon of Begin's success cannot be explained simply as manipulative recruitment of the masses by a demagogic leader, Netanyahu's success also has to be explained from the perspective of the counterhegemonic bloc that supported him.

CHARACTERISTICS OF ISRAELI TELEPOPULISM

Netanyahu used professional methods to manipulate the masses, but at the same time he offered them a political body in which the underprivileged classes could express their anger at their exclusion from the dominant social order. This was a system through which they could present their demands, and particularly their demand for recognition. This is precisely the dual nature of neopopulism. "Populism means at the same time a movement towards the people, in favor of the people, an echo of the people, and a strategy to dominate them or to acquire political power" (Taguieff 1995: 21). Populism oscillates between demagogy and protest. The liberal and especially the elitist view of populism thus oversimplifies this social phenomenon, as shown by analyses of populism in South America. "Populism has been a specific and concrete method of mass manipulation, but it has also been a means for expressing their concerns" (Weffort 1967: 625–26).

Many of the features of Netanyahu's telepopulism, particularly his news management, are characteristic of the leadership style of media-centered politics in general. In this there is a similarity between Barak and Netanyahu. However, other aspects characterize only a more specific group of leaders in contemporary politics, telepopulist leaders (Mazzoleni 2003). In order to understand this, we need to examine the specific manifestations of Israeli neopopulism of the 1990s, bearing in mind de la Torre's succinct description (De la Torre 1998: 88–89; also see Chapter 8 above).

In the Israeli case, these developments are not represented by a particular party (for example, Peronism) or a political movement (such as the agrarian populism in the United States). The populist trend in Israel is instead more amorphous and includes diverse societal groups. These are mainly groups of low- and middle-socioeconomic strata, which are in a process of mobility accompanied by status anxiety, but groups belonging to the nationalist-clericalist camp are also included in the neopopulist movement. As it does in Europe, Israeli neopopulism is to be found largely at the right-wing of the political map. This group includes elements of the two ideal types of populist movements — "nationalist populism," which emphasizes the ideology of national unity, and "protest populism," which emphasizes the internal social dimension (Taguieff 1995). However, telepopulism has spread to broader levels and has even penetrated the national culture as a whole because it is carried by television. Television culture encourages it, uses similar rhetoric and language, nurtures its discourse, disseminates central elements of its ideology, and, above all, glorifies popular culture.

In this respect, telepopulism possesses a dimension that did not previously exist in the various forms of populism. In the past, too, populist leaders used the media to convey their populist message. For example, Peron, in Argentina, used the radio as his main medium. However, the uniqueness of telepopulism lies in the fact that this time the dominant medium is not merely a tool. Television, by its very nature, structures the populist discourse, encourages and nurtures populist values. It does this because of its internal logic; telepopulism is therefore a process reinforced by the dialectical relationship between the medium itself and the use made of it by the populist leader. This is why telepopulism does not need to be confined to a political movement, as it was in the past, in order to be influential, because it extends over a much wider social spectrum.

The Israeli telepopulism of the 1990s, like other types of populism, is foremost an antistatus quo ideology. Populism is opposition, protest — of the losers, of the excluded, of the peripheral groups — against their marginal social status, against their lack of autonomy and inability to determine their own fate, against their exclusion from positions of power. It is a demand to rebalance power in society for the benefit of the majority (Kazin 1998). Therefore it is clear why the populist tradition arouses concern among groups who are satisfied with the status quo, those who are well served by the social order.

This central motif of neopopulism was still expressed by the champions of the populist trend in the Israel of the 1990s even after they rose to power; in fact, it actually grew stronger. "Prime Minister Benjamin Netanyahu hasn't changed much since he came to power," wrote Hemmi Shalev and Ben Caspit in *Maariv* on April 10, 1998, pointing out, among other things, the fact that, "as before, he still has trouble hiding the resentment and alienation that he feels toward the media and the elites alongside them." In various speeches, he repeatedly expressed anger and protest against the status quo, calling for the rescue of the nation and political renewal (Canovan 1999: 6).

The primary targets of the protest were the elites. In the Israeli populism of the 1990s, anti-elitism was the most salient and blatant element, compared with other elements of populism that were more hidden or implied. Yoram Beck, one of the few intellectuals who sided with Netanyahu and his government against the old elites, wrote:

It appears that Israeli democracy, despite the formal democratic structure, is a far cry from the Western model, which was distinctly a reign of the aristocracy. . . . It was a class in the full meaning of the word . . . and, like all the elites, they knew how to rationalize their domination in universalist terms. . . . But this reign had an Achilles' heel . . . it was aloof from the nation. . . . Netanyahu symbolizes the anti-elitist coalition, the coming together of all of the popular forces that rose up against the sophisticated and hypocritical government, and in this respect he is a threat to the very existence of the Israeli elite.[7]

In contrast, *Haaretz* writer Ehud Ashri attacked the Netanyahu government's anti-elitist policies.

What do the following have in common: the abortive appointment of Roni Bar-On [the lawyer who was appointed attorney general when his "common touch" was considered an advantage], the attack on public broadcasting, the flourishing of Channel 2, and the proposal to recognize *yeshiva* graduates as university graduates [a government proposal to enable those lacking higher education to be appointed to public roles for which an academic degree is mandatory]?

These are four examples of a single process, whose purpose is to upset the balance in Israeli culture between the elitist orientation and the popular orientation, in favor of the latter. . . . The deliberate process of reducing the power of the elites will inevitably lead to the diminution of elitism as a social value and to a general devaluation of cultural standards. Soon, nothing of quality will be able to survive here, unless it goes underground.[8]

As for Netanyahu himself, he began his assault against the elite in his own party, while he placed himself in opposition to the "princes" and built his power base by developing support from below, as the representative of the rank and file. Local strong-arm leaders suddenly became "cultural stars" in Netanyahu's camp. He promoted the concept of the marketplace, which he would visit from time to time and sweet-talk stall owners, the ones who would later set the tone in party conventions. When these stall owners were subsequently described as "a gang of loud-mouths, who think with their stomachs and breathe fire from their ears," Netanyahu and his supporters could point to such criticisms as further proof of the arrogant attitude of the elites and the media.[9]

From a populist point of view, the distinction between the two protagonists was clear-cut: the power bloc included the labor movement, the Ashkenazim, the intelligentsia, the cultural-artistic elite (of which the media are a part), academia, and the professional establishment, such as the legal system, the military and the defense establishment. The people were the Mizrahim, residents of peripheral neighborhoods, the lower socioeconomic classes, the orthodox and the ultraorthodox, and the new immigrants. Added to this second group, however, were also some whose socioeconomic status equaled that of the elite, but who were excluded from it due to the long-term hegemony of the labor movement.

Such was Netanyahu's father, Professor Ben-Zion Netanyahu. Son of a respected, wealthy family, an intellectual and an academic who lived in an aristocratic Jerusalem neighborhood, he nevertheless saw himself as part of the counter-Labor camp. In the 1950s he was not accepted by the Hebrew University of Jerusalem, imputing this to his right-wing views, as it was the left-leaning elites who had dominated the university. After this experience, he decided to take his family to the United States for several years. Like his father, Benjamin Netanyahu felt like an outsider, although he had studied at an elite Jerusalem school, Rehavia High School, and had been through the rite of passage of the Israeli elite, serving in the IDF commando unit.

In this respect Netanyahu followed in the footsteps of Begin, who had created the Likud by establishing a historic alliance between the counterelite of the largely Ashkenazi Herut movement and the mostly Mizrahi lower socioeconomic strata. Netanyahu created a new counterhegemonic bloc, which included the old Mizrahim and orthodox groups, along with new ones, the Russian-speaking immigrants. To build this bloc, Netanyahu was prepared to sacrifice the interests of his own party's apparatus. Like Begin, Netanyahu acted in this regard as the "signifier" described by Bourdieu, who, by the act of signification, "creates the [signified] group which creates him [as its representative]" (Bourdieu 1990: 62).

However, populism has an internal contradiction and a dual character. On the one hand, it speaks in the name of specific groups who are against the elite, and on the other, it claims to represent all "the people." This ambiguity of the people (*demos*) resurfaces with "the people" being at the same time the whole and part of the people — the better part. Populism simultaneously speaks of the united people and of part of it, "our people," the silent majority, the ordinary or common people, facing the privileged, educated, cosmopolitan elite (Canovan 1999: 5).

Ostensibly, Netanyahu spoke in the name of national unity, and in his Knesset speeches he repeatedly said, "We are one people." At the same time, he took advantage of every opportunity to inflame his supporters against the other camp, whispering words of incitement in their ears, "They hate us," as had happened with the "rabble incident." It was clear which of the two sides was the better part of the nation, because "virtue resides in the simple people, who are the overwhelming majority, and in their collective tradition" (Wiles 1969: 166).[10]

Netanyahu knew how to exploit the open-air markets, the *agora*, "and saw the public squares as an element in his political strategy," especially when his party was in the opposition.[11] But in most cases, particularly when he became prime minister, the public square served primarily as a stage or a setting for a television appearance. This demonstrates one of the differences between the old-style populism and telepopulism. Whereas the old populism had used the public square for political action, telepopulism prefers the TV studio and uses the square only as a backdrop for a TV spectacle.

The Israeli neopopulism was extremely critical of intellectuals. "Populism is anti-intellectual. Even its intellectuals try to be anti-intellectual" (Wiles 1969: 167). The intellectuals were accused by populist spokesperson of lacking roots in Jewish tradition, being deficient in national pride, imitating foreign cultures, importing Americanization, and being influenced by and even currying favor with foreigners in the world centers of power and culture, namely, the U.S. and the international media.

This conflict between the humanistic, universalist approach and the zealotry concerning particularist Jewish values has accompanied Jewish traditions for hundreds of years. The proponents of the former approach, primarily the intelligentsia, were labeled "Hellenists" in the Jewish tradition, referring to those who preferred the values of Athens to those of Jerusalem in ancient times. According to the Jewish nationalist approach, there is no room for compromise between the two poles:

> Since its birth, the Jewish people has been tested by its ability to stand up to the gentiles. Our forefather Abraham was called "Hebrew" because he stood on one side, while the rest of the world stood on the other [the word "Hebrew" comes from the same root as the words "beyond," "over," "cross over," and so on]. This is the essence of the Jew — he always faces up to the rest of the world, [and] the basic conflict between the Jewish people and the rest of the world remains unaltered.

Thus wrote Rabbi Yosef-Yitzhak Aharonov, editor of *Sichat Hashavua*, a journal of young Lubavicher Hassidim. This ultraorthodox movement, which had been at the extreme nationalistic pole since the 1980s, aided Netanyahu's success in the 1996 elections, campaigning under the slogan "Netanyahu is good for the Jews."

In the populist culture of the 1990s, the word "professors" became a derogatory word, and the high register of their speech was disparaged, as opposed to the popularist rhetoric that had been preferred in Israeli culture due to its direct, blunt nature (Katriel 1986). Similarly, Israeli populism glorified other expressions of folk culture, such as physical contact, including hugging and kissing between men, as well as shoulder-slapping. Politicians who exhibit these behaviors — like Haim Ramon or Binyamin Ben-Eliezer — are considered "good guys," while those who don't — such as Dan Meridor or Yossi Beilin — are regarded as elitist and arrogant.

The transformation of "popular" to "good" characterizes TV culture in general, which has rightly earned the title of "karaoke culture" after the entertainment genre that enables anyone to be a singer, even if he or she cannot sing at all. "It seems to me that all this 'inclusion' and democratization fosters a culture which values participation over ability and popularity over excellence: the karaoke culture," wrote Rory Bremner in the pro-Labor and progressive British opinion magazine *New Statesman*.[12]

When Netanyahu supported Knesset member Shaul Amor's candidacy for president against Ezer Weizmann, a member of the Israeli aristocracy, he used, among others, the argument that Amor was "a man of the people." In response, author Meir Shalev wrote scornfully about the cult of plebeianism, which had become the major criterion in the choice of a candidate for public office, whether for a professional role like the attorney general or a representative role like that of president. "Plebeianism is not necessarily modesty and simplicity," he wrote, "but a cover for the celebration of mediocrity and vulgarity, regression, inarticulateness, and other such positive traits."[13]

Perhaps even more than his choice of candidates for attorney general and president, Netanyahu expressed his attitude to the intellectual elite in his appointment of advisor on academic affairs. In contrast with the prime ministers before him, who had been proud to rub shoulders with intellectuals, artists, and writers, Netanyahu appointed an unknown scientist with no public standing whatsoever. Netanyahu's hostile attitude to intellectuals and academics led to a significant controversy when a group of senior professors protested after the Hebrew University of Jerusalem decided to confer an honorary doctorate upon him. A letter signed by twenty-three professors who were described as "the top league of academia" declared:

We are concerned that the prime minister, during his short term in office, has endangered and continues to endanger institutions and principles that any enlightened society holds dear, and which are the foundations of a proper democracy, such as the rule of law, the free press, and the government's duty to keep trust with the public. Mr. Netanyahu is trying to undermine public broadcasting; he had a hand, both actively and by omission, in severely harming the police, the prosecution, and the legal system, and has continuously violated the basic standards of government. He was instrumental in the appointment of a singularly unfit individual to the office of attorney general, even after the existence of corrupt motives for the appointment was brought to his attention.[14]

The professors' criticisms notwithstanding, neopopulism's perception that sees the people as an indiscriminate mass has several implications, some of which gave Israeli neopopulism its undemocratic character. For example, who belongs to the people, and who defines this belonging? One of the arguments voiced in Israel against the authority of the government, and even of the Knesset, to determine the fate of the occupied territories, was that the Land of Israel belongs to the people of Israel throughout the generations. Therefore, those living today have no authority to speak in the name of the people and certainly do not represent those who lived in the past or those who will live in the future. Another argument regarding the same matter was that the Knesset members include people who, although elected by Israeli citizens, do not belong to the nation because they are Arabs.

The presentation of "the people as one" negates the divisions and diversities of society. Politics becomes the struggle of the unitary people against the enemies of the people, "the other," contrary to the basic values of liberal democracy. Indeed, all the polls that examined voters' attitudes in the second half of the 1990s, divided into those who had voted for Netanyahu and those who had voted for Peres or Barak, showed that Netanyahu's supporters tended less to support liberal attitudes and had no deep conception of the liberal dimension of democracy, such as civil rights, pluralism, or tolerance.[15]

If the battle against elitism and the hegemonic bloc expresses the element of protest in Israeli populism, the perception of integral nationalism expresses its nationalistic character, and these two elements are closely intertwined. The nationalistic dimension has deep roots in the Israeli body politic. It derives from a long religious tradition that distinguishes between Israel and the gentile nations, was reinforced by the establishment of the national liberation movement, Zionism, and intensified in the wake of the hundred years of war against the Arabs, who opposed the establishment of a Jewish state in the Middle East. To all this, Netanyahu added the contemporary version of Huntington's *Clash of Civilizations*. In light of this tradition, it is not surprising that Israeli populism is manifested in intolerance of others, xenophobia, and suspicions of international conspiracy. In this sense, Netanyahu's neopopulism was no different from that of former Prime Minister Menachem Begin.[16]

The second component in the populist mixture is the leader of the movement. The leader is a particularly important element because unlike representative democracy, which is based on mediating bodies between the public and the political leadership, populism is built on the people-leader axis. Charisma is not a prerequisite, although many populist leaders were charismatic. Sometimes the populist leader claims that he is a "simple person, just like everyone else," and he thus represents the entire population and understands them much better than other politicians. This kind of leader bases his legitimacy not on his possession of outstanding political qualities, but rather on his being an outsider in the corridors of power — a representative of the people penetrating the loci of power of the elite and the establishment. This was the trump card played by Jimmy Carter in his first election (Canovan 1981: 268–69) and also the springboard for Fernando Collor de Mello's success in Brazil (Porto 2001). The same theme was used by "El Chino" (a friendly nickname often used for Asians in Peru), as the Peruvians called Alberto Fujimori, whose name and appearance testified to his Japanese origin. This outsider theme was also the basis for Netanyahu's legitimacy.

Lack of charisma has to be compensated for by an ability to control the central medium of telepopulism, to satisfy the needs of television, to adapt oneself and one's actions to it. Collor de Mello's campaign, for example, took advantage of the political scenario structured by television, not only in the news but mainly through soap operas, and when elected he established a spectacular and media-centered presidency. The ability to be a television tribune is a necessary condition of telepopulism, and it is no coincidence that the political pundits who estimated Netanyahu's telegenicity described it as "magic," a word often used to describe charisma.

The tendency for hyperpersonalization that characterizes populist movements was fostered by Netanyahu himself, by means of image building and image management, and was also manifested in his speeches. Netanyahu made extensive use of language emphasizing his special status. He and his spokespeople frequently used expressions such as "I instructed Minister so-and-so to do this or that," or, "The prime minister directed the chief of staff to act." This manner of speech, which was not common among previous prime ministers, emphasized that the prime minister was the direct, unmediated interpreter of the will of the people, and that he alone held the reins of power.

Cultural scholar Zohar Shavit, who analyzed speeches delivered by Netanyahu on special occasions, such as those he made on Israel's 50th Independence Day, Memorial Day, or on his visit to Auschwitz and Birkenau, showed the ways in which Netanyahu constructed his image — the populist leader. In these speeches,

Netanyahu places himself before the audience and Jewish history as a sort of mediator between heaven and earth, between the anonymous audience and the current reality, between the past and the future. He knows better than anyone how to read the historical process, and "history" has entrusted him with the helm, to steer Israel towards the future. All the others are passive spectators who willingly gave him the helm, or else they are doubters and skeptics afflicted with blindness.

Ostensibly these are speeches conveying a simple, practical message, using familiar symbols. But a more thorough reading shows that they are built with careful thought, based on complex rhetorical tricks. . . . There is only one clear statement in these speeches, glorification of Netanyahu. The unequivocal message is: I am the only leader in my generation, equal to the leaders of previous generations, if not greater. I am the embodiment of the wars, the Holocaust, the future; I am the past, the present, and the future; I am the flag, "L'etat c'est moi."

His texts are intended to connect Netanyahu with the honored pantheon of historic figures. But in his picture of the past, there are almost no key figures from Jewish or Land of Israel history. . . . When he has to refer to the actions of those who built the state . . . he uses the infinitive form of the verb to describe the action without mentioning those who carried it out, leaving them anonymous. So there is only "to arise," "to breathe fresh life into," "to take shape," instead of "they arose," "they breathed fresh life into," and so forth. The only time he uses the active form, singular or plural, is when he relates to himself and his actions, and thus he is the only figure that appears.

The only concrete personality in his jubilee speech was "I": This "I" has a clear face and a different form of speech. Now Netanyahu uses the present and future tense, relating the action to the speaker: "I am certain that," "I am full of hope." And he slides from "I" to "we" and to the symbols of the state, creating identity between himself, the collective, and the symbols.[17]

Just as he glorified the people, on the one hand, and himself as leader, on the other, Netanyahu tried to undermine the real mediating bodies of representative democracy. He revealed a clearly negative attitude not only toward parliamentarianism, for example by denying the legitimacy of the opposition, but also toward other institutions of government that mediate between the people and the leader. He and others who spoke in his name, such as Lieberman, repeatedly criticized the civil service, the foreign service, the judiciary, the police, and even the military top brass. His erosion of the separation of powers and his disdain for government institutions, to the extent of weakening the governing bureaucracy and the administrative bodies themselves can be seen clearly in this context.

This was the subject of a statement published by senior academics in Jerusalem, and it was also referred to explicitly by Michael Ben-Yair, who had served as attorney general during the governments of Rabin, Peres, and later Netanyahu. He stated, "The Netanyahu government is damaging the government system. The biting criticism of the civil service, of employees of the foreign office, of the top echelons of the military, of the attorney general's office, and the police — all of these injure the professional systems of the state."[18] The structure of the regime that developed in the second half of the 1990s was defined by Avnon as "a modern authoritarian regime." According to his description, the parliamentary opposition had lost its status, as the real opposition was inside the coalition. Furthermore, because of the built-in tension between the prime minister and his party, he had to create organizations that would help him in his work, particularly to promote his election. It was impossible to remain faithful to the formal process and at the same time efficiently make policy decisions. As a result, a system was devised to circumvent the formal structures of government. A series of alternatives to the governing bodies were presented, until it was no longer clear where decisions were made on national issues.

In this regime the democratic institutions and processes were ostensibly preserved but served as a means for the accumulation of personal power in the guise of taking care of the public needs, and concurrently the informal governing systems operated and there decisions were made. The court system, police, and the state comptroller became effective mediators in society, bypassing the parliamentary process and weakening democracy. In this state of affairs, the need for public opinion polls becomes clear; they may serve as an effective democratic process in conditions of a functioning parliamentary democracy, but when there is a crisis of democracy they strengthen the leader's authoritarian tendencies.[19]

Even if this description is exaggerated, it is revealing that Netanyahu has gone on record expressing support for Israel's becoming a presidential system. Added to this, a fairly high percentage of the Israeli public expressed preference for a "strong leader" (Peres and Yuchtman-Yaar 1998). Furthermore, the fact that there are political movements and even parties in Israel whose leaders are not elected, but rather acquire legitimacy by acclamation, recalls Karl Schmitt's version of populism (Schmitt 1994). Rabbi Ovadia Yosef of the Shas Party is a prime example of this.

In the last several chapters I pointed out the weaknesses that are endemic to media-centered democracies, which in fact are even more prevalent in populism. In telepopulism the weaknesses of both systems, mediapolitik and neopopulism, are interwoven. Therefore, the aspect of populism for which its supporters praise it most — for being a system that increases democratization and strengthens the participation of citizens in the political process — is merely an illusion. Populist and telepopulist leaders create only a false sense of inclusion and passive, not real, participation at most. Television creates relationships that are described by media scholars as "parasocial interaction" — a simulation of real social relations between the viewer and the image on the screen (Meyrowitz 1994). The telepopulist leader attempts to create similar relations by fostering an illusion of closeness between viewers and their political guide. Audiences begin to feel that they have a direct connection with the leader and that they are taking part in government and determining their fate and future. All of this is simply a mirage.

While so-called talk-show democracy was hailed by some American scholars for having energized the 1992 presidential campaign — although less was heard about this after 1996 — the role of elites as arbiters of civic understanding is indeed returning to the public. They are playing increasingly active roles in constructing social and political meaning of the mix of mediated narratives (Carpini and Williams 2000).

Similarly, the assessment that TV brings the masses closer to the social center and into the centers of power, is also in question. As explained by Bourdieu, television reproduces a new kind of elitism, esoterism, and demagogy. It appears to give access to a majority of people to certain fields of public life, but at the same time it deeply influences cultural production and the structure of research, denying autonomy to both politics and the media (Bourdieu 1999).

The case of Italian Prime Minister Silvio Berlusconi is a good example.

The combination of his economic power and control over media outlets enabled him to set up a social and cultural infrastructure (sports and entertainment) in the 1990s. When that was ready, he used it as a springboard to gain political power. Once in power, the media outlets could be used to praise the leader and consolidate his position. Thus, while the cultural products used by television in telepopulism are those of the masses, the real control over the tool — TV itself — is kept in the hands of the elite (Calloni 1998).

Many of telepopulism's weaknesses derive from the fact that the media are in fact not an effective tool of governance. The media agenda is not necessarily the most important agenda for the public: in the infotainment era the media deals with the "interesting" and not with the "important." "The news itself is not a suitable basis for political choice. The media provide a narrow and biased version of political reality, one that focuses on political game and weakens rather than strengthens the relations between the [American] people and their political leadership and institutions" (Patterson 2000: 264). Populism increases the pressure for short-term solutions to political problems and strengthens the danger that with mass attention focused on sociopolitical agendas, much official politics will be left in the hands of better-informed elites. As so many cases of telepopulism already showed, it also creates perfect conditions for the flourishing of manipulative measures and demagogues (Blumler and Kavanagh 1999: 226).

The need to reply to the passing moods of the public, as they are expressed by public opinion polls, to "blowing bubbles," is often not the most efficient way to deal with governance issues. At the end of the day, populism cannot compete with the institutionalized political mechanisms that integrate the masses in advanced democracies and make them participants in the public arena and power structures. It simply cannot replace the democratic mechanisms of articulation and integration of interests or the mechanism that enables it to steer the polity.

Urbinati correctly notes that entwined with the redemptive strand of democracy is a deep revulsion against institutions that come between the people and their action, and a craving for direct, unmediated expression of the people's will (Urbinati 1998). However, neither modern sophisticated media outlets nor plebiscites can act as substitutes for the bureaucratized and institutionalized mechanisms of governance. Populism has an attraction-power because it presents a model of personal and immediate politics, while the liberal democratic model is remote and bureaucratic. But even if populism has a seemingly magical appeal, democracy indeed needs these boring, gray, and cold institutions. And with all the pretensions to express the people's will, governments must take an institutional form that is far removed from spontaneous popular expressions in order to seriously conduct political life.

In the same way that a modern democracy cannot survive efficiently without these institutions, it cannot function well without parties. Two reasons in particular make the parties so vital. An effective party is, among other things, a disciplined organization that balances divergent interests to achieve a unified platform and legislative program. Parties also act as a means of providing some consistency over time and attention to long-term policies and issues. Governing without parties can accomplish neither end. Indeed, one cannot point to a successful democracy where parties have been replaced by mechanisms of direct democracy.

The Israeli case has shown that the media do not necessarily engender political passivity. However, they do cause a negative transformation of the public debate and the political discourse. The language of television is a language of acclamation, not a language of discussion (Urbinati 1998: 119). This is exactly the language of populism. An analysis of television rhetoric shows how similar it is to that of populism, how much the sound-bite culture and the logic of the small screen fit the political style of populism. In both, slogans and even artistic expressions replace arguments that have a universal and general validity. Furthermore, discourse is characterized by an emotional approach, rather than reason and sophisticated complex logical arguments.

In contemporary societies, the media, and foremost television, are not the most appropriate tools for the advancement of the democratic discourse: unlike political parties, the media do not involve debate by the public at-large with continuity and are not driven by a certain normative set of principles. Television operates by a normative system that does not have a clear moral or value-laden position concerning its environment. Its sole purpose is to increase its ratings — a principle that makes it apolitical. The criterion for newsworthiness is not a deviation from the normative — something that calls for a value judgment — but rather a deviation from the "normal." From this point of view, the more extreme the deviation, the more interest it creates, and the larger the audience that is attracted to the screens.

This is the reason why television deals with the odd, the piquant, and the deviant, and not with the "wrong" from a normative or value perspective. This is also the cause of television's focus on its own invented realities, not those of the outside world. Television, as Yatziv claims, "does not deal with the relations between the elements of reality that can be observed, but rather instructs the audience mainly to watch the fictitious world it creates, to ignore the reality in which the most important elements of their life are being determined, and to divert their attention from the processes that shape these elements" (1999: 97). Thus, the media lead the public away from rational discussions on the real problems of life to imagined, less meaningful problems, exactly like the imagined world that is created by populist and telepopulist rhetoric. After all, television editors of political programs admit, astonishingly enough, that they do not really want to encourage a political debate in the studio. Asked what is the profile of a good participant in such a discussion program, a senior producer on Israel's public Channel 1 replied:

> We believe that audiences have no patience to listen to someone who ponders and hesitates, or thinks while he talks. This causes people to think, something they don't like to do. People want new information, or known information brought to them in a new light, and it is important to spice it up with personal stories. The audience loves to watch an interviewee that knows what he or she says, but he or she should not be much wiser then they are. Therefore, program producers will never invite anyone who has an elaborate opinion. They always invite the same people over and over. To invite someone new needs extra production efforts, and who's got the time and the energy for that?[20]

This negative impact that television culture has on public discourse, in addition to the destructive impact of populism in bringing about deinstitutionalization, calls for a clear conclusion concerning the question of whether populism be regarded as a positive phenomenon.[21]

Contrary to those who argue for the virtues of populism in advanced democracies such as the United States (Kazin 1995), I tend to support the notion that neopopulism and telepopulism can be positive factors and enlarge the political field only under certain conditions, particularly only in democracies that have not yet reached maturity. In advanced democracies its detrimental effects far outweigh any advantages it might potentially offer.

CHAPTER ELEVEN

Netanyahu's War Against the Media

A COMPETITIVE MEDIA CONFRONTING
A POPULIST LEADER

Not unexpectedly, Netanyahu related to the media in his first "thank you" speech, immediately after his election in June 1996. "The media," he said, "play an important role in the fabric of democratic life in Israel. We must guard their position. Any debate on the functioning of the media in Israel should be civilized and responsible."[1] This was the kind of perfunctory interspersed with generous promises that every speechwriter of a prime minister-elect included in his speech of thanks. Beneath the surface, Netanyahu faced a rather complex problem. The political setup within which Netanyahu played in the second half of the 1990s was mediapolitik, in which the media did not behave like the domesticated pets every politician dreams of. The journalists' approach was not even adversarial, as it appeared on the surface, but actively confrontational. This model is based on the concept of conflict and challenge, mostly on the part of the media toward their political interlocutors, within the context of a search by the media for a power alternative to that exerted by political institutions (Cook 1998).

This pattern was formed as soon as Netanyahu entered Israeli political life, when he returned from the United States. At first, the media did not see him as a political actor with the potential to play in the major league. They regarded him as a lightweight compared to veteran political leaders like Shamir, Arens, Sharon, and Levy, and as a foreigner, an outsider, as opposed to the "princes," the pretenders to the throne of his generation. This unenthusiastic attitude continued even after Netanyahu surprised everyone by winning the leadership of the Likud, when the new political marketing style, and particularly the image building, that he imported to Israel increased the scornful attitude toward him.

If the confrontational model of media is problematic for any political leader, it is much more so for a neopopulist leader. According to the neopopulist approach, the media belong to the hard core of the hegemonic bloc and are partners in shaping the hegemonic belief system, which neopopulism seeks to destroy. The problem is further compounded for the telepopulist leader because this type of regime requires him to control the media, particularly television. This would surely arouse the media's resistance, as well as broad resistance among the public who support freedom of the press. This is an inherent contradiction between the democratic face of telepopulism and its antidemocratic character.

True to his neopopulist perception, Netanyahu saw the media elite in Israel as part of the "soft" liberal elite. In this respect he reflected the attitudes of American neoconservatives. In fact, he considered Israeli media even worse than its American counterpart, because there, "Although most journalists belong to the liberal wing . . . [and] professional ethics override personal opinions." In Israel, he argued, 80–90 percent of journalists belong to the Left and create a monopoly of ideas. "What is happening with the media in Israel is unlike anything in the Western world, and now even in the east. Even in many parts of the formerly communist world there is no example of such centralization, such conformism of thought and herd-like behavior." As a student of the revisionist school, he saw leftists as lacking backbone and failing to understand the nature of the cruel game of international relations, especially in the Middle East, where no one cares about Israel's existence and its survival depends on its military power. But he also saw the Left as a closed, arrogant clique that refused admission to others.

Journalists' attitudes toward Netanyahu, reserved at first and later sharply critical, fell on ripe soil. He had not really expected them to behave otherwise, though he had hoped that they might do so. This was a combination of psychological undercurrents and a rational worldview. The political journalists were against him because he was an outsider, while they were the friends of the party "princes." Furthermore, they also opposed him because they shared the worldview of the leftist elite he so despised. And so it was that Benjamin Netanyahu, son of an aristocratic family from a prestigious Jerusalem neighborhood, who had served in an elite IDF unit, felt more comfortable with the excluded groups in Israeli society, such as new immigrants from the former Soviet Union, the orthodox and the ultraorthodox, and the Mizrahim on the periphery.

This state of affairs naturally found expression in the media. In contrast to his complex and hostile relations with the national media, his relations with the sectarian media were another story entirely. He was the cultural hero of the Russian-language papers. He was a faithful and much admired political partner to the orthodox and ultraorthodox press, from the fundamentalist *Hashavua* to the National Religious Party's *Hatzofeh*. He was a faithful ally of the West Bank settlers' pirate radio station, Channel 7 and enjoyed the praise of the dozens of illegal radio stations run by Shas, which they called "the sacred channels."

Neopopulism seeks to effect radical reforms in the social structure, and the state of the media served Netanyahu as proof of the distorted state of Israeli culture and society. "The intellectual structure of Israeli society is off-balance. . . . It is monolithic. Everything leans to one side. There is no cross-fertilization between two sides . . . but rather an ongoing monologue of one inside cult, which both writes and interprets its own gospel, and expects everyone to worship it."[2] In the past, too, there had been periods of tension, suspicion, mutual accusations, and even real conflict between the prime minister and the media. During the tense "waiting" period before the Six-Day War in 1967, journalists and commentators had supported a fierce public campaign against Prime Minister Levy Eshkol, who avoided launching a preemptive strike against Egypt. On very rare occasions there was an extremely sharp dispute on issues relating to metadiscourse in communication, namely, when the differences of opinion between the political elite and the media elite concerned the actual definition of the role of the media and the government's media policy. This happened in 1981, when Defense Minister Sharon denied the media access to the Rafah Pass in the south of the Gaza Strip during the evacuation of Palestinians from the area. Newspaper editors, including the most conservative and security-oriented, like *Maariv* editor Shemuel Schnitzer, protested against the closing of an area and actually stood across from the barbed-wire fence, in a demonstration for media access. All of these incidents, however, paled in comparison with the depth of the conflict during Netanyahu's period, which was much sharper and different in principle, due to the new role played by the media in the telepopulist system.

THE AFTERMATH OF RABIN'S ASSASSINATION

If the mistrust in relations between Netanyahu and the media became apparent immediately on his entrance into political life, it was severely aggravated by the scandal of the "red-hot tape" in 1993. Just before the Likud primaries he appeared in a dramatic live broadcast on the evening news, announcing that he had been threatened that a videocassette apparently showing him having extramarital relations would be distributed. He said that he had discussed the matter with his wife and had asked for her forgiveness, and the two had patched things up. He accused his political rivals in the primaries — a veiled reference to David Levy — of the deed. The way in which Netanyahu exposed the story of his extramarital affair was a new departure in Israel's political culture, and it did not improve his standing in the political community. The latter, including the media, did not like the intrusion of the private sphere into the political arena, and the debate over this became a source of friction between them throughout the entire period of his office. He himself, who had broken down the barrier between the private and public sphere, accused the media of invading his private life, and they in turn politicized the private and were forced to defend themselves for doing so.

However, the disputes between Netanyahu and those who set the tone in the national media became much more intense due to Netanyahu's hard line toward the Rabin government after the Oslo Accords. They were less critical of his political attitudes than of his political behavior as head of the opposition, his extreme language, and his help of the extra-parliamentary groups on the extreme Right, which were sometimes even violent. On one occasion, he took part in a demonstration in Ra'anana with anti-Rabin placards followed by a burial casket. In another demonstration, the incensed crowd burned a placard bearing a likeness of Rabin dressed in a Nazi SS uniform. At this demonstration Netanyahu addressed the cheering crowd from a balcony overlooking Jerusalem's Zion Square, prompting comparison with other times in other places.

When Rabin was assassinated in November 1995, a media frame that saw the incitement against him as the main cause of his murder solidified and an accusing finger was pointed at Netanyahu (Wolfsfeld 1996). For the same reason the victim's widow refused to shake hands with Netanyahu, then head of the opposition, when he walked past her at the funeral, which was on a live TV broadcast. Further, she did not agree to his speaking at the first annual memorial ceremony, even though he was prime minister then.

This was the atmosphere at the beginning of the election campaigns for the 1996 Knesset. The political media did not behave as Netanyahu had expected, treating him and his rival, Shimon Peres, equally. Most journalists supported Peres, and their attitude was reflected in the op-ed pages, and even more in the influential columns of top political analysts. Netanyahu's supporters claimed that the television stations gave Peres much more coverage than Netanyahu.[3] Netanyahu saw this as proof of his argument that "journalists are part of the nomenclature of the old guard."[4]

In fact, some of these arguments were confirmed by journalists themselves. Criticism, they said, was common journalistic practice. Furthermore, they did not estimate Netanyahu's chances to be high, Peres seemed to be the favorite, and the media generally focus on the winner. Some of them even admitted that they harbored bitterness toward Netanyahu over Rabin's murder. One journalist defined it this way: "It was such an enormous tragedy that we felt obligated to Rabin's heritage, and Peres was the natural heir."[5]

The criticism of the media's bias, however, was a broad generalization. Although senior political columnists supported the Oslo Accords and therefore also supported Rabin and Peres, this support was not reflected in the role played by the media in the elections. Three studies on the media in the election campaign showed that on the whole, radio and TV news broadcasts, press news stories, and the style of campaign coverage were not biased, as distinct from the op-ed pages, which have less exposure and less influence. Quantitative studies showed that, contrary to Netanyahu's claim that Peres was given extra TV exposure, both channels gave equal coverage to the two candidates.[6]

Qualitative studies substantiated this finding, showing that the television treatment of terrorist acts, through the use of "a disaster marathon," namely, exaggerating the drama, hurling accusations at the government, and extensive exposure of the attitude of the opposition had aided the Likud campaign and Netanyahu (Liebes and Peri 1997; Liebes 1998). When the new government was formed, it brought with it added sources of tension toward the media. All of the parties forming the coalition shared the view of the media as the bastion of the old center, the arrogant elite, the Ashkenazi establishment of the labor movement and the liberal, secular, dovish world view, labeled by the overall term "leftist." These parties did not hide their intentions of settling their accounts with the media.

The latter did not hide their antagonism toward "the coalition of the rejected" and what it represented, either. They criticized the religious parties' growing influence on public life, the generous government subsidies given to settlers and settlements on the West Bank, and the diversion of budgets to the separate educational systems of Shas and to draft-dodging yeshiva students. Added to all this was the fear that the new government would halt the peace process. The new government was not granted the one hundred days of grace that the media usually grant new governments.

On the contrary, after the elections the media beat their breast over the fact that they had not exposed Netanyahu to the public as they should have done. They sought to repair this omission by trying to reveal both the enigma behind the mask and Netanyahu's life story. They began hostile probes into his private life, in many cases without any factual basis, even going so far as to publish strange tales of Netanyahu's impersonating various individuals or spying for the CIA. These allegations were found to be groundless, but this did not weaken the media's suspicion and animosity toward "the magician."

All of this served to reinforce his natural misgivings and anger at the media, as well as his division of the world into "those who are for us" and "those who are against us." "Let the creeps in," he would say to his bureau chief, referring to the journalists waiting to meet him. Nevertheless, he kept on meeting them just as often.[7]

A very widely publicized investigative story on Sara Netanyahu by *Yediot Ahronot* marked a high point in exposing the prime minister's wife, and a low point in the media's relations with the Netanyahu family. The picture that emerged was that of a woman with a problematic personality and marital relations very different from the ideal image that Netanyahu attempted to present. In the image war it was not at all relevant whether or not this was true. But it was this media frame that became fixed in the national media.

THE STRATEGY OF THE WAR AGAINST THE MEDIA

The bad blood between Netanyahu and the media placed him in a dilemma. On the one hand, his political strategy was based on the use of the media, particularly television. On the other hand, he understood that they would not allow him to implement this strategy. Moreover, in the first year following the elections, the parliamentary opposition almost disappeared. The Labor Party, sunk in postelection depression, was neutralized by internal struggles over the succession to Peres as leader of the party. This reinforced the sense of mission among journalists, especially those in *Haaretz* and television, who felt that it was up to them to take up the role of opposition to the government.

Netanyahu's task, therefore, was to control the media while neutralizing journalists themselves, and he chose a three-pronged approach: (1) to use his power as prime minister in order to gain control over the public news organizations; (2) to use media outlets to reach the public over the heads of the journalists; and (3) to launch a crusade to delegitimize the journalists and undermine their professional stature as an interpretive community. The last of these was meant to detract from journalists' ability to fulfill the role as interpreters of reality, as those who determine the significance of the collective experience (Zelizer 1992).

Gaining Control of Public Broadcasting

In his first appearances after the elections, Netanyahu declared his intention to privatize the Broadcasting Authority. Privatization was part of his overall approach to the economy, but in the case of the Broadcasting Authority he made no secret of the fact that it was also a political step. "A substantial part of the population feels that its opinions are not given expression on the airwaves and the TV screens," he said and explained that by privatizing the Authority, decentralizing and increasing the number of radio and television stations:

There will be a free market of opinions and channels in Israel. I believe that privatization is necessary to ease tensions in Israeli society and to encourage discussion. In this way, we will foster real tolerance of opinions other than our own. This legislation will lead to a change in the present situation, wherein the overwhelming majority of the media are not objective, and their reportage cannot be trusted. There is no greater dictatorship than a dictatorship of ideas. I see open discussion and the creation of a range of ideas as one of the important missions in our national life.[8]

Whereas these remarks sounded pluralistic and almost Jeffersonian, Netanyahu's bureau chief, Avigdor Lieberman, was more frank and revealed that he wanted to place at the head of the Broadcasting Authority "people who think like us." Netanyahu's intentions became clear before long. In one case in the summer of 1997, Netanyahu asked the CEO of the Broadcasting Authority, Motti Kirshenbaum, to help jam the radio broadcasts of The Voice of Palestine. Kirshenbaum refused to be a political tool in the hands of the government: he replied, "The Broadcasting Authority deals with broadcasting, not with jamming."[9]

Netanyahu nominated two subcommittees, one directed by him and the other by Communication Minister Limor Livnat, a longtime political and ideological partner of his. These subcommittees were supposed to assist in implementing the privatization plan. Concurrently, Netanyahu also held talks with businesspeople from among his wealthiest friends in the United States, including Ron Lauder and others, suggesting that they buy the Broadcasting Authority. He hoped that these people would ensure that the Authority would adhere to the right-wing political line, in the same way as Conrad Black, who had bought the *Jerusalem Post* in 1993, had changed the policy of that paper, which had hitherto supported the Labor Party.

However, the process ran into difficulties raised by the Broadcasting Authority employees, who feared for their futures as a result of privatization, especially when the cost of severance packages was calculated. Also the professional community was alerted to the danger of a political takeover under the guise of privatization. When it emerged that one of the two committees (the Zukerman Committee) also opposed privatization of the Broadcasting Authority, the prime minister shelved its conclusions and began taking alternative steps.[10]

Departing from the customary procedures, Netanyahu did not delegate ministerial responsibility for the Broadcasting Authority to one of the ministers but instead kept it for himself. He attempted to detract from the centrality and importance of the news broadcast on the public channel by weakening the status of public broadcasting, as well as by opening up a profusion of channels and entrusting them to the supervision and control of his coalition partners. Thus, he proposed to grant a license to the settlers' pirate station, Radio 7, and to establish another TV news station. His second tactic was to return to a system that had been used in the distant past, which gave the prime minister and the government in general more influence over public broadcasting.

Netanyahu used various means of pressure. He and his people continued to brandish the sword of privatization over the heads of the Broadcasting Authority employees in order to induce them to use more self-restraint, and they also introduced other "taming" techniques. They put pressure on the Authority constantly threatening to fire the director-general. They also used financial pressure, employing delaying tactics in setting and approving the Authority's budget, attempting to cancel the TV fees, and delaying the transfer of monies that had already been approved. Last but not least, they exerted pressure with regard to the contents of the broadcasts by closing sources of information to the Authority personnel. Throughout this period members of the government repeatedly attacked the contents of the broadcasts.

In marked contrast, Netanyahu was generous with his compliments to Channel 2 and gave it preference as regards interviews. Avigdor Lieberman also launched a public and legal campaign to besmirch Broadcasting Authority Director-General Kirshenbaum in an attempt to bring about his dismissal, together with other senior members of the Authority, on the grounds of mismanagement, political rather than professional motives, failures, and even alleged criminal offenses. The accusations were found to be groundless, but months of legal investigation, together with the other struggles, dealt a severe blow to the director-general and did not help to improve the mood at the Broadcasting Authority, which saw its CEO as the victim of a plot to undermine the freedom of the press.

The professional and psychological pressure on Broadcasting Authority employees took its toll, morale fell, and journalists, especially those in senior positions, began to leave. When the time came to appoint a new Broadcasting Council and director-general, Netanyahu appointed two political nominees. As chairman of the Broadcasting Authority he chose Gil Samsonov, a Likud activist and owner of an advertising agency, who had worked in the past in the party's public affairs department. He appointed Uri Porat director-general. Porat was a former journalist who had served in that role before, after serving as Prime Minister Menachem Begin's spokesman.

Porat, who was proud of his political worldview, made no secret of his intention to "clean out the stables." He wanted to make the Authority more efficient but also to set its political tone. He tried to remove from the airwaves programs with liberal and feminist approaches (such as Moshe Negbi's program on legal issues and Shelly Yehimovich's current-affairs program). He cancelled current-events programs with a critical or confrontational approach (foremost among them the weekly news magazine *Events of the Week*) and was often involved in litigation, as a result of frequent labor disputes, ostensibly on professional issues, but in fact on a political basis.

Using the Media, Bypassing Journalists

The second strategy employed by Netanyahu to harness the media for his own purposes was to use the media while bypassing journalists altogether. At first he tried to hide this technique, but over the course of time he spoke openly of it. On February 15, 1996, he was a guest of MSNBC on the internet. During the interview, 2,911 people visited the site, and about 10,000 had submitted questions beforehand. Netanyahu very much enjoyed the meeting: "It's an excellent tool for reaching hundreds of thousands of people directly, without the intervention of the media," he said.[11] Similarly, on January 20, 1999, he expressed his enthusiasm for the live television broadcasts of Knesset sessions on Channel 33, because they were unedited, and "because Channel 33 doesn't have commentators."[12]

Netanyahu also used the services of the Government Press Office more than his predecessors had done, and the Press Office even introduced its own TV news service. When the prime minister's office attempted to prevent Channel 1 and 2 camera crews from covering official events in which he took part and began sending videocassettes filmed by the new Video Division to news editors, the directors of both news companies responded angrily. "We will not accept that a public event be covered by a government body, and we will not accept material that was edited by someone unknown to us," said Channel 1 Director Ya'ir Stern.[13]

Above all, Netanyahu endeavored to appear on the evening news live and unedited. A few weeks after entering office, just after returning from his first meeting with President Clinton, Netanyahu waited for an hour in his plane in order to hold a press conference at the airport exactly at the beginning of the evening news. The Channel 2 news director, however, decided not to broadcast the press conference, and the prime minister appeared only on Channel 1.[14]

The second time Netanyahu did this with a press conference was during budget talks, and the third time was at the beginning of 1997, after the Knesset approved the Hebron agreement with the PA, whereby Israel would withdraw from Hebron. Instead of talking to journalists about the Hebron agreement, as he had announced to the directors of both channels, Netanyahu opened by addressing the public directly in a long speech describing the achievements of his government in the economic sphere. The Channel 2 news company responded by cutting off the broadcast in the middle. "We refused to broadcast according to the timetable set by the prime minister," said the director, Shalom Kital. "It's the prime minister's right to talk about whatever he wants, but it's our duty to edit the news. There is no justification for taking up half of the news broadcast with a 'State of the Union Message' just because he wants to speak during the news broadcast."

When the directors of the news divisions of both channels, Shalom Kital and Rafik Halabi, realized that this method was being used systematically by the prime minister, they decided in May 1997 not to broadcast the prime minister's appearances live during the news if journalists were not allowed to ask questions. Explaining that doing so would violate the principles of journalism, they announced their decision in a joint public appearance on May 17. However, this did not stop Lieberman from using the same method as the prime minister. At a press conference on November 16, 1997, he read an announcement and refused to allow journalists to ask questions. When they insisted, he ended the press conference and accused them of inappropriate behavior.

That same day, the Israel Press Association issued a statement saying, "The journalists of Israel will not be wax in the hands of the prime minister's director-general and will not accept dictates regarding their methods of press coverage. It is journalists' professional duty to ask questions and to convey information in the name of the public's right to know and not to serve as agents conveying messages in the service of the government." The next time this happened, at a press conference where Lieberman announced his resignation from his post, the representatives of the two TV channels decided not to broadcast the press conference. "If we can't interview you, there is no reason for us to participate in the press conference," they said and turned off the lighting.

Along with a "screen stealing" technique, Netanyahu also used another method. During television interviews, he would consistently turn his glance away from the interviewer and look straight at the camera, directly into the eyes of his audience. The subject he spoke about was sometimes totally unrelated to the interviewer's question or to the issue at hand, but rather to another message that he wanted to convey. The first time he did this, on January 22, 1997, his two interviewers, Dan Semama and Ehud Ya'ari, begged him, "Please, let's continue with the interview." Netanyahu replied, "In my naïveté, I thought that the prime minister was allowed to address the people directly." "Naive he is not, and it was out of line for him to exploit the cameras," commented *Maariv*'s TV critic, Meir Schnitzer, the next day. On another occasion, when Netanyahu appeared on *Popolitika*, the topic of the interview was decided on in advance of the program. But, in answer to the opening question, he began lecturing about another matter entirely. The moderator, Dan Margalit, was only able to stop the flow of his words by threatening to bring the program to an end.[15]

Netanyahu's success in using direct broadcasting techniques despite various expressions of protest resulted largely from the weakness of television itself. Excited by the suspense and drama aroused by live broadcasts, the news editors on both channels missed no opportunity to broadcast live. The live broadcast was perceived in the 1990s as the ultimate expression of the art of television, the closest thing possible to the realization of the journalistic ideal. The fact that this kind of broadcast actually expresses a regression in professionalism, virtually obviates the need for professional judgment, is socially harmful (Liebes 1998) and hastens the "end of journalism" (Katz 1992), has not stopped the news editors from making it a favorite routine.

Delegitimizing Journalists

The third strategy used by Netanyahu in his war against the media was a systematic, prolonged, and determined effort to undermine their legitimacy and thus divest them of their weapons and render them incapable of hurting him. This strategy was based on a profound understanding of mediapolitik. The power of the news media lies in the fact that they interpret reality. They are the ones who give meaning to things, to events. Journalists are not the only agents who perform this function; their major rivals are politicians. Journalists' status and their legitimacy stem from their credibility (Zelizer 1995), and their advantage over politicians is that the public believes that the latter are partisan and have vested interests. The public expects journalists to behave according to professional standards, namely, to be impartial and objective, presenting the facts "as they are," without bias. This simplistic positivistic approach has been largely abandoned over the last twenty years. Academic research in general, and research in the field of communication in particular, recognizes that "facts" are always established through power struggles and battles of interests. Nevertheless, the original view is still prevalent among the general public.[16]

The media's need to preserve their credibility is essential to their democratic function. It is even more relevant now that the media have become commercial, because "without credibility, news is worthless, either in terms of money or power" (Castells 1995: 314). In the case of a media-centered democracy, the media's situation is even more complicated because they can no longer maintain the distance required for "objectivity." They changed their position vis-à-vis the political actors when they became political actors themselves. But although they have acquired a more proactive political role than in the past, they still seek to guard their credibility, knowing that without this attribute they will lose the basis of their legitimacy. This dilemma has thus been thrust into the center of the media's self-contemplation in recent years.

Netanyahu knew how to draw the inevitable conclusion. Since the media are a political actor, just as parties are, they should be treated as political rivals are treated. They have to be controlled and converted into allies. If this does not work, one has to fight them and weaken their power. Since the media's vulnerable spot is their credibility, the most effective way is to undermine just that.

In order to do this, Netanyahu used two basic arguments, which he repeated endlessly. One of these was that the media did not operate according to professional norms. On December 26, 1997, at a prize-giving ceremony conferring the Prime Minister's Award for Literary Achievement, Netanyahu said, "The situation today is that the overwhelming majority of the media are not objective, and their reports cannot be trusted." It was important to him to emphasize that the media distorted information generally, in order to lay the groundwork for his claim that they were also mobilized against him. In a radio interview on Kol Israel on May 12, 1999, he said explicitly, "The press is not serious, it is engaged in brainwashing and demoralization. It is hostile, and beyond hatred, it is mobilized against me and in favor of Barak. . . . What is written about me is far from the truth, the only things that are correct in the newspapers are the date and the price." His second argument related to the societal base of the media, claiming that they supported one side of the political map, because they expressed the views of one social group and refused entrance to representatives of other groups. Netanyahu opened one of the first cabinet meetings of 1997 with the remark, "The media are run by my political opponents" (January 23), and he dealt with the same subject at the last cabinet meeting of that year (December 27, 1997). He said, "A large majority of the public suspects that the media are tendentious, and this makes them deeply frustrated. There is no freedom in broadcasting in Israel today."

The media were quick to understand that Netanyahu's battle against them was not like the disputes they had had with previous prime ministers. Netanyahu's verbal criticism of the media not only was more abusive than before, but also was received by his supporters as calls for action against journalists and broadcasters. On February 3, 1997, *Haaretz* retaliated with an unprecedented editorial under the headline, "A Government Hostile to the Media":

> We are witness to a phenomenon unlike anything seen before: the prime minister and his associates have declared war on the Israeli media. They do not just criticize specific publications, but are conducting a systematic propaganda war, designed to discredit the entire Israeli press in the eyes of the public. This unjustified tendency is a cause for great concern, and is liable to have harmful implications for the strength of the Israeli democracy and the validity of the rules of the game that have traditionally operated in it . . . . Netanyahu and his associates are behaving like people attempting to strike fear in the hearts of the press. This tendency should not be taken lightly.
>
> Netanyahu has already proven his ability to appeal to public opinion and send the public calculated messages using simplistic but effective propaganda methods. . . . His attitude to the media contradicts the use he himself makes of them and his stated views. The prime minister's world of political concepts was formed in the United States, the land of civil liberties and freedom of speech, and it is therefore strange to find that he has not internalized the rules of the game practiced there. Someone who advocates the principles of liberalism and pluralism should apply these beliefs also to the sphere of freedom of debate and freedom of expression.
>
> Previous governments, none of which was pampered by the media, learned to live with a critical press and never went to war against it. Over the years public figures learned to coexist with the media, to profit by the advantages they offer and bear their barbs. Netanyahu's government has brought to the arena a new type of public figure, who courts the cameras and the microphones while hounding the journalists.

The media sought to show that their criticism of Netanyahu did not stem from unprofessional motives, and particularly not from political bias. They did this by quoting extensive criticism of Netanyahu voiced by his political partners, especially government ministers. Columnist Amnon Dankner wrote, "Never was a prime minister so attacked, so slandered, so denigrated, and even hated. It is his duplicity that has brought upon him such hatred and contempt. . . . His suspicious, closed, and arrogant character . . . [has] brought Israel's political culture down to an unprecedented low."[17] Analysts Nachum Barnea and Shimon Shiffer added, "Netanyahu is loathed by ministers and Knesset members. He has lost his credibility not only with his rivals but also with his personal friends. . . .

His colleagues are more occupied with his character and his tricks than with his policies."[18] The press was also full of more direct quotes and graphic descriptions.

INCITEMENT AND ATTACKS AGAINST JOURNALISTS

Encouraged by his supporters, Netanyahu did not confine himself to parliamentary or constructive criticism, but instead stepped up his verbal assaults on the media, attacking them sharply. His supporters' response also took a more practical form. In the past there had been some cases of attacks on journalists, but these were carried out in the occupied territories by extremist settlers, who pushed or even tried to hit journalists whom they perceived as hostile. A case that gained greater attention occurred in 1995, when Nachum Barnea was attacked by settlers in Hebron. In 1997 the violence spread into Israel proper and to the political community of the government supporters, particularly among Likud and Shas supporters. At a meeting of the Herut Central Committee on March 2, 1997, cries of "death to the media" were heard. Similar cries, accompanied by posters prepared in advance, were heard at a Shas rally in Tel Aviv.

Following this, the Israel Press Association called an emergency meeting and its resolutions addressed the prime minister directly. "The Press Association warns the prime minister that his continuous verbal violence and incitement against the media is liable to deteriorate into physical violence and real injury to journalists by some elements in society." It also condemned the cries of "death to the journalists" at the conference of the Likud convention. "The verbal escalation against journalists' freedom of expression threatens Israeli democracy," said the announcement.[19] The Press Association also established an emergency committee to act against incitement.

Nevertheless, there were still incidents in which party activists attacked reporters who came to cover conferences of the Likud or Shas. The main victims of the curses, shoving, attempted beatings, and breaking of cameras were TV crews. In one case a crowd mobbed a Channel 1 mobile broadcasting unit that was covering a demonstration in support of Shas leader Arie Deri near his home. The driver sustained a head injury from a stone thrown at him and was taken to hospital for treatment, and a production assistant was knocked down. The demonstrators cut the tires of the van and threw smoke bombs. "They called us 'murderers,' 'death to the media,' 'man-eaters,' " said TV reporter Gilad Adin, who was an eyewitness.[20]

Television director Yair Stern attributed the incident to remarks by Netanyahu. "Our people really escaped by the skin of their teeth, these are not just words floating in the air, they are words that take on concrete form. The prime minister's attacks on Channel 1 border on incitement, and they were translated into action."[21] Broadcasting Authority Director-General Motti Kirshenbaum was more blunt: "Netanyahu incites against freedom of broadcasting instead of learning to live with a free press. This incitement and his very undemocratic reaction certainly worries me."[22]

After Rabin's assassination, "incitement" became a highly charged word in Israeli society, and accusations that Netanyahu used it against journalists recalled the criticism of his part in the incitement that preceded the assassination. Uzi Benziman, editor of the media critique magazine *Ha'ayin Hashevi'it*, commented:

The press will survive the prime minister's attacks. It has seen many national leaders come and go and has learned to stand up to their pressure and their threats. . . . There's never been a prime minister who has made such open, transparent use of the media to get his message across, even false messages about the media themselves. But the problem that Netanyahu presents to Israel's media community is the incitement embodied in his words. And that is something that should not be taken lightly.

In March 1997, as the Bar-On affair investigation drew to a close, the tension between the prime minister's office and Channel 1 rose even higher. Appearing on *Media File*, a TV program on the media, Kirshenbaum commented on the cries of "Death to the media!" at the Likud convention, and on the fact that Netanyahu egged on his audience. He blamed the prime minister directly: "It's a grave phenomenon. This is not criticism, this is incitement and de-legitimization to which the prime minister is an accessory."

In another interview with media critic Ehud Ashri in the March 11, 1997, issue of *Haaretz*, Kirshenbaum said:

What happened at the Likud convention was incitement to murder journalists, and it's time we realized this. In the climate of polarization and divisiveness in Israeli society there are customers for such incitement. When the crowd shouts "Death to the media!" and Netanyahu cups his hand behind his ear so that they'll shout louder, that is extremely dangerous. I'm not being paranoid. Do you want us to pretend we don't see until some journalists are murdered here?

The growing danger to journalists led the Broadcasting Authority to attach bodyguards to its correspondents covering political rallies, and indeed certain events might have ended tragically without this security precaution, especially when the prime minister appeared to be fanning the flames of anger against journalists in order to stir up his audience. The latter loved hearing these attacks, and sometimes even called out to

Netanyahu to give them a "show": "Talk about the media, talk about the media!" Netanyahu, for his part, when he saw that the 1999 campaign was not taking off, used the battle against the media as a stimulus, even instructing his campaign workers "to step up the attack on the media." At one rally he said, "We should attack the media more. Don't believe a word you read there."[23]

The reaction of his inflamed supporters followed swiftly. At a campaign rally in Jerusalem, *Maariv* correspondent Ya'akov Galanti reported, "The audience's glance kept going backward and forward between the prime minister and the press gallery. They were examining their leader and his prey." Photographer Orit Segev, who had covered many of Netanyahu's gatherings, heard the shouts all around and became frightened. "I really feared for my life," she said. They burned a hole in Galanti's coat with a cigarette.

On May 19, 1997, the subject was again raised at a meeting of the Broadcasting Authority, this time by military correspondent Carmela Menashe: "The next [after Rabin] to be injured by some crazy or hotheaded citizen will be a Broadcasting Authority reporter, and I don't want to see members of the Authority rolling their eyes up to heaven. . . . Authority correspondents in the field are under constant threat. They[24] can't go around with bodyguards. This isn't a police state." In February 1998, the issue was discussed by the official bodies of the Israel Press Association. The ninth convention expressed "grave concern at the continued incitement and verbal and physical violence toward the media, and the injury to journalistic freedom of expression." The convention appealed to the heads of government with a "demand to put an end to the malicious campaign against the media, blaming them for every setback and failure." The announcement ended with the sentence: "Israel's journalists will continue to struggle to uphold the principle of freedom of the press and the public's right to know."

The sharpest words were written by Hemmi Shalev in *Maariv* on April 2, 1999, in a story headlined "A Dead Journalist Walks." The story began:

At least one journalist who at this moment still lives and breathes is potentially a walking dead man. At best, they will beat him up and leave him lying there. At worst, they will put a bullet through his head and bury him. That's what happens to someone who betrays his profession, lies and slanders, joins battle in the service of the Left, and tries to subvert the leader of the national camp, Benjamin Netanyahu.

When it happens, Netanyahu will express deep horror and will call for the upholding of the law. He will claim that an errant few distorted his meaning, didn't understand, took his words out of context. He will remind us that he issued a statement of clarification, and in the archives we'll find that he is right. He will swear that he did not hear the cries of "Death to the journalists!" He will deflect the criticism and claim that we're trying to besmirch "half the nation" because of the deeds of a few crazies. The true incitement, he will say in all seriousness, is that committed by the mobilized media and the Left. He himself, he will claim, suffers character assassination day in day out.

Shalev built this scenario on fresh memories, because this was exactly what had happened after Rabin's assassination. In case his readers didn't understand his words, Shalev wrote explicitly:

> Netanyahu is again playing with fire beside a very combustible human pool, despite the fact that he's already been burned in the past. No other leader in the democratic world lashes out so violently against the press and the media. No other candidate for prime minister so cynically nurtures the darkest instincts of his supporters. If something happens and things get out of control, someone misunderstands him and is inspired to do something Netanyahu did not intend — then he will claim that his hands are clean. His advisors will whisper that the media are to blame, that they brought it upon themselves, exactly like last time.

In Netanyahu's last important appearance in the 1999 election campaign, the media were again the target of his attack. This time he called out to the crowd: "Do you know why they [journalists] behave this way [attack us]?" he asked, then answered, "Because they're scared." And when he felt the crowd stirring up, he repeated these words over and over in a steady rhythm: "They are scared, they are scared." This scene, broadcast repeatedly on various television programs, aroused disgust even among those who agreed with the prime minister's criticism of the media.[25]

In the 1999 elections, most of the national media took revenge on Netanyahu and joined in the battle against him with all their might. Only 25 percent of the political articles published in *Maariv* during the campaign were in favor of him, and 75 percent were against him (out of 419 articles). In *Yediot Ahronot*, the scales were tipped even further: 90 percent of the 277 articles published were against him. The balance in *Haaretz* is not even worth mentioning. That paper was mobilized entirely to the task of bringing down Netanyahu's government, and it devoted to this its editorial pages, as well as nearly all its other sections.

On July 14, 1999, Netanyahu was interviewed on TV for the first time since his defeat. He chose a talk show on Channel 2, moderated by Amnon Levy, a genial host who was known for being kind to his guests. Netanyahu portrayed an image of stocktaking. His big mistake, he said, was that he had not succeeded in explaining himself: "You did it and didn't explain — you didn't do it." And anyway, he said, he loved the entire nation all the time, but the Left thought for some reason that he hated them. Of course, that was not true, he insisted, but he conceded that he hadn't explained himself properly. It was the same with the media: "There should have been a better dialogue between us." Now, after the elections, did he really believe his own words, or was this, too, just part of the show, only this time with different conciliatory image, as most of the TV commentators believed?[26] Whatever the case, an analysis of Prime Minister Netanyahu's pattern of interaction with the media leads to an inevitable conclusion: his war against the media was not a miscalculation or a tactical error, but rather a defining component of entire approach — the telepopulism that Netanyahu sought to institute.

Nachum Barnea summarized the Netanyahu era in an article that touched on many of the points raised in these three chapters. He analyzed "the magician" thus:

Netanyahu suffered from emotional overload in his relations with the media. He liked the tools but did not like the tool-bearers. Until his last day as prime minister, he was tortured by the question as to why the Israeli media were so cruel to him. . . . The answer lies partly in his worldview: he was good at speaking to people on the Right, both in the United States and here. But those on the Left found it hard to listen to him. Basically, however, the answer is to be found elsewhere. Netanyahu built his coalition of voters around one common theme: hatred of the "old" Israel. This worked well in the polling booths, but it also extorted a price. The media, the stronghold of the old guard, could not help but see him as an enemy. His part in the incitement before Rabin's assassination added a moral aspect to the conflict.

And perhaps there was also some envy here on the part of journalists — envy of Netanyahu as a colleague. He was the first Israeli politician to understand how to talk on TV: in short sentences, four or five words long, articulate but lacking meaning. He was the first Israeli politician to understand how one should look on TV: he carried a makeup kit with him at all times and knew how to make himself up. He staged his photo-ops with care. Toward the end of his term, he took care to bleach his face daily. To everyone who met him he looked like a Kabuki actor who had forgotten to wash off his makeup, but in the camera lens he looked clean-shaven, fresh, and energetic.

He was the first prime minister who devoted his entire workday to the media, from the first morning meeting, which dealt with the headlines in the morning papers and the daily spin, to the spokesperson's evening statement, the final message for the morning headlines and the midnight news. He appeared daily on television, and towards the end on all the radio news broadcasts. Netanyahu did not for a moment leave the nation's bloodstream.

Perhaps he was ahead of his time. Journalists, who were accustomed to a different breed of prime minister, did not know how to swallow this new breed, the virtual prime minister. They wondered when their prime minister actually worked. During the first months, he enjoyed talking to them. He was as happy as a sandboy with his victory at the polls, with the power conferred by his office, the world leaders waiting at his door. . . . All this gradually faded. The fading was tragic, of Shakespearean dimensions. The critical media exposures played a certain part in his decline. Netanyahu convinced himself that he was about to lose the election because of the media. This was effective: his audience imputed to the media a demonic influence, like the influence that anti-Semites impute to Jews. It was convenient. . . . The election results showed that a large proportion of the voters did not want a tele-prime minister. Over-exposure has its price.[27]

BETWEEN TRUTH AND LIES: THE BATTLE OVER
THE INTERPRETATION OF REALITY

It was not, however, simply overexposure that damaged Netanyahu. Overexposure is like time; it is neither good nor bad, and its influence can work in either direction. What defeated Netanyahu was his failure in the battle with the media. Just as Netanyahu's need to dominate the media was essential for the fulfillment of his telepopulist project, the media's need to hurt him politically became an existential need for them, in order to prevent their own obliteration as significant political players. They used the same weapon that he had used against them: casting doubt on his legitimacy by undermining his credibility. Just expose the political construct that he seeks to build, and his methods are revealed; remove his mask to show the figure behind it, and he will lose his magical influence over the public. In the age of personal politics, it was clear that this battle would not be over policy or ideology, but rather over personality. The media aimed to peel away the persona and reveal the figure behind it.

Among the various criticisms leveled at Netanyahu by the media during his three years in office, the most common one related to the fact that he did not speak the truth. "The crookedness of the prime minister" was the headline of an article by one journalist. "The politicians and journalists who fell for Netanyahu's trick," wrote another. "A fraudulent political bandit who came from America" was a description that appeared in an article by a professor of philosophy.[28]

These were not, however, merely accusations that Netanyahu did not speak the truth, but a claim that his entire persona was a sham. Netanyahu tried very hard to present himself as a "strong man." Dan Margalit deconstructed him thus, "His big mouth threatens and he stands tall when photographed, but when an imminent confrontation is anticipated in the Knesset chamber, he is struck dumb. The weakness of his political nerves defeats the power of his understanding. He is purely and simply a political coward."[29] If he tried to present himself as an ideal family man, the media published stories of his twisted family relations. If he tried to demonstrate symbolic leadership as "leadership that can be trusted," the media published testimonies of his friends and close associates in the Likud leadership, government ministers, top civil servants who had working relations with him, and world leaders who had given him a chance at first, such as President Mubarak of Egypt or King Hussein of Jordan, but once burned, twice shy. They all referred to him explicitly as an untruthful person.

The issue of his credibility, or rather his lack of credibility, pursued

Netanyahu throughout his entire term of office. In December 1999, some radio and TV programs dealing with the media were devoted to the question: "Is Bibi a liar?" Most of the journalists who took part answered in the affirmative, vying with each other in their graphic descriptions of the phenomenon. As usual, it was the sharp-tongued Knesset member Yossi Sarid who most aptly expressed the prevalent image of Netanyahu, saying, "He hasn't yet managed to be caught saying one true word." And a book published in 1999, entitled *World of Lies*, dealing with psychological, philosophical, political, legal, literary, and artistic aspects of lying, devoted a special section to Netanyahu, summarizing his character as follows:

> The policy and behavior of Israel's prime minister, Benjamin Netanyahu, made him in the eyes of his opponents and rivals, and even many of his friends . . . the embodiment of falsehood, deception, duplicity, dissemblance, trap-setting, insincerity, false statements, cover-up stories, throwing dust in people's eyes, and more. This concentration of expressions of deceit was taken entirely from newspaper headlines and from the words of politicians and statesmen in Israel and abroad. (Adir Cohen 1999: 570)

In the end, Netanyahu's image was tarnished. A Gallup poll published in *Maariv* in April 1998 reflected the political stalemate in Israel — 51 percent were satisfied with the prime minister's functioning compared with 44 percent who were not. But to the question "Is or is not Netanyahu a credible politician in your opinion?" only 38 percent answered that he was credible, while 55 percent replied not credible. Even among those who had voted for him for the Knesset, 28 percent replied that he was not credible in their opinion.[30]

In symbolic politics, where the signifiers are more important than the signified, the winner is the one who succeeds in marketing his representations to the public. The media succeeded in their mission of showing to the public that there was a gap between Netanyahu's image and his underlying character. In the public's mind they exposed the character behind the mask, over which Netanyahu had labored so hard. With his credibility shattered, it was hard for Netanyahu to dictate the agenda, to determine the media frame, and to shape the symbolic reality.

Netanyahu attempted to repair his spoilt relations with the media through his devoted spokesman, Shay Bazak, who was positioned like a lightning conductor, a protective barrier, between Netanyahu and the media. But Bazak, who had been very popular among journalists when he had worked with Netanyahu as head of the opposition and had acquired a good reputation as a professional in the primaries, was forced so often to issue denials as the prime minister's spokesman that he lost all trace of credibility and was mockingly nicknamed "the denier."[31]

In the end, after two years, he was sent away by Netanyahu, to be Israel's consul in Atlanta. But his successor, a journalist from the IDF radio station and a professional highly regarded by his colleagues, also lost all of his credibility within less than a year. At this stage, the caricaturists, who for a long period had endeavored to find a prominent visual attribute to characterize Netanyahu, found a solution to their problem. Now they began to draw him as Pinocchio, whose nose grew every time he told a lie.

WILL TELEPOPULISM CONTINUE WITHOUT NETANYAHU?

The battle between the media and Netanyahu was not over on election night. Following his defeat, Netanyahu announced on that same night that he was resigning, at least temporarily, from political life. However, his ordeal was not over. He and his wife underwent a humiliating process of police investigation of alleged corruption. They were accused of employing staff in their own home and for their own private purposes at the expense of the state, as well as of taking home official gifts presented to the prime minister. Netanyahu was even accused of taking bribes. The affair finally ended after more than year with a decision by the attorney general and the state attorney not to indict him. But throughout that entire period Netanyahu was portrayed by the media as guilty beyond any doubt, in a massive campaign of critical coverage by the media, regularly fed by the police investigation department.

When the Barak government's standing began to shake, and it became clear that it would not last out its term, Netanyahu returned to the game, announcing that he would submit his candidacy for prime minister. His intentions, hinted at first and later stated explicitly, were received by the national news media with a wave of criticism. They reminded him of the failure of his government's policy, which had injured Israel's international standing, the failures of his government in various spheres of life, the unsavory administrative procedures he had introduced, and the government's inadequate management. But again the emphasis was on his personality.

During his two-year cooling off period, Netanyahu adopted a new policy toward the media. He endeavored to meet with senior journalists, developed a dialogue with intellectuals, and even attempted reconciliation with supporters of the Left. The thesis that he presented was the one he had stated on his first appearance on Amnon Levy's program. He partly admitted to the mistake he had made in arousing internal dissension in the nation, saying that he had learned from his experience and that in the future, as a national leader, he would take on reconciliatory, unifying, and healing roles. He also admitted his mistake in criticizing the media so sharply, although he did not retract the contents of the criticism. However, this attempt to present a new face was greeted with skepticism and cynicism by most columnists, who regarded it as yet another marketing ploy.

As for the public, it appeared that the number of Netanyahu's supporters had not shrunk, that the camp that supported him remained faithful, and that he was still the most favored leader of the Right. Public opinion polls close to the election date showed that his support was higher than that of the right-of-center leader, Prime Minister Ariel Sharon, and certainly higher than that of Ehud Barak. Ironically, it was the Direct Election Law, which Netanyahu himself had promoted, that prevented him from running in the 2000 elections. This law stipulated that if elections were held only for the prime minister, and not for the Knesset as well, only someone who was currently a member of Knesset could be a candidate, and Netanyahu had resigned from the Knesset after his defeat in the previous elections.

However, the support for his candidacy was so high that a majority of Knesset members passed an amendment to the law, determining that a candidate for the premiership did not have to be a member of the Knesset. Despite the amendment, which was even called the Netanyahu Law, he decided not to run for prime minister, out of tactical considerations. He knew that without a change in the composition of the Knesset, the new government would face unbearable difficulties. Most polls at the time, however, showed that if he had decided to compete, he would have swept the public along with him and returned to the prime minister's office with a resounding victory.

How can this phenomenon be explained? How did it happen that two years after his dramatic demise, Netanyahu once again became a national superstar? Why did Netanyahu still capture the hearts of close to half of Israel's citizens? One reason, of course, was the profound disappointment with Barak, who came after Netanyahu, and whose fall was even more dramatic. The collapse of Barak's initiatives weakened the Left and brought about an unprecedented strengthening of the Right, with Likud winning close to thirty votes for the Knesset and Labor only fourteen. But why was Netanyahu preferred over Sharon, whose policies were not substantially different? The answer lies in the bowels of the social sphere, rather than in the political sphere. It lies in Netanyahu's telepopulist project.

In retrospect it must be said that despite Netanyahu's first electoral failure, his populist project began to strike roots. It met the real needs of broad groups in the population, and therefore his failure in the 1999 elections did not mean total collapse for the campaign against the elite, the ideology of nationalist populism, the symbolic going to the market-place and encouraging folk discourse. This all gave the lower classes the sense that they were worthy of recognition, that they had rights and enti-tlements, that they were really partners in government.

Presumably, the fact that Israeli populism did not have an outstand-ingly authoritarian character blunted part of the resistance that might have grown toward him, as happened in the 1990s toward radical right-wing movements in Europe. Perhaps also the security crisis made larger sections of the public ready to accept, and even seek, an authoritative leadership.

However, the success of Israeli populism and its legitimization also stemmed from the cultural climate that was fostered by the media culture. Whereas during the Begin era, when politics ruled everything, his pop-ulism was mainly political, at the end of the twentieth century, with the growing dominance of the cultural sphere, the impact of cultural forces on the social system also grew, and culture in this period was affected pri-marily by the media. By means of television representations the populist discourse penetrated broader layers than ever before. The fact that televi-sion, more than other media in the past, deals with issues of the "the peo-ple" rather than those of the elite and the popular assumption that tele-vision images reflect the "authentic" social reality enhance the sense of inclusion of the people. Sitting in a circle on Dan Shilon's TV program or around the table in *Popolitika* creates in the viewers the sense of an egal-itarian, albeit virtual, national community. As Keane observed, "Television has created a new type of social space. It has reduced the dis-tance separating the mass from the elite. Thus, people think they have more direct access to power and culture. Politicians play to their interests with this "virtual nearness" (1996: 1–22). Despite the media's war against Netanyahu, he succeeded, through television, in answering the real needs of broad groups, and therefore they believed in him and were loyal to him. The more he was attacked by the media, the stronger their identification with his arguments against the hegemonic bloc, and their feeling that this bloc attacked him in order to preserve the existing social order, which he, Netanyahu, sought to uproot in the name of the people and for their sake.

Netanyahu did not run in the 2002 elections, and Sharon became prime minister. In January 2003, elections were held for the Knesset as well, and Netanyahu returned to the Likud's parliamentary caucus. He was appointed minister of finance in Sharon's new center-Right government and was generally thought of as next in line to lead the party. On his return to government, Netanyahu seemed to possess different character traits from those he had exhibited as prime minister. He was more balanced, more reflective, and less excitable. He was seen and heard less, appearing in the media less frequently than before. He came to be perceived as a bearer of economic wisdom, the person who would save Israel from the most severe economic crisis it had experienced since its founding. Netanyahu's return involved a combination of substantive policy and political style. The way in which he sought to rehabilitate the economy was rightly referred to by some as Reaganism or Thatcherism. It included comprehensive structural reform of the economy, liberalization, privatization, decreasing the national budget, and a substantial reduction in social services. This time, in contrast with the 1990s, his allies in this project were members of the highest economic strata of Israeli society: industrialists and merchants, manufacturers, economic experts and academicians, as well as professional civil servants in the Ministry of Finance. It seemed, though, that the rehabilitation of the economy would come at the expense of the weakest and most disadvantaged segments of society, which had long benefited from the state's large welfare budget. Those who considered themselves the potential victims of the new economic approach were members of the very same groups that Netanyahu had attempted to unite in the past as an antihegemonic bloc: the ultraorthodox and the Mizrahim; new immigrants and residents of economically peripheral areas; the weak and the disadvantaged. Indeed, in their campaign to defeat his economic program, these groups blamed Netanyahu for betraying them and for forging an alliance with the country's wealthy elites.

In Netanyahu's new incarnation, the divisive rhetoric he had used in the past was gone. There were no more attacks on the "treacherous Left" and no more public criticism of the media. In short, all the traits characterizing neopopulist leaders did not resurface. Netanyahu was still a politician in the era of mediapolitik, utilizing the media for public policy, but he was no longer a telepopulist. Had the mature Netanyahu come to view his erstwhile telepopulist project as essentially negative? Had he reached the conclusion that his former populism was a mistake, and that without the support of establishment groups — without the support of the media in particular — he would be unable to return to power? Whatever the answers to those questions may be, the potential for populism that existed in Israel in the mid-1990s neither disappeared nor weakened by the beginning of the twenty-first century. The media culture continues to nurture populism, and the social and cultural forces that led to its emergence remain. If Netanyahu becomes prime minister and wishes to head the populist movement again, he will be able to do so. Otherwise, the movement will need to wait for a new leader to appear — there is nothing to preclude that happening.

But telepopulism was not the only answer offered to the crisis of integration when the old mechanisms of mediation between society and state collapsed. Concurrently, another alternative began to develop. Instead of the concept of organic national integration with a leader who served as a figure for identification, where the link with him was created by the mainstream media, however, what now emerged was integration on a communal basis, particularist social consolidation of various co-cultures.

In a certain sense this is the opposite of the populist model. If telepopulism hastened the disintegration of the established frameworks and fostered a direct link between the masses and their leader, the alternative model laid the foundations for institutionalized frameworks — social organizations that answer the need for belonging, identity, and recognition, and are based on communitarianism. This was a return to the old pattern of the "camp parties."

PART THREE

Communitarianism
and the Alternative Media

CHAPTER TWELVE

Minority Media in a Sectorial Society

COMMUNICATION AND THE CONSTRUCTION
OF A NATIONAL IDENTITY

Many scholars of nationalism have referred to the central role of communication systems in the creation of national consciousness and the consolidation of a national identity (Deutsch 1966; Gellner 1983). Benedict Anderson's notion of "imagined communities," for example, ties the development of national identity to the spread of what he calls "print capitalism," of which the newspaper is a primary product. The reading of a newspaper, he argues, involves millions of people in a daily "mass ceremony," creating a community even in the midst of anonymity (Anderson 1983). This is truer than ever today. "In the present environment, one cannot consider identity without reference to new communication technologies (NCTs). NCTs have changed the backdrop against which identity is constructed; they have framed the generalized others and the 'generalized elsewhere from which the self takes its cues' " (Cerulo 1997: 397). Communication systems in the modern era also affect the nature of the political regime. In that way, Thomas Carlyle regarded the invention of printing, and similarly Tarde argued that the birth of the newspaper was a source of democratization, leading to the collapse of monarchic regimes. The newspaper, conveying information from place to place and from person to person, preempted the unique position of the monarch, who was hitherto the only one who knew what was happening throughout the country, due to his special communication system (Katz 1996). If Tarde had lived in our time, he might have used Foucault's apt image and said that the king was the only one in the panoptic position. The advent of the newspaper abolished this relative advantage.

In the 1960s, the proponents of the social development school conjectured that television would serve as the major nation-building and state-building tools in the new states that had just freed themselves from the yoke of colonialism. In this spirit, Katz and Wedell wrote, "Highest among the hopes for the broadcast media in the new nations is the hope that they will contribute to national integration" (1977: 171; see also Hallin 1998: 156).

The birth of the Zionist movement at the end of the nineteenth century and the growth of the Israeli community from the beginning of the 1920s are other examples of this hope. The cultural sphere, and particularly the revival of the ancient Hebrew language, formed the basis for the constitution of a collective national identity and later also for the consolidation of a new political identity (Z. Shavit 1998). As a result, the cultural elite sought a central place among the nation builders in the pre-state period, and the political elite attributed great importance to the communication systems in the process of nation building and national integration in the early years of the state.

This is particularly evident when we look at the roles played by Israeli national radio in the 1950s. Its founders saw it as John Reith viewed the BBC, as a "secular temple" with a national educational mission. This view persisted in Israel even after the radio was transferred, in 1965, from direct government control to the public Broadcasting Authority. Kol Israel ("the Voice of Israel") was not simply the major supplier of information to the public, it also set a common agenda for society and endeavored to maintain the public morale in times of crisis as in everyday life. It invented and promoted a common "Israeli culture" by injecting new contents into the traditional Jewish religious holidays and creating civil holidays, the most important of them being Independence Day. It molded and magnified the collective memory, cultivated the national myths, gave form and content to the national rituals, and promoted the rituals of the state. It taught the immigrants Hebrew, commissioned and broadcast Israeli music, and was the final arbiter in matters of taste, responsible for choosing the songs that would become popular (Liebes 1999).

Television followed in the footsteps of radio and, due to its special qualities, even surpassed radio's ability to construct a broad national identity. TV news broadcasts are one of the ways in which a modern society constructs its own narrative, and they play an important part in disseminating symbolic messages concerning social boundaries. The regular hour of the newscasts that are viewed by a large proportion of the members of the collective, the format that bolsters the feeling of simultaneity, the repeated use of items from the common cultural repository — all of these give television its singular social capability. Its newscasts transmit historical narratives that are versions of the joint existence and serve as cohesive material that binds the collective memory.

The development of multichannel commercial media, however, created a new situation. In the 1990s the national media were no longer a tool exclusively in the hands of the nation-building elite, and the expectations of them, on the part of both their operators and clients, were now different. Even more important is the fact that the hegemonic status of mainstream television was now threatened. The competitor that rose up to challenge it was the alternative, minority television (sometimes called "particularistic" or "sectorial" media), which was greeted with avid interest by media consumers of all kinds. This important fact was unnoticed by Israel's political leaders, who only paid attention to it after it had wrought a political upheaval in the 1996 elections. Thus, what had happened in Iran a decade earlier, on the eve of the Khomeini revolution, was repeated in Israel in the 1990s.

As Teheranian described so well (1979), under the Shah's modern regime, with the national media operating under secular supervision, there existed unseen a dense web of alternative communication, by means of which the Ayatollah Khomeini broadcast to the masses of his followers. From his exile in Paris, the Ayatollah sent messages to the believers in his movement through tapes, with the religious establishment serving as intermediaries. While the central government and foreign observers were convinced that what they saw on television, heard on the radio, and read in the newspapers reflected the reality of Iranian society, a parallel political body was in fact operating covertly. They were thus taken by complete surprise when they received word that a revolution had broken out in Iran, which then toppled the old order.

When a coalition of minority parties surprisingly won the 1996 Israeli election, it emerged that this, too, had not just sprung up from nowhere. In examining the causes of the political upheaval, one cannot ignore the minority media, which had hitherto been silent and invisible in Israel's hegemonic public space. However, the results of the 1996 elections not only expressed the enfeeblement of the hegemonic sector but also reflected Israel's new social fabric. As in the past, the media were a critical factor in constituting the awareness and the cultural identity of the elements of this new fabric. This time, however, it was not only the mainstream media that were so influential but also the minority media, which acted within the various cultural enclaves.

Toward the last decade of the twentieth century, a vast transformation occurred in Israeli society as a result of demographic changes and other social developments. The most important of these were the immigration of almost one million people from the former Soviet Union; consolidation of the Palestinian identity of the almost one million Arab citizens of Israel; the emergence of an ethnic identity of the religious and traditional

Mizrahi population; and the growing political power of two groups that had been peripheral in the past, the ultraorthodox and the nationalist-clericalist camp. Let me first clarify these terms.

The changes in Israeli society were reflected in the sociological discourse. In the 1960s, the founding father of Israeli sociology, S. N. Eisenstadt, imported Shils's concepts of "center" and "periphery." The entire sociological discourse was conducted from the perspective of the groups that dominated the center, and therefore the concept "culture" referred to the dominant national culture, while all the other groups were "subcultures." Later, under the influence of critical theories, the concepts "dominant" or "hegemonic" were added in reference to the central group and its culture, while the others were called "countercultures" or "cultural enclaves." The postmodernist and poststructuralist approach, which criticizes the technique of the social construction of reality by means of categorization, proposes the term "co-cultures," which avoids the negative or derogatory connotations of minority groups (Orbe 1998).

THE SIX TRIBES OF ISRAELI SOCIETY

Even during its formative period from the 1930s, Israeli society was far from being homogeneous. It was a divided society of the type known as "segmented pluralism," defined as the separation of society into co-cultures or political camps that were distinguished by religious and ideological differences, each with its own comprehensive network of political parties, educational, and cultural institutions, and other organizations acting in every sphere of life (Lorwin 1970–71: 141; Don-Yehiye 1997). The polder model in Holland, where three camps exist, is virtually the prototype of this kind of society. Israeli society was also divided into three sectors: the labor movement, the bourgeoisie, and the clericalist bloc (there was a fourth bloc, the Palestinians, but they were perceived by the Jews as an external group). Each of these blocs had several parties.

Despite these deep divisions, Israeli society as a whole subscribed to the ethos of the "melting pot," which was promoted by the ruling elite. In the 1950s this ethos won the recognition and support of academia, which eagerly embraced the theories of assimilation and acculturation of ethnic relations in the spirit of the Chicago Park-Whyte school (Van der Berghe 1981: 214). The ethos supported the idea of creating one new nation out of a jumble of cultures, although in fact, the solidarity, integration, and cohesion of society were achieved largely by virtue of the dominance of one camp, the labor movement, relying on partial consociational arrangements. Arend Lijphart, who dealt extensively with this political model, explains that it is an arrangement made by the elites of the various camps, who understand that without self-restraint and the consideration of minority groups, it is impossible to guarantee social integration and political stability in a deeply divided society (Lijphart 1968: 1995).

The nature of segmented pluralism is manifested by the structure of the media system. Every camp, or "pillar" in the language of the consociational school, had its own media. These were the party papers. However, there was also a public sphere common to all of them — public radio broadcasting. This sphere was controlled by the dominant party, and the members of the various cultural enclaves bowed to its privileged status, just as they had submitted to its control of the other national institutions. This submission demonstrates the meaning of the concept "dominant party."

Although the numerous party papers were controlled by the various parties and served as channels of internal communication, tools of socialization, mobilization, and social control of their own sectors, most of them also had a common denominator — the shared ethos of the Zionist enterprise and the wish to share in the project of nation building. The mobilized press thus had a dual role: it both served a particularist party and took the overall social responsibility of supporting the supreme national leadership.

This sectorial structure collapsed in the 1960s, and in the late 1980s and early 1990s a new structure was established (Yatziv 1999). On the one hand, the hegemony of the central stream was broken; on the other hand, the politics of identity and recognition led to the consolidation of new, fairly autonomous co-cultures, each with a distinct identity and clear boundaries. Unlike in previous years in which there was still a strong political center, a hybrid situation arose in the 1990s. In the same way that stateness was enfeebled, the centrality of the social center began to erode. Thus, a process of institutionalization of the sectorial structure occurred.

Since the 1990s Israeli society has been composed of six co-cultures.[1] True, the groups have a defined social core and boundaries, some of them with well-defined ethnic boundaries (Russian immigrants and Palestinians), but there is also a partial convergence of the various cultural groups. The nature of their boundaries differs, some of them are more integral and others more permeable, and similarly the strength of the internal bonds or the exclusivity of membership within the groups differs in the various sectors (Cerulo 1997). Thus, a constructionist, rather than an essentialist, approach should be adopted in examining these co-cultures, which sees collective identity as an ongoing, fluid, and flexible element of society.

Nevertheless, the dividing boundaries between the co-cultures are easily discernible: the rate of endogamous marriages exceeds the exogamous; there is a process of geographical separation of areas of residence; and there are separate institutional and sociopolitical systems, such as schools, clubs, marketing chains, social organizations, and even political align-ments at both the local and national levels. An important basis for exclu-sivity is the different lifestyle, with all its elements, particularly the use of a separate language. This is naturally most evident in the use of Arabic, Russian, or Yiddish, but it is also relevant to the differences between var-ious dialects of Hebrew (Kimmerling 1998: 264–308; 2001).[2]

THE RUSSIAN-SPEAKING CULTURAL GROUP

The newest group is that of the immigrants from the former Soviet Union. The first wave of Russian-speaking immigrants arrived in the 1970s, motivated by Zionist and anticommunist ideology. The second wave, which started in 1989, was much larger, more diverse in its social com-position and geographical origins, and motivated largely by pragmatic and instrumental considerations. By 2000 the Russian-speaking commu-nity numbered some 850,000, comprising 13 percent of Israel's popula-tion, with a high proportion of academics — 60 percent as opposed to 40 percent in the general population — and an intellectual class with strong self-awareness and cultural affinity to its former homeland.

This is a variegated population, with considerable cultural differences, for example, between those from European and those from Asian coun-tries in the former Soviet Union. Unlike other groups of immigrants in the past, this group also includes high rates of non-Jews, whose collective memory is very different from that of Israeli society (Sikron and Leshem 1999). However, the shared difficulty in integrating in the new society, and above all the tension between the host society and the immigrants, reinforced the internal bonds of this cultural group, while at the same time raising the barrier that separated them from the host society.

Studies on migration show that under certain conditions a group of immigrants will not be assimilated in the local population and culture but will retain its separate identity (Van der Berghe 1981). The case of the Russian-speaking immigrant group matches these conditions: it has a crit-ical mass; it has its own cultural and political elite; and it has a judgmen-tal attitude toward the assimilating society. The Russian-speaking immi-grants did not see the move to Israel as "ascent," but rather as emigration for the purpose of improving their living conditions. Consequently, they were not submissive toward the local society. On the contrary, they were highly critical of it, even feeling a sense of superiority.

All these conditions did not exist with regard to waves of immigration from other countries, and thus they strengthen the probability that this group will not seek to be assimilated in the host society, but will guard a separate and distinct identity, even if this identity may not be the original identity but rather a combination of Russian and Israeli elements. This new group is more likely to adopt another communicative strategy, that of accommodation. "Those functioning from this perspective insist that the dominant structures reinvent, or in the least, change the rules, so that they incorporate the life experiences of the co-cultural group" (Orbe 1998: 15).

Indeed, in the 1990s it became clear — to the surprise of veteran Israelis — that the Russian-speaking immigrants were behaving differently from previous waves of immigrants. Not only did the group preserve its internal links and encourage cultural distinctness, but also it consolidated its own political expression. Unlike the frequent failures of groups of immigrants to establish ethnic parties in the past, the new party of the Russian-speaking immigrants, Yisrael Be'aliya, won seven seats in the elections for the 14th Knesset and entered Netanyahu's coalition government with two portfolios. In the 15th Knesset elections three lists competed for the votes of this population. One of them did not reach the qualifying threshold, but the other two, Yisrael Be'aliya and the new party, Yisrael Beitenu, headed by Avigdor Lieberman, together won ten seats, supported by the overwhelming majority of the Russian-speaking immigrants from European countries in the former Soviet Union (the immigrants from Asian countries, approximately 10 percent of all the immigrants, with a much lower social profile, tended to vote for Shas).

Another phenomenon that astonished the Israeli public was the wealth and variety of the internal culture of the immigrants from the former Soviet Union, with the mass media as part of it. It included libraries, cultural centers, a network of schools, music groups, and more. In the past, there had been only one Russian-language newspaper, *Nasha Strana*, which was one of six foreign-language newspapers owned by the Labor Party (Mapai), drawing its material from the mainstream Israeli press and serving as a tool of the elite in its dealings with the new immigrants. This was a newspaper *for* the immigrants but *of* and *by* the assimilating society.

As soon as they began to arrive, at the end of the 1980s, the Russian-speaking immigrants developed a rich print media market in their native language. By the end of the 1990s this comprised more than one hundred and twenty publications, including four dailies, close to sixty weeklies and local papers, more than forty monthlies and bimonthlies, and another ten magazines devoted mainly to the arts and literature. The combined circulation of all the Russian-language papers and magazines is estimated at 250,000 on weekends.[3] Unlike the newspapers for immigrants during the 1950s, most of them are privately owned. Added to these are newspapers and journals printed in the former Soviet Union and imported to Israel. Surveys on the population's exposure to the media conducted in the second half of the 1990s reveal that only about 10 percent of the second wave of Russian-speaking immigrants read daily papers in Hebrew.[4]

Television, and to a lesser extent radio, are part of the minority media setup of the Russian cultural group, but there is a fundamental difference between these and the print media. Although the newspapers are produced by immigrants for immigrants (even if they are mostly owned by Israelis of long-standing), television programs — viewed by two-thirds to three-quarters of all the members of this cultural group — are relayed to Israel from Russia on the three Russian channels, ORT, RTR, and NTV, via satellite and cables (Fein 1995).

Israeli television also allocates several hours weekly for broadcasting in Russian, on TV Channels 1, 2, 23 (educational TV), and 33. These channels, however, have the flavor of government-sponsored broadcasting, similar to the style of Kol Israel broadcasted for many years. This is even more evident in the radio broadcasts, which are made quasi government; first by Kol Israel, and since 1999 by a special immigration and absorption network, financed by the Ministry of Immigration and Absorption and also targeting Jews living in Russian-speaking countries. There is also a Russian-language program on the Jerusalem regional radio — Channel 7 — as well as on a few pirate radio stations in areas that have large Russian-speaking communities.

The Russian media developed as a result of two factors: the desire of the Russian group to preserve and foster their particular co-culture, as well as their reaction to being rejected by the mainstream media. As Riggins says, "Mainstream mass media have tended to ignore ethnic minorities or to present them essentially in terms of the social problems they create for the majority" (1992: 2). This was also the case in Israel. The Russian-speaking immigrants express harsh criticism of the mainstream media, saying that the media ignore them and their problems, deny them access and hence exposure to the Israeli public, and if the media do give them exposure, they do so out of a negative approach, using negative stereotypes. The Russian cultural group's feelings of alienation and anger against the mainstream media were so great that they became a major subject of political discussions, leading to the establishment of the immigrants' political parties.

A content analysis of Russian-language newspapers in Israel reveals how the press was a central factor in building and promoting the Russian counterculture (Kimmerling 1998: 287). These newspapers refer extensively to the Hebrew media and publish translations and comments on what appears in the electronic and print media. However, this takes place in the context of a fierce debate with the Hebrew media, characterized by skepticism, criticism, and even arrogance. This is most noticeable at times when media events unite the Israeli collective and emphasize communal solidarity, as happened with Rabin's assassination in 1995. The publishers of articles in the Russian press criticizing the Israeli public's emotional reactions to the assassination underlined the unique culture of the Russian community.

A new technological reality helped to promote their cultural uniqueness. This was the first time in Israel that a large population of immigrants could maintain daily contact with the old homeland by means of TV broadcasts transmitted directly via satellite. This media consumption enabled the Russian mnemonic community to preserve its cultural origins. Combined with their confrontation with the national media, which they perceived as antagonistic, it helped to construct the collective identity of this cultural group. Concurrently, the minority media helped to consolidate and promote the group's communitarian dimension.

THE ULTRAORTHODOX COMMUNITY

The ultraorthodox community in Israel is estimated at approximately 650,000 people in about 130,000 households. This sector comprises those who see themselves as committed to the ultraorthodox religious tradition, as opposed to the stream that attempted to combine a religious lifestyle with modernity, on the one hand, and Zionism, on the other. The neotraditional ultraorthodox society includes several main subgroups, about 30 percent of them organized members of "courts," largely identified with the Agudat Yisrael Party and led by its religious council. Among the main "courts" are the Hassidim of Gur, Viznitch, Belz, and Chabad. In addition, the Lithuanian stream numbers nearly 30 percent of the ultraorthodox and is identified politically with the Degel Party, which was established by Rabbi Shach at the end of the 1980s. There are also smaller groups of Hassidim, who preserve the names and traditions of the places they came from in Europe (the ultraorthodox Mizrahim are a separate cultural group). All these share the view that the axis around which the lives of the individual and the community revolve is religion. Hence, Torah study is the imperative value and a superior way of life to productive work; this is described as "a learning society" (Friedman 1991). Therefore, the religious leaders are the social and political leaders, and hence the negative attitude to secular Zionism and to the regime and secular institutions of the state (Friedman 1991).

What distinguishes the ultraorthodox cultural group from the others is the explicit prohibition on its members using the national communication outlets, although the severity of the prohibition differs from one court to another. One example of the implications of this prohibition was during the 1991 Gulf War. During this time, when Iraq attacked Israel with missiles, many ultraorthodox had to tune in to the radio or even television so as to hear the emergency announcements broadcast by the military, but after the war was over, radio and TV sets were collected and burned in a public square (Liebes and Peri 1998).

The minority media of the ultraorthodox community are extremely varied, as are the media strategies used by this community both internally and vis-à-vis the outside world. They include five outlets: newspapers, synagogue newsletters, placards, taped sermons, and radio broadcasts. Unlike most of the newspapers in the Russian sector, which are commercial and privately owned, the media in the ultraorthodox sector are owned by the various communities and are at the service of the heads of these communities. This is a similar pattern to the parallelism that existed in the early days of Israeli society. The proliferation of ultraorthodox newspapers in recent years reflects the divergence within this sector. Each group uses its newspaper both for its own internal needs and for its battle against other groups in the community, and, of course, against the common external enemy — secular society, and in most cases the Zionist State of Israel.

Until 1984, the ultraorthodox scene was dominated by *Ha'modia*, the official daily of Agudat Yisrael, established in 1950. Rabbi Shach left the Council of the Holy Sages and created a new party, Degel, and with it a new newspaper, *Yated Ne'eman*. The next split was when Rabbi Ovadia Yosef and his supporters founded the Shas Party and the daily paper, *Yom Le'yom*. Other ultraorthodox groups have their own organs. *She'arim* — which was a daily paper for some time and later became a weekly — belongs to Po'alei Agudat Yisrael. *Ha'mahane Ha'haredi* is the mouthpiece of the Belz Rabbi's Hassidic court. *Ha'eda* and *Ha'homa* are the papers of Ha'eda Ha'haredit and Neturei Karta, respectively; these are the two most extreme anti-Zionist groups in the ultraorthodox enclave. In the 1990s the growing strength of Chabad, followers of the late Lubavicher Rabbi who believed and still believe that he is the Messiah, was reflected in the increased circulation and influence of this movement's papers, headed by the journal *Kfar Chabad*.

In the 1990s a more modern style appeared in the press of the ultraorthodox community, on a commercial basis and with no direct link to any of the sects. These included the two weeklies, *Yom Shishi* and *Erev Shabbat*; a color magazine, *Hamishpaha*; the organ of the world of Hasidism, *Ha'shavua*; and *Hila*, a glossy commercial women's magazine. All these are more modernized in terms of their use of better quality paper, color, and some photographs, and above all their content. Recently, the number of local papers has grown, most of them commercial. Currently there are four: *Hashavua Bapetach Tikva, Dati Tzfoni, Dati Dromi*, and the Jerusalem-based *Kolbi*. Altogether, it is estimated that the dailies and weeklies in the ultraorthodox community reach more than 100,000 households concentrated in four large urban centers, more than half of them in Jerusalem and Bnei Brak (35 and 30 percent, respectively).

A special channel of communication in the ultraorthodox community is the synagogue newsletter. This is a vehicle also used by the fourth cultural group, the national religious, who, in fact, were the first to introduce it. There are some 3,800 synagogues in Israel, accommodating hundreds of thousands of worshippers each week.[5] Accelerated political processes in the religious public sphere in the 1980s — the establishment of Shas, the split in Agudat Yisrael, Chabad's entrance into politics and the National Religious Party's shift to the right — generated a need for intensive communication among the members of these cultural groups. One of the new solutions was the establishment of synagogue newsletters.

These are weekly bulletins distributed in the various synagogues, reflecting the internal division of the religious community into many sects, which are identified with political parties and social communities. Initially these newsletters were meant to deal with religious issues, primarily the biblical reading of the week, but they soon became a social, cultural, and political medium of communication for the various religious groups, reflecting the internal division of the religious community into many sects, political parties, and social communities (Rappel 1991). It is estimated that more than half a million of these newsletters are distributed weekly in the various synagogues, and in certain periods up to 800,000 a week.

A third channel of communication unique to the ultraorthodox community is the *pashkevilim* — placards stuck on walls in ultraorthodox neighborhoods. They appear at irregular intervals, depending on the pace of events that occupy these communities. They deal with the various issues that concern the community, including both internal matters such as disputes between different groups in the community and the struggle against the secular. They are mostly produced on behalf of the leadership of the various groups, and in this sense they are no different from newspapers or synagogue newsletters. This is an effective social control mechanism because they are disseminated quickly; the placards are usually printed and pasted on the walls overnight. Because the ultraorthodox live in their own separate neighborhoods, they reach most members of the community quickly and have a powerful impact.

In contrast to the pashkevilim, which characterized ultraorthodox communities back in Europe, in the 1970s a more modern tool of communication began to develop in Israel — the cassette tape (Blondheim and Kaplan 1993). First, tapes of religious music circulated, but in the 1980s an industry producing everything from children's stories to bible studies, family guidance, housekeeping advice, as well as recordings of political rallies and events emerged. The most popular are the tapes of public sermons, containing passages from the Torah, explanations of current events, preaching the virtues of a religious lifestyle, criticism of secular society, practical advice, and so forth.

The tapes are in great demand in ultraorthodox circles. Many thousand of different tapes are produced and can be bought very cheaply, at about a dollar a tape, or exchanged at hundreds of special libraries in ultraorthodox population centers. Tapes calling on people to return to religion are distributed free or for a small donation at road junctions, mostly by people who are "born again."

A very large part of these sermons is devoted to attacking the secular media, using various puns to describe them as wicked liars. In some of the sermons, the popular preacher, Amnon Yitzhak, who constantly attacks the mainstream media, explains the sacred verse: many evils threaten the righteous, and He will save us from all of them. "What are the evils that we have to be saved from? [Spelling out the word "evil" in Hebrew, which is formed by the initial letters of the words radio, newspaper, video, television]. That is where all the dirt is" (Blondheim and Kaplan 1993).

The very popular use of these tapes among the ultraorthodox community recalls the fundamentalist Shi'ite tapes in Iran, distributed by the opponents of the Shah. In contrast to the subversive use of the tapes in Iran — this communication network was hidden from the public eye — in Israel not because of a totalitarian regime but because the mainstream media simply ignored the various cultural enclaves and their media.

The fifth communication channel of the ultraorthodox is electronic broadcasting. Some religious traditions interpret the Second Commandment, "Thou shalt not make unto thee a graven image, even any manner of likeness" as including television, and therefore only very small groups among the ultraorthodox permit television viewing. The religious dimension notwithstanding, it is impossible not to see the political consideration behind this prohibition. The strictly preserved boundaries are designed to restrict the contact between this group and the surrounding society, as a distinct strategy of social control (Sivan 1991).

The spread of radio is also limited among the ultraorthodox, although televisions are even more scarce, and that is why they have made no attempt to penetrate the latter. One estimate is that more than 25 percent of the households in this community do not possess radio sets.[6] However, the use of radio demonstrates how the ultraorthodox community's strategy toward the mainstream media has evolved over time. Throughout the years they accused the national media of corrupting the nation and presenting a distorted picture of ultraorthodox society. In the 1990s they changed their strategy, engaging in accelerated development of alternative media.

During this period they set up scores of pirate radio stations, especially in their main population centers such as Jerusalem and Bnei Brak. These stations began by broadcasting the tapes that already filled the market, but then they switched to live broadcasting, both of music and of verbal matter. Those mainly involved in developing the pirate radio stations were the Mizrahi ultraorthodox, encouraged by Shas. For them the subversive broadcasting filled a twofold purpose — to give expression to both the religious and the Mizrahi voices — two communities that had been mute and had not succeeded in reaching the mainstream radio. The pirate radio stations, the "sacred channels" as they were called by the Shas leaders, were designed to replace the national media, which they called "the devil's regiments."

The conventional view of fundamentalist religious groups as conservative, totally faithful to tradition and adhering to the ways of the past, ignores their readiness to adopt innovations and even their entrepreneurial nature. The media world is a distinct example of this. From the adoption of print by Luther's pupils in order to disseminate the Protestant message in the sixteenth century, through the use of the developed steam for transportation by U.S. evangelist groups who sought to spread the gospels, to the American tele-evangelists, we see a strong link between religious groups and the development of communication technology. In Israel, the ultraorthodox party Shas was the first to develop a network of satellite broadcasts as a political broadcasting technique.

In the early 1990s Shas began to broadcast the weekly lesson delivered by its spiritual leader, Rabbi Ovadia Yosef, in his religious college in Jerusalem, which was then relayed throughout the country by satellite to 150 clubs where the movement members and supporters gather. These televised broadcasts began as religious teaching but soon acquired a political flavor, serving to foster collective consciousness and promote community solidarity despite the geographic distance. These broadcasts were so successful, particularly in the 1996 elections, that the National Religious Party emulated the approach and constructed a parallel system starring its spiritual leader, Rabbi Mordecai Eliahu.

Some interesting evidence on this issue comes from attorney Avraham Doron, a journalist who edited religious programs on Kol Israel for twenty years and was formerly director-general of the Ministry of Communication, chairman of the Public Council for cable TV, and a central Shas propagandist:

Between the national media and Shas there is an ongoing dialogue of the absurd, a dialogue of the deaf. The media does not understand Shas and cannot interpret its language. Rabbi Ovadia Yosef uses the media more than the media understand him. The rabbi burst into the modern media back in the 1960s, when he converted his rabbinical *responsa* literature into a popular radio program that put him on the map and paved his way to his first office as Rishon LeZion [chief rabbi of the Mizrahi communities].

When he established Shas, he took a brave decision: to participate in televised election broadcasts, which had hitherto been boycotted by the ultraorthodox. Without the TV campaign starring Yosef, it is doubtful whether Shas would have passed the qualifying threshold. The next stage was the rabbi's decision, before the era of satellite communication, to transmit his weekly lesson via satellite to 150 outlets in Israel and abroad. In this he was ahead of all the prophets of the advanced media.[7]

THE ISRAELI PALESTINIANS

The population of Israeli Palestinians numbered about 1.2 million at the end of 1999 (compared with 150,000 in 1948). Like the ultraorthodox, most Palestinians are concentrated in certain areas, mainly in the Galilee, in the "triangle" of Arab villages in the center of the country, and in the Negev Desert (these are mostly Bedouin). They are divided into several subgroups by religion (mainly Muslims and Christians, but also ethnic groups such as Circassians and Druse), by geographical links, tribal affiliation, political division (for many years the Communist Party was predominant; now the Islamic movement predominates), and by other criteria. Despite these subgroup divisions, the Israeli Palestinians are a distinct national minority with a separate collective identity.

This group is the most distant from the Israeli political center by virtue of the fact that Israel was defined in the Declaration of Independence as a Jewish State, and its dominant ideology is of that of ethno-nationalism rather than political nationalism (Peri 1988). The Israeli Palestinians are the only group that comprises members of a different national minority, with a different religion, culture, and language. Moreover, the fact that they belong to the Arab nation, which is in conflict with Israel, heightens the barrier of alienation and hostility between the Jewish majority and the members of the Arab-Palestinian minority group, who are nevertheless citizens of Israel. Our tragedy, the Israeli Palestinians often say, is that our nation, Palestinian, is in conflict with our state, Israel.

The separate attributes of Palestinian society and their exclusion from the Israeli national collective makes this cultural enclave much more closed to the dominant Jewish national culture, and its internal cultural system more developed. This was not, however, the situation with regard to their media. Although the Palestinians speak Arabic and many do not know Hebrew, they did not have extensive media outlets in the past and lacked a national newspaper of any importance. This was largely a result of the "divide-and-rule" policy adopted by the Jewish hegemony since the establishment of the state, systematically thwarting any attempt to consolidate a countrywide Palestinian national movement (Lustick 1980).

In addition, the inner divisions and the living conditions of the Israeli Arabs after the establishment of the state did not provide fertile ground for the growth of a press. This was largely a rural society, only 8 percent urban; the educated urban class had fled or been expelled in the War of Independence, and the entire society was in a state of shock caused by the *Nakba*, their term for the disaster that was the outcome of the war. The newspapers that appeared in Arabic were *El Youm*, published under the auspices of the Jewish establishment (the government, the Trade Union Federation, and the Labor Party), and even written and edited by Jews for many years, and *El Itihad*, the paper of the Communist Party, the Israeli Arabs' main antisystem party. This paper started as a weekly, then appeared twice a week, and in 1982 became a daily.

El Itihad, like the Communist Party, was a legitimate tool of expression or a safety valve to release political pressure for the Israeli Arabs, who still lived under military government for part of this long period (until the mid-1960s). The controversy between this paper and *El Youm* was very bitter and reflected the extreme hostility between Mapai, which embodied the Jewish hegemony in Israel, and the Communist Party. "For a considerable period the two papers reflected the polarization and lack of pluralism in the Arab sector. If you are on the side of the government — you are a reader of *El Youm*; if you are against the government — you read *El Itihad*" (Jobran 1999).

Toward the end of the 1950s some new, small, party newspapers appeared, the main one being *El Marsad*, the organ of Mapam, the largest party in this sector. When the Israeli administration prohibited the activity of political movements that it deemed illegitimate, such as the national movement, El Ard, it also closed their publications. At the same time, the political climate was more conducive to the development of literary and social weeklies and monthlies that did not deal with political issues. Such were *El Mujatama, El Shark, El Mukab, Muakaf, Lakaa-Mifgash*, and others that helped to develop Israeli Arab culture.

The era of parallelism in the Palestinian media came to an end later than in Jewish society, only in the 1980s. Concurrently, a local and a commercial press began to flourish. In the 1990s the only daily was *El Sinara*, a commercial paper that was published in Nazareth, and there were a number of weeklies with a circulation of a few thousand, the largest being *El Bustani* and *Panorama*. In addition, some local papers appeared in the Galilee, the "triangle," and the large towns.

The Jewish establishment, for its part, continued using the mass media as a vehicle for political indoctrination of the Israeli Palestinian minority. This was done on the two main channels, Kol Israel Arabic radio broadcasts, belonging to the Broadcasting Authority, and a few hours of daily broadcasting in Arabic on TV Channel 1. Unlike the Hebrew radio and television, these channels in Arabic recall the work methods, management style, and even the contents of the mobilized Hebrew media that existed in Israel in the 1950s and 1960s, and are in fact perceived by the Arabs as the official mouthpiece of the state. It is not surprising, therefore, that when the "skies were opened" in the early 1980s, there was an outbreak of subversive electronic media, first pirate radio stations (numbering twenty-seven in 1999), and later also pirate television stations, most of them at the local level.[8]

Commercial interests of entrepreneurs from this cultural group allied with journalists' ambitions to find an independent professional vehicle, but mainly with the wish to give expression to this group's cultural and political aspirations. When the Second Authority inaugurated fourteen regional radio stations, it included one broadcasting in Arabic, Radio 2000 — Kol Arav Beyisrael. Like the others, this was a local station, but because the Israeli Palestinians are concentrated mainly in their own regions, Kol Arav Beyisrael reaches more than 10 percent of them. This is a station run by and for Israeli Palestinians, expressing critical attitudes toward the Jewish hegemony and battling against the government on various issues that are common to the Arab minority in Israel. "It's time the Israeli [namely, the Hebrew] media stopped setting our agenda," said Mouin Halabi, the director of the station.[9] Nahman Shai, CEO of the Second Authority and responsible for the fourteen regional stations (he was previously an IDF spokesman and commander of Galei Zahal, the IDF broadcasting station), responded by saying, "So long as they do not declare an independent state and do not harm Israel's democratic foundations, they can broadcast whatever they want."

This is still regional, not national, radio. It is not surprising that the Palestinian political parties that seek to achieve cultural autonomy for

Israeli Arabs, although they express satisfaction that "At last Arab media people run the radio, edit the broadcasts, and present them," most of them demand the establishment of a countrywide Arabic radio station. The link between three phenomena is important to see here. First, over the years more and more members of this cultural group have come to define themselves as Palestinians, or Palestinian Israeli citizens, as opposed to the old definitions of Arabs, or Israeli Arabs. Second, voting patterns have changed, and more and more Palestinian voters support their national parties, abandoning their traditional pattern of voting for Zionist parties. Third, there has been a growth of minority media in Arabic. The collective definition, political behavior patterns, and media environment are all intertwined.

THE NATIONAL RELIGIOUS COMMUNITY

I expanded above on the description of the ultraorthodox internal media system, and in particular the Mizrahi ultraorthodox who belong to Shas, because that cultural enclave makes the most diverse use of the various media outlets. The national religious camp, which is the religious wing of the Zionist movement, was one of the three camps that made up the consociational structure of Israeli society before the establishment of the state. Unlike the ultraorthodox, who sought to minimize their interactions with the secular majority, the national-religious camp was in favor of integration in modern life and participation in the Zionist enterprise. This perception was also manifested in their attitude toward the national media. The communication strategy of this camp thus combined penetration of the mainstream media with the promotion of an autonomous media system. The growing strength of the ultraorthodox wing of religious Jewry after the 1980s, and especially the success of Shas, led the religious Zionist camp to redouble their efforts with regard to both aspects.[10]

Since 1938, the National Religious Party (NRP) has had its own newspaper, *Hatsofe*, one of the very few party newspapers that still exist. Its circulation is about 10,000 and it is still subsidized by the party and continues to serve as its organ. In 1998 it was redesigned and given a fresh new look after its veteran editor Moshe Ishon — the last of the old school of editors — retired, and a young editor was appointed in his place. In the 1980s the party took advantage of its control of the Ministries of Education and Religious Affairs and allocated government budgets for the development of synagogue newsletters. This was done under the heading of religious services, but the newsletters soon became a political, even a party, tool. Ultraorthodox organizations also enjoyed this channel of communication, but the national religious community needed it more because they possessed fewer media outlets.

Other media of the national religious enclave are not directly connected to the party but to other social and cultural organizations belonging to this cultural group. There is, for example, the monthly *Nekuda*, which is formally the organ of the Council of Settlements in Judea and Samaria but is in fact the major ideological platform of the settlers, the founders of *Gush Emunim*. There are also some smaller publications that are not known at all in society at-large. As previously mentioned, prior to the elections of 1996, the NRP began to broadcast their spiritual leader's weekly lesson in narrowcasting, and since then this satellite channel has served the party. However, one of the greatest successes of the national religious media was the introduction of the pirate radio station, Channel 7, in 1989. This was followed by other pirate stations belonging to this co-culture, but Channel 7 achieved a special status. It is the largest and most established of all the pirate stations, being the only one that can be heard throughout the country. It has become the flagship of the national religious camp, particularly of the settlers.

At the end of the 1990s, Channel 7 was at the center of a stormy and complex political controversy, which indicates the major role played today by the media in Israel's political body. The station's transmitters are installed on a boat anchored off the coast, but the studio operates from Bnei Brak, near Tel Aviv. Channel 7 broadcasts a mixture of Israeli popular or folk music (equivalent to country music in the United States) and religious music, a combination that has made it very popular, but its true importance lies in its political messages. In fact, this station is the clear, sharp voice of the settlers in the territories and the nationalist-clerical camp; therefore, it also enjoys the public and political support of secular nationalists. Just before the 1996 elections, prime ministerial candidate Benjamin Netanyahu demonstrated his support for this illegal radio station, when he made an official visit to the boat.

Channel 7 took an extreme line against the Rabin-Peres government, especially after the Oslo Accords, and did not balk at broadcasting open incitement against the prime minister. Following Rabin's assassination, Communication Minister Shulamit Aloni tried to have the station closed down but failed due to sharp opposition from the Right, ironically supported by left-wing intellectuals and devotees of the arts and culture. The latter argued that it was important to understand the distress and respond to the demands of this broad political and cultural group that had no means of expressing itself in the national media, even if the broadcasts were illegal.

Although the attempt to close Channel 7 failed, the demand to shut it down because of its illegal nature continued during the Netanyahu government. Cabinet ministers who sought to remove the threat to the station tried to introduce a special law, authorizing this specific channel without legalizing the dozens of other pirate channels. Because this plan smelled strongly of illegality, the legislation process lingered on throughout the entire period of the Netanyahu government, until, under pressure from the NRP, just before the end of the Knesset's mid-1999 term, the government pushed through a law at the last minute.

This situation was most irregular. The attorney general described it as unconstitutional and announced that if an appeal was submitted to the Supreme Court citing the government for illegal legislation, he would not be able to defend it. In fact, such an appeal was submitted by three Knesset members, and the court ruled in an interim decision that the law could not be enacted until the matter had been considered in depth by the court. Meanwhile, the result is that the station's operation was not legalized but it was not closed, either. It continues to broadcast illegally as in the past.

The national religious sector's struggle to preserve its independent radio station and develop separate communication channels coheres with the other aspect of its media policy, namely, the effort to penetrate the mainstream media more deeply. In the 1990s this community began to train cadres of journalists and television workers, even opening a special vocational school in Jerusalem for this purpose — Ma'aleh. In an internal memo distributed in the educational system, Matty Dagan, director of the Religious Education Administration in the Ministry of Education, wrote:

Media people assert their right to shape culture and provide a solution to the capitalist hegemony over the masses, to mold public opinion, guiding it subjectively — and sometimes maliciously — toward parts of the public. It is our duty to act for the integration of media trends and encourage graduates of religious education to enter all branches of the media, while preparing to struggle with pressures from those in charge of the various systems and their attempts to ignore the religious public and surrender to popularity and to opinions that are detrimental to the values of Judaism.[11]

The NRP used its political power and its control of budgets and government machinery to place its people in the public news organizations. It succeeded in increasing the number of skullcap wearers (the emblem of the national religious) among journalists doing their military service at the IDF radio station. It strove for representation on the councils of the Broadcasting Authority and the Second Authority, and in the 1990s one of its representatives, Micha Yinon, was chairman of the Broadcasting Authority Council. It achieved similar success in the Educational Television Authority, which is under the supervision of the Ministry of Education.

The fifth cultural group, which I call the "southerners," is harder to characterize than the four cultural enclaves described above. It has no separate national background like the Palestinians; it is not a group of new immigrants like the Russian speakers; its boundaries are not as impermeable as those of the ultraorthodox, and it lacks internal cohesion, just as the national religious community itself. Its hybrid character is also expressed in the fact that its communication system is the least developed of all the groups. Nevertheless, it can be very clearly located on Israel's social and media map.

The term "southerners" is taken from Israeli slang and is not to be found in books on the political sociology of Israel, where the common term is Mizrahim, as compared to the Ashkenazim. Although this group includes a high percentage of people of low socioeconomic status, in the absence of class consciousness or class discourse, several attempts to define it as a lower class have not succeeded. The rise of the politics of identity has heightened its members' ethnic consciousness, and they therefore prefer the term Mizrahim.

The advantage of the term "southerners" as opposed to Mizrahim (literally "Eastern") is that it emphasizes the cultural dimension, rather than primordial ethnic elements. This also arises from a study on leisure culture in Israel in 1998, which found that there is not full convergence between Eastern ethnic ascription and the Mizrahi ethnic identity. Nor is there full convergence between ethnic ascription and the desire for Israel to have a Mizrahi culture. In other words, there are people of Eastern ethnic origin who do not see themselves as Mizrahim (some 40 percent), and an approximately equal number who do not want Israel to have a Mizrahi culture.[12]

"Southerners" have more positive attitudes toward religious tradition than "northerners"; they also promote their ethnic traditions, such as the Maimouna Festival of Moroccan Jewry or the Saharana of those from Kurdistan. Although its members are scattered throughout the various parties, the majority of them vote for the Likud (with the realignment of the 1970s, the rate has risen from two-thirds to more than three-fourths). They have a common denominator in social geography, living on the periphery of Israel, in development towns in the North and particularly in the South, on the outskirts of the cities in the center of the country.

Of particular relevance are this group's unique patterns of cultural consumption, in lifestyle, cuisine, and especially in their preference for certain types of entertainment, such as the music that is known as Mizrahi or Mediterranean music. Unlike the northerners, they prefer more "popular" types of entertainment to "high" culture such as opera or theater, watch more "popular" television programs, and read tabloids more than highbrow papers.[13]

The fact that this group is less distinct and structured than the religious, the Arabs or the Russian immigrants is also reflected in the media. Isolated attempts to create separate media (like *Ha-Patish* magazine, a supplement of *Hadashot*, and others) failed miserably.[14] The southerners have no newspapers of their own. The main reason for this is that the "melting pot" policy, which branded any form of ethnic grouping as illegitimate, prevailed during the period when the immigrants from North Africa were the group with the most potential to develop ethnic particularism. For this reason there were scarcely any attempts to establish a separate enclave (an initiative to establish a separate school system, *Kedma*, failed). The major effort since the 1970s has been to penetrate the center and have influence in shaping its symbolic order.

Their cultural endeavors focused on fighting the exclusion of this group's characteristic music, "Mizrahi music," from the mainstream media. This was a battle that continued for many years with regard to radio and later spread to television, but it had much broader significance. "Popular culture's ability to produce and articulate feelings can become the basis of an identity, and that identity can be the source of political thought and action . . . in particular politics of citizenship, the right to belong, and to be recognized" (Street 1997: 10, 12). The exclusion of this music from the radio led to the flourishing of a musical co-culture, which came to be known as "cassette culture." These were privately produced tapes of music sung by Mizrahi singers and groups. Although sold in huge quantities, the tapes were not sold in mainstream music stores. Rather they were available in special stores and even from street stalls in southern neighborhoods, such as Tel Aviv's central bus station.

The shift to multichannel commercial electronic media and producers' drive for high ratings provided the southern culture with broader opportunities for expression. Thus, the media revolution aided the empowerment of the southern culture.[15] More than television, the open skies of radio made it possible to fulfill and express the particularist cultural identification. In the 1990s some 150 pirate radio stations sprang up. Of these, approximately 40 have a political-cultural character; these are the religious stations, many of them belonging to Shas. However, the other two-thirds are commercial stations, specializing in certain specific varieties of Mizrahi music and expressing the southern cultural group (Limor 1998). Improvement of the southerners' political standing in the 1990s, along with growing recognition of their demands for cultural representation, led to their increased presence in the national channels, although they are still underrepresented.

The last cultural group in the mosaic of Israeli society is the one that has dominated the center since the formative years of Israeli society, the Ashkenazi group, situated on the higher rungs of the ladder of education, occupation, income, environment, and power, controlling the cultural and symbolic means of production and distribution. This is the group that has succeeded more than others in integrating in globalization processes. Because this group controlled the various loci of power in society and saw itself as reflecting "Israeli society" as a whole, it did not need separate cultural channels to emphasize its cultural distinction, although it might be argued that such institutions as the opera, the philharmonic orchestra, or *Haaretz* are exclusive cultural channels of the northerners' enclave. However, the nature of the hegemony is that it appropriates the national space in two ways: it controls public tools such as the national radio and TV channels, yet its separate platforms are regarded as expressing the entire general public sphere.

In Israel in the 1990s this hegemony, whereby the northerners were perceived as expressing the broad national culture, and not as one group among many, collapsed. At the end of the decade, this was still the dominant group, but it had lost its legitimacy as the exclusive representative of the symbolic order. This was a dramatic reversal. For the first time in Israel's history, it had a government in which the majority were immigrants from Russia, ultraorthodox, religious Zionists, and southerners (Ben-Simon 1997). For the first time the old "central" cultural group faced a situation whereby its hegemonic status was undermined. The melting-pot policy was now attacked not because it was an attempt to create a new type of Israeli, but because it was perceived as a program to impose northern "Israeliness" on all the other cultural groups while assimilating them. Instead of the melting pot, there now arose a demand to grant legitimacy to pluralism, if not to multiculturalism.

In the same way that the minority media helped in the construction of the separate collective consciousness of each of the co-cultures, control of the national media became one of the major battle sites between the various groups that sought to shape the Israeli collective and influence its policy sphere. The battle over what was called the designated channels was one of them.

In negotiating with the Likud over joining the Netanyahu government, Yisrael Be'aliyah conditioned its partnership, among other things, not only on having representatives in the Broadcasting Authority Council but also on the establishment of separate radio and television channels in Russian. By the same token, the NRP demanded legitimization for the illegal Channel 7, and Shas demanded legalization for its "sacred channels," those forty pirate radio stations. In March 1999, the Knesset amended the law and determined that radio stations that had operated continuously for five years could receive legal concessions to broadcast. This was illegal legislation and the Supreme Court froze it. The pressure of the minority groups led Limor Livnat, minister of communication in the Netanyahu government, to approve the establishment of five new channels designated for the various cultural enclaves. This would have been a fatal blow to the Broadcasting Authority as the public sphere in which all the streams flowed, even if they were not equally represented.

After the fall of the Netanyahu government the representatives of the co-cultures conditioned their partnership in Barak's government on implementation of the program. At a certain stage, a committee of ministers headed by Justice Minister Yossi Beilin was about to approve the establishment of two national radio stations for Shas and one for the NRP — Channel 7. However, the religious parties were not satisfied and demanded a separate broadcasting authority like the First and Second Authorities. In fact, this was an initiative to implement sectorialism in the public broadcasting system, whereby each sector would receive a license from the state to maintain a separate independent broadcasting system. This battle continued throughout the duration of Barak's government and was not resolved only because of the political crisis that led to the government's collapse. Leaders of the co-cultures viewed the fierce resistance to these recommendations on the part of politicians, media professionals, and academics as a desperate attempt of the old northern elite to continue its control of the national media and thus of society as a whole. A year later, as a result of continued pressure, the Russian-speaking channel and the channel devoted to religious affairs were established.

CHAPTER THIRTEEN

Will the Public Sphere Survive?

MINORITY MEDIA AND COMMUNITARIANISM

The changes that took place in Israeli society were not confined to the collapse of the old party system, as in many European countries. During this period a new sectorial social structure was also formed, whereby various cultural groups competed over the definition of the collective identity and the nature of the new political order. The upper echelons — the possessors of political, economic, and symbolic resources, who profited from globalization — continued to stay in the loci of power of the media-centered democracy and to preserve their status. The co-cultures — the minority groups and the lower classes — did not have access to the new forms of power and needed to find other political mechanisms for expressing their interests, voicing their needs for recognition and identity, influencing the policy sphere, and shaping the social and symbolic order.

Neopopulism was one of the practices that appealed to many people in these groups. They joined the antihegemonic bloc and followed the telepopulist leader Netanyahu, challenging the social order and seeking a radical change in the system. But telepopulism had some outstanding disadvantages, one of which was the nature of parasocial relations with the leader. Neopopulism did not meet the need for strong community ties and clear identification with a solid social framework. This was what the new sectorial structure could offer: membership of a cultural group with a deep sense of affiliation based on grounds perceived as primordial, such as ethnic origin, language, extended family ties, and above all close cooperation in systems that supply vital social services.

The sociocultural movements of the 1990s in sectorial Israel embraced this communitarian solution. These movements also assumed a political aspect, resembling the "camp parties" that had existed during the pre-state period (Lissak 1998). Shas was the most prominent example of these sociocultural movements. Within a short period of time, Shas successfully established an extensive framework of social services, similar to non-Jewish fundamentalist movements, which included educational and health services, employment, housing, and welfare. Other sectors varied in their levels of development, with the small media playing a major role in consolidating a new social movement, building up the status of the leadership and functioning as a tool of mobilization and social control. These media helped to define the collective boundaries by fighting with the "other" — particularly the groups that occupied the old national center.

In this case, the familiar role of the Israeli media in the dynamic process of collective identity construction occurred not at the nation-state level but at the subnational level of cultural groups, minorities, or diasporic communities (Riggins 1992: 2). In the same way that the particularist media helped the creation of an Iranian diaspora in California (Naficy 1993), the gay press reinforced the collective identity of the gay community in the United States (Gross 1993), and the black media aided the emergence of a black public sphere in Chicago (Herbst 1994; see also Dayan 1996b: 109), the minority media in Israel instituted the sectorial discourse and strengthened the particularist collective identity of the various cultural and co-cultural groups.

This analysis of the minority media evidently supports the constructivist view in media research. In contrast to the instrumentalist approach, which regards the media as a vehicle used by the group to disseminate its message, the constructivist approach argues that the media influence the construction processes of the group itself. Proponents of this approach argue that the action of the media is not measured by the extent to which the group succeeds in using them to spread its messages, but by the way in which the media's coverage of the group shapes its self-constitution (Zoonen 1996).

If the elections of 1996 were marked by the advent of a new telepopulist leader and influenced by his leadership style, the 1999 elections revealed the drawing power of the communitarian solution. Combined, the two major parties that represented the old center lost twenty-one seats, having already lost eighteen in 1996, and now together commanded not more than forty-five seats, the lowest number ever. The real victory in the elections was that of the various co-cultures, which bore the flag of the communitarian alternative. Invited by Barak to join his government, they did not reject his offer on the spot, despite their vastly different political opinions. The possibility of gaining a share in the national budget in order to supply services directly to their members seemed much more important to the leaders of these parties than the overall national issues with which Barak was concerned, such as the peace talks.[1]

The establishment of particularist media systems in each of the co-cultures puts great pressure on the public sphere, threatening it with disintegration and fragmentation. The picture that emerged at the end of the 1990s was one of a fierce struggle over control of the general public sphere while at the same time questioning its centrality and simultaneously strengthening the small public spheres, the "public micro-spheres" (Dahlgren 1994), or "sphericules" (Gitlin 1999). These developments raise a major question as to the effects of the segmentation of the public sphere: Does such fragmentation of the public sphere testify to the weakness of the mechanisms of solidarity and social integration, to the point of collapsing the common ethos and disintegrating Israeli society?

The fear of the minority media's disintegrative effect in Israel reflects a state of mind that prevailed among media scholars in the 1990s, especially in the United States. Many media scholars feared that the development of the new media and the rapid spread of broadcasting would lead to diminution of the national commitment and fragmentation of the collective culture. The empirical data particularly from the United States (Turow 1997) and the concept of disintegration or even loss of the public sphere (Habermas 1989) deepened this fear.[2] In Israel, the concern about the proliferation of channels was expressed by Elihu Katz (1996), whose argument merits special attention:

> With the rapid multiplication of channels, television has all but ceased to function as a shared public space. . . . Unlike the replacement of radio by television, as radio underwent a similar process of segmentation, there is no new medium in the wings to replace television that is likely to promote national political integration. . . . Thus is mass democracy deprived of its last common meeting grounds, and . . . cohesion of the nation-state itself is in jeopardy. (Katz 1996: 22)

Katz sees this as particularly relevant with regard to Israel:

> Television served Israel as a powerful unifying force. It deepened the sense of attachment to the center both in its focus on collective concerns and in its communal way of doing so. . . . The years of monopolistic public television in Israel have almost certainly had an effect on the forging of the national identity, enhancing the sense of belonging, promoting civil religion and the continuity of traditional sentiments. . . . The new era of segmentation will support the growing liberal spirit of individualism, self-fulfillment, hedonism, and privatization. By definition it will not do much good to altruism, patriotism, collectivity orientation, ideological politics, or the civic need for a shared public space. (Katz 1996: 22–32)

Katz, more than others, expressed concern about the fragmentation and segmentation of the Israeli public sphere and the extinguishing of the "tribal bonfire." As a world-renowned media scholar who was also as a practitioner (he headed the team that set up Israeli television at the end of the 1960s), Katz was associated with the "social development" school, a prevalent sociological paradigm of that period. This was a time when the development of new societies in the "third world" was at its height, being at the end of the decolonization period. Like other scholars, Katz saw television as a major tool for national integration and nation building.

To Katz, the loss of the "tribal bonfire," around which most Israelis sat every evening and shared in interpreting the common text with its repeated stress on the characteristics and contents of the collective identity, was the loss of the public sphere, which he saw as a condition for the shared existence. The media revolution scattered the Israelis into many small groups, each in its own territory, each within its closed boundaries. Katz saw the Israeli phenomenon as a particular case of the postmodern process that many contemporary societies were undergoing, notably the United States. But was he right? Is there really no difference between the Israeli and American cases? Regardless of the comparison, three questions are pertinent here. First, does the proliferation of channels mean division and destruction of the public sphere? Second, is Israeli society really more divided today than in the past? Third, does the minority media's restructuring of the collective identity of the various co-cultures inevitably lead to the dismantling of the overall social bonds?

The salient difference between the American and the Israeli case is that in the United States the audience was divided by narrowcasting (Turow 1997). The aim of this technique is to create "consumer groups," classified by age, gender, interests, values, or taste, based on differential consumption patterns, in order to focus on the advertisement of products preferred by specific, and thus relatively limited, groups of consumers. Even the division into ethnic or cultural groups stemmed largely from commercial considerations. Mass audiences have been divided into distinct groups for the purposes of gearing certain products and services toward these targeted groups.

This is not, however, the case in Israel, and the critical difference between the two results mainly from the size of the market, that is the difference between a market of 6 million and another of 280 million. More importantly, niche marketing prevails in the United States, and consequently consumer groups are created by the advertisers. In the case of Israel, however, these are cultural groups whose members maintain interactions within the group and share interests and a consciousness of a common identity. The groups in the United States are "conceptual categories" (Meyrowitz 1993: 44), which are fluid and are constantly shifting, while in Israel they are identity groups, some of them traditional, combining ethnic origin, a cultural system, and a community base.[3]

In terms of consumption of political media, there lies another difference between Israel and the United States. In the United States, "mass audiences have been broken down or segmented in the present era into strategic groups for which highly personalized messages and delivery systems are constructed by the growing ranks of pollsters, strategists, and spin doctors who work behind the scenes of modern democracies" (Bennett and Entman 2000: 17). The difference is that 70 percent of the American public receive most of their political information solely from television (Entman 1989: 23), and if they watch one channel that is geared only to them they will not know exactly what was broadcast on another channel, while in Israel most TV viewers also read a daily paper. Thus, it is hard to speak of a process of atomization of this society due to differential media consumption.

Has the proliferation of channels really led to the disappearance of the one public sphere? The reasoning is that so long as there was one national television channel in Israel, most of the population viewed the same news broadcast every evening. In 1990, 63 percent of households viewed the news broadcast. The establishment of the multichannel structure split this population, with more of them now watching the news on Channel 2. Altogether some 40 percent watch the nightly newscasts (Katz and Haas 1995; Tokatly 2000: 239).

These figures are problematic, particularly with regard to the earlier period, because of the changes in measurement methods over the years. In the 1970s the measurement procedure was "time budgeting," that is to say, respondents were asked to complete diaries detailing all their activities during a twenty-four-hour period. In the 1980s telephone interviews were used and the questions were based on "recall" ("Did you watch the news last night?"). In the late 1990s, another method (the "people meter") was introduced and used (Adir Cohen 1999).

Furthermore, one may ask, does viewing the news on two separate channels mean viewing two different newscasts, thus providing no basis for a joint discourse of the two viewing groups? This argument would be valid if there were a significant difference between the broadcasts, and someone seeing one of them did not know what was in the other. But that is not the case. The convergence process has eliminated the difference; the items in the lineup of both broadcasts are similar, about 80 percent of the items appear nightly in both, and the same people are interviewed on both channels. In fact, they participate in the same discourse.

More important is the argument that it is not the television newscast alone that forms the Israeli tribal bonfire, but rather the sum total of the political broadcasts, including programs on current events and talk shows. From this point of view, the Israeli public sphere has not shrunk due to the proliferation of channels; it has grown, just as it grew in other places due to the blurring of genres (Bennett and Entman 2001: 21). The conclusion is that the fear of disintegration of the public sphere as a result of commercial multichannel television appears to be unfounded.

IN WHAT DIRECTION WILL THE PLURALISTIC
STRUCTURE DEVELOP?

Is Israeli society in the twenty-first century more polarized than it was in the past? Arguably it was no less divided in previous years, but the division was less visible. The press, the main communication medium during the pre-state period and the first ten years of the state, was no less divided during the era of parallelism. For example, at that time it would not have occurred to an ultraorthodox Jew from Jerusalem to read *Al Hamishmar*, or to a Mapai kibbutz member to read *Hamodia*. Even when the consociational arrangements were weakened and Israeli society appeared to be growing more homogeneous, the dividing lines between the various co-cultures still remained below the surface. The illusion of unity was created because of the hegemony of the dominant camp and its control of the national culture.

But the fact that Kol Israel newsreaders, for example, spoke only in a "correct" Hebrew accent does not mean that there were not broad groups that spoke in different accents, in a Yiddish dialect or a French-Moroccan accent. By the same token, does the fact that Kol Israel avoided broadcasting Mizrahi music indicate the absence of a large consumer market for this cultural product? In fact, it was precisely because of Kol Israel's virtual ban of this music that the alternative industry of taped Mizrahi music flourished.

The hegemony hid the division but did not eliminate it. As co-culture theory argues, "The mainstream media have tended to ignore ethnic minorities or to present them essentially in terms of social problems they create for the majority" (Riggins 2001: 2). The dominant groups in society view the minority groups negatively and ignore them. They create communication systems that reflect their hegemonic status and force the weaker groups to adjust to an inferior and marginal state (Orbe 1998: 11), in which their experiences are often made invisible by the pervasiveness of the dominant culture. The fact that the dominant culture did not succeed in bringing the other cultural groups to accept it and become assimilated in it led to the "revolt of the peripheries" in the 1990s.

Thus, what happened was not the deepening of social divisions but the undermining of the foundations of social solidarity and enfeeblement of some of the mechanisms of conflict resolution and management. The end of the dominant party regime, the creation of a competitive bipolar system, the political impasse, and the ongoing crisis generated by the colonial situation are some of the causes. At the same time, there was growing recognition of the existence of the divisions, awareness of conflicts, and concern about their consequences. These were certainly influenced by the media, for the simple reason that the media exposed them and gave voice to them.

In the old sectorial society, in which contact between secular and ultra-orthodox Jews was minimal, there was less awareness of the divisions. When representatives of both camps sat around the table haranguing each other on a televised political talk show, many more became aware of the actual depth of the division and started fearing its potential dangers. Although exposing conflicts and divisions through the media does not cause social segmentation, it does bring about the mobilization of counterforces by raising awareness of existing divisions and conflicts.

A different but much more significant question is whether the cultivation of separate cultural identities in separate media systems strengthens disintegrative processes. The concern expressed in "and deliver us from segmentation" is that the fostering of the separate identities will destroy national unity. This was the underlying concern of the advocates of the melting-pot approach that prevailed in Israel until the 1990s, and this was the justification for the assimilationist approach, the attempt to eliminate cultural differences, causing them to lose any distinctive characteristic in order to fit the dominant cultural group. For this reason, the assimilationists opposed every separate ethnic cultural organization. But surely national integration can be achieved by other means than the melting pot. A strategy of accommodation — the development of appreciation, independence, and communication skills to effectively work with persons from other cultures — seems to be a possible alternative. Functioning from this perspective requires that the dominant structures reinvent, or at least change the rules, so that they incorporate the life experiences of each co-cultural group (Orbe 1998: 15). There are some who believe that this is definitely possible:

> There is no doubt that the maintenance of diversity may involve a rejection of universalism. . . . It may foster the decline of that universalist model of the nation-state. . . . Yet particularistic motives are not doomed from the beginning. They can involve a rejection of universalism but not necessarily so. In fact, the discourse of particularism is far from monolithic. The media that insure the continued survival of certain groups tend to offer these groups competing versions of their identity. Some are lethal, some are not. There are many types of particularist rhetoric, and many ways of mediating the knowledge required for community construction. Constructing identities, and maintaining identities, involves various processes. (Dayan 1996: 105)

This argument is also supported by empirical research. Naficy, for example, who studied groups of Iranian émigrés in California, showed how their microspheres served as a stage in the process of their entrance into the national sphere. "Far from exclusivity protecting traditional lifestyles, the construction of exile cultures served as a rite of passage into, and an instrument of acculturation to, the host society" (Dayan 1998: 110).

A similar debate arose in the 1990s, following the massive immigration from the former Soviet Union. In the ongoing public discourse — but also in the academic, particularly sociological, discourse — two voices could be heard. One argued that the fact that the Russian-speaking immigrants trying so hard to preserve their cultural identity, unlike previous immigrants, testified to their wish to remain separate from Israeli society, to "ghettoization," and was liable to erode the national bonds (Lissak and Leshem 1995). The second voice argued that this was a new pattern of integration, replacing the previous acculturation pattern, which had involved the old identity components.

This new pattern creates a new breed of "Israelis with a Russian flavor." There are Russian-Israelis, to borrow Gitlin's play on words, and "the affirmation of the left side of the hyphen becomes a way of affirming the right side" (Gitlin 1998: 173). In the same way, there are Palestinian Israelis or ultraorthodox Israelis. According to this view, when Israelis recognized the fact that there is more than one way of being Israeli they also reached the awareness that it is possible to maintain a new pattern of national integration, accepting the existence of various breeds side by side, without attempting to destroy the uniqueness of any of them.[4]

Now that the melting-pot approach has gone, what will replace it? In what direction will Israeli society develop and what will be the nature of its pluralism? Smolicz's schematic structure presents the range of possibilities. He discerns six strategies for relating to different cultural groups: assimilation, cultural diversity, residual multiculturalism, transitional pluralism, segregation, and interactive multiculturalism (Smolicz 1981, 1997). In the period of mass immigration in the early years of the state, the assimilation strategy was unquestioningly adopted, both by the authorities and by the immigrants themselves. However, concepts such as "melting pot" and "generation of the wilderness," which characterized the 1950s, disappeared in the 1970s, and by the 1990s had become negative points of reference, "the mistakes of the 1950s" (Leshem and Lissak 1998).

With time, cultural diversity gained legitimacy, albeit to a limited extent, and mainly from an ethnographic, folklorist standpoint. The Arabs were still prohibited from fostering their political identity, and the southerners from fostering their ethnic identity. This has been described as culinary multiculturalism. Later, a growing number accepted the residual multiculturalism model, which is one step up in the acceptance of people's right to be different and preserve their distinct character. However,

those who hold these views are at heart advocates of transitional pluralism: they believe that diversity is a temporary phenomenon that will pass
when the generation of the wilderness disappears and a new generation
grows up speaking Hebrew (Horowitz and Leshem 1998: 303).

By contrast, in the 1990s, a demand arose for the first time in Israel,
that the principles of interactive multiculturalism — which sees coexistence, cross-fertilization, and mutual enrichment as the best solutions to
pluralism — be adopted. From this point of view the Russian immigrants'
impact on Israeli culture was quite revolutionary. The stated wish of these
immigrants to preserve their culture and their language, and to pass them
on to their children, was a significant factor in the development of interactive pluralism. They were supported in this by the popularity of multicultural ideas brought to Israel by the intellectual and cultural elite. In a
society based on multicultural principles, the minority media can fill its
dual role without its two components being perceived as an irreconcilable
contradiction. On the one hand, the minority media contribute to ethnic
cohesion and cultural maintenance; on the other hand, they may also
encourage the assimilation of their audience to mainstream values
(Riggins 1992: 4).

The question of language is also critical. In the 1950s the "imparting
the language" campaign was more than just an endeavor to teach the new
immigrants Hebrew; it was also pressure to stop the use of foreign languages, as part of the process of severing the immigrants from their
Diaspora past and of building the new nation. The official policy also
influenced the social norms, and Israelis were sometimes coerced into
changing their family names and adopting new Hebrew names. For the
same reason, foreign-language newspapers were held in contempt, even
though some of Israel's best journalists wrote for them.

The Russian speakers were the first group of immigrants who used
political tools to fight for official recognition of their language, so much
so that in the 14th Knesset a private bill was submitted to make Russian
one of Israel's official languages. For the first time in the history of immigration in Israel, these immigrants established a parallel education system
of supplementary studies operating in the afternoon, with the lessons
conducted in Russian. The proliferation of Russian-language newspapers
can be seen not only as a means of supplying information to those who do
not speak Hebrew but also as an educational effort to preserve the language. Therefore, they are likely to survive for the foreseeable future.

The question of language applies also to some of the other co-cultures.
The nonuse of Hebrew among the Palestinian cultural group is not so
much due to lack of knowledge as to the intention to preserve this distinguishing cultural component. Similarly, the prohibition on using the
mainstream media among the ultraorthodox is designed to seal off the

boundaries between their community and society at large, which inevitably intensifies the use of the alternative, minority media. Thus in the 1990s, the period of growth and flourishing of co-cultures and of the sectorial structure, the proportion of foreign-language dailies and periodicals in Israel rose considerably.[5]

THE MEDIA IN A MULTICULTURAL SOCIETY

The key to the question of solidarity and integration in Israeli society is to be found less in the growth of the number of commercial channels in the national media, and much more in the direction of development of the minority media. The concern expressed by Katz recalls a similar situation in the mid-1970s, when local newspapers began to spring up and it was feared that they would "cause a decline in the centralizing power of the national establishments," or "consolidation of a local identity" (Caspi and Limor 1992: 69). In a small country like Israel, with its centralized government structure and national rather than localized problems, these fears soon proved to be groundless.[6]

Nevertheless, in the near future, the minority media and their relations with the national media might have a greater impact on how pluralism develops in Israel. The extent to which the minority media foster animosity and alienation toward the national media, or avoid doing so, will affect the development of Israeli pluralism in the direction of multiculturalism, segregation, or even disintegration. An examination of the Russian-language press conducted in 1995 found indications of three approaches toward the host society: adaptation, segregation, and integration (Lissak and Leshem 1995). Thus, various possible directions of development exist.

The attitudes of minority media tend to be influenced by the attitudes of the national media toward the co-cultures, and many studies conducted worldwide show that the tendency is usually to ignore these cultures (Riggins 1992). Hitherto, this has been the case with Israel.[7] The more the national media give expression to the representatives of the various co-cultures, reveal what happens within these groups, and reflect their symbolic order, the more the barriers dividing the sphericules will be relaxed.

If the national media ignore the co-cultures and the minority media — refraining from broadcasting their music, giving a stage to journalists and broadcasters from these co-cultures, or covering what happens in their communities — these groups will increasingly turn to their internal media and become alienated from the national media. In addition, the spiral of ignorance of the majority concerning the cultural enclaves will grow, deepening the misunderstanding and antagonism toward them.

There was a dramatic precedent for this in the 1990s. In retrospect, one of the major shortcomings of the national media in Israel was their failure to describe social and cultural developments affecting the immigrants from the former Soviet Union who arrived in such large numbers. Consequently, Israeli society at large remained unaware of developments affecting close to one-fifth of the population, and policymakers were completely blind to these issues. Therefore, the important developments in this cultural enclave, including their political organization and their success in the elections to the 14th Knesset, were unanticipated.

If the co-cultures have access to the mainstream media, even if the minority media continue to coexist alongside the mainstream media, the minority media is more likely to complement the national media instead of being antagonistic toward them. In this context, the national media's ability to use, or even create, common identity symbols, even of a "virtual" nature, will be very important. The fact that these symbols will be polysemic, capable of interpretation in various ways, is not necessarily negative. On the contrary, it has the advantage of permitting social solutions in the spirit of "constructive ambiguity."[8]

The difference in the professional cultures of the mainstream media and the minority media is one of the factors that affect their relations. A basic principle among journalists of the national media is "the public's right to know." This does not apply to the ultraorthodox media, however. "We repudiate this principle and we are proud of the public's right not to know. . . . We will give information only up to the point where it might violate our principles," wrote Moshe Akiva Druk, editor of the ultraorthodox *Hamodia*, in March 1986 to Education Minister Yitzhak Levy (Levy 1989: 247). The general press is characterized by negative writing. "With us it is forbidden to write bad news about crime, sex, and the like." And Rivka Flok, a journalist who writes for ultraorthodox newspapers, offers an explanation for this policy: "Exposure arouses devils and increases crime."[9]

That is why journalists in the religious press willingly accept the decisions of the "supreme council," which represents the community leadership, sitting every evening in the editorial room and serving as the final arbiter of what will be published and what rejected. This is a practice that is completely in contradiction with the principle of professional autonomy of the national press. While the national media embrace the principle of even-handedness, giving the injured party the right to react, the minority media object to this. "That approach, whereby every attitude also has a legitimate opposing attitude, is exactly what leads you to relativism. We have one clear truth."[10]

This is exactly the phenomenon described by White in his work on differing conceptions of professionalism in the mainstream and minority media. Because minority media are more concerned with journalists' responsibility to a community or movement, there may be active rejection of autonomous professionals, whose standards are set internally, in favor of a participatory approach to communication that welcomes citizen input. The result may not necessarily be the most objective reporting of events (White 1989).

Basic principles upheld by a large part of the minority media are unacceptable to journalists in the national media, who relate to such a professional code in the same way as hegemonic groups in liberal democracies relate to traditional, nonliberal practices in their co-cultures, such as kosher slaughter of animals, clitoridectomy, or the arranged marriage of young girls. "I accept multiculturalism, provided that they behave according to liberal game rules," said Avirama Golan, a columnist in *Haaretz*.[11] Is it possible to bridge such a deep normative gap?

In the past decade this question has increasingly occupied the multicultural discourse, which distinguishes between shallow and deep multiculturalism. The solution is easy in the case of shallow multiculturalism, where cultural differences are tempered by the acceptance of liberal principles. But to what extent can a liberal society accept the existence of nonliberal codes in the name of multiculturalism? Can there also be deep multiculturalism, in which liberal cultures live side by side with nonliberal ones?

Yael Tamir believes that this is possible (Tamir 1998), and in her opinion such coexistence does not match some moral principle but constitutes a compromise solution that suits the interests of both sides. This is a modus vivendi that is achieved by the liberal community out of respect for the other, and by the nonliberal community out of recognition of its inferior status. The liberals will lower their demands and expectations regarding the kind of agreements they can achieve with nonliberal groups, while the latter will understand that compromise is the best solution because all the alternatives are worse.

This solution is feasible in a sectorial society, but only on one condition: although not all the groups sharing a public sphere have to be committed to the basic principles of liberal democracy, they do have to share in the consensus regarding the constitutional order. Not every stable democracy has a consensus on liberal principles; however they do possess social mechanisms that enable them to prevent the nonliberal movements from destroying liberal democracy, as happened in Germany or Italy between the two world wars. For example, there is the Scandinavian experience, when some of the symbols of the protofascist movements were "domesticated" and integrated into the parliamentary tradition. The same thing happens in the United States, where even fascist or religious groups that openly oppose liberal values undertake to uphold the constitutional order and conduct their ideological battle, finding justification and support for it in the Constitution.[12]

There is a debate regarding whether at the beginning of the twenty-first century, the groups in Israel that do not accept liberal principles are stronger than they were in the past. More important, though, is the fact that largely as a result of the colonial situation and the intense conflict over collective identity, the groups challenging the constitutional order have gained strength. They have even received support from the very heart of the political establishment. The most extreme demonstration of their strength, both in practical and symbolic terms, was the assassination of Yitzhak Rabin and its aftermath, but at a less dramatic level attacks on, and the infringement of, the constitutional order are much more prevalent. The fact that Channel 7 is still broadcasting is just one minor example of this.

So long as there is agreement on the constitutional order, society can incorporate co-cultures that behave according to nonliberal principles, but as soon as this agreement on the constitutional order ceases to exist the social bonds will be broken. The same applies to the minority media. So long as these groups accept the constitutional principles they can maintain different professional norms within their own sector, even if these are not compatible with the liberal model. But if they castigate the constitutional order they are liable to undermine the common basis of the broad social system.

The proliferation of national commercial channels in itself is no cause for concern over the collapse of the Israeli public sphere. But the direction of development of the minority media and the growth of separate sectorial formations might indeed encourage this phenomenon. What is clear is that, in view of the weight of the national and minority media in constructing the collective identity, they will have considerable influence on the direction in which Israeli society is heading. Journalists' lower status in the co-cultures, particularly the religious ones, will lead to a situation whereby the spiritual and political leadership will largely determine the nature of their groups' relationships with the center.

That said, the new status of the national media elite in media-centered democracies makes them as powerful as politicians, sometimes even more powerful. Are they aware that they are no longer simply reporters, interpreters, and intermediaries, but policymakers as well? Are they aware of their heavy new responsibility? Do journalists and editors understand that in the new democracy they must be concerned not only with the morality of intentions, but also with the morality of results?

Conclusion

"Mediapolitik" and the Future of Democracy

THE ELITES' CONNECTION

The media have acquired power and status equal to politicians in the new media-centered politics. Now the media are full partners in policy making, and the logic of media drives the fusionist system. No one, from Gutenberg to the students of McLuhan, dreamed this might be possible. Urgent questions arise: Are the media aware of their new role, status, and responsibility? Or, are they intoxicated by power and enjoying its fruits, and thus reluctant to accept the restrictions and rules of behavior that bind leaders in a democracy? These questions lead our discussion as we conclude this study of telepopulism.

The democratic theory of the media ascribes great importance to professional autonomy. For the media to be able to fulfill their function in the public sphere, there must be a separation of powers and the media must be independent from the establishment. The more autonomous the media are, states this theory, the better they can act as watchdogs of democracy, or as the so-called fourth estate. For this reason, the competitive model was adopted by the media in the United States in the 1960s, in Western European countries in the 1980s (Bono and Bondebjerg 1994), and in many emerging or consolidating democracies toward the end of the twentieth century. Autonomy is thus perceived as an expression of democratization. But what happens in the fusionist model of mediapolitik, where this separation of powers does not exist, in which even the myth of objectivity cannot hide the political nature of the press, and in which politics is practiced by "going public" and news making?

A shift occurred in Israel from the parallel to the competitive model of journalism. However, social, political, and professional factors restricted the media's freedom of action. If the political change and the adoption of the principles of competitive journalism could have neutralized some of these factors, the symbiosis created by media-centered democracy precluded the possibility of developing the professional autonomy that is called for in a polyarchic regime (Dahl 1989). The resultant situation is more reminiscent of a battle between subelites within a one-party system than between different elites in a multiparty polity.

The first factor detrimental to structural pluralism is the strong social bond between media and political elites. The two groups belong to the same social strata and are similar in patterns of socialization, education, places of residence, patterns of consumption, and lifestyle (Etzioni-Halevy 1993). This type of elbow-rubbing affects the media's mode of functioning. Avraham Burg's election as speaker of the Knesset in 1999 is a case in point. After the general elections in 1999, Prime Minister Ehud Barak's candidate for speaker was Knesset member Shaul Simchon, one of his most ardent supporters, but the media made no secret of the fact that they preferred Burg, a member of the "Octet" in the Labor Party and an intraparty rival of Barak. In the internal vote conducted in the Labor Party, Burg won. Simchon's reaction expressed his anger and frustration:

> I don't think those media stars opposed me on ethnic grounds [Simchon is Mizrahi, Burg Ashkenazi]. Nor do I think they are racist. But I do think that they are elitist yuppies, snobbish and arrogant, who are cut off from the Israeli reality and are biased in favor of politicians who mix with them all the time. They eat with them and invite them a thousand times to the same talk shows. All the others simply don't exist for them.[1]

Comments of this nature are heard frequently.

The social affinity between journalists and politicians gives the Israeli media one of their major advantages: they are extremely knowledgeable concerning what happens in the corridors of power. Their mastery of internal information is impressive, even compared to countries in which professional journalism is more developed. Diplomats and reporters stationed in Israel corroborate this fact. But does journalists' easy access to information strengthen their independent and critical position? Or is it detrimental, distancing them from the general public and positioning them as part of the hegemonic bloc, thus weakening their capacity for self-reflection?

Close ties between journalists and politicians have existed since the beginning of the Zionist movement, when journalists accepted the hegemony of the political leaders. In the 1980s another common relationship pattern between the two groups existed. Instead of "court scribes" or "adjutants," who fully identify ideologically with their sources, some journalists became "associates." These are journalists who, in exchange for precious inside information, are prepared to pay the price for cultivating the source, becoming dependent on it, and in the end losing their independence and their legitimacy. Only very few of the political correspondents in Israel can be defined as truly independent journalists, that is, those who have managed to develop variegated sources of information from diverse political directions while at the same time being privy to government secrets. In the end, this reinforces the cartel-like character of political parties and the symbiosis between politics and the press.

A man who drew attention to the norm of rubbing shoulders with politicians was *Haaretz* editor Gershon Schocken. An intellectual from an aristocratic class of German Jewry, Schocken adhered to the rule whereby an editor does not develop friendships with politicians and members of the elite about which his paper writes, and he preached this principle to his journalists. His behaving so differently from the norm underlined the common practice, and he remained an exceptional figure on the Israeli journalistic scene.

In Israel's professional community a journalist's status is measured largely by how close he or she is to the inside and the favors he or she receives by being close to the loci of political power. There are many such favors. Newspaper editors, for example, accompany the prime minister on his plane on state visits abroad, their seats paid for by the prime minister's office. Economic analysts are also invited to the finance minister's bureau to help him prepare a new economic plan, and military correspondents are made privy to security secrets. Such inside status makes it difficult for journalists to take an independent and critical stance.

Further intertwinement of media and political elites is evident in the appointment of journalists to government positions as spokespeople, responsible for public affairs, advisors to ministers, or heads of bureaus. Others join the diplomatic service as cultural or press attachés, or even as consuls-general. Some are appointed to prestigious positions that have no connection with the professional field of journalism. The appointment of a journalist to undertake an official role on behalf of the state while he or she is still working as a journalist can be particularly problematic. This was the case with *Maariv* editor Ya'akov Erez, who was appointed in 1999 to be Israel's representative in a joint committee with the Palestinian Authority on the issue of preventing propaganda.[2]

A related problem is the "revolving door," with journalists moving back and forth between journalism and the political world (McEnteer 1991; Wolfson 1991).[3] In some cases, it is a one-way move from journalism to politics: Journalist Yossef (Tommy) Lapid is one case in point. He was preceded by such other examples as Yossi Sarid, the *Meretz* leader, and Yossi Beilin, one of the Labor Party leaders, who began their careers as journalists. The advantage of such a move consists of journalists-turned-politicians' exposure to the inner workings of government. The practical experience not only enriches their knowledge but also changes their perception of the way government functions. For example, journalists tend to believe conspiracy theories and are surprised to discover that a state of earnest confusion is more prevalent in government than willful deception. Many journalists who have entered government service admit they learned a great deal about the journalistic profession from the other side of the desk. When they return to journalism from their government posts, they tend to be much more skilled as a result of these eye-opening experiences, much of which was not flattering (McEnteer 1991: 8, 9).

The revolving door also carries many disadvantages, especially in terms of journalists' image and their legitimacy in the public eye. In a model in which the media and politics are intertwined more than ever, the problem increases manifold. The revolving-door method supports the argument that the media are a political class. This is particularly salient when journalists become government envoys to the media, as in the case of Uri Porat. As a result, journalists' ability to act as representatives of civil society — as independent agents between citizens and the govern-ment — is perceived to be hindered. This further strengthens the public's cynical view of the collaboration of political and media elites.

The revolving door is especially detrimental to military correspon-dents. Nachman Shay was a military correspondent with Channel 1 tele-vision, became director of the IDF radio station, Galei Zahal, and later spokesman of the IDF and director-general of the Channel 2 Authority. Another case was that of Ron Ben Yishay, who was a Channel 1 military correspondent, became a military analyst for *Yediot Ahronot*, was appointed commander of Galei Zahal, and then went back to work for the independent commercial newspaper.

The operational mode of the media in Israel also adds to the blurring of boundaries between the press and politics. Editorial structures and control in the news organizations are gray areas. Comparative studies of news organizations show that there are considerable differences in the division of labor between reporters and editors, in styles of working in the newsroom, in the editorial structure, and in the role perception of the reporter. Thus Esser (1998) and others before him (Kepplinger and Kocher 1990) found that in Britain, as compared to Germany, there is more centralization in the newsrooms, as well as a high degree of division of labor. In Britain there are distinct separations among the tasks of the reporter, who collects news and reports on it; the subeditor in the edito-rial office, who corrects texts and formulates titles or headlines; and the commentator or "leader writer," who contributes texts expressing opin-ion. In Germany there is less separation between the tasks of reporter and subeditor, and there is not such a sharp separation between those two tasks and writing opinion articles.

The division of labor practiced in Germany generates more direct contact between the reporter and the final product of his work and greater possibility of influencing opinion pieces, while the division of work and the increased specialization in the British case separates the source from the final journalistic product. The same is true of the press in the United States. While only 7 percent of journalists in Germany said that the news they prepared was edited by somebody else in the newsroom in order to increase audience interest, in the United States this figure is 36 percent (Donsbach 1995). In Israel the editors have considerable influence over the finished product, although not in the case of articles filed by top political reporters. These writers enjoy great freedom, and the published product, sometimes even the headlines, is closer to the original text that they wrote. Thus, the influence of the link between the political source and the journalist is evident in the finished text.

The changes that have occurred recently in journalists' working styles have clouded yet further the distinction between reporters dealing with news and writers of opinion articles. In the past, too, there was less separation in Israel between the department dealing with the editorial pages and that dealing with the news pages, compared with the convention in quality papers in the United States. Representatives of these two departments take part in daily editorial meetings, and the editors of the opinion pages are informed about what subjects will be dealt with in the news pages. In the past, however, there was greater division among the writers in the different sections of the paper.

This situation began to change in the 1980s, with the introduction of "new journalism" to the Israeli press and the blending of news and opinion in the same text, all in a personal literary style. This trend gathered strength in the context of the newspapers' preparations to face the challenge of television. Interpretive articles began to fill the news pages. This phenomenon reached its peak when the style of the personal columnists spread. Salient examples of this are Nachum Barnea in the newspaper and Amnon Abramovich on television, both of whom combined news whose classic place was in the news columns, together with very personal interpretation.

Furthermore, if in the past there was complete separation between news and opinion pieces, that is no longer the case today. The political reporter writes a news item on the front page and expresses an opinion on the editorial pages. The educational correspondent attends a press conference and reports on it but also expresses his opinion on the subject in an interpretive article on the op-ed page. The small size of the market and the limited resources of the media organizations restrict the ability to employ a large number of writers, which is necessary in order to maintain a higher level of specialization. However, the professional culture that sees nothing wrong with such a blend of news and opinions has also contributed to this phenomenon.

Another cause of the growing indistinctness between journalism and politics is the domination of celebrity culture over the press. This phenomenon, taken for granted in a commercial TV culture such as the United States, was new and somewhat alien to Israeli society, in which journalists not so long ago were regarded as educators and had a sense of social mission like teachers or writers. From the mid-1990s, TV producers began to replace professional journalists as program hosts with celebrities, singers, models, or actors, whose advantage is their star power rather than journalistic skills. The politicians interviewed on these programs have been pleased because in the absence of journalistic skill, programs that were supposed to put the politician under a microscope become pure entertainment. However, journalism has suffered. The definitions of the profession have become blurred. Moreover, the public does not distinguish between professional and unprofessional behavior and ultimately does not get a product that conforms to the rules taught in schools of journalism.

The loosening of the professional constraints also comes from the opposite direction. Journalists end up becoming celebrities, and they exploit this status for profit in a way that often damages their professional integrity. This began when they started appearing in TV and radio commercials, in contravention of the code of professional ethics. The public had no way of knowing when a journalist was appearing as a commentator, a social critic, or when he was selling goods as an advertiser or a merchant. A few years later, journalists began appearing on television as entertainers or as hosts of entertainment shows. One day you are an entertainer joking with a politician on an entertainment show, and the next day you are a professional journalist in a program of investigative journalism. These shifts between roles further blurred the distinction between genres, between entertainment and journalism, and also between journalistic and commercial considerations. Whereas hitherto the commercial considerations were those of the proprietors of the media outlets, they were now rivaled in importance by individual journalists' commercial interests.

The mechanisms designed to safeguard the professional ethics of journalists were ineffective in face of the new celebrity culture. Complaints were lodged with the Press Council and the Press Association against journalists who took part in commercial advertising, but even these organizations were unsuccessful in imposing their authority. In cases where the professional bodies were adamant, the accused—Israel's top journalists—preferred to leave the association rather than jeopardize their high earnings. They also knew that their public and professional status would not suffer in the slightest as a result.

The fusion of politics and journalism grew with the increasing number of politicians who served as political analysts. These were the politicians who appeared not as representatives of political camps or as advocates of particular viewpoints, but rather as people who knew how to adapt themselves to the role of journalist. They assumed a "neutral" and populistic interpretive style of the type that television likes (for example, they often seasoned their analysis with analogies from the world of sport). Because they were able to transform themselves in the media, they gained much greater exposure than politicians who could not or would not dare to deviate from the "party line."

Two figures who stood out particularly in this group were former minister and Knesset member for Labor Uzi Baram, and former mayor of Tel Aviv Ronny Milo of the Likud. The latter was so successful that in 1998 the editor of the weekly news commentary program *Saturday Game* invited him week after week to appear as an analyst on his program, even after Milo announced that he intended to run for prime minister.

Because politicians with telegenic, celebrity-type personalities grew in status also among the politicians themselves, a kind of gray area developed between the three groups: politicians, journalists, and entertainers. They all belonged to the same social category of actors who are celebrities, and in the 1990s politicians and public figures appeared in the role of journalists, as guest-interviewers alongside the hosts of radio and television programs, and even as hosts of their own programs. Today you interview and tomorrow you are interviewed, whether you are a journalist or a politician. Thus, the symbolic character of the relations between the media and politics is not confined to the macro, structural level, but is in fact put into practice by the agents themselves.

THE PUBLIC'S LACK OF TRUST IN THE MEDIA

Other characteristics of Israeli journalism have further intensified the negative repercussions of the fusion of politics and journalism and are indeed detrimental to journalism's professional standards. First, the media deal extensively with politics. They do so not only to the point of ignoring other fields and issues but also by offering politicians a platform for airing opinions on any issue in any context, even when their words have no news value whatsoever. In addition, the print press, and particularly broadcast journalism, focuses on coverage of the geographical and social center, largely ignoring the periphery. This is evident, for example, in the inadequate, stereotyped, and derogatory coverage of Israeli Palestinians, as well as in the coverage of developing towns (Avraham 1998; Avraham, Wolfsfeld, and Aburabiya 2000).

Acting as an even greater influence are the forces of homogenization, mainstreaming, and passivization that intensified in the 1990s and brought about a cumulative outcome. George Garbner, along with a team of researchers from the Annenberg School of Communication, first exposed the impact of TV on cultural attitudes and attitude formation: television blurs traditional social distinctions; it blends otherwise divergent groups into the mainstream; and it bends the mainstream in the direction of the medium's interest in profit, populist politics, and power.[4] Television encourages and disseminates similar consensual opinions, which win the support of a broad social common denominator.

Pack journalism — the tendency to deal with the same subjects that colleagues deal with, to write about what they write about, in the same spirit and using the same language — also had a negative impact on the profession.[5] This was similar to the homogenization phenomenon, which stems from the centralization and competitiveness of market-driven journalism and which limits the scope of topics and variety of opinions. McNair provides an excellent description of pack journalism: "When a story is deemed to have become 'news' by one organization the others feel compelled to follow suit. This is not necessarily because the story has 'objective' importance, but will often be a product of editorial assumptions that to be left behind by the pack is dangerous for an organization's commercial position and legitimacy as a news provider" (1995: 62–63).

Though Israeli journalists lamented this particular characteristic, which was the cause of the 1973 "Blunder," they did not effectively resist pack journalism. On the contrary, in the 1990s the phenomenon expanded. Journalists' passivization increased its negative effect even more; that is, journalists tend not to go looking for news, but rather are tempted to use information that is submitted to them by the large army of press secretaries, public affairs officers, spokespersons, publicity experts, and spin doctors. These days it is very common to hear on the radio "an exclusive news item" that was distributed to many journalists by a press secretary, via beeper. Gone are the days when a reporter felt the need to modify the news item, not to mention verifying it or getting comments from other interested parties.

The development of the political-media complex elicited a dialectical response from the public. On the one hand, it heightened the recognition of the media's importance in the new politics. Media consumption grew, media celebrities became cultural heroes, media-related professions were the most sought-after careers among young people, and new media studies departments opened in a half dozen universities, after thirty years during which there had been only one such department — at the Hebrew University of Jerusalem.

On the other hand, there was growing criticism of the profession and a decline in the level of trust in the media. In March 2000, 38 percent of Israel's population said that journalists were not credible (an additional 39 percent said that they were only credible to a limited extent). In 2002 it was 47 percent.[6] Surveys conducted during the 1990s revealed that the level of trust in the media was low when compared with other national institutions.

There is a correlation between the level of trust and the power of the media in the new political system. The more the public feels that the media are powerful, that they have influence over public opinion and government, the less it trusts them. A large majority of the Israeli public — 78 percent — thought in 1997 that television had great influence on the formation of public opinion. Sixty-two percent thought that TV had great influence on the government and that politicians were unable to curtail or restrict its freedom of action.[7] This was also measured with regard to specific issues on the national agenda. In 1998, 61 percent estimated that the media influenced public attitudes toward the peace process to a large or very large extent, and only 33 percent ascribed little influence to the media on this subject.[8]

There is also a link between seeing the press as biased and ascribing influence to it. Those who believe that the press is not objective tend to impute more power to it. In the peace index poll of July 1998, only 34 percent replied that the Israeli media reported objectively on the peace process, while 59 percent thought that media reports were not objective (46 percent thought that the media tended to support the process, and 13 percent thought that they tended to oppose it).[9]

A low degree of trust in the media is a phenomenon common to all democratic societies. In a poll conducted by the American Society of Newspaper Editors at the end of 1999, some 78 percent of the newspaper readers in the United States accused the newspapers of bias and said that newspapers were either not open-minded and neutral about facts or that they pursued an agenda and shaped the news to conform with it. Eighty percent accused the press of sensationalism and of publishing items without thinking of the potential damage this might cause. Comparative research has shown that in the more developed democracies, there is greater mistrust of the media. In the World Value Survey conducted between 1997 and 1998, more than 80 percent of those polled in Austria and Germany expressed low trust in the media. In the United States the rate is almost 70 percent, and in Scandinavia, between 60 and 70 percent; whereas in Ghana, India, and Brazil, the figure was about 30 percent. In the last study done in Israel in January 2003, 47 percent expressed low confidence in the media.[10]

Even if the level of trust in the Israeli media is somewhat higher than in other developed democracies, the media still suffer from a lower degree of trust than other national institutions. In the 2003 study, more than 88 percent expressed trust in the IDF, and 60 percent expressed trust in the Supreme Court. The government is less trusted than the media: only 33 percent expressed confidence in it. And the political parties scored especially low: only 7 percent expressed trust in them.

The main cause of the low level of trust in the media in Israel is the divergent perceptions of journalists and the general public concerning the balance between freedom of the press and national security needs (Segal 1996).[11] While journalists see little reason to restrict the freedom of the press in wartime, most of the public disagrees. Forty-five percent even support the view that "the risk of minimal damage to security justifies real restriction of the freedom of the press" (Peres and Yuchtman-Yaar 1998). While almost all the journalists interviewed for the purpose of this book saw the media's involvement in the GSS affair of 1985 as one of their most important professional achievements, a large majority of the public believes that the media should not have exposed the fact that GSS officers had murdered Palestinian terrorists, thus instigating a campaign of criticism against the GSS and its leaders. This gap in attitudes recurs every time an incident connected with security comes to light.

The gap between journalists' and the public's perceptions of the role of the press goes far beyond security issues. As far back as 1988, the majority of the top journalists (97 percent of the print press and 90 percent of the broadcast media) replied that "the press should reveal all the information to the public, even if it is not pleasant or suitable," and only about half said that "they should be careful in reporting subjects that might lower the national morale." By contrast, most of the public supported the opposite attitude (Shamir 1988). At the beginning of 2003 we examined the differences in attitude toward various aspects of the profession between Israeli journalists and the public. Once again, we found a difference in attitude toward the role of the media in national security affairs. More than half of the journalists (about 51 percent) agreed with the sentence, "The Israeli media is patriotic and biased to an extent which damages its professionalism" (21 percent "very much agreed"; 33 percent "somewhat agreed"). Only 40 percent of the general population responded similarly.

But significant statistical differences were found in other issues as well.

Eighty-four percent of the journalists did not agree with the assumption that the media in Israel has a liberal bias. (In Israeli studies, the term used is Leftist, not liberal.) By contrast, half the public agreed with this statement and only one-fifth (22 percent) expressed total disagreement.

Gaps between journalists and the public were also found with respect to other matters. Approximately 94 percent of the general public considered the value that "a journalist should always be neutral" to be important, compared with 86 percent of journalists who held that view. Only 2 percent of the public, compared with 4 percent of journalists, considered that value to be of no importance at all.

Whereas 80 percent of the public agreed with the sentence "the media is motivated too little by moral considerations, and too much by a concern for ratings" (more than half reported that "they very much agreed" with this statement), of the journalists polled, 71 percent agreed. (Among the latter, 24 percent "very much agreed.") It was also found that while journalists tended to criticize the media for being overly mobilized and making factual mistakes, the public tended to criticize the media for being biased, for behaving unethically, and for not reporting enough good news.

THE MEDIA'S LACK OF REFLECTIVE THINKING

The growing public criticism of the media and the decline in public trust did not cause the media to reflect on its new roles and perceptions. Some in the media are still intoxicated by the rapid development that began in the 1990s and has not yet slowed down, with more and more new channels, programs, and production companies, as well as new stars emerging overnight and huge sums of money changing hands in the industry. The best print journalists also reach television, if not as hosts then as guests. Even the economic crisis that began with the outbreak of the El Aksa Intifada in September 2000 did not diminish the optimism that the media would continue to flourish. There is also another reason to ignore the criticism. It is the need to defend oneself against the political attacks on the media, which have increased since the 1990s. In this respect, Netanyahu's war against the media had a boomerang effect. The need to defend themselves against his attacks led even those who might usually admit to the faults and failures of the media to spring to their defense, in order to prevent the populist leader from injuring them and exploiting them for his own purposes.

The public's negative view of the free and critical press strengthens Israeli journalists' feeling that they really are free and critical and in fact prevents them from seeing the facts — that the opposite is true, that they are not independent enough, and that they are much less critical than they ought to be. In the past, such criticism would have been waved aside and would have disappeared (like Harshefi's book). At the end of the 1990s, however, the first seeds of systematic criticism began to appear from media critics in *Haaretz*, the magazine *Ha'ayin Hashevi'it*, and a few books by academic researchers.[12] However, this is still a marginal phenomenon compared with the amount of professional critical literature published in the United States, for example.

The gap between journalists' attitudes and those of the public, especially politicians, led to the fact that over the course of the 1990s, several attempts were made to restrict the freedom of the press and to reduce its power. Close to twenty bills were proposed in the Knesset that were designed to clamp down on the press, to prevent the publication of names of people suspected of criminal offenses, or to enforce the "right of reply" in a size and position identical to the original item. Some of the bills even proposed that anyone who published a report about a lawsuit without a reply from the accused would be liable to a fine and a one-year term of imprisonment.[13]

There were also many proposals to impose various restrictions on publication in newspapers. These ranged from various publication prohibitions — the name of a suspect so long as he or she had not been indicted, the personal details of the victim of a crime, the name and photograph of a person killed or wounded in an accident or disaster without the permission of the victim or a family member — to a prohibition of advertising the services of prostitutes or horoscopes.[14]

There were also bills, like that of Knesset member Avraham Katz-Oz (Labor), which sought to impose licensing on journalists. He explained his proposal: "Due to the fact that journalists possess great power — power that is sometimes abused — I believe it is necessary to impose certain requirements (such as studying and taking certification tests) for the training of anyone who wants to engage in journalism, which will be a condition for employment as a journalist."[15] This attempt, like most of the others that arose from time to time, failed, mainly due to pressure by editors and journalists on the legislators. Although they were not approved, the bills had a negative effect on journalists themselves. The need to defend themselves against the intention to limit their freedom of action and restrict their freedom of speech finally led journalists to turn a deaf ear even to justified criticism of the weaknesses, failures, and defects of the media and to rally to their defense against any criticism whatsoever.

The Israeli media as an institution and journalists as a profession are not yet aware of the new situation created by mediapolitik. They are still intoxicated by the atmosphere generated by the entrance into the new era, the era of privatization, deregulation, and "open skies." The bonds released after many years of external political supervision have led most journalists to feel that they have finally reached the promised land. They regard multichannel commercial television, operating in the free market, as capable of fulfilling the highest ideals of the profession, while also being lucrative.

Since journalists are not aware that the media have become part of politics, they are also unaware of the new ethical problems created by this situation. Their professional consciousness lags behind the new reality. A few are sensitive to the problems generated by the concentration of ownership and express concern about the potential danger to the public resulting from the continued trend of cross-ownership. The new problem caused by mediapolitik, however, is completely foreign to them — it has yet to appear on their radar screens.

In particular, there is no awareness of the fact that the media have crossed the line into politics. They are supposed to be part of the public sphere, the representative of civil society and of the citizens. According to democratic theory, the media should serve as a check on the government and as a guarantor of citizens' rights. They also should ensure that citizens take part in decisions that determine their fate. A condition for the fulfillment of these two goals is the free flow of variegated information, outlooks, and opinions. Instead, the media have become part of politics, even part of government.

So long as the media were assigned their original role, theoreticians and architects of democracy did not hesitate to give them great power. This was a condition for the ability to face up to the government. Now, however, in media-centered democracy, excessive concentration of power in the media's hands was liable to be contrary to the interests of the citizens, distancing them from the ideals of equal control of policy agendas, inclusive deliberation, and decision-making processes, which are the foundations of polyarchy. Doesn't the new positioning of the media call for a new professional conception, a formulation of different professional values, new ethics?

But how can the circle be squared? How is it possible on the one hand to defend the freedom of the press so that it can function as a public arena and a counterbalance to the various arms of government, and on the other hand to restrict it in order to ensure that it does not erode civil rights and liberties but remains responsible and accountable?

The internal conflict over these dilemmas led the president of the Supreme Court, Justice Aharon Barak, a creative reformer, to propose a new idea for public discussion. In a lecture on free speech delivered in

1996 at Tel Aviv University, he called for the application of some of the principles of public law to the private media.[16] According to Israeli law, said Barak, the public media — television and radio — constitute a government authority. As such, they have obligations defined by law. For example, the doctrine of equity, or the right of access to the media applies to them, meaning that they are obligated to allow the public access in the name of free expression, which they can limit only if they have almost certain knowledge of imminent danger to the public welfare.

But what is the fate of the private press, which operates as a private owner and does not need the airwaves, which are public property? Does the private newspaper have an obligation toward the individual — whether regular citizen or journalist — to give him a platform to voice his opinions? Such an obligation is imposed on the Broadcasting Authority because it is a government authority, but the private press is not part of government. Does this duty apply to one who is not part of the administration? Justice Barak proposed a question for discussion. Aware of its pros and cons, he explained that he was not taking a stand and wished only to open a public debate. He wrote:

> A private newspaper may be perceived as a hybrid, a two-dimensional or dual-natured body. On the one hand, it is a body which is subject to private law. On the other hand, it might be argued that it fulfills a public role and therefore is like a public utility. The media are common carriers of public discussion.
>
> According to this line of argument, the private newspapers are the most important public platforms in a democracy. . . . Anyone who dominates this platform controls an asset that is vital to a democracy. He controls a kind of "natural resource". . . . Indeed, private newspapers control the platform by means of which democracy exists and which protects its existence. Private newspapers control the air that is the breath of democracy. . . . This platform is not just private property governed by the law of private property; it is also public property, which the newspaper holds as a public trustee.
>
> Therefore, it should enjoy all those rights and obligations of a private corporation, but at the same time it should be subject to the principles of public law, which are necessary in order to preserve the public platform and prevent improper domination of it. In this respect newspapers belong to the category of dual-natured bodies, hybrids that are not part of the administration and formally are private bodies, but that fulfill a public role (like the electric company, the trade union federation, government and municipal companies, etc.), and the court imposes on them "normative duality": both private law and the basic principles of public law.

The idea raised for discussion by Justice Barak was that alongside the private ownership of newspapers, there should also be recognition of their obligation of public trusteeship of the platform they provide, "since the newspaper is not just a speaker, it is also a very powerful public platform that is vital for democracy and essential for the self-expression of the individual and the search for truth." Justice Barak rejected the idea of licensing for journalists, explaining that the approach he advocated, "is not designed to impose external censorship on the private press. It is designed to prevent inappropriate internal censorship; it is designed to prevent the domination of the public platform by a few; it is designed to impose restrictions on power — this time private, not governmental, power."

The well-known adage that absolute power corrupts absolutely is true not only in the public sphere but in the private sphere as well. The rules of trusteeship are designed to restrain power, whatever its source. Indeed, private newspapers are entrusted with the public interest of the free flow of information, and this power calls for supervision and restraint, in order to prevent its abuse. Thus, freedom of expression is not negative freedom — to use Isaiah Berlin's term. It is not only a defense against state intervention, it is also positive freedom, the sword that defends the freedom of speech. It entails newspapers' obligation to act fairly, objectively, without conflicts of interest, as public servants of any type should act. Justice Barak added:

Our tradition is based on what may be called the first generation of problems with freedom of expression. It is nourished by the classic paradigm of relations between the individual and government. It is based mainly on the existence of freedom of expression, which the government can restrict only if there is almost certain knowledge that it will endanger the public welfare. This is the negative aspect of freedom of expression, and it is a firmly established tradition. But the main problem today is in those aspects of freedom of expression that our tradition has yet to contend with. This is the second generation of problems connected with freedom of expression. These are the problems concerning relationships between individuals, and particularly between individuals and the private media. In these relations the media are not just the speakers, they are also the platform. They themselves can be perceived as figures of authority and as bodies with a public function. This is the positive aspect of freedom of expression, and for this positive aspect another model is needed alongside the classic model — to serve as a basis for freedom of expression in Israel.

Although he explained repeatedly that these were only ideas for discussion, not legal rulings, Justice Barak's radical suggestion was met with substantial criticism. Some of the legal principles in which it was grounded generated disputation, but the articles expressing the sharpest dissent were written by editors and in newspapers. These critics rejected his suggestion out of hand, giving voice to their fear of intervention by external elements into the newspapers' messages.[17] An editorial in *Haaretz* stated that the proposal conflicted with a ruling of the High Court of Justice in March 1995, which determined that a newspaper's obligation to publish a reply applied only in the case of a public journal that had public funding and was especially influential. The president of the Supreme Court, Justice Meir Shamgar, warned of the danger of "the exclusive idea market," resulting from the concentration of the media in the hands of a few, but supported the approach in the United Kingdom and the United States, which does not impose on private newspapers the obligation to publish responses or opinions.[18]

One typical reaction was:

> Justice Barak's proposal violates the principle of freedom of expression. If the role of a publisher and editor includes public trusteeship, that means that he must not subordinate the content of the paper to other interests than those of the public, as he understands them. If an editor has to edit according to considerations of the court and not his own considerations, that substantially impairs freedom of expression. . . . In order for the press to fulfill its role properly, it must act as a private element, with minimal restrictions and intervention from the state.[19]

And another:

> Barak is right in his assumption that the main danger to the Israeli press today is not from "the authorities." There is a danger that newspapers will be too strong, concentrated in too few hands. One of the greatest dangers lies in the tendency to make concessions to the readers and not to tell them what it is their duty to know. This happens mainly out of commercial considerations, here and there out of real laziness. But according to Barak's suggestion, the courts will become "super-editorial boards" responsible for the fairness of the newspaper. . . . His suggestion appears to reflect faith in the omnipotent power of the law to order all spheres of life.[20]

The fear of possible infringement on the freedom of the press that seemed to be implicit in Justice Barak's suggestion caused many of his polemicists not to deeply examine the dilemma he addressed. After all, it is hard to see Justice Barak as unconcerned with the freedom of the press, and he emphasized this in his words: "The attitude proposed is not designed to impose external censorship on the private press, it is intended to prevent improper internal censorship." Under Barak's presidency, and previously in a series of judgments, the Supreme Court has been among the bodies that, in the absence of a constitution, promotes the freedom of the press and freedom of expression in Israel. The ruling of the Supreme Court determined that "Freedom of expression is vital to democracy and is a supreme right. Government that takes upon itself the right to determine what is good for the citizen to know, will in the end decide what is good for the citizen to think." The Supreme Court ruled that freedom of the press does not run counter to the right of security, but rather that it constitutes a component of security. Under Barak the.Court has limited military censorship, ruling that publication would not be forbidden unless there was almost certain knowledge that the security of the state would be seriously jeopardized.[21]

Journalists who disputed Barak were anxious that a legal restriction imposed on them by the court might restrict their freedom of expression. In reality, however, they merely expressed the old perception of freedom of the press without entering into the depth of the dilemma that Chief Justice Barak was concerned with. An interesting distinction made by Michael Schudson with regard to models of journalism in the United States — the market model, the advocacy model, and the trustee model — might perhaps clarify Justice Barak's approach and further the discussion (Schudson 1998).

TIME FOR NEW MEDIA POLICY

For many years, the advocacy model existed in Israel, whereby journalists serve the public by being agents for the transmission of a political party perspective. This model emerged at the beginning of the Zionist movement at the end of the nineteenth century, accompanied the national endeavor to achieve independence in the middle of the twentieth century and continued after the establishment of the state in 1948, with the effort for nation- and state-building. According to the advocacy model, journalists have a social mission. They are expected to supply news from the perspective of the national leadership and social movements. The aim of news gathering is to advance the interests of the party. Here journalism is a secondary or subsidiary institution deferring to the party, rather than a wholly autonomous business enterprise. Even after the media revolution and the political upheaval at the end of the twentieth century, this model still exists in parts of the Israeli media, that is, in the sectarian media and to some extent in the public radio and TV channels.

However, in the Israel of the late twentieth century, the majority of journalists scorned and abhorred this model, which they perceived as shameful and unprofessional. Young journalists still hear stories of the era when one had to be a card-carrying party member in order to write for a newspaper and editorials were dictated over the telephone by party leaders. The lack of autonomy lowers professional respect and self-esteem. This generation of journalists regarded the market model of journalism as a solution to the fundamental problems of the profession, and they became ardent supporters of this model, whereby journalists serve the public by providing whatever the public demands. Consumer demand is the ultimate arbiter of the news product.

In the United States, says Schudson, market-model journalism is anathema to journalists. They may use it to apologize for what they do or to explain why their best efforts are often thwarted, but they seldom refer to it as an ideal. In the case of Israel, the opposite is true. The long tradition of party journalism left journalists with a deep sense that only the free market could guarantee freedom of the press, and that only in those conditions could journalists fulfill their democratic role of serving the general public and not political bosses. The reaction against the old model was so strong that the supporters of the new model ignored the fact that in the market model journalists' behavior is dictated by the profit motives of news organizations. Journalists lose their autonomy no less than in the old model, but now they become enslaved to public opinion and public taste, captives of their ratings.[22]

In fact, the sovereignty of the news consumer is also an illusion. He or she can choose only from commercially viable options. Consumers' tastes are formed by the manufacturers who dominate the means of representation. In the end, the commercial media create new needs and a new system that supplies them, so that in fact there is no autonomous behavior in the conditions of a free market. He who pays the piper calls the tune. Commercial logic influences the public's behavior, and its translation into the language of ratings determines the behavior of journalists. Thus, journalists are in fact enslaved to the wishes of the public, which is now beholden to commercial and consumer logic, in contradiction to the ideals of democracy.

So long as the pendulum of professional awareness has swung away from the advocacy model and is still moving toward the market model, journalists are still intoxicated by a false sense of freedom. Only a few of them know that there also exists a third model of journalism, which offers them a much higher degree of autonomy, and which in the end will enable them to better serve the public interest. This is the trustee model, based on the principle that journalists provide the news that they believe citizens should receive in order to be informed participants in a democracy. In the trustee model, journalists should provide news according to what they as a professional group believe citizens should know. The professional journalist's quest for truth and fairness, exercising sound and critical judgment as measured by a jury of his or her peers, should dictate what news should be.

> In this model, journalists imagine a public that is often too preoccupied and too distracted to be active citizens. Therefore, citizens entrust a measure of their sovereignty to journalists, just as people entrust a measure of control over their bodies to doctors. Journalists are professionals who hold citizenship in trust for us, and we rely on their experience or political analysis when we want information about the state of the country. (Schudson 1998)

The trustee model that was described by Schudson is the model to which Justice Barak referred. In the United States the model has undergone many changes, particularly the crises of Vietnam and Watergate, which provoked a great deal of external and internal criticism of conventional journalism and deepened the sense that, like any other professional group, journalists could conspire against the public. Following these scandals, the model underwent reform, but in essence it supplies a clear answer to the question as to who decides what is news. And the answer is neither a party nor the marketplace, but rather journalists themselves.

The conservative and maladroit nature of public broadcasting in Israel, the heavy cost of its maintenance compared with the commercial media, and above all the fact that it is still largely under government supervision have made it very unpopular, especially among journalists. For this reason, the revolutions that occurred in Western Europe did not occur in Israel. In those countries there was a reaction to the commercial market in the media, with the growing recognition that public-service broadcasting is the major and one of the few communication domains that provide space for nonprofit-derived public debate, thereby creating a public sphere where real information can be exchanged at a minimum of market intervention.

Israel, by contrast, is still at an earlier stage of development. There is increased willingness to devalue public broadcasting and ongoing endeavors to privatize it, accompanied by manifestations of contempt for its importance. With the changes in the ethos of Israeli society, public broadcasting is perceived as a relic of the Bolshevist era, like the principles of the welfare state, something that curtails the freedom of the individual and contradicts the spirit of democracy. Therefore, innovative ideas such as "responsible journalism" or "social media," which are discussed in developed democracies, have yet to reach Israel. Even concepts such as public journalism are gaining attention in Israel as echoes of the old advocacy model, although they are usually rejected outright without serious examination. What can be done to solve the problems created by the excessive dependence of government on the media and the media's deep involvement in politics? How can we put the most important actor — the independent, thoughtful, enlightened citizen — back into the center of the equation?

Despite the difficulty of reversing processes that appear inevitable, it is nevertheless possible to think of a series of steps that may address the problems created by mediapolitik. This may be done in four areas: changes in the nature of political institutions; changes to the media structure; change in media-politics relations; and finally, civic education of media consumers and media professionals alike.

The first area to be addressed is the strengthening of political institutions, whose weakness enabled the media to become as powerful as they are today. This refers primarily to the weakening of political parties.

Despite Pizzoreno's claim in 1987 that "parties are a passing phenomenon, a thing of the past," there are growing signs in Europe of parties' vitality and ability to adjust to the new conditions, though there will be no return to the structure and patterns that existed in the past (Yishai 2002). Here, too, the Americanization thesis must be taken with a grain of salt.

The fact is that the major parties in Israel recognized how destructive the direct election of the prime minister was to them, and in 1999 they repealed the Law of Direct Election and reverted to the previous parliamentary structure with some improvements. In the end, a strong and vital party system is essential to a democracy. This, however, is only the first step. Parties should go through a process of democratization, particularly regarding internal elections to their different institutions, so they can regain their true representative nature. To achieve the same goal they should also bring about a reform of the Knesset elections and introduce the regional element through the constituency system.

Another, less difficult, change that is required is in the structure of the media. The commonly heard solution of multiplication of media outlets is not enough in itself. In today's media environment, multiple media outlets have not generated a proliferation of opinions or a variegation of attitudes. Although the number of media outlets has grown, they are all affected by the powerful forces of competition and concentration, which lead precisely to "excessive sameness," the increasing homogenization of content and opinion. Heightened awareness of the damage that homogenization causes to the public discourse may strengthen legislators who advocate the restriction of centralized ownership.

It is more important, however, to raise the awareness of journalists and broadcasters to the new reality, to help them recognize that the profession they are engaged in today is not the same profession that it was fifty or twenty-five years ago — that journalism now is politics. Such recognition could become the basis for structural changes in the media market. One way would be to increase the power of the citizen vis-à-vis the media by strengthening the interactivity of the media, which would enable citizens to take a more active part in public dialogue. On-line newspapers already have regular columns for readers' responses, as well as chat rooms. Technological innovations, along with older methods such as town hall meetings, can be applied to the print and broadcast media.

It may be impossible to change the fast-paced, picture-driven, image-conscious style of today's coverage, but the strengthening of public broadcasting may help to weaken some of the commercial dimensions of the media and to limit the power of owners. This will also help to strengthen the representatives of the public in decision-making bodies. In the Bar-On

Hebron affair it was the public service channel, not a commercial channel, that had the courage to go into battle against the threat to democracy in Israel.

The third area that must be changed is politicians' and officials' special relationship with the media. The former have become much too dependent on the media, both in terms of their reliance on the media for news itself and in their use of the news in making political decisions. Another dimension of the problem lies in the weakness of alternative channels of communication between politicians and the public. This dependence may be reduced by improved understanding of the importance of media policy. At present, few decision makers, in the Knesset, for example, reveal any interest in or understanding of this issue. As a result they have become passive actors instead of leading new processes. The remedy is to introduce legislation that will ensure as much diversity as possible, to build media institutions that will reduce the dependence on the few existing channels.

One of the ways to do this is by strengthening alternative channels of communication between politicians and the public. Direct broadcasting of government events, debates in public institutions, lectures, conferences, seminars, and press conferences will expand the volume of information flowing between policymakers and the public. C-Span in the United States is a good example. Although the viewing ratings of these programs are not high, they are nevertheless viewed by the chattering and writing classes.

In Israel the Internet started being used for political purposes at the beginning of the 1990s, which has opened the way to many new, exciting developments. Today there are about a half-dozen news organizations on-line. The largest of these are, indeed, the sites of the papers *Yediot Ahronot, Maariv,* and *Haaretz,* but others include *Walla* and *Nana,* as well as information agencies operated on-line by private entrepreneurs or financial concerns that seek to reach a broad public through the drawing power that the news has in Israel. These portals and channels of information occupy an increasingly important place in the daily diet of Israel's news-consuming public. They raise a new set of professional and ethical problems, such as violations of libel laws, the invasion of privacy, and the spreading of rumors and unreliable information. However, their advantages are obvious, and there have already been quite a number of cases when early information on the Internet — in security matters, for example — forced the newspapers to follow in their footsteps.

The most important area for reducing the media's fusion with politics is the fourth: civic education of media consumers, and changing journalists' professional consciousness. Today, a decade after the beginning of the era of media-centered politics, a large segment of the public still harbors misapprehensions with regard to the media, does not understand their meaning, and is not aware of their working patterns. The Israeli reader has yet to acquire the habits of critical consumerism. There are no bodies in Israel — neither academic, private, nor nongovernmental organizations — that deal with the follow-up and accountability of the media. Simply put, the knowledge gap is growing, and there is no one to keep watch on the guards.

At the same time, there is broad scope for action among journalists themselves. While other associations of free professions, such as the Bar Association, hold periodical refresher courses, no such training exists among journalists. Apart from the initiatives of politicians that are often motivated by negative intentions, there is no original thinking with regard to ways of improving journalists' working methods in order to increase their accountability. Journalists should reveal to their readers and viewers what they cover and what they prefer to ignore, they should publicly discuss newsworthiness criteria and editing principles, and they should be responsive to the public's requests.

Empowerment of existing mechanisms such as the ethics committees of the Press Council and the Journalists Association is a need that should be self-evident but has not yet been recognized. Above all, it is essential to enhance journalists' awareness of the importance of their new position. Just as the aristocracy created the concept noblesse oblige, professional education should promote the awareness that power requires self-restraint and self-discipline.

To achieve this, the media have to arrive at a self-awareness of their new status in the era of mediapolitik and its implications. There is a need for new rules of behavior, a code of ethics suitable to their new role. Until such a new ethical code is formed, the media should adhere carefully to the existing code: admitting mistakes and publishing corrections, strengthening mechanisms like the ombudsman, making themselves more accountable to the public, and regarding their readers and viewers as citizens rather than consumers. Above all, they must practice self-restraint and set unambiguous rules that clarify that such a concentration of power, even when well intended, is by its very nature a threat to democracy.

The Israeli media have had some substantial successes over the past twenty-five years in confronting ministers and heads of government and exposing corruption in government. Such exposition occurred, for example, in 1977 when *Haaretz*'s Dan Margalit brought the illegal bank account held by Prime Minister Yitzhak Rabin in the United States to light, leading to the latter's resignation. It also happened in the 1990s, when Mordechai Gilat of *Yediot Ahronot* exposed the bribery of Minister

Arie Deri, leading to his trial and incarceration. Toward the end of the decade, Yoav Yitzhak of *Maariv* was instrumental in causing the first police investigation of an incumbent president in Israel, following his revelation of donations that President Ezer Weizmann had received from his friends. This led to the president's early retirement in the middle of 2000. Similarly, Channel 1, the public TV channel, prevented the appointment of Bar-On to the post of attorney general, thus diminishing the likelihood that criminal elements might influence the attorney general's office.

More meaningful than these successes was the determination the media displayed in their battle against Prime Minister Benjamin Netanyahu. Whereas the other struggles were conducted within the system, this was a battle over the system itself. It was an attempt to prevent a neopopulist leader from taking over the media and establishing a telepopulist system in which they would be tools in his hands. Their resistance was partly triggered by their refusal to return to the old system of advocacy or party journalism.

Despite these achievements, there remains a long list of faults and failures that have weakened the press and have cast doubt on its ability to successfully perform its proper role in a democracy. These faults have become increasingly serious and their danger to the democratic system more significant following the media's new position in the system of mediapolitik. There is a need for real reflection and stocktaking, and the solution lies not only in legislation but primarily in self-awareness of the media themselves and the willingness of their leaders, followed by the entire professional community, to take up the burden that their new status brings with it. Will they rise to the task?

Notes

1. Peretz Bernstein, the leader of the General Zionists, was the editor of the daily *Haboker*; Meir Bentov, a leader in Mapam, was the editor of *Al Hamishmar*; Rabbi Berlin Bar-Ilan of the National Religious Party was the editor of *Hatzofe*; Moshe Sneh, the leader of the Communist Party, was the editor of *Kol Ha'am*, and so on.

2. All of the terms and statistics mentioned here and in the remainder of the Introduction are developed and referenced throughout the book. In order not to interrupt the flow of the Introduction, I will not reference them here.

3. Sheldon Titlebaum, *Yediot Ahronot*, October 2, 1998.

4. Israel holds the eighteenth position on the world scale of globalization, but is fifth on "personal contact" index; see "Globalization at Work," *Foreign Policy* (January/February 2002): 39.

5. On camaraderie in Israel, see Blondheim 1997: 62.

6. The most recent and extensive analysis of the relations between media and neopopulism is Mazzoleni et al. 2003.

7. See Kop 2000.

8. The "southerners" are described in detail below in Chapter 12. I will explain there why I prefer using this term rather than the term more commonly used, "Mizrahim."

1. I elaborate this point in subsequent chapters.

2. Dahaf public opinion poll, *Haaretz*, April 3, 2001.

3. *Haaretz*, February 4, 2002.

4. In Italy, the phenomenon that occurred in the early 1980s was called the "ethereal revolution," see Mazzoleni 1987. On the concept "media revolution," see Abramson et al. 1988. On the proliferation of channels, privatization, and commercialization in Europe, see McQuail and Siune 1998.

5. Interview with former president, Yitzhak Navon, March 2, 1997.

6. Educational Television, granted to Israel as a gift by the Rothschild philanthropic foundation, had been broadcasting to schools since March 24, 1965.

7. Interview with Hanna Zemer, former editor of *Davar* and close friend of Levi Eshkol, November 5, 1998.

8. Yehuda Koren, *Yediot Ahronot*, April 10, 1998.

9. The same thing happened with VCRs. In the United States they spread to 11 percent of the households in the first ten years, compared with 50 percent in Israel. Also see Blondheim 1997: 60.

10. Source: official publication of the Ministry of Communication: http://www.moc.gov.il/moc/dows/Serve/itemEnglish/1/1/6/2/5/1/2/html. Again, for the purpose of comparison, in the United States, which was the pioneer in cable broadcasting, the rate of connection reached an average of 70 percent only forty years after the public was first exposed to cable at the end of the 1950s.

11. For data from different surveys, see Tokatly 2000: 110–17. For TV viewing by children, see *Haaretz*, December 31, 1998.

12. Nevertheless, the trend of expansion and differentiation of the press continued, with a growth of 40 percent in the various local periodicals, mostly weeklies, dealing with specific subjects, many of them culture, leisure, and entertainment.

13. See Zvi Harel, *Haaretz*, August 2, 2002; Aviv Lavie, *Haaretz* supplement, May 19, 2000. Another typical case of the change in the nature of management was in television. The TV company Reshet, for example, when first established was administered by journalist Dan Shilon. When he resigned in 1988, the person appointed in his place was Yochanan Zangen, an expert in financial management.

14. Interview with the Secretary-General of the Journalists Association, Razi Gutterman, June 10, 1999.

15. *Yediot Ahronot*, May 15, 1995.

16. Former editor of *Lamerhav*, David Pedatzur, *Davar*, May 22, 1992.

17. Archives of the Press Council, complaint number 85/89.

CHAPTER 2

1. According to a TGI survey on newspaper reading, at the beginning of 2000 more than 50 percent of the adult population in Israel read *Yediot Ahronot* (1,645,000); 26 percent read *Maariv* (849,000); 7 percent read *Haaretz* (225,000); and 3 percent read *Globes*, the financial magazine (100,000). In Israel, newspapers are not published on Saturdays, and the Friday paper includes the weekly magazine. On Fridays approximately two-thirds of the population read *Yediot Ahronot*. This is an interesting sociological and cultural phenomenon, which merits research. Very few countries exist where almost half the adult population reads the same daily paper.

2. *Haaretz*, April 21, 1998.

3. In the summer of 1999, when Fishman wanted to increase his control in *Yediot Ahronot* beyond 25 percent, he was prevented by the Anti-Trust Authority, on the grounds that it would be considered a merger of *Monitin-Globus* with *Yediot Ahronot* (*Haaretz*, May 6, 1998; July 7, 1999; and February 1, 2000).

4. In a conference on "The New Media Map in Israel: Challenges, Dangers, and Balances," Hebrew University, Jerusalem, January 2–3, 1999.

5. Attorney Didi Lachman-Maser in an interview, May 5, 1999.

6. See details and a wealth of bibliographical references in Limor 1997: 34–35.

7. See Report of Zadok Commission, 1997.

8. Knesset Finance Committee hearing, January 21, 2000.

9. *Globes*, April 24, 2001.

10. Arie Caspi, *Haaretz* weekly supplement, February 26, 1999.

11. Its editor, David Bar-Ilan, later became the editor of the *Jerusalem Post*. From 1996 until Netanyahu's defeat in the elections of May 1999, Bar-Ilan was media advisor to the prime minister.

12. Aviv Lavie, *Ha'ir*, July 5, 1998.

13. Yonatan Nasi, *Haaretz*, February 22, 1999.

14. Lilach Segan, *Haaretz*, February 24, 1999.

15. Aviv Lavie, *Ha'ir*, November 20, 1998. See also a special broadcast on Channel 1, summing up twenty years of TV broadcasting in Israel, July 1998.

16. This definition was provided by journalist and culture critic, Adam Baruch, who publishes a weekly column in *Maariv*'s Friday culture supplement. See also Moshe Shnitzer's summary of six years of Channel 2 broadcasting, *Maariv*, September 10, 1999.

17. Yael Chen, in an interview with Ya'akov Bar-On, *Pnai Plus*, December 24–30, 1998.

18. Interview with Uzi Peled, assistant to the head of the team that established television, and later CEO of *Tel-Ad*, one of the three commercial channel concessionaires, August 10, 1997.

19. See special issue devoted to these topics: *Communication Theory* 8, no. 4 (1998), particularly the editor's introduction.

20. Adam Baruch, *Maariv*, Friday supplement, November 11, 1998.

21. In an interview with Neri Livneh, *Haaretz* supplement, March 23, 2001.

22. Nir Efrimi, *Yediot Ahronot*, December 28, 1998.

23. Meir Shnitzer, *Maariv* culture supplement, September 10, 1999.

24. An interview with Kirshenbaum, *Yediot Ahronot* September 21, 1988. On the rating culture, see also Ehud Oshri, *Haaretz*, November 6, 1996.

CHAPTER 3

1. See *Foreign Policy* 1 (January–February 2001).

2. Democratic Index of Israel-Diaspora Institute, 2003, Jerusalem.

3. Survey by the Israel Democracy Institute, Jerusalem, January 2000.

4. Michael Ben-Yair in *Maariv*, October 25, 1996.

5. With regard to Europe, see Mair 1998; and Smith 1998.

6. See, for example, Webb 1995: 319.

7. It remained in power for forty-four years after winning the elections to the world Zionist movement, the Jewish Agency. The only comparable case was that of the Swedish Socialist Party, which stayed in power uninterrupted for forty-three years after World War II. Parties that maintained power for long periods also ruled in Japan and Mexico, but these are states of a different nature.

8. See Goldberg 1992, following Sartori's classification.

9. *Haaretz*, August 30, 1999.

10. On cartel parties see, for example, Katz and Mair 1995.

11. On the evolution of the struggle over partition in the Zionist movement, see Galnoor 1995.

12. Chaim Shibi, *Yediot Ahronot*, December 22, 1998.

13. *Yediot Ahronot*, November 12, 1994.

14. *Yediot Ahronot* and *Maariv*, March 14, 1996.

15. Chronicles of the 13th Knesset, session 299, January 16, 1995.

16. Interview with Knesset Speaker Burg, June 13, 2000.

CHAPTER 4

1. *Journalists Yearbook* 1950: 254–60.

2. Some additional examples: the veteran leader of the Agudat Yisrael Party, Rabbi Menachem Porush, was the publisher and editor of the party daily *Hamevaser*, and the editors of *She'arim*, the paper of Poalei Agudat Yisrael, were the party heads, B. Mintz and K. Kahane. Moshe Sneh, who headed the Communist Party during the last stage of his politically turbulent life, was editor of the party paper, *Kol Ha'am*. On the Right, Dr. Yochanan Bader, parliamentarian and finance minister in the Herut movement's shadow cabinet, was also publisher and editor in chief of the party paper, *Herut*. In *Davar* there were some who had roles in the party while working on the newspaper, such as Knesset member Herzl Berger, who wrote the leading articles in the paper throughout all the years he served as a member of the Knesset.

3. In matters of politics and security, he was a dove and moderate and, therefore, opposed the policy of the right-wing parties, headed by Herut. In terms of social policy he was antisocialist and thus opposed the parties of the Left. According to Blumler and Gurevitch's model, *Haaretz* was on the third level in the scale of five descending levels of partisanship (1995: 65).

4. Quotation from Ben Gurion, taken from the Labor Party archives, Bet Berl, file 24/49. On the need for subordinating the military organization to the party, see Peri 1983: 38–69.

5. One expression of this attitude was published by Ben Gurion in a programmatic article in the *Government Yearbook* for 1951, "Missions of the Spirit and Pioneering in Israel." On Ben Gurion and the intellectuals, see also Keren 1983.

6. *Communication Theory* 6, no. 2 (1996): 143–66.

7. Interview with Lea Porat, director of radio programs in the 1960s; see Mishal 1976.

8. Zalman Shazar, *Davar*, July 26, 1963.

9. These were characteristics similar to those described in Blumler and Kavanagh 1999: 211.

10. Many examples of this can be found in N. Cohen 1998.

11. *Al Hamishmar*, June 18, 1954.

12. Haim Isaac, *Davar*, Jubilee edition, May 30, 1975. The editorial in *Haboker*, the paper of the General Zionists, declared, "The party paper is a pio-

neer in the political struggle, and a large camp of supporters follows its lead" (*Haboker*, September 30, 1955).

13. A typical example was the press treatment of Israel's reprisal actions in Qibia in 1953. Israel officially denied the fact that an IDF force had entered an Arab village in Jordan and caused heavy civilian casualties. The press repeated the official version, knowing that it was not true. See Morris 1996: 33–46.

14. The resolutions of the convention appear in the archives of the Journalists Association, container 3, file 3–16. "Code of Professional Ethics for Members of the Journalists Association, 1958," from the preamble published by the association.

15. In 1983 another concept was added, "the public's right to know," and it was determined that "the freedom of the press and the public's right to know are among the fundamental principles of society in a democratic regime" (Clause 1 in the code of 1986).

16. Another interesting distinction in this context is between "sacerdotal" and "pragmatic" orientations of journalists toward the political institutions whose activities they cover and report (Blumler and Gurevitch 1986).

17. For a detailed description of the affair, see Gutman 1995. *The Storm in the GSS*. Tel Aviv: *Yediot Ahronot* Press.

18. Moshe Ishon, *Hadashot*, June 13, 1990.

19. Ofer's book, like *The Debacle*, came out in a limited edition after the Yom Kippur War and is almost unobtainable now.

20. The original article was published after the Yom Kippur War and reflects many articles in this spirit written about journalists during that period, in the *Journalists Yearbook* of 1994 and 1995.

21. Some of these were Hanoch Marmari in *Haaretz*, Alon Shalev and before him Moshe Vardi in *Yediot Ahronot*, Ido Dissenchik and later Ya'akov Erez in *Maariv*, Yoel Esteron in *Hadashot*, Adam Baruch in *Globes*, and others, including the present writer in *Davar*.

22. Interview with Ilana Dayan, October 24, 1999.

23. See Pfetsch 1998, who cites a number of studies. On the development of negativism in Sweden throughout the years, see Westerstahl and Johansson 1986. Other examples in Europe may be found in Kepplinger and Kocher 1990.

24. These attitudes stood out in a comparison of political reports and articles from the 1950s and 1960s and the 1980s and 1990s, as well as in quantitative studies on people in the media.

25. *Journalists Yearbook* 1995: 167–69.

CHAPTER 5

1. In 1999, Mazzoleni and Schulz (1999: 247–61) distinguished between mediated and mediatized politics. In their opinion, until the 1980s the late democracies were characterized by mediapolitik. Indeed, there was a rise of the news media as a political institution, but basically the media engaged in mediation, which is "an act of intervening, conveying, or reconciling between different actors, collectives, or institutions." The new situation that prevailed in the third period of the polit-

ical media, was different in principle. These authors call the new structure "mediatized" politics. To describe this concept, I mainly use the term "mediapolitik," but also "media-centered democracy." As the description will show, these terms are clearly much closer in meaning to what the previous authors call mediatized politics.

2. For further analysis of indexing, see Althaus et al. 1996.

3. In the U.S. presidential elections in 2000, television developed sophisticated weapons against the spin doctors by adding a third level of political commentary. First, it presents a political event, such as a speech by a presidential candidate. Then it cites the interpretation that is influenced by the spin doctors, but after that it adds interpretation to the interpretation, showing how the candidate's media experts try to manipulate the political message.

4. *USA Today*, June 7, 1995.

5. One should distinguish between Carter's (1959) fourth branch and the "fourth estate" that Thomas Carlyle ascribed to Edmund Burke in the nineteenth century.

6. Interview with Knesset member Dedi Zucker on Channel 1, February 8, 1999.

7. In a radio program on legal issues, *Din Udevarim*, January 18, 1999.

8. Only 15 percent thought that party activity was more effective, as opposed to 26 percent who chose the media (Galnoor and Peres 1992).

9. Other such examples were the planned appointment of Danny Naveh as commander of the IDF radio station, Galei Zahal, in 1990, and the proposed appointment of Danny Yatom of the Mossad as sergeant-at-arms of the Knesset in 1998.

10. See Edswall, November 9, 2000, as well as other pieces by him in the same paper during that period, such as March 26, in which he provides interesting statistical details on the new voting patterns that appeared in those elections, when the Democratic Party was losing the traditional support of the lower social classes and enjoying more support from higher social classes, who identify with liberal attitudes on issues such as abortion, weapons, death sentences, and the environment.

11. *Haaretz*, October 1, 1999.

12. On the growing importance of funding in Israeli politics in the 1990s, see Hofnung 1993, 1998.

CHAPTER 6

1. On the Histadrut election campaign, see Peri 1996.

2. Media consumption surveys, see *Otot* 20 (December 1998): 49.

3. Sources: TGI, *Haaretz*, July 21, 2000; national media survey, *Otot* 99, no. 221 (January 1999): 27.

4. For a review of this concept, see Carpini and Williams 2000.

5. On President Reagan's success as a result of the entertainment factor, see Alger 1998: 53.

6. Barak's fall was swift due to the failure of the peace talks with the Palestini-

ans and the rise of Palestinian terrorism in 2000. In the elections of March 2001 Ariel Sharon was elected, an elderly politician from the old school. But this happened because of a temporary conjuncture. Sharon had replaced Netanyahu at the head of the Likud when the contestants from the younger generation were deeply divided. In this respect his situation was similar to that of Shamir, who had followed Begin as a temporary agreed candidate due to the battle between the young pretenders to the title. In both large parties, the pretenders to the throne at the beginning of the present decade all belonged to the generation of mediapolitik.

7. Akiva Eldar, *Haaretz*, April 26, 1999.

8. On the campaign headquarters' operation, see Azulay-Katz 1999; Kfir and Caspit 1999.

9. Sara Yitzhki-Kaplan, *Otot* (March 1997).

10. Interview with Knesset speaker Shevach Weiss, July 21, 1998.

11. Interviews with Ministers Benny Begin and Yair Tsaban, July 21, 1998.

12. Brigadier-General Rafi Noy in an interview with Nachum Barnea, *Yediot Ahronot*, December 4, 1998.

13. This suggestion was included in a policy paper I submitted to Prime Minister Rabin in 1975, when I was his political adviser.

14. Interview with Kalman Gayer, November 1996.

15. Interview with former Knesset Speaker Shevach Weiss, October 21, 1998.

16. Nachum Barnea, *Yediot Ahronot*, January 2, 1999.

17. Shimon Shiffer, *Yediot Ahronot*, August 25, 2000.

CHAPTER 7

1. For a description of the origins of videomalaise and a fairly broad review of the literature, see Norris 2000.

2. For an interesting discussion of the media discourse, see Yatziv 1999.

3. See also others quoted in Graber 2001: 86.

4. *Yediot Ahronot*, January 1, 1997.

5. *Foreign Policy*, January 2002.

6. Sources: State of Israel, Ministry of Finance (1998). Report on expenditure on salaries in public bodies in 1997: 133, table G 10. Annual report for 2000 of the National Insurance Institute, Jerusalem. Also Swirski and Connor 2000.

7. Shlomo Ben-Ami, who later became foreign minister in Barak's government, was among the first to warn of this combination. See his book of 1998.

8. In Habermasian terms, populist politics are in essence a response to the divide between world system and lifeworld that is endemic to modern and modernizing societies, and to the preference of the peripheral groups of direct social interaction and relationship over large-scale system integration. For an enlightening analysis of Habermas's thesis and elaboration of the populist and communitarian politics, see Calhoun 1988.

9. With the electoral law, Shas had only eleven seats in the 2003 elections.

CHAPTER 8

1. On the radical Right, see, among others, Betz 1994; and Betz and Immersfeld 1998.

2. There are some who use the term "televisual political system," or "televisual politics" (Statham 1996). Habermas terms it "telematic populism" (quoted in Calloni 1998: 98).

3. Ionesco and Gellner's 1969 book was for years the classic text in the critical analysis of this phenomenon. Radical researchers, by contrast, claim that the book expresses the liberal approach to populism as "legitimate criticism-turned-unrestrained polemic" (Taguieff 1995: 24).

4. The journal *Constellations* 5, no. 1 (1998), devoted a special issue to the subject of population, based on an international conference on "Democracy Between Populism and Oligarchy," held at Princeton University in 1996.

5. In the American presidential elections of 2000 the pundits made considerable use of the term "populism." The election campaigns included many features of populism — for example, Bush's attack on the Washington establishment (which did not prevent him from building for himself an administration that included members of that establishment) and Gore's attack on large business concerns, both of which were attacks made in the name of the ordinary people, the nation.

6. The highbrow paper *Haaretz* in May 1998 devoted a special jubilee issue to this very subject.

7. Uzi Benziman, *Haaretz*, January 11, 1976.

8. Similarly, Filk, in analyzing Israeli society, claims, using Laclau's terminology, that populism can also be seen as a democratic project, in that it broadens the boundaries of the political field. This happens "in cases when there is a historical, contra-hegemonic bloc which includes social groups that were previously marginalized, and are now entering the political arena and being constituted within it as subjects through their participation in the historical bloc" (Filk 1996: 224).

9. For the rules of impression management, see Adatto 1993: 97.

10. See also Ari Shavit, *Haaretz* supplement, April 30, 1999, 24.

11. *Haaretz*, May 16, 1999.

12. Anat Balint, *Ha'ayin Hashevi'it* 11 (October 1997): 6–11.

13. See also journalist Ben Caspit, one of the authors of the book, *Netanyahu, the Road to Power*, and *Ha'ayin Hashevi'it* 11.

14. It was none other than Motti Kirshenbaum, who was CEO of the Broadcasting Authority during the first part of Netanyahu's term in office, and who later went over to work as a reporter on Channel 2. Channel 2 news magazine, October 30, 1998. Later, Prime Minister Barak was found to have used similar methods. For example, he would sit on a chair higher than his guests.

15. Avner Hofshtein, *Jerusalem Weekly*, January 3, 1997.

16. *Haaretz*, December 1996.

17. Ze'ev Segal, *Haaretz* legal commentator, August 4, 1997. Others expressed similar sentiments.

18. Uzi Benziman, *Haaretz*, December 17, 1998.

19. Hemmi Shalev, *Ha'ayin Hashevi'it* 4 (May 1998): 24–25.
20. *Newsweek*, March 10, 1997, 16.

CHAPTER 9

1. In the case of the breakdown of the talks with the Palestinian Authority at Camp David in the summer of 2000, for example, Barak's spin defeated the media frame that Arafat had tried to sell.

2. This aspect became so central that the media invented a new Hebrew term (*hitnahalut*) to express this combination of a behavior pattern arising out of personality. The terms closest to it in English — conduct, self-management — do not emphasize the psychological element sufficiently. See Drucker 2002.

3. Interview with Prime Minister Yitzhak Rabin, November 29, 1994.

4. Ibid.

5. Benziman, *Haaretz*, February 26, 1999.

6. Shay Reuveni in an interview with Naomi Levitsky, *Yediot Ahronot*, June 6, 1997.

7. But the practice became established and Barak did not change it. When he was at Camp David in 2000 in his last talks with Arafat, the talks whose failure led to Barak's downfall, he too used the polls. Before agreeing on the historic decision to cede neighborhoods in Jerusalem, he asked Stanley Greenberg to examine the reaction of the Israeli public to the idea. Greenberg returned with a clear message. The Israelis were not prepared to be "suckered" and would not give up the Temple Mount, but Barak would have the support of the public regarding neighborhoods in East Jerusalem (Eldar 2000: 3b).

8. A selection of Netanyahu quotes against the Rabin government which was compiled and appeared in the weeklies *Kol Ha'ir* and *Kolbo*, November 10, 1995.

9. In Israel, "Left" and "Right" refer to hawkishness and dovishness rather than to economic worldviews.

10. The "iron wall" is a concept used by the founder of the Revisionist movement, Ze'ev Jabotinsky, to express the idea that there is no chance of reaching understanding and coexistence with the Arab world in the foreseeable future. The passage quoted from Netanyahu is taken from the most comprehensive interview conducted with him during his period of office as prime minister (Shavit, *Haaretz* weekend supplement, November 22, 1996). See also another profile of him (Shavit, *Haaretz* weekend supplement, December 26, 1997). Netanyahu presented the essence of his political worldview in a programmatic speech at a graduation ceremony at the College of National Security on August 14, 1997.

11. Rino Tsror, *Ha'ir*, January 3, 1997.

12. Interview with Simcha Dinitz, July 28, 2000. Dinitz was Israeli ambassador to the United States and also a member of Knesset.

13. *Otot* no. 209 (January 1998): 14.

14. Prime Minister Shamir's spokesperson, Yossi Ahime'ir, *Otot* no. 209 (January 1998): 14.

15. Amir Oren, *Haaretz*, April 24, 1998.

16. Special interview with Netanyahu on political and state affairs and the

media, conducted for the *Journalists Yearbook* of 1998. See also *Haaretz*, November 21, 1996. Many statements by journalists on these subjects are quoted in Elishar-Malca 1999.

17. Shalom Yerushalmi, *Maariv*, February 21, 1997.
18. Aluf Ben, *Ha'ayin Hashevi'it* (February 7, 1997): 17.
19. Yossi Verter, *Haaretz*, January 24, 1999.
20. Nachum Barnea, *Ha'ayin Hashevi'it* (March 19, 1999): 4–5.
21. Ehud Ashri, *Haaretz*, June 5, 1997.
22. *Haaretz*, December 17, 1996.
23. *Haaretz*, September 17,1997.
24. Roni Dagan, *Ha'ayin Hashevi'it* (July 1998): 7.
25. Nachum Barnea, *Ha'ayin Hashevi'it* (May–June 1996): 3.
26. Baruch Kera, *Ha'ayin Hashevi'it* 13 (February 1998): 9.
27. Shalom Yerushalmi, *Maariv*, October 1, 1999.
28. Yossi Verter, *Haaretz*, December 10, 1999.

CHAPTER 10

1. Ari Shavit, *Haaretz*, March 4, 1999.
2. *Haaretz* supplement, January, 29, 1999. For an analysis of Yitzhak Rabin, see Peri 1998.
3. For example, in an interview with Amos Regev, in which he spoke of his love of desert treks, *Maariv*, March 31, 1999. Although he only reached the rank of lieutenant during his military service, he succeeded in building for himself the image of a professional solider whose status and experience equaled those of his political rival when running for prime minister against Lieutenant-General Barak.
4. Avi Shlaim, "His Royal Highness: King Hussein and Israel," *New York Review of Books*, July 15, 1999, 14–19.
5. *Haaretz*, November 22, 1996.
6. On the concept of the "freier" in Israeli culture, see R. Bloch 2000. On Netanyahu's image as a wheeler-dealer, someone who pulls wool over everyone's eyes, see Oshri, *Haaretz*, June 5, 1997; and on Netanyahu as "not a freier," see Shiffer, *Yediot Ahronot*, April 10, 1998. Netanyahu even defined himself using this term.
7. *Haaretz*, June 2, 1997.
8. *Haaretz*, January 24, 1997.
9. Eitan Haber, *Yediot Ahronot*, July 18, 1998.
10. In this sense, Netanyahu's populism resembles all the other types, in that it includes elements of primitivism, and expresses the concept of the "noble savage" (McRae 1969).
11. Nachum Barnea, *Yediot Ahronot*, February 20, 1998.
12. *New Statesman*, September 25, 1998, 24.
13. *Yediot Ahronot*, February 20, 1998.
14. This letter was published in all the major newspapers in Israel.
15. Effi Yuchtman-Yaar and Yochanan Peres, "Aspects of Democracy: Tolerance, Nationalism and Trust in Institutions," *Panim* 2 (1997): 33–40.

16. On Begin's methods and tactics, see Gertz 1995: 67–83.

17. Zohar Shavit, *Haaretz*, May 29, 1998.

18. From a conversation with Justice Michael Ben-Yair and also from his remarks at a conference on the danger of fascism in Israeli society, Tel Aviv, 1998.

19. From a lecture by Avnon during a conference at the Israel Institute of Democracy, Jerusalem, April, 2000.

20. Orna Kazin, *Haaretz*, September 7, 1999.

21. A special issue of *Constellations* 5, no. 1 (1998) is devoted to this very topic.

CHAPTER 11

1. This appears in an interview with Netanyahu in the *Yearbook of the Israel Press Association* 1998: 9–21 (Tel Aviv: Maor Press), marking the 50th Jubilee of the State of Israel. Interviewers were Razi Gutterman and Israel Landers. The following quotes are also taken from there.

2. Interview with Ari Shavit, *Haaretz* supplement, November 22, 1996.

3. A summary of the data of the Association for the Public's Right to Know, on the number of appearances of Peres and Netanyahu in the months before the 1996 elections, appeared in *Ha'ayin Hashevi'it* 5 (September–October 1996): 23–25.

4. *Haaretz* supplement, November 22, 1996.

5. An entire issue of *Hatikshoret* (The media) was devoted to an analysis of the behavior of the media toward Netanyahu during the 1996 elections. *Hatikshoret* 33, June 1996.

6. See the studies by Arian, Weiman, and Wolfsfeld in Arian and Shamir 1996. Also Wolfsfeld and Weiman 1999.

7. Testimony of bureau chief David Agmon, in an interview with Shalom Yerushalmi, *Maariv*, February 12, 1997.

8. *Maariv*, December 27, 1996.

9. Testimony of Kirshenbaum, *Maariv*, August 4, 1997.

10. Arnon Zukerman, *Ha'ayin Hashevi'it* 21 (July 1999): 28–29.

11. *Haaretz*, February 16, 1996.

12. *Ha'ayin Hashevi'it* 19 (March 1999): 53.

13. *Yediot Ahronot*, February 16, 1996.

14. Aviel Linder, *Ha'ayin Hashevi'it* 7 (February 1997): 15.

15. A similar threat was voiced by Nissim Mishal, who was hosting an election debate, when Netanyahu suddenly revealed to the camera graphs to illustrate his arguments. Mishal saw this as a violation of the rules of the game.

16. See *Annal*, no. 560 (November 1998), edited by Katz and Strange, which is devoted entirely to this topic.

17. Dankner, *Maariv*, December 18, 1998.

18. Barnea and Shiffer, *Yediot Ahronot*, December 11, 1998.

19. *Haaretz*, March 4, 1973.

20. *Yediot Ahronot*, April 23, 1997.

21. *Haaretz*, April 23, 1997.

22. *Yediot Ahronot*, April 23, 1997.
23. *Haaretz*, April 2, 1999.
24. *Haaretz*, May 20, 1997.
25. Threats and attacks on journalists continued throughout the election campaign and afterward. See *Ha'ayin Hashevi'it* 20 (May 1999).
26. For example, Orit Shochat, *Haaretz*, July 16, 1999.
27. *Ha'ayin Hashevi'it* 21 (July 1999): 4–5.
28. See Akiva Eldar, *Haaretz*, December 17, 1999; Joel Marcus, *Haaretz*, December 15, 1999; Yirmiyahu Yovel, *Yediot Ahronot*, December 24, 1999.
29. *Haaretz*, December 17, 1998.
30. *Maariv*, April 10, 1998.
31. Interview with Orna Kadosh, "Shay deny Bazak," *Sofshavua* (*Maariv* weekend supplement), March 14, 1997.

CHAPTER 12

1. Kimmerling, who describes "the end of hegemony and the onset of cultural plurality," relates to two more countercultural groups: the Ethiopians and the noncitizen workers (1999, 2001).
2. The formation of tribes explains why the large international chains such as Toys 'R' Us, Super Office, and others, which opened huge stores in Israel, failed so miserably. Their strategic error lay in seeing the Israeli market as one market of six million potential buyers, ignoring the fact that the population comprises different co-cultures with different consumer behavior. See Michael Etgar, *Haaretz*, December 21, 1998.
3. Aviva Laury, *Haaretz*, March 12, 1999, 42.
4. One survey showed 8 percent (Lissak and Leshem 1996), and another survey showed 11 percent (Omri Dolev, *Ha'ir*, February 12, 1999). Twelve percent read weekend papers in Hebrew.
5. Nadav Cohen, *Davar Rishon*, March 24, 1996.
6. According to *Hamigzar Haharedi Beyisrael*, Information Kit of BSD Publicity, February 1998.
7. Shlomo Tsasna, *Maariv* supplement, April 16, 1999. Rabbi Ovadia Yosef introduced another innovation of religious significance in 1998, when he approved the establishment of a special radio station operated by women for ultraorthodox women, despite the religious tradition that forbids women's voices being heard in public.
8. Ronnie Shaked, *Yediot Ahronot*, February 12, 1999.
9. *Yediot Ahronot*, "7 Nights," February 12, 1999.
10. For a detailed analysis of the communicative strategies, or practices, of cocultures, see Orbe 1998.
11. A memo issued by director-general of Religious Education Administration; see also *Haaretz*, October 28, 1996.
12. The Bracha Report, *Israel's Culture Policy*, Van Leer Institute, Jerusalem, 1999.

13. Consumer habits of the southerners compared with the northerners are monitored and analyzed by *Geocartographia* market research in Tel Aviv.

14. For a review of these attempts, see David Hemmo, *Maariv*, September 20, 1998.

15. The long hours devoted to phone-in programs on Galei Zahal during the war in Lebanon, when soldiers at the front called in sending songs to their families, compelled the directors of the radio stations to play the songs requested. This weakened the barriers limiting the amount of Mizrahi music broadcast on the radio station.

CHAPTER 13

1. In the 2003 elections, this situation changed. Following the Intifada, the abolition of direct prime ministerial elections, and the internal crisis in Shas, Likud won in a landslide, attaining thirty-eight seats, and together the two major parties had fifty-seven seats. However, that change in the balance of power within the Knesset did not alter the sectorial base of Israel: society generally.

2. This is true both of those who agree and of those who disagree with Habermas's criticism of the monolithic character that he ascribes to this sphere. On this, see Rawlins 1998: 374.

3. It is true that some of the broadcasts in the United States also target such groups, for example, broadcasts in Spanish. But even with regard to them Meyrowitz argues that the broadcast does not lead to division but to another kind of integration.

4. A reflection of this change may be found in the Education Ministry's decision in March 1998: "In an attempt to introduce a multi-cultural approach and avoid repeating the mistakes in the absorption of eastern immigrants in the 1950s, the educational system today encourages the immigrant students . . . to learn the languages, tradition and culture of their countries of origin" (*Haaretz*, March 31, 1998). Education Minister Yitzhak Levy is quoted as saying, "Assimilation and absorption in Israeli society does not mean giving up family traditions and turning one's back on one's origins."

5. Of the forty Hebrew-language newspapers that had appeared in 1948, only seven (18 percent) remained, while among the twenty-one foreign-language newspapers from the same period, ten (48 percent) still appeared in 1999, and added to these were the new papers. See Limor 1999. On the growth in the circulation of foreign-language papers, see also *Daily Newspapers and Periodicals Published in Israel, 1995* (January 1998), Central Bureau of Statistics, Jerusalem.

6. Similarly, the projection at the beginning of the 1990s that the establishment of fourteen local radio stations would develop local community identity also proved erroneous. Most of the local stations suffered from a low listener rating and financial difficulties, and only three succeeded in recovering their investments. The few that succeeded flourished, because they managed to assume a distinct character and to locate suitable audiences, particularly young people who liked certain kinds of music.

7. Toward the end of 1996 fierce attacks on the national secular media

appeared in the ultraorthodox newspapers. "Most of this nation who put the Netanyahu government in power voted first and foremost against the media," wrote Mordecai Gerlitz in *Hamodia*, the organ of Agudat Yisrael. See also Shachar Elan, *Haaretz*, November 4, 1996.

8. In this case it will be possible to promote segmental integration, based on fostering of the groups without their losing their identity. See Portes 1996.

9. *Documedia* (a radio and TV show on media affairs), August 27, 1999.

10. Ultraorthodox journalist Dudi Hershlag, in a symposium on the ultraorthodox press.

11. Avirama Golan, in a symposium on the media and the elections, Van Leer Institute, Jerusalem, April 29, 1999.

12. This idea was developed by S. N. Eisenstadt in a colloquium on the future of Israeli society, the Steinmatz Institute, Tel Aviv University, May 5, 1998.

CONCLUSION

1. Rami Rosen, *Ha'ir*, July 16, 1999, 65.

2. A few examples bear witness to this point: TV correspondent Amiram Nir was appointed by Shimon Peres in 1985 as advisor to the prime minister on counterterrorism. Journalist Eitan Haber was spokesman for and later bureau chief of Prime Minister Yitzhak Rabin. Uri Oren, also of *Yediot Ahronot*, became spokesman to Minister David Levy and later ambassador to South Africa. Arie Mekel, Kol Israel correspondent, was appointed media advisor to the prime minister and later consul-general in Atlanta, Georgia.

3. Outstanding in this category are journalists like Dan Patir, who worked for *Davar*, then became media advisor to Prime Ministers Yitzhak Rabin and Menachem Begin, and finally returned to work as a journalist. Eitan Haber, a journalist with *Yediot Ahronot*, became spokesman to Defense Minister Yitzhak Rabin. When Rabin was elected prime minister, Haber became his bureau chief and closest confidant. After Rabin's assassination, Haber left government and went into business but continued to write opinion pieces in *Yediot Ahronot*. For full disclosure I have to say that I was a journalist with *Davar*, a spokesman for the Labor Party, a political advisor to the prime minister, and then went back to *Davar* as editor in chief.

4. See *Journal of Communication* 30 (1980): 10–29.

5. Rogel Alper, *Ha'ir*, February 19, 1999, 69.

6. The poll in 2000 was conducted by the Smith Institute and the question related to trust or lack of trust in journalists. It was published on May 22 in the program *Documedia* on Channel 1. The poll in December 1994 was conducted by the Dahaf Institute and published in the paper *Shishi*.

7. Orly Bar-Kima, *Haaretz*, January 16, 1997.

8. Peace index poll, *Haaretz*, July 5, 1998.

9. For a good summary of the subject of the credibility of the various media, see Edelstein, Ito, and Kepplinger 1989.

10. A detailed study, the first of its kind, about public trust in the media was undertaken as part of a comprehensive project which I have been conducting

together with my colleague Yariv Tzfati, under the auspices of The Chaim Herzog Institute for Media, Politics and Society at Tel Aviv University. Our assumption is that in general, the level of confidence in the media in Israel is lower than our poll showed. The 2003 data was probably affected by the impact of the Intifada. As is well known, in times of war, there is a tendency towards increased trust in national institutions (Peri and Tzfati 2003).

11. For an extensive analysis of the Israeli concept and practice of freedom of the press, see Segal 1996.

12. For example the books of Dor 2001; Yaron 2001.

13. See details in Limor 2001.

14. *Haaretz*, February 22, 2002.

15. A letter from Knesset member Katz-Oz to the president of the Press Council, Yitzhak Zamir, archives of the Press Council, files 1988–1990.

16. Lecture delivered at Tel Aviv University, May 13, 1996. The text of the lecture was published in the journal *Devarim Achadim* under the heading "The Tradition of Freedom of Expression in Israel and Its Problems," vol. 1 (1977): 3–26.

17. For example, the article by retired justice Hana Avnor, *Haaretz*, June 4, 1996.

18. Editorial, *Haaretz*, May 20, 1996.

19. Tal Chasin, *Haaretz*, May 22, 1996.

20. Tom Segev, *Haaretz*, May 15, 1996. The writer referred to the well-known tendency of Justice Barak to uphold the status of the courts in the public system, an approach known as "judiciary imperialism."

21. Petition 680/88, Schnitzer versus the Chief Military Censor, Judgment 42 (4); also a letter from the defense minister, dated May 17, 1989, to the chairperson of the Editors Committee, Hanna Zemer, archives of Editors Committee.

22. The opinions quoted here do not only reflect moods, they represent opinions voiced at a fascinating meeting I had with scores of young journalists in the summer of 1999 at Mishkenot Sha'ananim, Jerusalem.

Works Cited

Abramson, Jeffrey B., F. Christopher Artherton, and Garry R. Orren. 1988. *The Electronic Commonwealth*. New York: Basic Books.

Adatto, Kiku. 1993. *Picture Perfect*. New York: Basic Books.

Adoni, Hanna, and Hillel Nossek. 1997. In *Communication and Democracy in Israel* (in Hebrew), ed. Dan Caspi, 97–115. Tel Aviv: Hakibbutz Hameuchad.

Akzin, Benjamin. 1970. The Role of Parties in Israeli Democracy. In *Integration and Development in Israel*, ed. S. N. Eisenstadt, Rivkah Bar-Yosef, and Chaim Adler, 9–46. New York: Praeger.

Alger, Dean E. 1989. *The Media and Politics*. Englewood Cliffs, N.J.: Prentice Hall.

Almog, Oz. 2000. *The Sabra*. Berkeley and Los Angeles: University of California Press.

Altheide, David L., and Robert P. Snow. 1991. *Media Worlds in the Postjournalism Era*. New York: Aldine de Gruyter.

——. 1979. *Media Logic*. Beverly Hills, Calif.: Sage.

Althaus, Scott, et al. 1996. Revising the Indexing Hypothesis: Officials, Media, and the Libya Crisis. *Political Communication* 13, no. 4: 437–54.

Anderson, Benedict. 1983. *Imagined Communities*. London: Verso.

Arian, Asher. 1998. Parties in Accelerated Change. In *The Demise of Parties in Israel*, ed. Dan Koren, 91–128. Tel Aviv: Hakibbutz Hameuchad.

Arian, Asher, and Michal Shamir, eds. 1999. *The Elections in Israel—1999* (in Hebrew). Jerusalem: The Israel Democracy Institute.

Arian, Asher, Gabriel Weiman, and Gadi Wolfsfeld. 1999. Even-handedness in Covering the Elections. In *The Elections in Israel—1996* (in Hebrew), ed. Asher Arian and Michal Shamir. Jerusalem: The Israel Democracy Institute.

Avnon, Dan. 1998. The Israeli Basic Laws' (Potential) Fatal Flaw. *Israel Law Review* 32, no. 4: 535–66.

——, ed. 1993. *Political Parties Law in Israel* (in Hebrew). Tel Aviv: The Israel Democracy Institute.

Avraham, Eli. 1993. *The Media in Israel: Center and Periphery* (in Hebrew). Tel Aviv: Breirot.

Avraham, Eli, Gadi Wolfsfeld, and Isam Aburabiya. 2000. Dynamism in the News

Coverage of Minorities, The Case of the Arab Citizens of Israel. *Journal of Communication Inquiry* 24, no. 2: 117–33.

Azulay-Katz, Orly. 1999. *The Man Who Defeated Himself* (in Hebrew). Tel-Aviv: Miskal.

Baram, Uzi. 1996. Reshuffling of the Political System. In *The Electoral Revolution* (in Hebrew), ed. G. Doron, 215–18. Tel Aviv: Hakibbutz Hameuchad.

Barnhurst, Kevin G., and Catherine A. Steele. 1997. Image-Bites News: The Visual Coverage of Elections on U.S. Television, 1968–1992. *Press/Politics* 2, no. 1: 40–58.

Bar-Tal, Daniel, Dan Jacobson, and Aaron Klieman, eds. 1999. *Security Concerns, Insight from the Israeli Experience*. Stamford, Conn. and London: JAI Press.

Barzilai, Gad. 1992. *A Democracy in Wartime: Conflict and Consensus in Israel*. Tel Aviv: Sifriyat Hapoalim.

Barzilai, Gad, and Yossi Shain. 1991. Israeli Democracy at the Crossroads: A Crisis of Nongovernability. *Government and Opposition* 26, no. 3: 345–67.

Bar-Zohar, Michael. 1994. *Ben Gurion: A Political Biography* (in Hebrew). Tel Aviv: Am Oved.

Begin, Benny. 1996. Primaries — The Price of Democracy. In *The Electoral Revolution* (in Hebrew), ed. Gideon Doron, 207–13. Tel Aviv: Hakibbutz Hameuchad.

Ben-Ami, Shlomo. 1998. *A Place for All* (in Hebrew). Tel Aviv: Hakibbutz Hameuchad.

Ben Gurion, David. 1953a. The Press and Life. In *Journalists Yearbook 1953* (in Hebrew), 193–95. Tel Aviv: Maarac.

———. 1953b. *War Diary* (in Hebrew). Tel Aviv: Maarac.

Bennett, W. Lance. 1998. The Uncivic Culture: Communication, Identity, and the Rise of Lifestyle Politics. *PS: Political Science and Politics* 31, no. 4: 741–61.

———. 1990. Towards a Theory of Press-State Relations. *Journal of Communication* 40, no. 2: 103–25.

———. 1983. *News: The Politics of Illusion*. New York: Longman.

Bennett, W. Lance, and Robert M. Entman, eds. 2001. *Mediated Politics*. New York: Cambridge University Press.

Ben Porat, Yeshayahu. 1944. *Typewritten Memories*. Tel Aviv: Zmora-Bitan.

Ben-Porat, Yeshayahu, Yonathan Gefen, Uri Dan, Eitan Haber, Hezzy Carmeli, Eli Landau, and Eli Tavor. 1974. *The Debacle* (in Hebrew). Tel Aviv: Special Publication.

Ben-Simon, Daniel. 1997. *A New Israel* (in Hebrew). Tel Aviv: Arie Nir Publications.

Betz, Hans-Georg. 1994. *Political Right-Wing Populism in Western Europe*. New York: St Martin's Press.

Betz, Hans-Georg, and Stefan Immerfeld, eds. 1998. *The New Politics of the Right: Neo-Populist Parties and Movements in Established Democracies*. London: Macmillan.

Bhabha, Homi K. 1990. Introduction: Narrating the Nation. In *Nation and Narration*, ed. Homi K. Bhabha, 1–7. London: Routledge.

Bloch, Daniel. 1990. We Must Take Stock. In *From Our Military Correspondent*, ed. Tali Zelinger, 73. Tel Aviv: Defense Ministry Publications.

Bloch, R. 2003. Who's Afraid of Being a Freier?: The Analysis of Communication Through a Key Culture Frame. *Communication Theory* 13, no. 2: 125–59.

Blondheim, Menahem. 1998. Israel. In *Global Media and Economics*, ed. Allan Albrran and Sylvia Chan-Olmsted, 233–52. Ames: Iowa State University.

———. 1997. Communication Technology and the World of Knowledge: The Universal Construct and the Israeli Example. In *Communication and Democracy in Israel* (in Hebrew), ed. Dan Caspi, 47–70. Tel Aviv: Hakibbutz Hameuchad.

Blondheim, M., and K. Kaplan. 1993. "Wicked Broadcasting" — The Media and Video Cassettes in the Ultra-Orthodox Society (in Hebrew). *Kesher* 14: 51–62.

Blumenthal, Sidney. 1982. *The Permanent Campaign*. New York: Simon and Schuster.

Blum-Kulka, Shoshana, and Tamar Liebes. 2000. Peres versus Netanyahu: Television Wins the Debate. In *Televised Election Debates: International Perspectives*, ed. S. Coleman, 66–92. London: McMillan.

Blumler, Jay G., and Michael Gurevitch. 1998. Change in the Air: Campaign Journalism at the BBC, 1997. In *Political Communications: Why Labor Won the General Election of 1977*, ed. I. Crew, B. Gosschalk, and J. Bartle London, 176–94. London: Frank Cass.

———. 1995. *The Crisis of Public Communication*. London and New York: Routledge.

———. 1986. Journalists' Orientation to Political Institutions. In *Communication Politics. Mass Communication and the Political Process*, ed. Peter Golding, Graham Murdock, and Philip Schlesinger, 67–92. Leicester: Leicester University Press.

Blumler, Jay G., and Dennis Kavanagh. 1999. The Third Age of Political Communication, Influences and Features. *Political Communication* 16, no. 3: 209–30.

Bono, Francesco, and Ib Bondebjerg, eds. 1994. *Nordic Television, History, Politics and Aesthetics*. Copenhagen: Department of Film and Media Studies.

Bourdieu, Pierre. 1999. *Sur La Television* (Hebrew trans.). Tel-Aviv: Bavel.

———. 1990. *The Logic of Practice*. Stanford, Calif.: Stanford University Press.

Brants, Kees. 1998. Who's Afraid of Infotainment? *Journal of European Communication* 13, no. 3: 315–35.

Brokaw, T., J. Fallow, K. Jamieson Hall, M. Matalin, and T. Russert, with M. Kalb. 1997. Talk Show Democracy '96. *Press and Politics* 2, no. 1: 4–13.

Brzezinski, Zbigniew, and Samuel Huntington. 1963. *Political Power, USA/USSR*. London: Chatto and Windus.

Calhoun, Craig. 1988. Populist Politics, Communications Media and Large-scale Societal Integration. *Sociological Theory* 6, no. 2: 214–19.

Calloni, Marina. 1998. Neopopulism and Corruption. *Constellations* 5, no. 1: 96–109.

Canovan, Margaret. 1999. Trust the People! Populism and the Two Faces of Democracy. *Political Studies* 47, no. 1: 2–16.

————. 1981. *Populism*. New York and London: Harcourt Brace Jovanovich.

Cappella, Joseph N., and Kathleen Hall Jamieson. 1997. *Spiral of Cynicism*. Oxford and New York: Oxford University Press.

Carpini, Michael Delli, and Bruce A. Williams. 2000. Let Us Infotain You: Politics in the New Media Environment. In *Mediated Politics*, ed. W. Lance Bennett and Robert M. Entman, 160–81. Cambridge: Cambridge University Press.

Carter, Douglas. 1959. *The Forth Branch of Government*. Boston: Houghton Mifflin.

Caspi, Dan. 1996. American-style Electioneering in Israel, Americanization versus Modernization. In *Politics, Media, and Modern Democracy*, ed. David Swanson and Paolo Mancini, 175–92. Westport, Conn., and London: Praeger.

————. 1982. How Do Knesset Members Assess the Mass Media as Suppliers of Cognitive Needs? *State, Government and International Relations* no. 16: 507–20.

Caspi, Dan, and Yehiel Limor. 1992. *The Mediators* (in Hebrew). Tel Aviv: Am Oved.

Caspit, Ben, et al. 1996. *Netanyahu: The Way to Power* (in Hebrew). Tel Aviv: Maariv.

Castells, Manuel. 1997. *The Power of Identity*. Malden, Mass.: Blackwell Publishers.

————. 1996. *Information Age: The Rise of the Network Society*. Malden, Mass.: Blackwell Publishers.

Cerulo, Karen A. 1997. Identity Construction, New Issues, New Directions. *Annual Review of Sociology* no. 23: 385–409.

Chalaby, Jean K. 1998. A Charismatic Leader's Use of the Media: De Gaulle and Television. *Press and Politics* 3, no. 4: 44–61.

Cohen, Adir. 1999. *Lies*. Haifa: Amatzya.

Cohen, Akiba. 1998. Between Content and Cognition, On the Impossibility of News. *The European Journal of Communication Research* 23, no. 4: 447–61.

Cohen, Nathan. 1998. The Status of the Israel Public Broadcasting Authority (in Hebrew). Ph.D. dissertation, Dept. of Communication, Hebrew University, Jerusalem.

Cook, Timothy E. 1998. *Governing with the News: The News Media as a Political Institution*. Chicago: University of Chicago Press.

Cotteret, Jean-Marie. 1991. *Gouverner c'est Paraitre* [Governing is appearance]. Paris: Presses Universites de France.

Crozier, Michael, Samuel Huntington, and Watanuki Joji. 1975. *The Crisis of Democracy*. New York: New York University Press.

Curran, James. 1986. The Impact of Advertising in the British Mass Media. In *Media, Culture and Society*, ed. R. Collins et al., 309–35. London: Sage.

Dahl, Robert. 1989. *Democracy and Its Critics*. New Haven, Conn.: Yale University Press.

Dahlgren, Peter. 1995. *Television and the Public Sphere*. London: Sage.

————. 1994. *Media and the Public Sphere*. London: Sage.

Dahrendorf, Ralf. 2000. *The Global Class and the New Inequality*. Lecture at the Israel Academy of Science, Jerusalem.

Dayan, Daniel. 1996a. Maintaining Identities, Constructing Identities, Particularistic Media and Diasporic Communication. In *Media and Knowledge, The Role of Television*, ed. Jostein Gripsrud, 27–45. Bergen: University of Bergen Press.

———. 1996b. Particularistic Media and Diasporic Communications. In *Media, Ritual and Identity*, ed. Tamar Liebes and James Curran, 103–13. London: Routledge.

Dayan, Daniel, and Elihu Katz. 1992. *Media Events: The Live Broadcasting of History.* Cambridge, Mass.: Harvard University Press.

De la Torre, Carlos. 1998. Redemptive Populism in Latin America. *Constellations* 5, no. 1: 85–95.

Deutsch, Karl W. 1966. *Nationalism and Social Communication.* Cambridge, Mass.: MIT Press.

Di Tella, Torcuato. 1965. Populism and Reform in Latin America. In *Obstacles to Change in Latin America*, ed. Claudio Veliz, 47–74. London: Oxford University Press.

Donsbach, Hans. 1995. Lapdogs, Watchdogs and Junkyard dogs. *Media Studies Journal* 9, no. 4: 17–30.

Don-Yehiye, Eliezer. 1997. *The Politics of Accommodation: Settling Conflicts of State and Religion in Israel.* Jerusalem: The Floersheimer Institute for Policy Studies; Tel Aviv: Hakibbutz Hameuchad.

Dor, Daniel. 2001. *Newspapers Under Influence* (in Hebrew). Tel Aviv: Babel.

Doron, Gideon. 1998. Real Parties and Virtual Parties. In *The Demise of the Parties* (in Hebrew), ed. D. Koren, 215–23. Tel Aviv: Hakibbutz Hameuchad.

———. 1996. *The Electoral Revolution* (in Hebrew). Tel Aviv: Hakibbutz Hameuchad.

Dror, Yehezkel. 1998. The Demise of Parties and the End of Zionism. In *The Demise of Parties in Israel*, ed. D. Koren, 54–64. Tel Aviv: Hakibbutz Hameuchad.

Drucker, Raviv. 2002. *Harakiri. Ehud Barak: The Failure* (in Hebrew). Tel Aviv: Miskal.

Duverger, Maurice. 1963. *Political Parties.* New York: Wiley.

Eco, Umberto. 1990. A Guide to the Neotelevision of the 1998s. In *Culture and Conflict in Postwar Italy*, ed. Zygmunt G. Baranski and Robert Lumley, 245–55. New York: St. Martin's Press.

Edelman, Murray. 1985. Political Language and Political Reality. *PS: Political Science and Politics* no. 8: 10–19.

———. 1974. *The Symbolic Uses of Politics.* Urbana, Chicago, and London: University of Illinois Press.

———. 1971. *Politics as Symbolic Action.* Chicago, Ill.: Markham.

Edelstein, A. S., Y. Ito, and H. M. Kepplinger. 1989. *Communication and Culture: A Comparative Approach.* New York: Longman.

Edwards, Lee. 2001. *Mediapolitik.* Washington, D.C.: The Catholic University of America Press.

Elishar-Malca, Vered. 1999. *The Influence of Netanyahu's Government on the*

Role of the Media in the Peace Process (in Hebrew). M.A. thesis, Dept. of Communication, Hebrew University, Jerusalem.

Entman, Robert, M. 1989. *Democracy Without Citizens*. New York and Oxford: Oxford University Press.

Esser, Frank. 1999. Tabloidization of News: A Comparative Analysis of Anglo-American and German Press Journalism. Paper presented to the 49th Annual ICA Conference, San Francisco, Calif., May 27–31.

———. 1998. Editorial Structures and Work Principles in Britain and German Newsrooms. *European Journal of Communication* 13: 375–405.

Esslin, Martin. 1982. *The Age of Television*. San Francisco: W. H. Freeman.

Etzioni-Halevy, Eva. 1993. *The Elite Connection and Democracy in Israel* (in Hebrew). Tel Aviv: Sifriyat Hapoalim.

Ewen, Stuart. 1988. *All Consuming Images: The Politics of Style on Contemporary Culture*. New York: Basic Books.

Ezrahi, Yaron. 1997. *Rubber Bullets, Power and Conscience in Modern Israel*. New York: Farrar, Strauss and Giroux.

———. 1992. Technology and the Civil Epistemology. *Inquiry*. 35, nos. 3/4: 363–76.

Fallows, James. 1997a. *Breaking the News: How Media Undermine American Democracy*. New York: Vintage Books.

———. 1997b. Did You Have a Good Week? *The Atlantic Monthly* no. 274: 32–33.

Fein, Aharon. 1995. *Immigrants from the Former Soviet Union — Survey of Media Exposure* (in Hebrew). Jerusalem: Tatzpit Research Institute.

Filk, Dani. 1996. Post Populism in Israel: Netanyahu's Latin American Model. *Theory and Criticism* no. 9: 217–32.

Fiske, John. 1996. *Media Matters*. Minneapolis: University of Minnesota Press.

———. 1987. *Television Culture*. London and New York: Routledge.

Franklin, Bob. 1994. *Packaging Politics, Political Communications in Britain's Media Democracy*. London, New York, Melbourne, and Auckland: Edward Arnold.

Friedman, Menahem. 1991. *The Ultra-Orthodox Society — Sources, Trends and Processes* (in Hebrew). Jerusalem: Institute for the Study of Jerusalem.

Galnoor, Itzhak. 1998. Parties, Communication and the Israeli Democracy. In *The Demise of Parties in Israel*, ed. D. Koren, 195–214. Tel Aviv: Hakibbutz Hameuchad.

———. 1996. The Crisis in the Israeli Political System, the Parties as a Stabilizing Factor. In *Israel Towards the Year 2000*, ed. M. Lissak and B. Knei-Paz, 144–75. Jerusalem: Magnes Press.

———. 1994. *Territorial Partition: Decision Crossroads in the Zionist Movement* (in Hebrew). Jerusalem: Magnes Press.

———. 1982. *Steering the Polity*. Beverly Hills, Calif.: Sage Publications.

Galnoor, Itzhak, and Yochanan Peres. 1992. Whoever Votes, Influences. In *Democracy* (in Hebrew), 29–31. Tel Aviv: The Israel Democracy Institute.

Gamson, William A., and A. Modigliani. 1989. Media Discourse and Public

Opinion on Nuclear Power: A Constructionist Approach. *American Journal of Sociology* 95: 1–38.

Gellner, Ernest. 1983. *Nations and Nationalism.* Ithaca, N.Y.: Cornell University Press.

Gertz, Nurith. 1995. *Captive of a Dream: National Myths in Israeli Culture* (in Hebrew). Tel Aviv: Am Oved.

Giddens, Anthony. 1991. *Modernity and Self-Identity: Self and Society in the Late Modern Age.* Stanford, Calif.: Stanford University Press.

———. 1990. *Sociology.* London: Polity Press.

———. 1984. *The Constitution of Society.* London: Polity Press.

Gidron, Beni. 2000. *The Third Sector in Israel, 2000* (in Hebrew). Be'er-Sheva: Ben-Gurion University.

Gil, Tzvi. 1986. *The Diamonds Building.* Tel Aviv: Sifriyat Hapoalim.

Gilboa, Eytan. 2000. Mass Communication and Diplomacy: A Theoretical Framework. *Communication Theory* 10, no. 3: 275–309.

Gitlin, Todd. 1999. Public Sphere or Public Sphericules? In *Media, Ritual and Identity,* ed. Tamar Liebes and James Curran, 168–74. London: Routledge.

———. 1995. *The Twilight of Common Dreams: Why America Is Wracked by Culture Wars.* New York: Pantheon.

Goldberg, Giora. 1992. *Political Parties in Israel — From Mass Parties to Electoral Parties.* Tel Aviv: Ramot.

Gould, Philip. 1998. *The Unfinished Revolution: How the Modernisers Saved the Labour Party.* London: Little, Brown.

Graber, Doris A. 2001. *Processing Politics.* Chicago: University of Chicago Press.

———. 1996. Making Sense of International News: Can Citizens Meet the Challenge? Paper presented to the 46th Annual ICA Conference, Chicago, Ill., May.

———. 1989. Say It with Pictures. *The Annals of the American Academy of Political and Social Science* 546: 85–96.

———. 1985. *Candidate Image: The Impact of Audio-Visual News on Public Opinion Formation.* Paper presented at the Annual Meeting of the Midwest Political Science Association, Chicago, Ill.

———. 1984. *Processing the News.* New York: Longman.

Griffin, Michael. 1992. Looking at TV News: Strategy for Research. *Communication* 13: 121–41.

Gross, Larry. 1993. *Outtested Closet: The Politics and Ethics of Outing.* Minneapolis and London: University of Minnesota Press.

Guo, Zhongshi, and Patricia Moy. 1997. *Medium or Message? Predicting Dimensions of Political Sophistication.* Paper presented to the political communication division of the ICA, Montreal, Quebec, May.

Gurevitch, Michael. 1993. The Globalization of Electronic Journalism. In *Mass Media and Society,* ed. James Curran and Michael Gurevitch, 178–93. London: Edward Arnold.

Gusfield, Joseph R. 1963. *Symbolic Crusade.* Urbana: University of Illinois Press.

Gutman, Yechiel. 1995. *The Storm In the G.S.S.* Tel Aviv: Yediot Aharonot.

Habermas, Juergen. 1989. *The Structural Transformation of the Public Sphere.* Cambridge, Mass.: MIT Press.

————. 1984. *The Theory of Communicative Action*. Boston: Beacon.

————. 1976. *Legitimation Crisis*. Cambridge: Polity Press.

Ha-Ilan, Neta. 1999. *Making Sense of "The Administered Territories" in Israeli Television*. Ph.D. dissertation, Hebrew University, Jerusalem.

Hallin, Daniel. 1998. Broadcasting in the Third World. In *Media Ritual and Identity*, ed. Tamar Liebes and James Curran, 153–67. London and New York: Routledge.

————. 1994. Speaking of the President. In *We Keep America on Top of the World*, 113–32. London and New York: Routledge.

Harshefi, Yoela. 1977. *Not in the Headlines* (in Hebrew). Tel Aviv: Ya'ad.

Hart, Roderick P. 1994. *Seducing America: How Television Charms the Modern Voter*. New York: Oxford University Press.

Hay, F. 1986. *Photojournalism*. Englewood, Calif.: Prentice-Hall.

Hazan, Reuven Y. 1998. Not Parliamentary and Not Presidential: The Change in the Election System and the Israeli Regime (in Hebrew). *Politica* no. 2 (December): 97–111.

————. 1997. Executive-Legislative Relations in an Era of Accelerated Reform, Reshaping Government in Israel. *Legislative Studies Quarterly* 22, no. 3.

Heclo, Hugh. 2000. Campaigning and Governing: A Conspectus. In *The Permanent Campaign and Its Future*, ed. Norman J. Ornstein and Thomas E. Mann, 1–37. Washington, D.C.: American Enterprise Institute and the Brookings Institution.

Held, David. 1991. Democracy, the Nation-State and the Global System. *Economy and Society* 20, no. 2: 138–72.

Herbst, Susan. 1994. Race, Domination, Mass Media and Public Experience, Chicago 1934–1960. In *Politics at the Margin, Historical Studies of Public Experience Outside the Mainstream*. Cambridge: Cambridge University Press.

Herman, Tamar, and Ephraim Yuchtman-Yaar. 2000. Israeli Attitudes Towards Political Protest. In *The Assassination of Yitzhak Rabin*, ed. Yoram Peri. Stanford, Calif.: Stanford University Press.

Herold, Susan. 1986. A Synthesis of 1,043 Effects of Television on Social Behavior. In *Public Communication and Behavior*, vol. 1, ed. George Comstock. New York: Academic Press.

Hertzgaard, Mark. 1988. *On Bended Knee, The Press and the Reagan Presidency*. New York: Farrar, Strauss and Giroux.

Hofnung, Menachem. 1998. The Candidate, the Investor and the Voter: Financing Parties and Primaries in 1996 Elections. In *The Demise of Parties in Israel* (in Hebrew), ed. Dani Koren, 91–128. Tel Aviv: Hakibbutz Hameuchad.

————. 1993. *Funding of Parties and Funding of Elections in Israel*. Jerusalem: The Israel Democracy Institute.

————. 1991. *Israel Security Needs vs. the Rule of Law*. Jerusalem: Nevo.

Horowitz, Dan, and Eli Leshem 1998. In *Profile of Immigration* (in Hebrew), ed. Sikrun and E. Leshem. Jerusalem: Magnes Press.

Horowitz, Dan, and Moshe Lissak. 1989. *Trouble in Utopia: The Overburden Polity of Israel* (in Hebrew). Tel Aviv: Am Oved.

Ionesco, Ghita, and Ernes Gellner. 1969. *Populism, Its Meaning and National Characteristics*. London: Weidenfeld and Nicolson.

Iyengar, Shanto. 1991. *Is Anyone Responsible? How Television Frames Political Issues*. Chicago: Chicago University Press.

Jamieson, Kathleen Hall. 2000. *Eevrything You Think You Know about Politics . . . and Why You Are Wrong*. New York: Basic Books.

———. 1996. *Packaging the Presidency*. New York and Oxford: Oxford University Press.

Janeway, Michael. 1999. *Republic of Denial*. New Haven, Conn.: Yale University Press.

Jobran, Salem. 1999. The Arabic Press in Israel (in Hebrew). *Kesher* no. 25 (May): 83–87.

Kadman, Yitzhak. 1998. The Role of the Press in Shaping the Knesset's Agenda Concerning Welfare Issues. In *Mass Media in Israel*, ed. D. Caspi and Y. Limor, 579–93. Tel Aviv: Open University.

Kalb, Marvin. 1991. Forward. In *The Media and Foreign Policy*, ed. S. Serfaty, xiii–xvii. New York: St. Martin's Press.

Katriel, Tamar. 1986. *Talking Straight "Dugri" Speech in Israeli Sabra Culture*. Cambridge: Cambridge University Press.

Katz, Elihu. 1996. And Deliver Us from Segmentation. *The Annals of the American Academy of Political and Social Science* 546 (July): 22–33.

———. 1992. The End of Journalism? Note on Watching the War. *Journal of Communication* 42, no. 3: 5–13.

Katz Elihu, and Hadassa Haas. 1997. Twenty Years of Television in Israel: Are There Long-Run Effects on Values, Social Connectedness, and Cultural Practices? *Journal of Communication* no. 47: 3–20.

Katz, Elihu, and Jeffrey J. Strange, eds. 1998. The Future of Facts. *The Annals of the American Academy of Political and Social Science* 560 (November).

Katz, Elihu, and George Wedell. 1977. *Broadcasting in the Third World: Promise and Performance*. Cambridge: Cambridge University Press.

Katz, Elihu, et al. 1992. *Leisure Culture in Israel 1970–1990* (in Hebrew). Jerusalem: Israel Institute of Applied Social Research.

Katz, Richard S., and Peter Mair. 1995. Changing Models of Party Organization and Party Democracy: The Emergence of Cartel Party. *Party Politics* 1 , no. 1: 5–28.

Katzman, A. 1999. Between Two Editors — The Liberal Path of *Ha'aretz* (in Hebrew). *Kesher* no. 25: 20–27.

Kazin, Michael. 1998. U.S. Democracy Betrayed and Redeemed. *Constellations* 5, no. 1: 75–84.

———. 1995. *The Populist Persuasion*. New York: Basic Books.

Keane, John. 1996. Structural Transformation of the Public Sphere. *The Communication Review* no. 1: 1–22.

Kellner, Douglas. 1995. *Media Culture*. London and New York: Routledge.

Kepplinger, Hans M., and Renate Kocher. 1990. Professionalism in the Media World? *European Journal of Communication* no. 5: 285–311.

Keren, Michael. 1996. *Professionals Against Populism* (in Hebrew). Tel Aviv: Ramot.

———. 1988. *Ben Gurion and the Intellectuals* (in Hebrew). Jerusalem: Ben Gurion University Press.

Kernell, Samuel. 1986. *Going Public, New Strategies of Presidential Leadership.* Washington, D.C.: Congressional Quarterly Press.

Kimmerling, Baruch. 2001. *The Invention and Decline of Israeliness.* Berkeley and Los Angeles: University of California Press.

———. 1999. Elections as an Arena of Battle for the Collective Identity. In *The Elections in Israel — 1996* (in Hebrew), ed. Asher Arian and Michal Shamir, 27–44. Albany: New York State University Press.

———. 1998. The New Israelis — A Multiplicity of Cultures Without Multiculturalism (in Hebrew). *Alpayim* 16: 264–308.

———. 1985. Between Primordial and Civil Definition of the Collective Identity: Eretz Yisrael or the State of Israel. In *Comparative Social Dynamics*, ed. Eric Cohen, Moshe Lissak, and Yuri Almagor, 262–83. Boulder, Colo.: Westview Press.

Kircheimer, Otto. 1969. *Politics, Law, and Social Change: Selected Essays of Otto Kircheimer.* Ed. F. S. Burin and K. L. Shell. New York: Columbia University Press.

———. 1966. The Transformation of the Western European Party System. In *Political Parties and Political Development*, ed. J. LaPalombara and M. Weiner, 177–200. Princeton, N.J.: Princeton University Press.

Kop, Yaakov, ed. 2000. *Allocation of Social Resources to Social Services* (in Hebrew). Jerusalem: Center for the Study of Social Policy.

Koren, Dani. 1998. *The Demise of Parties in Israel.* Tel Aviv: Hakibbutz Hamenchad.

Lachman-Messer, Davida. 1997. The New Map of Israeli Media Map (in Hebrew). *Dvarim Ahadim* no. 1: 66–87.

Laclau, Ernesto. 1977. *Politics and Ideology in Marxist Theory.* London: Verso.

Landi, Oscar. 1994. Theses sur la video-politique en Amerique Latine. In *Amerique Latine, Democratie et Exclusion*, ed. Hames Cohen, 219–31. Paris: L'Harmattan, Futur Anterieur.

Leshem, Eli, and Moshe Lissak. 1998. In *Roots and Routes* (in Hebrew), ed. Shalva Weil, 135–71. Jerusalem: Magnes Press.

Levy, Amnon. 1989. *The Ultra-Orthodox* (in Hebrew). Jerusalem: Keter.

Liebes, Tamar. 2001. There Is a Need for Two to Create a Scandal (in Hebrew). *Panim* no. 16: 11–19.

———. 2000. A Socio-schematic History of Broadcasting in Israel. In *De-Westerninzing Media Studies*, ed. J. Curran and M. J. Park, 305–24. London: Routledge.

———. 1998. Television's Disaster Marathons: A Danger for Democratic Processes? In *Media, Ritual and Identity*, ed. Tamar Liebes and James Curran, 77–86. London: Routledge.

Liebes, Tamar, and Elihu Katz. 1990. *The Export of Meaning: Cross-Cultural Readings of "Dallas."* New York: Oxford University Press.

Liebes, Tamar, and Yoram Peri. 1997. Electronic Journalism in Segmented Societies: Lessons from the 1996 Israeli Elections. *Political Communication* 15, no. 1: 27–44.

Lijphart, Arend. 1968–69. Consociational Democracy. *World Politics*: 207–25.

———. 1968. *The Politics of Accommodation, Pluralism and Democracy in the Netherlands*. Berkeley and Los Angeles: University of California Press.

Limor, Yehiel. 2001. *The Israel Press Council as a Mechanism of Self-regulation* (in Hebrew). Ph.D. dissertation, Bar Ilan University, Ramat-Gan.

———. 1999. *Mass Media in Israel*. Tel Aviv: Open University.

———. 1998. *Pirate Radio in Israel, the Situation in 1998* (in Hebrew). Research report, Smart. Institute of Communication. Hebrew University, Jerusalem.

———. 1997. The "Little Prince" and the "Big brother," or, the Media Industry in Israel in an Era of Change. In *Communication and Democracy in Israel* (in Hebrew), ed. Dan Caspi, 29–46. Tel Aviv: Hakibbutz Hameuchad.

Lipset, Seymour Martin. 2000. The Indispensability of Political Parties. *Journal of Democracy* 11, no. 1: 28–55.

Lissak, Moshe. 1998. The Demise of the Parties and the Sectorial Blossom. In *The Demise of Parties in Israel* (in Hebrew), ed. D. Koren, 129–40. Tel Aviv: Hakibbutz Hameuchad.

Lissak, Moshe, and Dan Horowitz. 1989. *Trouble in Utopia: The Overburdened of Israel*. Albany: State University of New York Press.

Lissak, Moshe, and Eli Leshem. 1995. The Russian Intelligentsia in Israel, Between Ghettoization and Integration. *Israel Affairs* 2, no. 2: 20–36.

Lomsky-Feder, Edna, and Eyal Ben-Ari. 1999. *The Military and Militarism in Israeli Society*. Albany: State University of New York Press.

Lorwin, Val R. 1970–71. Segmented Pluralism. *Comparative Politics* no. 3: 141–75.

Lustick, Ian. 1993. *Unsettled States, Disputed Lands*. Ithaca, N.Y.: Cornell University Press.

———. 1980. *Arabs in the Jewish State*. Austin: University of Texas Press.

Machill, Marcel. 1999. The Effect of the Commercialization of Swedish Television on Journalistic Culture. *Press and Politics* 4, no. 2: 103–11.

Mair, Peter. 1989. Western Europe, the Dangers of Apathy. In *The Demise of Parties in Israel*, ed. D. Koren, 23–32. Tel Aviv: Hakibbutz Hameuchad.

Mancini, Paolo. 2000. How to Combine Media Commercialization and Party Affiliation, The Italian Experience. Unpublished paper.

———. 1999. New Frontiers in Communication Professionalism. *Political Communication* 16, no. 3: 231–45.

Mann, Raphael, and Tzippy Gon-Gross. 1991. *Galei Zahal — Around the Clock* (in Hebrew). Tel-Aviv: Ministry of Defense.

Margalit, Dan. 1997. *I Have Seen Them All* (in Hebrew). Tel Aviv: Zmora-Bitan.

Mazzoleni, Gianpietro. 1995. Towards a Videocracy? Italian Political Communication at a Turning Point, *European Journal of Communication* 10, no. 3: 291–319.

———. 1987a. Media Logic and Party Logic in Campaign Coverage: The Italian General Election 1983. *European Journal of Communication* no. 2: 81–103.

——. 1987b. The Role of the Private TV Stations in Italian Elections. In *Political Communication Research*, ed. David Paletz, 75–87. Norwood, N.J.: Ablex.

Mazzoleni, Gianpietro, and Winfried Schultz. 1999. "Mediatization" of Politics, A Challenge for Democracy? *Political Communication* 16, no. 3: 247–61.

Mazzoleni, Gianpietro, Julianne Stewart, and Bruce Harsfeld. 2003. *The Media and Neo-Populism*. Westport, Conn., and London: Praeger.

McChesney, Robert W. 1999. *Rich Media, Poor Democracy*. Urbana: University of Illinois Press.

McEnteer, James. 1991. *Changing Lanes on the Inside Track: The Career Shuttle Between Journalism, Politics and Government*. Discussion Paper D-8, the Joan Shorenstein Barone Center, Harvard University.

McLeod, Jack M., Gerald M. Kosicki, and Douglas M. McLeod. 1994. The Expanding Boundaries of Political Communication Effects. In *Media Effects: Advances in Theory and Research*, ed. Jennings Bryant and Dolf Zillmann, 123–62. Hillsdale, N.J.: Lawrence Erlbaum Associates, Inc.

McNair, Brian. 1995. *An Introduction to Political Communication*. London and New York: Routledge.

McQuail, Denis. 1990. Western Europe, Mixed Model Under Threat? In *Questioning the Media*, ed. J. Downing et al., 25–138. London: Sage.

——. 1989. *Mass Communication Theory: An Introduction*. London: Sage.

McQuail, Denis, and Karen Siune. 1998. *Media Policy: Convergence, Concentration and Commerce*. London: Sage.

McRae, Donald. 1969. Populism as an Ideology. In *Populism, Its Meaning and National Characteristics*, ed. Ghita Ionesco and Ernest Gellner, 153–65. London: Weidenfeld and Nicolson.

Merten, K. 1994. *Konvergenz der Deutschen Fernsehprogramme. Eine Langzeituntersuchung 1980–1993*. Munster/Hamburg: Lit.

Messaris, Paul. 1997. *The Role of Images in Advertising*. Thousand Oaks, Calif.: Sage.

Meyrowitz, Joshua. 1994. The Life and Death of Media Friends. In *American Heroes in a Media Age*, ed. Robert Cathcart and Susan Drucker. Cresskill, N.J.: Hampton Press.

——. 1992. The Power of Television News. *The World and I*: 453–80.

——. 1985. *No Sense of Place*. New York and Oxford: Oxford University Press.

Meyrowitz, Joshua, and John Maguire. 1993. Media, Place, and Multiculturalism. *Society* 30, no. 5: 41–48.

Mishal, Nissim. 1976. *The Broadcasting Authority, Political Dynamics*. M.A. thesis, Dept. of Political Science, Bar-Ilan University, Ramat-Gan.

Mizroeff, Nicholas. 1999. *An Introduction to Visual Culture*. London and New York: Routledge.

Morris, Benny. 1996. The Israeli Press in the Qibia Affair, October-November 1953 (in Hebrew). *Theory and Criticism* no. 8: 33–46.

Nachmias, D., and I. Sened. 1998. The Decline of the Parties and Public Policy. In *The Demise of the Parties* (in Hebrew), ed. D. Koren, 243–50. Tel Aviv: Hakibbutz Hameuchad.

Naficy, Hamid. 1993. *The Making of an Exile Culture*. Minneapolis and London: University of Minnesota Press.

Negbi, Moshe. 1995. *Freedom of the Press in Israel — The Legal Aspect*. Jerusalem: The Jerusalem Institute for Israel Studies.

Netanyahu, Benjamin. 1995. *A Place Under the Sun* (in Hebrew). Tel Aviv: Yedioth Ahronoth.

Nissim, Moshe. 1996. The Primaries System: Out of the Frying Pan, into the Fire (in Hebrew). *Ha'uma* no. 125: 28–33.

Nordhaus, William D. 1975. The Political Business Cycle. *Review of Economic Studies* no. 42.

Norris, Pippa. 2000. *A Virtuous Circle, Political Communication in Postindustrial Societies*. Cambridge: Cambridge University Press.

———, ed. 1999. *Critical Citizens, Global Support for Democratic Governance*. Oxford: Oxford University Press.

Norris, Pippa, John Curtice, David Sanders, Margaret Scammel, and Holli A. Semetko. 1999. *On Message: Communicating the Campaign*. London: Sage.

Orbe, Mark P. 1998. *Constructing Co-Cultural Theory*. Thousand Oaks, Calif.: Sage.

Ornstein, Norman J., and Thomas E. Mann. 2000. *The Permanent Campaign and Its Future*. Washington, D.C.: American Enterprise Institute and The Brookings Institution.

Paletz, Davis. 1999. *The Media in American Politics*. New York: Longman.

———. 1998. The Media and Public Policy. In *The Politics of News, The News of Politics*, ed. Doris Graber, Denis McQuail, and Pippa Norris, 218–37. Washington, D.C.: CQ Press.

———, ed. 1987. *Political Communication Research*. Norwood, N.J.: Ablex.

Panebianco, Angelo. 1982. *Models of Parties*. Bologna: Il Mulino.

Patterson, Thomas E. 2000. The United States, News in a Free-Market Society. In *Democracy and the Media*, ed. Richard Gunther and Anthony Mugham, 241–65. Cambridge: Cambridge University Press.

———. 1998. Time and News: The Media's Limitation as an Instrument of Democracy. *International Political Review* no. 19: 55–68.

———. 1996. Bad News, Bad Governance. *The Annals of the American Academy of Political and Social Science* no. 546 (July): 97–108.

———. 1994. *Out of Order*. New York: Alfred A. Knopf.

Patterson Thomas E., and Wolfgang Donsbach. 1996. News Decisions: Journalists as Partisan Actors. *Political Communication* no. 3: 455–68.

Payne, James L. 1980. Show Horses and Work Horses in the United States House of Representatives. *Polity* 12, no. 3: 428–56.

Peres, Yochanan, and Ephraim Yuchtman-Yaar. 1998. *Between Consent and Democracy: Democracy and Peace in the Israeli Mind* (in Hebrew). Jerusalem: Israel Democracy Institute.

———. 1992. *Trends in Israeli Democracy*. Boulder, Colo., and London: Lynne Rienner Publishers.

Peri, Yoram, ed. 2000a. *The Assassination of Yitzhak Rabin*. Stanford, Calif.: Stanford University Press.

————. 2000b. Media, War, and Citizenship. *Communication Review* 3, no. 4: 1–29.

————. 1998. Afterword. In *Yitzak Rabin: The Rabin Memoirs*, 339–93. Berkeley and Los Angeles: University of California Press.

————. 1996. The Age of New Politics. *Journalists Yearbook 1994–1995* (in Hebrew), 79–93. Tel Aviv: Journalists' Union Press.

————. 1989. *Electoral Reform in Israel*. Report nos. 5 and 6 (May and August) of the International Forum on Electoral Reform. Tel Aviv: Israel Diaspora Institute.

————. 1988. From Political Nationalism to Ethic-Nationalism — The Case of Israel. In *The Arab-Israeli Conflict, Two Decades of Change*, ed. Yehuda Lukas and Abdalla M. Battah, 41–53. Boulder, Colo.: Westview Press.

————. 1983. *Between Battles and Ballots: Israel Military in Politics*. Cambridge: Cambridge University Press.

Peri, Yoram, and Yariv Tsfati. 2003. Index of Public Trust in News Media. Report No. 1, March. The Chaim Herzog Institute for Media, Politics, and Society. Tel Aviv University, Tel Aviv.

Pfetsch, Barbara. 1998. *Government News Management, Strategic Communication in Comparative Perspective*. Paper presented at the ICA Conference, Jerusalem, July 20–24.

————. 1996a. *Comparing Political Television Formats in Germany*. Paper presented at the 46th Annual ICA Conference, Chicago, Ill., May 23–27.

————. 1996b. Convergent Through Privatization: Changing Media Environments and Televised Politics in Germany. *European Journal of Communication* 11, no. 4: 427–51.

Pharr, Susan, Robert Putnam, and Russell Dalton. 2000. A Quarter-Century of Declining Confidence. *Journal of Democracy* 11, no. 2: 5–25.

Piccone, Paul. 1995. Postmodern Populism. *Telos* 103 (spring).

Pizzoreno, Allesandro. 1987. Politics Unbound. In *Changing Boundaries of the Political*, ed. Charles S. Maire, 27–62. Cambridge: Cambridge University Press.

————. 1981. Interest and Parties in Pluralism. In *Organizing Interests in Western Europe, Pluralism, Corporatism, and the Transformation of Politics*, ed. Suzanne Berger, 249–84. Cambridge: Cambridge University Press.

Portes, Alejandro, ed. 1996. *The New Second Generation*. New York: Russell Sage Foundation.

Porto, Mauro P. 2001. *Mass Media and Politics in Democratic Brazil*. Paper presented to the conference "15 years of Democracy in Brazil," Institute of Latin American Studies, University of London, London, February 15–16.

Postman, Neil. 1986. *Amusing Ourselves to Death*. New York: Penguin Books.

Preuss, Ofra. 1997. Implementing the Permanent Campaign in Israel, A Guide for Effective Leadership. Unpublished paper, Kennedy School of Government, Harvard University.

Protzel, Javier. 1996. Disbelief, Media, and Terrorism in Peru. In *Political Communication in Action*, ed. David Paletz, 53–96. Cresskill, N.J.: Hampton Press.

Putnam, Robert D. 1995. Bowling Alone: America's Declining Social Capital. *Journal of Democracy* 6, no. 1: 65–78.

Rahat, Gideon, and Neta Sar-Hadar. 1999a. *Intraparty Selection of Candidates for the Knesset List and for Prime-Ministerial Candidacy 1995–1997* (in Hebrew). Jerusalem: The Israel Democracy Institute.

————. 1999b. The 1996 Primaries and Their Political Implications. A Position Paper, No. 12 (in Hebrew). Jerusalem: The Israeli Democracy Institute.

Rahat, Menahem. 1998. *Shas — The Spirit and the Strength* (in Hebrew). Tel Aviv: Alpha Tikshoret.

Ram, Uri. 1999. Israel in the Era of the Global Village (in Hebrew). *Israeli Sociology* no. 1: 99–144.

Rannis, Peter. 1992. *Argentine Workers, Peronism, and Contemporary Class Consciousness.* Pittsburgh, Pa.: University of Pittsburgh Press.

Rappel, Yoel. 1991. Synagogue Newspapers (in Hebrew). *Kesher* no. 10: 109–12.

Rawlins, William K. 1998. Theorizing Public and Private Domains and Practices of Communication, Introductory Concerns. *Communication Theory* 8, no. 4: 369–80.

Ricci, David M. 1993. *The Transformation of American Politics.* New Haven, Conn., and London: Yale University Press.

Riggins, Stephen H. 1992. *Ethnic Minority Media: An International Perspective.* Newbury Park, Calif.: Sage.

Robinson, Michael J. 1976. Public Affairs Television and the Growth of Political Malaise: The Case of "the Selling of the Pentagon." *American Political Science Review* 70, no. 2: 409–32.

————. 1975. American Political Legitimacy in an Era of Electronic Journalism: Reflections on the Evening News. In *Television as a Social Force: New Approaches to TV Criticism*, ed. Douglas Cater and Richard Adler, 97–139. New York: Praeger.

Roeh, Yitzhak. 1994. *Another View of the Media* (in Hebrew). Jerusalem: Reches.

Rozental, Rovik. 2000. *Hazira Haleshonit* (in Hebrew). Tel Aviv: Am Oved.

Sabato, Larry J. 1991. *Feeding Frenzy: How Attack Journalism Has Transformed American Politics.* New York: The Free Press.

Scheer, Leo. 1994. *La democratie virtuelle.* Paris: Gallimard.

Scheuer, Jeffrey. 1999. *The Sound Bite Society.* New York: Routledge.

Schmitt, Carl. 1994. *The Crisis of Parliamentary Democracy.* Cambridge, Mass.: MIT Press.

Schudson, Michael. 1998. The Public Journalism Movement and Its Problem. In *The Politics of News, the News of Politics*, ed. Doris Graber, Denis McQuail, and Pippa Norris, 132–49. Washington, D.C.: CQ Press.

————. 1997. Towards a Troubleshooting Manual for Journalism History. *Journalism and Mass Media Quarterly* 74, no. 3: 463–76.

————. 1995. *The Power of News.* Cambridge, Mass.: Harvard University Press.

————. 1982. The Politics of Narrative Form: The Emergence of News Convention in Print and Television. *Dedalus* 111, no. 4: 97–12.

Schultz, Winifred. 1999. Television and Declining Political Trust: How Germans React to Changes of the Media System. Paper prepared for the 49th Annual Conference of ICA, San Francisco, May.

Segal, Zeev. 1996. *Freedom of the Press: Between Myth and Reality* (in Hebrew). Tel Aviv: Papyrus.

Seymour-Ure, Colin. 1998. Are the Broadsheets Becoming Unhinged? In *Politics and the Media*, ed. Jean Seaton, 43–54. Oxford: Blackwell.

———. 1991. *The British Press and Broadcasting since 1945.* Oxford: Blackwell.

———. 1974. *The Political Impact of Mass Media.* London: Sage.

Shabat, Gad. 2001. *The Political Agenda Setting Function of the Media: Social Issues in the Media and in the Parliament.* M.A. thesis, Bar Ilan University, Ramat-Gan.

Shah, Hemant. 1996. Modernization, Marginalization, and Emancipation: Towards a Normative Model of Journalism and National Development. *Communication Theory* 6, no. 2: 143–66.

Shamir, Jacob. 1988. Israeli Elite Journalists: Views on Freedom and Responsibility. *Journalism Quarterly* no. 65: 589–94.

Shamir, Michal, and Asher Arian. 1999. Collective identity and the 1996 elections. In *The Elections in Israel—1996* (in Hebrew), ed. Asher Arian and Michal Shamir, 57–83. Jerusalem: The Israel Institute of Democracy.

Shamir, Michal, and Jacob Shamir. 1995. Competing Values in Public Opinion: Conjoined Analysis. *Political Behavior* 17: 107–33.

Shapiro, Yonathan. 1996. *Politicians as a Hegemonic Class* (in Hebrew). Tel Aviv: Sifriyat Hapoalim.

———. 1989. *Chosen to Command* (in Hebrew). Tel Aviv: Am Oved.

———. 1978. *Democracy in Israel* (in Hebrew). Tel Aviv: Masada.

Shavit, Z. 1998. *The Construction of the Israeli Culture, The History of the Jewish Community in Pre-State Israel Since the First Zionist Immigration* (in Hebrew). Jerusalem: Bialik Institute.

Sheafer, Tamir. 2001. *Charismatic Resources, Political Communication and Politics* (in Hebrew). Ph.D. dissertation, Hebrew University, Jerusalem.

Shilon, Dan. 1998. *Live* (in Hebrew). Tel Aviv: Miskal.

Siegel, Arthur. 1966. *Politics and Media in Canada.* Toronto: McGraw-Hill.

Sikron, Moshe, and Elezer Leshem. 1999. *A Profile of Immigrants.* Jerusalem: Magnes Press.

Singer, Jerome L. 1980. The Power and Limitation of Television: A Cognitive-Affective Analysis. In *The Entertainment Functions of Television*, ed. Percy H. Tannenbaum, 31–65. Hillsdale, N.J.: Erlbaum.

Sivan, Emanuel. 1991. On Cultural Enclaves (in Hebrew). *Alpayim* no. 4: 45–98.

Skocpol, Theda, and Fiorina P. Morris. 1999. *Civic Engagement in American Democracy.* Washington, D.C.: The Brookings Institution Press.

Slater, Don. 2001. Political Discourse and the Politics of Need: Discourses on the Good Life in Cyberspace. In *Mediated Politics: Communication in the Future of Democracy*, ed. W. Lance Bennett and Robert M. Entman, 117–40. Cambridge: Cambridge University Press.

Smith, Gordon. 1998. The New Labor Party: A Social Democratic Ideal? In *The Demise of Parties in Israel*, ed. D. Korn, 33–44. Tel Aviv: Hakibbutz Hameuchad.

Smolicz, Jerzy. 1981. The Three Types of Multiculturalism. In *Community Languages: Their Role in Education*, ed. M. Garner, 1–12. Melborn: River Seine.

Smolicz, Jerzy, and Richard J. Watts, eds. 1997. *Cultural Democracy and Ethnic Pluralism*. New York: P. Lang Publishers.

Smooha, S. 1993. Social, Ethnic and National Divisions and Democracy in Israel. In *Israeli Society: Some Critical Aspects* (in Hebrew), ed. Uri Ram, 172–202. Tel Aviv: Breirot.

Sparks, Colin. 1992. Popular Journalism: Theory and Practice. In *Journalism and Popular Culture*, ed. Peter Dalgren and Colin Sparks, 24–44. London: Sage.

Sparks, Colin, and John Tulloch, eds. 2000. *Tabloid Tales*. New York: Rowman and Littlefield.

Statham, Paul. 1996. Berlusconi, the Media, and the New Right in Italy. *Press and Politics* 1, no. 1: 87–105.

Stewart, Agnus. 1969. The Social Roots. In *Populism, Its Meaning and National Characteristics*, ed. Ghita Ionesco and Ernest Gellner, 180–96. London: Weidenfeld and Nicolson.

Stone, Gerald. 1987. *Examining Newspapers: What Research Reveals about America's Newspapers*. Beverly Hills, Calif.: Sage.

Street, John. 1997. *Politics and Popular Culture*. Philadelphia, Pa.: Temple University Press.

Swanson, David L. 1997. The Political-Media Complex at 50. *American Behavioral Scientist* 40, no. 8: 1264–82.

Swanson, David L., and Paolo Mancini. 1996. *Politics, Media, and Modern Democracy*. London: Praeger.

Swirski, Shlomo, and Etti Konor, eds. 2000. *The Social Picture*. Tel Aviv: Adva Center.

———. 1998. *A Social Report 1998* (in Hebrew). Tel Aviv: Adva Center.

Syvertsen, Trine. 1997. Paradise Lost: The Privatization of Scandinavian Broadcasting. *Journal of Communication* 47, no. 1: 120–27.

Taggart, Paul. 2000. *Populism*. Buckingham: Open University Press.

Taguieff, Pierre-Andre. 1995. Political Science Confronts Populism: From a Conceptual Mirage to a Real Problem. *Telos* 103 (spring): 9–43.

Tamir, Yael. 1998. Two Concepts of Multiculturalism. In *Multiculturalism in a Democratic and Jewish State*, ed. Menachem Mautner, Uri Sagi, and Ronen Shamir, 79–92. Tel Aviv: Ramot.

Teheranian, Majid. 1979. Iran, Communication, Alienation and Revolution. *Intermedia* 7, no. 2: 6–12.

Thompson, John B. 1995. *The Media and Modernity: A Social Theory of the Media*. Stanford, Calif.: Stanford University Press.

Tokatly, Oren. 2000. *Communication Policy in Israel* (in Hebrew). Tel Aviv: Open University.

Tolson, Andrew. 1996. *Mediations, Text and Discourse in Media Studies*. London: Arnold.

Trautman, K. G., ed. 1997. *The New Populist Reader*. Westport, Conn.: Praeger.

Turow, Joseph. 1997. *Breaking up America: Advertisers and the New Media World*. Chicago: University of Chicago Press.

Urbinati, Nadia. 1998. Democracy and Populism. *Constellations* 5, no. 1: 210–24.

Van der Berghe, Pierre. 1981. *The Ethnic Phenomenon*. New York and Oxford: Elsevier.

Vardi, Ronit. 1997. *Benjamin Netanyahu — Who Are You, Mr. Prime Minister?* (in Hebrew). Tel Aviv: Keter.

Wagner-Pacifici, Robin E. 1986. *The Moro Morality Play: Terrorism as Social Drama*. Chicago: University of Chicago Press.

Walzer, Michael. 1998. Democracy and the Politics of Assassination. In *Political Assassination* (in Hebrew), ed. Charles Liebman, 13–21. Tel Aviv: Am Oved.

Weaver, P. 1975. Newspaper News and Television News. In *Television as a Social Force*, ed. D. Carter and R. Adler. New York: Praeger.

Webb, P. 1995. Are British Political Parties in Decline. *Party Politics* 1, no. 3: 299–322.

Weber, Max. 1961. *Politik Als Beruf* (in Hebrew). Tel Aviv: Schocken.

Weffort, Francisco C. 1967. Le Populism dans la Politique Bresilienne. *Les Temps Modernes* (October): 624–49.

Weiman, Gabriel. 1996. Cable Comes to the Holy Land, the Impact of Cable TV on Israeli Viewers. *Journal of Broadcasting and Electronic Media* no. 40: 243–57.

———. 1995. Zapping in the Holy Land, Coping with Multichannel TV in Israel. *Journal of Communication* no. 45: 97–103.

Weiman, Gabriel, and Ayelet Goren. 2001. Sobriety and Ratings Met Halfway (in Hebrew). *Panim* no. 16: 4–10.

Westerstahl, Jorgen, and Folke Johansson. 1986. News Ideologies as Moulders of Domestic News. *European Journal of Communication* 1, no. 2: 133–49.

White, Robert A. 1989. Social and Political Factors in the Development of Communication Ethics. In *Communication Ethics and Global Change*, ed. Thomas W. Cooper et al., 40–65. White Plains, N.Y.: Longman.

Wiles, Peter. 1969. A Syndrome, not a Doctrine, Some Elementary Theses on Populism. In *Populism, Its Meaning and National Characteristics*, ed. Ghita Ionescu and Ernest Gellner, 166–79. London: Weidenfeld and Nicolson.

Wolfenson, Avraham. 1975. *The Party Press in the Political Process* (in Hebrew). Ph.D. dissertation, Hebrew University, Jerusalem.

Wolfsfeld, Gadi. 2001. Political Waves and Democratic Discourses: Terrorism Waves During the Oslo Peace Process. In *Mediated Politics*, ed. W. Lance Bennett and Robert M. Entman, 226–51. New York: Cambridge University Press.

———. 1998. *Constructing News About Peace: The Role of the Israeli Media in the Oslo Peace Process*. Tel Aviv: Tel Aviv University, the Tami Steinmetz Center for Peace Research.

———. 1997. *Media and Political Conflict*. Cambridge: Cambridge University Press.

———. 1996. *Critical Events and the Struggle over Meaning, Competing Media Frames of the Rabin's Assassination*. Unpublished paper. Dept. of Communication, Hebrew University, Jerusalem.

Wolfsfeld, Gadi, Yoram Peri, and Rami Khouri. 2002. News about the Other in

Jordan and Israel: Does Peace Make a Difference? *Political Communication* 19, no. 2: 189–210.

Wolfsfeld, Gadi, and Gabriel Weiman. 1999. Agenda Setting in the 1996 Election Campaign. *Politika* no. 4: 9–26.

Wolfson, Lewis W. 1991. *Through The Revolving Door: Blurring the Lines Between the Press and Government.* Research Paper R-4, the Joan Shorenstein Barone Center, Harvard University.

Woodward, Bob. 1995. *The Agenda.* New York: Pocket Books.

Yatziv, Gadi. 1999. *The Sectarian Society* (in Hebrew). Jerusalem: The Bialik Institute.

————. 1997. *Introduction to Normative Sociology* (in Hebrew). Tel Aviv: Sifriat Haminhal.

Yishai, Yael. 2002. The Return of Civil Society: Post Cartel Parties in Israel (in Hebrew). *State and Society* 1, no. 1: 11–30.

Yuran, Noam. 2001. *Channel 2 — The New Statehood* (in Hebrew). Tel Aviv: Patish.

Zadok Commission. 1997. *Report of the Public Commission for Press Laws.* Jerusalem.

Zaller, John R. 1998. Monika Lewinsky's Contribution to Political Science. *PS: Political Science and Politics* 31 (June): 182–89.

Zelinger, Tali, ed. 1990. *From Our Military Correspondent* (in Hebrew). Tel Aviv: Defense Ministry Publications.

Zelizer, Barbie. 1992. *Covering the Body: The Kennedy Assassination, the Media and the Shaping of Collective Memory.* Chicago and London: University of Chicago Press.

Zisser, Baruch, and Asher Cohen. 1999. From Ordering Democracy to Crisis Democracy: The Struggle over the Israeli Collective Identity (in Hebrew). *Politica* no. 3 (June): 9–30.

Zoonen, Liesbet van. 1996. A Dance of the Devil: New Social Movements and Mass Media. In *Political Communication in Action*, ed. David L. Paletz, 201–22. Cresskill, N.J.: Hampton Press.

Index